The 360 Music Industry

Second Edition

By

Larry E. Wacholtz

Edited by

Beverly Schneller

ISBN 978-1-948715-01-0 Second Edition-hardback/color

ISBN 978-1-948715-00-3 Second Edition-paperback

ISBN 978-1-948715-02-7 Second Edition-ebook

The rights of Larry Wacholtz as the author of this work are in accordance of the United States Copyright Law and Section 17 to include the six exclusive rights of ownership. All rights reserved. No part of this book may be reprinted or reproduced or utilized in any form or by any electronic mechanical or other means now known or thereafter invented without the written permission of the publishers.

Trademarks are used only for identification and without intent to infringe.

Library of Congress Cataloguing or In Publication Date (TBD)

© Copyright Thumbs Up Publishing 2018

The 360 Music Industry

Thumbs Up Publishing

3100 West End Cir

#201

Nashville, TN 37203

(615) 732-5736

lwacholtz@mac.com

Pictures by Larry Wacholtz

Cover photo, art work, some additional photos, and infographics licensed through Adobe Stock.

© Copyright Thumbs Up Publishing 2018

Dr. Larry Wacholtz is Professor of Entertainment and Music Business at Belmont University in Nashville. A consultant to industry professionals, he is a member of NARAS, USASBE, MEIEA, IFBPA, and the Academy of Entrepreneurship. He was the former Director of Music Business Entrepreneurship at Belmont University, has written extensively on the entertainment and music business, and has presented research papers at many national conferences. Earlier in his career, Wacholtz owned a psychographic research company (Entertainment Industry Research) that provided consumer behavior and image research to MCA and Word Records. Other publications by Wacholtz include:

- *Monetizing Entertainment,* (Taylor & Francis) with companion Website www.routledge.com/cwd/wacholtz (Instructor and Student Guides)

- *Off the Record: How the Music Business Really Works, 3rd Edition* with Instructor's and student guide (Thumbs Up Publishing)

- *Off the Record: How the Music Business Really Works 2nd Edition* (Thumbs Up Publishing)

- *Off the Record: How the Music Business Really Works* (Thumbs Up Publishing)

- *Breaking News/Broken News* (Editor) (Thumbs Up Publishing)

- *Chivalry is Not Dead: Boston* (Editor) (Thumbs Up Publishing)

- *The Business of Songwriting* (Thumbs Up Publishing)

- *Star Tracks: Everything You Really Need to Know about the Music Industry* (Thumbs Up Publishing)

- *How the Music Business Works* (Thumbs Up Publishing)

- *Inside Tracks* (Thumbs Up Publishing)

- *Inside Country Music* (Billboard Publications/Watson-Guptil)

Making music is about passion, inspiration, emotion and creative talent.

However, it is not just a gift of human nature: it also requires an extraordinary amount of hard work, time, effort and sustained investment.

An enormous supporting cast of skilled, dedicated and passionate people are devoted to helping make the artist and their music a success.

This behind-the-scenes community works in hundreds of different ways, in countless different roles, to support the artist and to take their work to a large audience of fans, often spanning the globe.

It is no less important in today's music landscape than in the past – in fact it is more important. In a world of digital diversity and complexity, this help is needed more than ever before.

PLÁCIDO DOMINGO

CHAIRMAN, IFPI[1]

---

1 "Looking for industry knowledge? Our range of resources and reports cover everything from analysis on digital music, to how labels invest in music." Investing in Music - IFPI - Representing the recording industry worldwide. 2016. Accessed July 23, 2017. http://www.ifpi.org/investing-in-music.php.

Preface

Oh No, Not Another Book!

There are so many books on the music business available for consumers to buy and read, that in most cases when you're done, all you've discovered is that your more confused than when you started. And I've written some of them! Even Passman's in his book *All You Need to Know About the Music Business* defines his book's title by stating "There is no way one book (even one filling several volumes) could poke into every nook and cranny of a business as complicated as the music business".[1] Passman's has long been considered one of the best in the industry, just as Krasilovsky's publication of *This Business of Music* and Baskervillle's *Music Business Handbook* have contributed to a better understanding of the industry in the past.

However, much of what they and I have written about in the past, no longer exist as the industry has reinvented itself due to digital technology, personal devices, non-enforcement of copyright laws, safe harbors, and consumers' demand for free music and entertainment products. Therefore, I encourage you to first realize that all the information you need is not found in one book. Passman is a highly successful attorney and is to be praised for the success of his book. However, he also presents the industry from a legal side of the business. As such, he is less concerned with the types of business knowledge often required for success in the creative, administrative, and entrepreneurial sides of the business. His excellent book appears to be written for the acts who have achieved building a sizable fan base and buzz that has been noticed by label executives. He is an attorney advising his clients about deals and the basics of what they may need to know about the deal.

But what about everyone else who is not at that level in the industry? What

---

1 PASSMAN, DONALD S. ALL YOU NEED TO KNOW ABOUT THE MUSIC BUSINESS: p.5, ninth edition. 9th ed. S.l.: VIKING, 2017.

about the students who don't know the first step to take toward putting a band together, creating a wow song, recordings, marketing, pitching themselves as an act to a promoter, or club owner for a show? Where does radio fit in? What can companies such as CD Baby and websites really achieve for an aspiring new act? The list goes on and on about what is not in the three previous mentioned books.

This edition of *The 360 Music Industry* includes much (but not all) of the information many who want careers in the industry will need to know. Passman and the others usually offer their legal opinion on what to do to become a successful part of this industry. That is important, but so is the information in this text from over 250 citations from a variety of sources such as The Security and Exchange Commission, Corporate Reports, to information news releases, to *Billboard, Pollstar*, and many other industry sources. The entertainment network provides comments and advice from legendary industry insiders Mike Curb, songwriter L. Russell Brown, and record producer, Jimmy Bowen.

Take a few minutes to look these iconic leaders up on the Internet and you'll understand why their success in the industry, their quotes, and contributions are relevant to your success. So, by all means read Passman and others, but don't think you'll know all you need to know to be successful in the business. However, reading this book along with the others will place you ahead of the others who don't. Indeed, this industry changes so quickly that once you in it, you'll be learning new things all the time if you want to stay in it successfully.

Grab every bit of knowledge you can from networking with successful industry leaders, read and create your own mindset on what the industry is (from your perspective) to determine where you can contribute to its success. It's your job to determine where you best fit in, maybe it's as a local vocalist, or as a superstar rock act performing in front of thousands. Maybe it's as an attorney or an audio engineer providing the live sound locally or for the superstar act. Who knows, but that's up to you to figure out and create.

This is not a simple industry to break into and it never has been. As the labels have moved toward the 360 business model it's gotten more complicated and the ripple effects have changed much of the rest industry. Look at each section of this book as a "cube of knowledge" consisting of layers that you'll need to know before you'll "grasp" or "understand how the "cube" becomes a building "block" in your "wall of knowledge" about the structure, administration, and opportunities you'll find in the business.

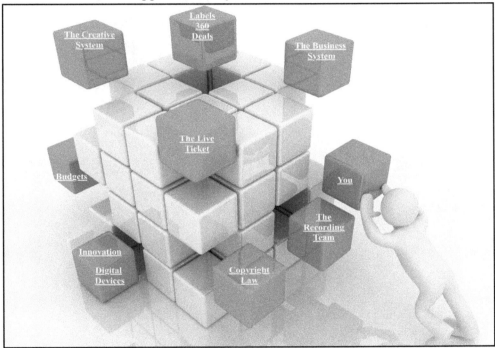

You may want a career in the creative side as a songwriter, musicians, recording artists or producer. Or, maybe you're more into the business side of the industry as a label executive in administration, sales, marketing, promotion or publicity. You may also be more of a "people person" who wants to work in artist representation such as personal management, or as a booking agent or business manager or as a concert or event promoter. You may want to own your own night club, be an attorney or work in the traditional media such as radio or TV or help with analytics or be in social media.

The available opportunities are up to you to learn, so get to know yourself as much as possible. What creative and business skills are you really good at and then follow your passions. However, remember that in today's world to be successful, you'll often need to work as a team member instead of by yourself, and at the same time, you'll also have to help others become successful. Therefore, use this book as an inclusive overview of the industry and use it to figure out where you best fit in with your dream career. Reading this book will deepen your knowledge and understanding of the points made in other books and introduced you to what they often missed. It will also help you better understand what you really what to do and need to know to become a leader in the entertainment industry.

> *There are a lot of people who find the music business exciting and glamorous- and sometimes it is.*

> *But, there are also times when the music business will challenge everything that you have experienced in your entire lifetime.*

> *It makes no difference if you are an employee, producer, songwriter, or record company owner, the music business is unlike any other business because you have to live it, realizing the uncertainties and negatives are far outweighed by the positive fulfillment that comes from building successful careers for artists and employees.*

> *I want to encourage others to believe in the music business and most of all have faith in themselves.*
>
> *- Mike Curb*[2]

---

[2] Mike Curb, with Don Cusic, Living the Business. Nashville, TN: Brackish Publishing, 2017: 378.

Contents

CHAPTER 1   31

The Psychology of Entertainment   31

The 360 Music Industry   32

Access   35

Consumers   36

Being Human   37

What Do Entertainment Products Mean to Us?   38

    The Play Theory of Humanity   39

    Our Brains on Music   40

    Emotions of Entertainment   41

    Constructivism   42

Lifestyle Segmentation   43

The Global Market   46

Summary   48

CHAPTER 2   55

The Power of Innovation   55

Entrepreneurship and the Early Labels   55

    The Printing Press   56

    Film, Microphones, The Phonograph, & Batteries   58

The Early Labels   62

  RCA 63

  Capital Records 63

  Warner Bros. Records 63

  Motown 63

  MCA 64

  A & M 64

Inventions & Technology as a Commodity 65

  Terrestrial Radio & Television 66

  Computers 70

  The Internet 72

  Digital Transmissions 73

  MP3 74

  Personal Digital Devices 75

Social Media 76

Word of Mouth 79

Music as a Commodity 80

What Happened 81

Equity Lost 81

The First Bombshell-EMI 82

Summary 84

Chapter 3 87

The Value of Creativity 87

The Traditional Music Business Model 88

  The Creative System 89

  The Business System 92

360 Economies of Scale   94

360, 270, & 180 Business Models   98

Summary   100

CHAPTER 4   103

Copyright Laws- The Legal Foundation of Creativity   103

    A Very Brief History of Copyrights   104

    How Copyright Laws Began   104

    The Statute of Anne   105

    The United States Constitution   107

Acquiring a Copyright   108

What is a Copyright   108

Duration   109

The Exclusive Rights of Ownership   114

Fair Use Right-An Exception to the Exclusive Rights   115

The Compulsory License-Another Exception to the Exclusive Rights   116

Safe Harbors   116

Intellectual Properties   117

    Copyrights (©)   117

    Trademarks (TM, SM, & ®)   118

    Patents   118

Copyrightable Protected Works   119

Authorship & Ownership   120

Copyright Registration   121

    Registration of Copyright- eCo   121

    Certificate of Registration   123

Certificate of Recordation   124

Deposit Copies   125

"Pitching" Creative Works   125

The Texas Two-Step   129

Summary   132

Chapter 5   139

Songwriting & Music Publishing   139

Song Formulas   140

Connecting Lyrics & Emotions   140

Creative Networking   141

The Filtering System   143

The Production Matrix   144

The First Step   145

Referrals   145

What Publishers Do For Songwriters   146

The Free Internet Marketplace   146

Wow Songs   147

Projected Values   147

Types of Music Publishers   148

Songwriter/Music Publishing Deals   150

Splits & Shares   150

Ask Questions   152

Types of Music Publishing Deals   153

Work-Made-For-Hire Deal   154

Indie Deal   156

Staff Deals   156

        Quotas 158

    Co-Publishing Deal 159

    Administrative Music Publishing Deal 161

    Shark Deal 162

Licensing Published Songs 163

Types of Licenses 164

    Reproduction (Mechanical License) 164

    Public Performance (Blanket License) 164

    Synchronization License 165

    Master License 165

    Folio License 165

The National Music Publishers Association of America (NMPA) 166

Mechanical Licenses 166

The Harry Fox Agency (SESAC) 167

The Statutory Rate, Compensation, and Licensing 169

    The Controlled Composition Clause (CCC) 171

Indie Recordings of Cover Songs 173

Interactive Streams & Digital Configuration Mechanicals 173

Sampling 175

Public Performance (or Blanket Licenses) 176

    ASCAP 177

    BMI 179

    SESAC 180

Consent Decree 182

    Synchronization Licenses 183

    Master License 184

    Folio and Print Sheet Music 184

Other Licenses   185

Selling Copyrights/Selling the Publishing Company   185

Professional Organizations   186

Nashville Songwriters Association International   187

Summary   188

CHAPTER 6   193

Breaking In-Career Entrepreneurship   193

Creating Recording Artists   195

Artist's Career Timeline-Beginnings   195

The Digital Advantage   196

Business Plan   198

Getting Discovered   198

Entrepreneurship Lesson   202

Types of Businesses   203

    Sole Proprietorship   203

    Partnership   204

    Corporation   204

    Limited Liability Corporation (LLC)   204

Why Start a Label?   204

Indie Labels   185

Timing   206

Indie Label Entrepreneurship   206

Perceived Value of Acts   207

Summary   208

CHAPTER 7 211

Labels (Multiple Rights Organizations) 211

Traditional Market Economies of Scale 212

Recoupable Label Budgets 212

Defining Multiple Rights 216

Retail 217

Physical Sales 217

Digital Downloads 217

Freemium 218

Multiple Rights Revenues 218

Streaming 219

Music Publishing 224

Image & Branding 224

Merchandise Fulfillment 226

360 Deal Strategic Management 226

    More Artists Run 227

    Brand-Driven 227

    Price Flexible 227

    Cross-Promotional 227

    Able to Connect Artists with Technologists 228

    More Diversited into Live Events & Culture 228

The Glue 228

Five Territories 229

Local Repertoire 230

The Music Business Connection to Entertainment & Media 231

Cinema Revenues 233

Books and other Publishing Sources   233

Advertising Revenues   233

Computer & Digital Games   234

Summary   234

Chapter 8   237

Creating Profits Out of Creativity   237

Administration   238

Weekly Meeting   239

The Financial Formula   240

Department of Artists & Repertoire (A&R) 242

 Signing Acts & Songs - Deal Points 244

 Exclusive Recording Agreement   245

Executive Experience   247

Recording Budget   248

Artist Development   248

Department of Promotion & Publicity   250

 Radio   251

 Radio Programming   252

 Radio Tours   252

 Promotional Copies   252

 Mass Media - Passive Communication   253

 Day Parts   254

 Social Media   254

 Social Media - Interactive Communication   255

Marketing and Sales Department 256
    Market Research 257
Distribution Department 260
    Recorded Music 260
    Retail Sales 261
    Free Goods 261
    ISRC Codes 262
    UPC Codes 262
    Digital Downloads 263
Spotify 265
Streaming Revenues vs. Sales 265
Different Royalties 265
Legal/Multiple Rights 267
Summary 269

CHAPTER 9   273

The First Year 273
The Artist's Perspective 273
Live Ticket 275
The New Act's First Year 277
    Representation 277
    Studio 277
    Label Relations 278
    Artist Development 278
    Branding 278
    Promotion 278

Publicity 279

Marketing 279

Live Show & Tour 280

The Label's First Year 280

Label Analysis of Tour Numbers 282

Computing Royalties 282

Sound Exchange 283

The Small Print in the Deal 284

Multiple Rights Payments 289

Branding 289

Merchandise 289

Corporate Sponsorships 290

Label Kickback 290

The Recording Industry Association of America (RIAA) 290

Gold, Platinum, & Diamond Awards 291

The International Federation of the Phonographic Industry (IFPI) 291

Nielsen 291

Billboard 292

Variety 292

Buzz Angle 293

Summary 293

CHAPTER 10   297

Creating Recordings 297

Shift of Focus 298

Studios 300

The Recording Team   302
    Producers   302
    Independent Producers   303
    Studio Musicians   303
    Audio Engineers   304
    Royalty Artists   306
    Studio Singers   306
Aesthetics   307
Microphones   307
    Dynamic   308
    Robbin   308
    Condenser   308
Pickup Patterns   309
Consoles/Boards   309
Recorders/Software   310
Speakers   310
Effects   311
Studio Schedules   313
The Recording Process- Setting the Stage for Success   313
    Pre-Production   313
Stages of a Recording Session   316
    Basic Tracks   317
Digital vs Analog Recordings   318
    Overdubbing   318
    Mixdown   319
    Mastering   320
Unions   321

    SAG-AFTRA   321

    The AF of M   321

    Right-to-Work States   323

    The AF of M Sound Recording Labor Agreement   323

    The Special Payments Fund   324

    The Sound Recording Trust Agreement   325

    The SAG-AFTRA National Code of Fair Practice for Sound Recordings   325

    SAG-AFTRA Contingent Scales   327

Recording Budget   328

Recording Rate Scales   328

The Technical Legal Requirements   332

The Recording Budget All-Ins   332

Promotion and Publicity Budgets   333

Summary   334

Chapter 11   337

Artist Representation   337

Chain of Events   338

"Getting Discovered"   338

The Label/Management Connection   340

The Strategic Management Plan   341

The Management Team   341

    Personal Manager   342

The Artist Personal Manager Contract   345

    Power of Attorney   350

Types of Personal Mangers 350

Commission Base and Rates 350

Gross Revenues 351

Business Managers 351

Booking Agents 351

Tour or Road Managers 352

Attorneys 353

Outsourcing 353

Termination of the Deal 353

The Label Connection 354

Promoters 354

The Catch-22 355

Summary 355

CHAPTER 12 359

Generating the Stage Show 359

Creating a Show 359

    The Band's Legal Business 360

    The Band, Crew, & Equipment 360

The Live Ticket Show 362

    Transportation 363

    Hotels & Food 363

    Merchandise 364

    Self-Promoting 366

    Venues 368

Pitching the Deal 368

Show Production 369

Website & Press Kits 369

Creating the Tour 369

    The Rehearsal 370

    AF of M Road Show Scales 371

    Pricing the Show 371

    Baseline Budget 372

The Asking Price 377

The Value of the Act 377

The Price Range 378

    Booking Agent Fee 379

    Opportunity Vs. Risk 379

    Merchandise 383

    Tour Financials 384

    Tour Gross 385

    Paying the Label, Personal & Business Managers 386

    Artist's Mail Box Money 386

Artist Growth 387

Celebrity Access 387

Talent Agencies 388

Creative Artists Agency (CAA) 388

International Creative Management (ICM) 389

United Talent Agency (UTA) 389

William Morris Endeavor Entertainment (WME2) 390

Talent Agents 391

IEBA 391

NACA 392

Stage Names   392

Summary   393

CHAPTER 13   397

Launching the Concert Event   397

The Two-Week Notice   397

Creating Demand   399

Connecting the Dots   399

Revenue Streams   400

The Live Ticket   401

The Concert Business   402

The Staging Process -Recap   402

The Label's Buy In   403

Selling the Show- Recap   403

Bid Sheet   404

    Signatory   404

    Venue   405

    Promoter's Projected Expenses   405

    Pre-Show   406

    Sponsoring Radio Station   407

    Social Media   407

    I.A.T.S.E. Crew   407

    Ticketmaster   407

    The Promoter's Legal Business   408

Promoter's Show Expenses   409

    Talent   409

Security	409	
Operation Personnel	410	
Artist Riders	410	
Production/Tech Rider	410	
Medical Standby	410	
Fireman	411	
I.A.T.S.E. Crew (Show)	411	
Piano Rental	411	
Chairs	411	
Catering	412	
Equipment & Extra Professionals	412	

Post- Show Expenses   412

Projected Event Expenses   413

Ticket Sales Projected Revenues   415

Scaling the House/Ticket Prices   416

    The Scaling Formula   416

The Types of Deals   418

    Straight Guarantee   419

    Guarantee Plus a Percentage of the Net (Gate)   419

    Guarantee Versus a Percentage of the Net   419

    Guarantee Plus a Bonus   420

Concert Promotion Process   420

Profit Margins   420

Merchandising   421

Serious Music Market   422

AEG Live   423

On Stage Entertainment   423

Feld Entertainment   424

Cirque du Soleil   424

Virtual Corporations   425

Awards Shows   425

    The Grammys   425

    The Emmys   426

    The Oscars   426

Summary   427

Chapter 14   431

Careers   431

How We Got Here   431

The North American Industry Classification System NAIC   434

NAICA Jobs for Creative Artists & Technicians   439

The Future   442

Epilogue   443

Index   445

Chapter 1

The Psychology of Entertainment

If you want a career in today's entertainment and music industry, you've got to understand how much the business has changed over the past few years. It's not the same old let's pick up a guitar, learn how to sing, put on a few local shows, get discovered, sign a label deal, and become rich and famous. It's better than the old business by far for both artists and business- minded people who want to break into the business. Yet, it's more difficult to make serious money, as it's almost impossible to sell albums.

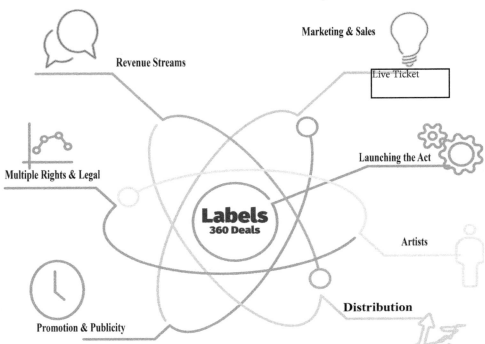

Only two albums sold platinum in 2017 in the U.S.A.[3] Yet, labels are still the banks and the engine that provide the knowledge, experience, and money

---

3 BuzzAngle Music 2017 US Year End Report." BuzzAngle Music. Accessed January 26, 2018. http://www.buzzangle-music.com/us-2017-ytd-report/.

(usually between $500,000 to $2,000,000) to launch artists, their recordings mass and social media, and branding, to consumers. Thus, the industry has changed business models to the 360 deal. According to Honeyman (2015),

> The old music industry is dead. We're standing in the ruins of a business built on private jets, Cristal, $18 CDs and million-dollar recording budgets. We're in the midst of the greatest music industry disruption of the past 100 years. A fundamental shift has occurred—a shift that Millennials are driving. For the first time, record sales aren't enough to make an artist's career, and they certainly aren't enough to ensure success. The old music industry clung desperately to sales to survive, but that model is long gone.[4]

THE 360 MUSIC INDUSTRY

In today's world, inventions, innovation, and digital technology have reinvented almost everything we do, every day of our lives. Netflix, Spotify, e-books and all the other Internet-based programming we consume are actually in competition for our spare time and available dollars. Iconic recording act's recordings are harder to sell. In some ways, they are not as important as they were in the past, because our understanding of fame and what is talent have changed over time. Years ago, we listened to the radio, bought a record or sometimes caught our favorite band or singer on a TV show. Now, there are so many ways to be entertained using digital tools that you can access whatever you want when you want it at the touch of your finger on a screen.

Record labels once used their "gut" feelings and local connections to tip them off about prospective new recording artists to sign. Now labels use an analysis of real Internet "hits" and psychographic research, metadata, analytics, and an accountant's financial projections of potential profits from album sales, branding, live ticket performances, merchandise sales, licensing and corporate endorsements before considering acts to sign.

---

4 Honeyman, Thomas. "How One Generation Was Single-Handedly Able To Kill The Music Industry." Elite Daily. June 6, 2014. Accessed May 30, 2015. http://elitedaily.com/music/how-one-generation-was-able-to-kill-the-music-industry/593411/.

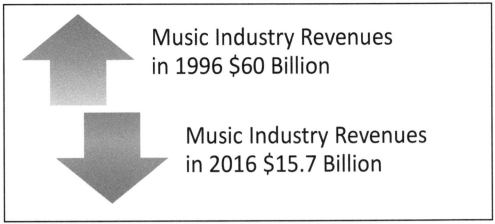

Figure 1.1: The music industry has dropped from an estimated gross, adjusted for inflation, of about $60 billion in 1996, down to about $15.7 billion in 2016. In addition, how we listen has changed dramatically from purchasing CDs and other recorded music formats to free and subscription streaming.[5,6] The numbers are frustrating. The difference between the previous gross revenues and the current gross income indicates a value gap in the money collected currently for streaming compared with album and singles sales.

The popularity of home recordings using ProTools and other types of computer-based software is reducing, and maybe even destroying, the fundamental need for demo studios, where aspiring artists cut their first recordings. However, few musicians can achieve the same level of inspired quality required to produce hit recordings without some use of live musicians working together in the creative atmosphere of a real recording studio.

Marketing, promotion, and publicity are also more difficult to sustain. The lines of distribution are switching from radio stations and major TV networks (who are losing their audience base at a shocking rate) to streaming of audio and video programming on sites currently protected by Safe Harbor laws (discussed in Chapter 3). Streaming simply doesn't pay close to the revenues generated by album sales as 1,500 streams equals the revenue and royalties generated by the sale of one album. At the same time, cable TV consumers are dropping their cable in favor of the Internet and Wi-Fi

---

5 Hogan, Marc. "How Much Is Music Really Worth?" How Much Is Music Really Worth? | Pitchfork. April 16, 2015. Accessed July 24, 2017. http://pitchfork.com/features/article/9628-how-much-is-music-really-worth/.
6 "An explosion in global music consumption supported by multiple platforms." Facts & Stats - IFPI - Representing the recording industry worldwide. Accessed July 24, 2017. http://www.ifpi.org/facts-and-stats.php.

(without the cable TV) and using social media sites for news, sports, online education, and entertainment.

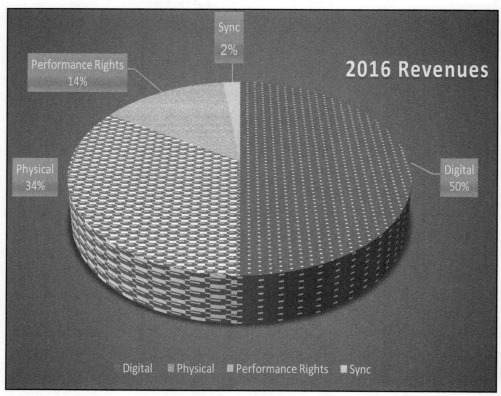

Figure 1.2: In 2016, the music industry grossed $15.7 billion total sales. Fifty percent ($7.85 billion) were digital revenues defined as free and subscription streaming, and digital downloads. Thirty-four percent ($5.3 billion) were physical sales of CDs and other types of physical formats. Fourteen percent ($2.2 billion) in PRO licensing, and two percent ($354 million) were Sync Licensing.[7]

In addition, most of us are actually dependent on our digital devices. Let's be honest, we are certainly emotionally connected to them, and why wouldn't we be? We can "see" our friends, live chat with tech support, and create new content, not to mention find and apply for jobs, take courses online. Instead of going to a library to find information or to read the newest book free while sitting in the library, we can download whatever we need in seconds. When it comes to entertainment, we don't have to sit and wait for the local radio station to play our new favorite songs. Furthermore, we use YouTube,

---
7 "An explosion in global music consumption supported by multiple platforms." Facts & Stats - IFPI - Representing the recording industry worldwide. Accessed July 24, 2017. http://www.ifpi.org/facts-and-stats.php.

Spotify, or one of the other 400 legal streaming sites to hear them. Who needs to call and talk to anyone? Text them your message, anytime, anyplace, and, hopefully not while you are driving your car. As discouraging as the numbers may appear to be, the fact is this is simply a different type of industry than the one in 1996. Music is music, yet the ways consumers find out about it, acquire it, and in some cases, use it has changed for the better.

We are at the beginning of the new music business revolution based on the 360 deals labels now offer their artists. That deal, where the labels receive part of the live ticket and part of the artist's gross revenues, has saved the business. It has driven the labels and personal management teams to work together to the advantage of the artist's successes and profits for all involved in the acts' career.

ACCESS

Digital devices and personal consumer preferences for streaming music and movies online has also saved consumers billions of dollars. They can acquire entertainment content anywhere, anytime. It is free or they pay a low subscription rate. However, many in the industry use the term "value gap" to describe the differences between the money generated from an album sale and the 1,500 streams that are supposed to equal one unit sold. It's a numbers game. As consumers continue to stream music products, the gap will continue to narrow. And streaming is increasing at nearly a double rate, which means in a few years, we'll be back to the profits the industry generated in 1996.

The R.I.A.A. (Recording Institute of America), who represent record labels in the United States, and the I.F.P.I (International Federation of Phonographic Industry), who represent labels worldwide, note some of the changes occurring in the industry (2017). Their research highlights the economic and consumer consumption trends in entertainment,

- Record labels are estimated to annually invest $4.5 billion worldwide in Artist & Repertoire (the Department of A&R), responsible for the signing of new acts, songs, studio recordings and artist development) combined with Marketing (The Department of Marketing), which is responsible for distribution, promotion, publicity and sales of the signed acts.[8]

- The major labels combined have around 7,500 artists on their rosters and tens of thousands more are signed to independent labels.[9]

- While each deal is different, the investments made by labels for advances, recordings, video production, tour support, and promotion, are between $500,000 to $2,000,000 to break a new act into the music market.[10]

- Research from the IFPI in 13 leading digital music markets (globally) shows that 69% of the Internet users have used a licensed digital music service in the past six months.[11]

- The primary driver of growth was a doubling of paid streaming music subscriptions which helped the American music business experience its biggest gain since 1998.[12]

CONSUMERS

Given the speed of how we use technology, there are numerous articles and

---

[8] "Record companies discover, nurture and promote artistic talent. They are by far the largest investors in artists' careers." Investment - IFPI - Representing the recording industry worldwide. Accessed July 24, 2017. http://www.ifpi.org/investment.php

[9] "Record companies discover, nurture and promote artistic talent. They are by far the largest investors in artists' careers." Investment - IFPI - Representing the recording industry worldwide. Accessed July 24, 2017. http://www.ifpi.org/investment.php.

[10] "Record companies discover, nurture and promote artistic talent. They are by far the largest investors in artists' careers." Investment - IFPI - Representing the recording industry worldwide. Accessed July 24, 2017. http://www.ifpi.org/investment.php.

[11] "Music fans have more choice of licensed digital music services." Consumer Research - IFPI - Representing the recording industry worldwide. Accessed July 24, 2017. http://www.ifpi.org/consumer-research.php.

[12] "News and Notes on 2016 RIAA Shipment and Revenue Statistics." RIAA. Accessed July 24, 2017. https://www.riaa.com/reports/news-notes-2016-riaa-shipment-revenue-statistics/.

books being published about how our brains have adapted to the software that drives our phones and computers. Let's take a closer look at how we have integrated technology into our daily routines and what that means to the entertainment and music business. In the new 360 music industry, the industry has to understand the consumers better then ever before. We will start with a quick look at our brains. As you can see, the ways consumers acquire and use music, recordings, and artists for personal enjoyment is the key to success in this industry now more than ever!

BEING HUMAN

Humans have been on the planet about 7 million years. According to some scientists, we evolved into our current stature only in the last 200,000 years. More amazing is that we have only been what some people like to call "civilized" for about 6,000 years.[13] Most of us, except the Chinese, mark our calendars with the arrival of Christ (BC) and After Christ's Death (AD). In the big picture of time, 2000 years is a blink of the eye. Some even claim that we are living in the "post- Christian Era", although the calendars have not changed.

Have you noticed things seem to keep speeding up when it comes to how we connect and interact with each other? Are you aware of how technology has been struggling to adapt to the changes as quickly as possible? Of course, all of this is just the next step in the technical digital delivery revolution for acquiring information and entertainment products that started well over 600 years ago. The speed of the technological advances has offered all of us an overwhelming menu of "choices" when we are seeking to entertain ourselves.

To understand what I am suggesting, we need to gain a deeper understanding of how consumers perceive the entertainment products we buy, use and enjoy as valuable. Before you think I'm going off the deep end, consider that

---

[13] Howell, Elizabeth. "How Long Have Humans Been on Earth?" Universe Today. December 23, 2015. Accessed May 10, 2017. https://www.universetoday.com/38125/how-long-have-humans-been-on-earth/.

we have to perceive as valuable the entertainment products we buy, use, and enjoy or we will look for fun and fulfillment elsewhere. The question "Why do we value what we do?" is key to understanding and, eventually, managing consumer preferences, which is especially important in the entertainment and music business. With all the choices, and all the ways to acquire entertainment products, we need to understand what people value and want in order to create demand for the products and artists that labels and others are investing in. This is explained further in Chapters 8, 9, 10, and 11.

What Do Entertainment Products Mean to Us?

As we evolved into more modern societies, we started to realize we had some spare time to actually think, create, connect, and dispute our own sense of realities. Where you grew up, in what type of family, how much money you had and have, and what kind of education you have and will have, as well as what kinds of entertainment you like are part of what we call our "frame of reference".

This means that our tastes in everything from clothing to food to entertainment and what we fundamentally believe are linked our past experiences, and future desires and goals. When we can't figure stuff out, we frequently ask others to help us understand the situation or ourselves better. On our trip to self-discovery, we ask people we know and people we have never met, our "friends" on social media, to help us understand ourselves better.

Let's start with the basics about how we might think and process information now compared to the past. While what you have just read may raise questions about where we headed in this discussion, we are trying to uncover mindsets and behaviors of people who are also the consumers to whom the music industry wants to sell stream music, sell CDs, merchandise, and tickets for live events. Our need to emotionally create feelings for ourselves has not changed, but the processes used in the creation of entertainment and artistic products, along with their delivery, market share, laws, and the related, adjusted business models certainly have. If you are in the music industry, and you want to sell entertainment to customers, the best strategy is to know why consumers enjoy music. Let's start there!

The Play Theory of Humanity

If we are going to have a chance at success in the entertainment and music industry, we have to commit ourselves to figuring out how to create a demand for industry's entertainment products and what draws consumers to certain types of products and not others. While recording artists express their creativity through their recordings and live shows, others have jobs geared toward drawing profits out of the emotional relationships consumers' build for themselves when listening or watching their favorite acts. Creating a demand for the recordings, shows, and brands is only part of their job. The clincher is selling it or having businesses and consumers use it (as in streaming) to make profits.

When consumers make the personal connection to feeling something, be it happy or sad, they accept the marketed creative product as a desirable form of entertainment, which we hope they want more of, as that creates revenue for the business. Insight into the fundamental links between why we might use our imagination to play perceptual games in our own minds can be found in *Humo Ludens: A Study of the Play-Element in Culture.* This book was written by Huizinga back in the early 1900s, as cognitive psychology was developing as a science. Consider some of these concepts from Huizinga's theory of play and imagination and what they may have to do with entertainment,

> *Play only becomes possible, thinkable, and understandable when an influx of mind breaks down the absolute determinism of the cosmos.*

> *Any thinking person can see at a glance, that play is a thing on its own, even if his language possesses no general concept to express it.*

> *No other language in the world has the exact equivalent definition of the English word "fun". French has no correspond term, German tries by combining the word spass (which is related to having a good time at work), and Witz together.*

> *The reality of play extends beyond the sphere of human life . . . to animals such as dogs and others.*[14]

A little deep of course, but one study of mine found that what executives want in potential employees is the ability to THINK and SOLVE PROBLEMS. So, a basic understanding of how entertainment products and how they are used by consumers to connect emotionally through imagination or mental playfulness, makes sense to me. In the quote below, I have added some entertainment industry language to Huizinga's claims to suggest how you can make them match,

> *. . . try to take play as the player (consumer) takes it: in its primary significance. If we find that play (entertainment products such as music) is based on the manipulation of certain imagination of reality (i.e. its conversion into images), then our main concern will be to grasp the value and significance of these images and their imagination".*[15]

Huizinga, whose work became one of the foundations in game design philosophy, goes on to argue that most languages, laws, wars, poetry, and philosophy are simply elements of human play. Is it then a stretch to investigate the connection of our minds and capacity for self-play to the business of entertainment, music products, and performances? Let's take a look at how our brains use entertainment products and why we select various types of products to spark our sense of inner, imaginative play.

OUR BRAINS ON MUSIC

Every heard of passionate fans? Why does a person become a fan of a recording artist? What about branding? Savvy industry professionals use the

[14] Huizinga, Johan. Homo Ludens: a study of the play-element in culture. 2nd ed. Boston: The Beacon Press, 2009.
[15] Ibid.

value consumers associate with the recording artists, songs, and how the artist looks or sounds to sell products. Again, the question is why and how does this work?

Researcher and author Daniel Levitin takes our examination of the relationship of entertainment, imagination, and the development of the human mind a few steps deeper. He says music, specifically, over the last 10,000 years, has helped shape our brains in six ways, including how we experience knowledge, friendship, religion, joy, comfort, and love.[16] Levitin says,

> ... *at least in part, the evolution of music and brains over tens of thousands of years and across the six inhabited continents. Music, I argue, is not simply a distraction or a pastime, but a core element of our identity as a species, an activity that paved the way for more complex behaviors such as language, large-scale cooperative undertakings, and the passing down of important information from one generation to the next. This book explains how I came to the (some might say) radical notion that there are basically six kinds of songs that do all of this. They are songs of friendship, joy, comfort, knowledge, religion, and love.*[17]

EMOTIONS OF ENTERTAINMENT

Fans appear to create as many as a dozen different emotions when listening to various forms of music, but how the emotions are turned into meanings specific to an individual emotion is still not fully understood. However, Susanne K. Langer (1951) suggests in her book *Philosophy in a New Key: A study in the Symbolism of Reason, Rite, and Art* the ranges of emotions, art, and ritual (such as a concert) can produce in people (see the table below). [18]

Now, with all our devices, we use music and our ear buds to walk through our days in any emotional state we want and may need. We can be listening

---

16 Levitin, Daniel J. "Chapter 1: Taking from the Top." In *The World in Six Songs: How the Musical Brain Created Human Nature*, 3- 4. First ed. New York, New York: Dutton/A Penguin Group, 2008.
17 Ibid.
18 Langer, Susanne K. "The New Key." In *Philosophy in a New Key: A Study in the Symbolism of Reason, Rite, and Art*, 1-19. 3d ed. Cambridge, MA: Harvard University Press, 1957.

to our favorite hits if we're in a world of joy or even if we're stuck in a world of controlled darkness. We have now come to our second strategy that's important to understand as we examine how consumers experience music and entertainment products differently.

Sadness	Seriousness	Excitement	Happiness
Relaxation	Amusement	Sentiment	Longing
Patriotism	Devotion	Irritation	Want to dance

CONSTRUCTIVISM

George Kelly's *Theory of Personality* provides some clues into how and why we change our minds. Knowing this is especially helpful when you are trying to create something that satisfies both what you want to communicate to a consumer and what the consumer will gravitate toward as an entertainment product. As mentioned above, we want to try to understand what makes people "think differently" as part of our role in understanding what consumers want when it comes to entertainment products.

One of Kelly's theories is we tend to select the types of music, books, films, plays, and events that help us understand, define, or celebrate who we are. This may be the "who" of our subconscious sense of self and how we define reality. How odd is it that we seem to want to use some form of fantasy to figure out reality? Funny, isn't it? Maybe some of the realities of the world are better off not being thought about at all.

After many replications of the same or like experiences, what Kelly called impressions, the selections we make about how we answer who we are seem to help us shape the pathways in our minds that become our belief system (of what the world is really about) and our personality (how we fit into it). This is a more sophisticated way of thinking about how we develop those frames of reference I mentioned earlier in the chapter. In the music industry, the marketing departments put these concepts to use to help create a demand for the acts, their recordings, and brands in an attempt to connect the consumers to the products.

Electronic nerve signals and brain chemical reactions to music, books, and movies serve as a cognitive stimulus. If our subconscious chooses, it seems we can make an emotional connection instantly. Yet, why one person enjoys one type of entertainment and others don't is part of the game. Indeed, what we enjoyed as a kid we probably don't laugh at now, as we get older. Do listening to and watching entertainment products enrich our life? Of course, because it is FUN! Now, if we can make money at the same time, why not go for it! In today's entertainment industry, we use big data and analytics to determine what type of person prefers what type of entertainment products. Then, we market specifically to the people who will most likely buy or use them. Guess whose job that is?

The third step in better understanding potential music entertainment consumers is to know where they live, work, and play, and why they shop for or listen to various types of entertainment and music products, such as recordings, and why they seek out certain live performances.

LIFESTYLE SEGMENTATION

Here is where things get really interesting. We do not all see or psychologically "perceive" events the same way. Everyone is different and unique, yet marketing executives use data on our personal buying habits and decisions (at the subconscious level it appears) to "fit" us into 68 lifestyles in the United States. According to Claritas,

> *Savvy marketers are challenged with understanding the consumer. PRIZM® is the industry-leading lifestyle segmentation system that yields rich and comprehensive consumer insights to help you reveal your customer's preferences. PRIZM combines demographic, consumer*

behavior, and geographic data to help marketers identify, understand and reach their customers and prospect... PRIZM defines every U.S. household in terms of 68 demographically and behaviorally distinct types, or "segments," to help marketers discern those consumers' likes, dislikes, lifestyles and purchase behaviors. Used by thousands of marketers within Fortune 500 companies, PRIZM provides the "common language" for marketing in an increasingly diverse and complex American marketplace[19]

If we believe Kelly and Construct Theory, entertainment and music are perceived as "playful mental events" used to help us shape, understand, and celebrate our personality, position in life, and other things. Within us, shifts in perception happen at a subconscious level so fast we don't even know they're happening. However, we do seem to know when we are experiencing the emotions of happiness, sadness, and any of the others on Langer's list. Why are we conflicted and feeling different? Could it be our subconscious is trying to tell our conscious mind that something is going on and that we need to take a few moments and try to figure it out?

One way we appear to accomplish making connections between perceptions, emotions, and reason is by dreaming. According to a recent article in *Medical News Today* (2017), researchers are speculating on the necessity of dreaming to brain development. The list below is some of the ways they see dreaming linked to both the intellect and the imagination:

- *... consolidates learning and memory tasks.*
- *... is active during mind wandering and daydreaming.*
- *Dreaming could be seen as cognitive simulation of real life experiences.*
- *Participates in the development of cognitive capabilities.*
- *... incorporates three temporal dimensions: experience of the present, processing of the past, and preparation for the future.*

---

19 "Segment Details." Claritas MyBestSegments. Accessed June 19, 2017. https://segmentationsolutions.nielsen.com/mybestsegments/Default.jsp?ID=30&pageName=Segment%DEtails.

- *... serves the need for psychological balance and equilibrium.*[20]

Dreaming, it appears, can help us learn and develop long-term memories.[21] Think about the similarities between our emotions and feelings about ourselves when we listen to music. A recent article from the *Psychology of Music* (2014) says we listen to music for three reasons including [22]

- *... to regulate arousal and mood,*
- *... to achieve self-awareness,*
- *... as an expression of social relatedness*[23]

We seem to know what we need to choose to entertain ourselves as an instant experience of "What if?" Our subconscious seems aware of when it is healthy for us to distract our minds and consciousness and enter into a world of play and imagination.

Can you think of someone whose company has made well over a billion dollars doing exactly that? Ever heard of Walt Disney? Sometimes we become comfortable with our constructed sense of reality in order to grow into the types of people we are right now. But how do we grow mentally over time? That is when something throws us a curve ball and we are once again placed into a mental state of questioning what's real and what it means to me. Here's an example to help explain what I mean.

Let's say you are driving your car approaching a green light. We drive through it because we know the cars approaching the red light will stop. But, let's say another car runs the red light and smashes into you. Shock, nailed, bewildered! Guess what? The next time we approach a green traffic light, we'll probably slow down a little and look both ways before driving on. Why did your behavior change? Because we discovered the "reality" that going through a green light may not be as safe as we thought it was!

---

20 Nichols, Hannah. "Dreams: Why do we dream?" Medical News Today. February 23, 2017. Accessed June 04, 2017. http://www.medicalnewstoday.com/articles/284378.php.
21 Ibid.
22 "The Psychology of Music: Why We Listen to Music and How It Affects The Mind." Reflectd. October 20, 2016. Accessed June 04, 2017. http://reflectd.co/2014/06/17/the-psychology-of-music/.
23 Ibid.

Why do kids enjoy Mickey Mouse and Donald Duck when very young and later don't care for it? Why do many college students have a liberal attitude about politics, saving the world, etc., and then become politically conservative later in life? There are not any right or wrong answers. No judgment is being prescribed, just a thought about how our minds work and how we can change our minds, tastes and actions over time, based on our engagement and experiences in the world without even knowing our minds are doing it.

Let's take a deeper look into why listening to music can be perceived as a valuable experience to consumers. Remember, if we want to be in the business of creating and selling music it might be wise to understand why consumers consider it valuable. According to researchers Miendlarzewska and Trost (2014) "listening to music influences the cognitive development of our brains."[24] North (2012) suggests, "music influences our perceptions",[25] while Kawakami and colleagues (2013) claim listening to "sad music makes us feel better."[26] On the other hand, Ziv and colleagues (2011) claim that "listening to music increases our perception of hope".[27] Notice the connections these separate writers make between music and brain development, music and emotion, and music and a sense of well-being. These are key in understanding how to find and market music to potential consumers.

THE GLOBAL MARKET

Why did we dive into all the psychological stuff? Because labels and artists understand consumers' wants and needs and how to best reach them through various types of traditional and social media. If you want to be in this business, you need to have a basic understanding of it also. Now you

---

24 Miendlarzewska, Ewa A., and Wiebke J. Trost. "How musical training affects cognitive development: rhythm, reward and other modulating variables." Frontiers in Neuroscience. 2013. Accessed June 04, 2017. https://www.ncbi.nlm.nih.gov/pmc/articles/PMC3957486/.
25 North, Adrian C. "The effect of background music on the taste of wine." British Journal of Psychology. September 07, 2011. Accessed June 04, 2017. http://onlinelibrary.wiley.com/doi/10.1111/j.2044-8295.2011.02072.x/abstract;jsessionid=6AD00446F7EC5E4B7C9B17160772223E.f01t03.
26 KAWAKAMI, AI, Kiyoshi Furukawa, Kentaro Katahira, and Kazuo Okanoya. "Sad music induces pleasant emotion." Frontiers. May 14, 2013. Accessed June 04, 2017. http://journal.frontiersin.org/article/10.3389/fpsyg.2013.00311/full.
27 Ziv, Naomi, Anat Ben Chaim, and Oren Itamar. "The effect of positive music and dispositional hope on state hope and affect." Psychology of Music. March 24, 2010. Accessed June 04, 2017. http://journals.sagepub.com/doi/abs/10.1177/0305735609351920.

do! As one lady I was talking to recently said to me, "Listening to music is pure inspiration". This is a business, and understanding the consumers and what they want is vital for not only the label and the acts' successes, but yours, also. Clearly, consumers place a very high value on music. It is not wrong to think of music as an extension of one's sense of self. The record labels' job is to provide recordings, acts, and shows that have the ability to give consumers what they will most enjoy and in the process, make a profit.

With the Internet and digital technology, the market has also changed from local and national to a global market full of thousands of new entertainers, venues, and new forms of products, such as computer games. With all the content creators, distribution channels, and evolving markets, it makes hitting the "big time" much more difficult for the emerging artist or new entertainment company.

The sheer mass of products and services and the speed of availability has made our job of selecting products much more difficult. Instead of hundreds of choices, we now have hundreds of thousands to millions all available at the same time, which tends to make our ability to choose an overwhelming experience. This makes the kind of data labels and entertainment companies need to collect to build the psychological profiles of their consumers more of an adventure then in the past. Ever heard of metadata? Metadata and analytics are windows into how consumers' use digital technology.

This type of data further reveals the significant number of consumer choices available in selecting technology and the significant number of choices in selecting various types of entertainment products. Managing the catalogs for global businesses takes skills in understanding consumer culture and the consumer's culture. Executives and leaders in the entertainment and music business are familiar with regional tastes and preferences, the aspirations of the entertainment marketplace as a global player, finance and global currency, laws, consumer preferences, and many other tangible and intangible characteristics that make up the consumers and the marketplace culture. Because the world is different today, no one person can do all of the above. Existing companies, in particular, need you and others with the ability to solve their problems so that they can continue to grow the business and their profits.

Summary

Consumers project a value into and onto the entertainment products they are using or watching to help them feel good about themselves. Ever get excited at a concert? Want to spend money on overpriced t-shirts and merchandise? There is a job for you as a creative artist or an employee in the business if you can make "the it" experience happen. Consumers use their emotional connection to an act or products to feel excitement or obtain a better understanding of an experience. It's the industry's job to create "the it" experience and to sell it, preferably around the world. To do that, you have to know your market. You need to collect marketing data on fans in multiple ways, as we saw earlier in the chapter, by using the zip code based purchasing data as collected by Claritas for US consumers, for example. The more known about consumers the easier it is to sell them concert tickets, branded items, merchandise, and other revenue generating items.

Are you starting to see the entertainment and music industry is much larger and more varied than what you may have thought when you said you wanted to "be in the industry"? Entertainment companies are actively seeking people like you who can be part of or lead teams to solve their on-going need to find the right products that will make enough money to sustain and grow their businesses. If you can demonstrate abilities in market research, psychographics, finance, business modeling, and add in some understanding of law, politics, and the culture of the place where you find yourself working, that makes you valuable.

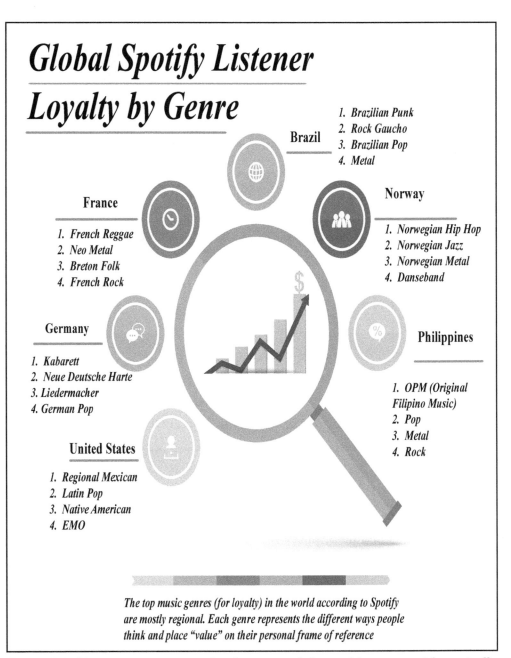

Figure 1.4: It's a surprise to see what fans around the world connect with musically. According to the Spotify data, it appears the most loyal fans in the U.S. listen to Regional Mexican and Latin Pop, while in Norway it's Norwegian Hip Hop. The music and entertainment industry make their money supplying the types of music genre fans most want to hear and enjoy. As an artist, musician, label executive, we need to understand how people think differently around the world if we want to be successful.[28]

28 Buskirk, Eliot Van. "Which Music Genres Have the Loyalest Fans?» Insights. October 09, 2015. Accessed August

You never want to lose the desire to investigate the connection of our minds and imaginations (self-psychological play) to almost everything about our lives, including the way we think, and more directly, to how the business of entertainment, music products and performances works. Let's summarize our look at how our brains use entertainment products and why we select various types of products to spark our sense of inner imaginative play.

Think of the songs, films, media, etc., that got us through falling in and out of love, personal problems, illness, other events affecting our daily moods and life. What's being created, marketed, and sold as entertainment are packages of the best and worst of humanity and most everything in between.

By now, it should be clear how entertainment products are sought out by consumers to help them enjoy life. Subconsciously, consumers engage in an immersion process that frees their minds, imaginations, and emotions for a cognitively driven sense of play. When we have imaginatively played a role in the entertainment we just experienced-think of playing air guitar with Eric Clapton- we have built a bond between what we have heard and who we want to be. Can you start to understand that once we start to see the world and ourselves in it differently, then we may become motivated or inspired to continue to improve our lives? This, as Shakespeare says, "is the stuff that dreams are made of".

Ours is one heck of a great business if you know what you are doing and have the talent to actually write, create, produce, market, and sell entertainment products to consumers who perceive those products as having innate value to how they live their lives and who they think they are. Now that we began a dialog about of why and how consumers value entertainment products, let's take a look at how we got to where we are in the entertainment and music business today through the development of technology

08, 2017. https://insights.spotify.com/us/2015/04/02/loyalest-music-fans-by-genre/.

and entrepreneurship. The question is. . . do you now have a better understanding of how consumers "value" entertainment products after reading this chapter? Have you also gained a better understanding of how music and other entertainment products communicate a stimulus to consumers who may then use it psychologically to help themselves "emotionally and cognitively" connect to their essence?

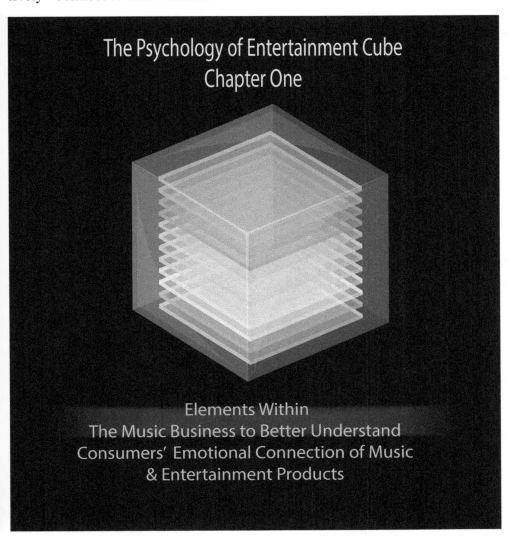

Think of each chapter in this book as a "block of knowledge" made up as a cube with "layers of information". If we understand each layer, then we'll also understand the meaning of each cube or block. Assume the music industry is really a bunch of "building blocks" stacked on top of each other.

At the end of each chapter you will see a cube representing one of the building blocks full of the corresponding "layers of information". Take some time to make sure you know each layer of information and how it's related to the other layers of information. Once you've accomplished that, you should have a good understanding of "what makes up the block of knowledge" and then be ready for the next chapter in the book and it's corresponding block of knowledge. By the end of the book you'll be able to put the blocks together and have a much better understanding of how this industry really works and where you fit in.

Chapter 2

The Power of Innovation

The music industry has confronted the reality of change, adapt, or die. In reality, it's how people think and psychologically "use" entertainment products that creates the opportunity to turn consumer's enjoyment of music into a business. Now, let's take a quick look at the innovations and inventions that had to be developed to create, record, and distribute music before we there was an actual business. Why are we reviewing the inventions and such corresponding businesses such as radio, the social media, the Internet, and personal devices? Because they play a significant role in the creation, distribution, promotion, and publicity in today's typical 360 deal processes that lead to successes for artists, tour promoters, merchandising sales, branding, and label profits.

ENTREPRENEURSHIP AND THE EARLY LABELS

Making money in the music business has depended on the use of inventions and technology that were available at the time to innovatively capture "new market shares" of consumers with products they would use or buy. That's what businesses do, offer in exchange for money, either a product or a service, or both. That's an important lesson that most of the people who create entertainment products on their computers and then upload them to websites such as YouTube tend to forget. You are a business if you're trying to make money or use another person or company's property, such as a song, video, or musical recording, which we call a copyrighted product.

The Printing Press

Welcome to the 1400s or the Age of Enlightenment and the Gutenberg printing press with movable type. Consider the impact of the work one inventor had in revolutionizing access to both educational and entertainment products with movable type:

> *The first man to demonstrate the practicability of movable type was Johannes Gutenberg (1398–1468), the son of a noble family of Mainz, Germany. A former stonecutter and goldsmith, Gutenberg devised an alloy of lead, tin and antinomy that would melt at low temperature, cast well in the die, and be durable in the press. It was then possible to use and reuse the separate pieces of type, as long as the metal in which they were cast did not wear down, simply by arranging them in the desired order. The mirror image of each letter (rather than entire words or phrases), was carved in relief on a small block. Individual letters, easily movable, were put together to form words; words separated by blank spaces formed lines of type; and lines of type were brought together to make up a page. Since letters could be arranged into any format, an infinite variety of texts could be printed by reusing and resetting the type.*[29]

The invention of the printing press was a trailblazer in the development of many different types of businesses. Here is a look at how *Time Magazine* evolved far from its roots as a weekly news magazine. *Time Magazine*, which eventually became part of Time Warner, is related to the Warner Music Group record label. Briton Hadden and Henry Luce created Time Publications in 1922. According to an analysis of its history provided by Kelly (2003), "*Time* was first published on March 3, 1923, as a newsmagazine which summarized and organized the news so 'busy men' could stay informed".[30]

Warner Music was created in 1811 as Chappell & Co., a sheet music and musical instrument store in London.[31] In 1923, Harry, Jack, Albert, and Sam

29 Kreis, John S. "The Printing Press." *The History Guide, Lectures on Modern European Intellectual History.* September 11, 2014. Accessed June 25, 2016. http://www.historyguide.org/intellect/press.html.
30 "History of TIME - Archive Collection." Time. Accessed June 20, 2017. http://content.time.com/time/archive/collections/0,21428,c_time_history,00.shtml.
31 Warner Music Group. "Time Line", http://www.wmg.com/timeline, (accessed June 18, 2013)

Warner founded Warner Bros. Films, and, in 1925, they purchased exclusive rights to the invention of the "Vitaphone" which allowed them to turn silent films into "talkies."[32] One thing led to another and these entrepreneurs had products to develop, manage, and deliver to consumers through three markets, print, music and movies.

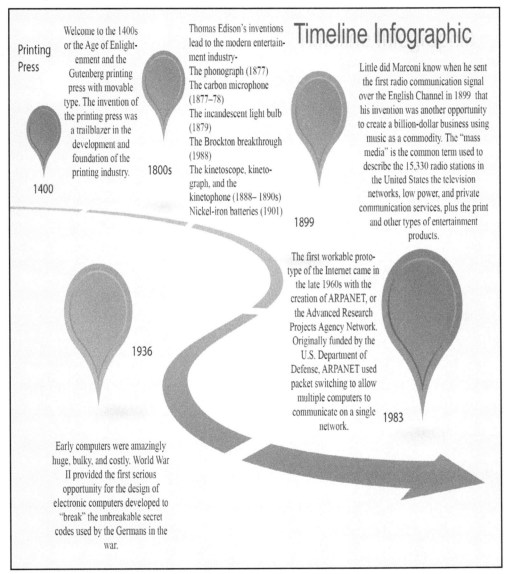

Figure 2.1: It's the inventions and the innovations over the last couple of centuries that have provided the foundation for the entertainment business.

---

32 "Warner Music Group | Culture." Warner Music Group Official Website. Accessed June 20, 2017. http://www.wmg.com/culture

FILM, MICROPHONES, THE PHONOGRAPH, & BATTERIES

We often limit our recognition of creative people to artists, painters, and symphony conductors, but Thomas Alva Edison (1847-1931) was also a brilliantly creative inventor of *devices*. The scientific discoveries he and others made developed into innovative tools that by and large still sustain the majority of entertainment products we enjoy. The creation of these new entertainment devices and techniques really started with fresh ways to use electricity. Some of the most important discoveries came initially from the Serbian (now Croatian) innovator Nikola Tesla (1856–1943), whose idea of alternating electrical current, as opposed to Edison's application of direct current, led to the foundation of wireless communication systems, the design of the modern generator, and other engineering-based inventions.

Between Edison and Tesla, who came to America to work with Edison, the first light bulb, camera, projector, microphone, and sound recorder (a cylinder device) that led to the phonograph were all designed, tested, improved upon, and patented. Edison's inventions when used by some very bright businessmen and women led to recorded music, radio programs, films, movies, and, eventually, computer games. In essence, Edison created how most of us receive our entertainment products delivered over radio, TV, Internet, and in live theater. According to the site *Howstuff-works.com*, Edison invented-

- *The phonograph (1877)—Edison earned his nickname "The Wizard of Menlo Park" in November 1877 when he invented the world's first method of recording and playing back sound.*

- *The carbon microphone (1877–78)—Alexander Graham Bell may have invented the telephone, but it was Edison who invented a microphone that turned the telephone from a promising gadget into an indispensable machine with real, practical applications.*

- **The incandescent light bulb (1879)**—*Without a doubt, the light bulb is Edison's most famous invention. Scientists and inventors had been racing against each other for years, trying to invent artificial light. Edison cinched the win by creating an incandescent bulb with a carbon filament that could be practically reproduced.*

- **The Brockton breakthrough (1883)**—*Once the world had light, it needed a way to power that light. In the tiny town of Brockton, Massachusetts, Edison set out to construct one of the world's first three-wire electrical power plants as a way to show the world that electric power was safer and more efficient than gas power.*

- **The kinetoscope, kinetograph, and kinetophone (1888–1890s)**—*Edison and his assistant William Dickson first invented the kinetoscope, a boxlike contraption that enabled a single viewer to watch a motion picture short through a peep- hole. Films were recorded with a motion picture camera called the kinetograph; later, the kinetophone attempted to add sound to moving pictures.*

- **Nickel-iron batteries (1901)**—*Before steam- and gasoline-powered engines were popularized, some of the world's first automobiles were powered by batteries. Edison's nickel-iron batteries were an improvement, in terms of both ecological impact and charging time, over the more commonly used lead- acid batteries of the day.*[33]

---

33 Gerlinda Grimes "What did Thomas Edison invent?" 12 January 2011. HowStuffWorks.com. <http://science.howstuffworks.com/innovation/famous-inventors/what-did-thomas-edison-invent.htm> 26 May 2017

It didn't take long before some investors converted the invention of recording music into a business. The story of the sound recording industry on phonograph discs spans the invention of the phonograph in 1877 to the 1940s, when new technologies such as television emerged. The original major labels in the industry were Victor, Columbia, and HMV (which originally stood for His Master's Voice) until the end of World War II. These companies all got their start in the 1890s, when the phonograph was still young.[34] Nevertheless, Columbia Records claims to be the first actual label.

According to columbiarecords.com (2017),

> *While working on refining the telegraph in 1887, Thomas Alva Edison hit on the idea of transcribing sounds on a cylinder wrapped in tinfoil, and the patent for his "phonograph" was issued on February 19, 1878. With this technology and the leadership of Edward Denison Easton, the Columbia Phonograph and the American Graphophone Company became the beginnings of what would evolve to be Columbia Records, a company famed not only for its music but also the entire history of the American recording industry and its impact on modern life.*[35]

Thomas Edison's 1877 invention of what eventually became the phonograph was followed by most notably the "graphophone", which became the basis of the Columbia Records Company.[36] Both inventions used a cylinder with groove in it until Columbia invented the flat disk. The original primary markets for the label were businessmen, lawyers, court reporters, and others who used stenography to capture important thoughts or compose letters. Marconi (who is credited with the invention of radio) created the "Velvet Tone" disc that boosted sales for the label to an unheard of $150 million a year in 1919. In 1948, Columbia Records was owed by the

---

34 "125 Years of Columbia Records - An Interactive Timeline." Columbia Records Timeline. Accessed June 20, 2017. http://www.columbiarecords.com/timeline/#!date=1909-01-01_20:16:39!
35 "125 Years of Columbia Records - An Interactive Timeline." Columbia Records Timeline. Accessed June 20, 2017. http://www.columbiarecords.com/timeline/#!date=1909-01-01_20:16:39!
36 University of California, Santa Barbara. Library. Department of Special Collections. "Cylinder Preservation and Digitization Project." Index. November 16, 2005. Accessed June 20, 2017. http://cylinders.library.ucsb.edu/history-early.php.

Columbia Broadcasting System, (CBS TV) when it introduced the 33 &1/3 LP (long play) album on a vinyl disc, which became the industry standard. In the 1960s, the label introduced Columbia House direct mail order record club to the public, using the idea of direct marketing of books into the home by the German company, Bertelsmann A.G.[37]

Edison was aware his inventions likely had great value as industrial products and that others would pay for them. He didn't just invent devices the industry could use; he was also an *entrepreneur*, having started the Edison General Electric Company in 1892.[38] His company eventually became General Electric, one of the largest energy companies in the world, and he was the largest single shareholder. Edison's role in the development of the business of entertainment is also notable as he launched the first movie production company in 1893, called *The Black Maria,* which was the nickname of his Kinetographic Theater.[39] Through this company, he improved on late nineteenth century European efforts to design a movie projection system.

His inventions also led to the development of sound recordings, motion capture techniques, and projectors used in early film theaters notably in his groundbreaking 1903, reel *The Great Train Robbery,* which was filmed by a cameraman who had worked with Edison.[40] Can you see the correlations between Edison's inventions and the business of entertainment and music business, as we know it now? Consider the invention of the computer chip, add the brilliant Steve Jobs and Apple, and look at what happened to the music industry.

*****

---

37 Bill Damain, "The History of the Major Labels," Performing Songwriter Magazine, July/August, 2003
38 The Editors of Encyclopædia Britannica. "General Electric (GE)." Encyclopædia Britannica. February 16, 2017. Accessed June 21, 2017. https://www.britannica.com/topic/General-Electric.
39 "Thomas Edison Most Famous Inventions." Thomasedition.org. 2015. Accessed September 21, 2015. http://www.thomasedison.org/index.php/education/inventions/.
40 "Adventures in Early Movies: The Great Train Robbery and "Broncho Billy" Anderson, Pt. 1." White City Cinema. April 20, 2015. Accessed June 21, 2017. https://whitecitycinema.com/2012/07/23/adventures-in-early-movies-the-great-train-robbery-and-broncho-billy-anderson-pt-1/.

The Early Labels

Usually, new business models and markets are created by entrepreneurs, who are often the only ones wild and crazy enough to reinvent the wheel. Labels, in the early stages of the business, were launched by entrepreneurs who were either creative artists themselves or executives who visualized the potential profits of marketing live performances.

According to a *Performing Songwriter Magazine* article (2003), most of the early labels were entrepreneurial ventures that "blew up" into huge multiple billion dollar corporations. The article is used below as a basic element to provide a summary of the early labels.[41]

---
41 Bill Demain, "The History of the Major Labels," Performing Songwriter Magazine, July/August, 2003

- **RCA Records** (Recording Corporation of America) began as a by-product label from the establishment of the Victor Talking Machine Company in 1901 by Emile Berliner and Eldridge Johnson. The company label under the name Victor connected to HMV (the English label – His Master's Voice) and grew into a very successful label with recording artists Enrico Caruso, Al Jolson, and then later under the RCA label with Tommy Dorsey, Glenn Miller, Perry Como, Dinah Shore, Dolly Parton, David Bowie, and Elvis Presley.[42]

- **Capitol Records** was founded in 1942 by songwriter Johnny Mercer, movie producer and songwriter Buddy DeSylva, and retail record storeowner Glenn Walichs. Capitol Records' major success came after it was purchased by EMI (Electrical Music Industries) in 1956 and its release of very successful albums by the Beach Boys and The Beatles.[43]

- **Warner Bros. Records** was established by movie mogul Jack Warner in 1958. He used many of Warner Bros TV shows and movies to sell music by connecting the two in cross marketing efforts using artists in hit shows such as Kookie, Edd Byrnes from (77 Sunset Strip) and comedian Bob Newhart to sell recorded products. …The Everly Brothers and Frank Sinatra joined the roster along with Dean Martin and Sammy Davis Jr. Other great acts who recorded for the label under the supervision of Mo Ostin including The Kinks, The Grateful Dead, Joni Mitchell, The Doobie Brothers and Fleetwood Mac.[44]

- **Motown** launched by Berry Gordy Jr had the sign "Hitsville, USA" in front of his house in Detroit when he started the label in 1959. A songwriter himself, "Lonely Teardrops", Gordy used $800.00 of borrowed family money to start his company. The R&B recordings

---
42 Ibid.
43 Ibid.
44 Ibid.

from his label crossed over into top 40 radio with Smokey Robinson & The Miracles, The Temptations, Diana Ross, Marvin Gaye, The Commodores, the Jackson 5 and Stevie Wonder making him rich.[45]

- **MCA** (Music Corporation of America) was founded in 1924 as a Chicago-based talent agency by medical student Julies Stein, who booked bands on the side to get through school. It has gone through many different owners including Matsushita Electrical Industrial of Japan and Seagram Liquor of Canada. Chairman Edgar Bronfman added the number one entertainment company at the time PolyGram N.V. owned by Philips (the one "l" is the correct spelling), in 1998 for $10.6 billion.[46] Bronfman changed the name of the company to Universal, which is its current moniker and then sold the entertainment company and the liquor company to Vivendi of Paris, France for $32 billion. Later, MCA records was merged with Geffen Records, officially wiping the name of the company founded in 1924 by Stein and later run by the Lew Wasserman.[47]

- **A & M Records** was opened by Herb Alpert and Jerry Moss as Carnival Records in 1962 with $200. Later, they found out the name Carnival was already being used so they changed the name of their label to A&M Records using the first initials from their family names. After seeing a bullfight in Tijuana, Mexico, Alpert and Moss recorded a brassy sounding instrumental titled "The Lonely Bull" in their garage. It sold over 700,000 copies, which they shipped from the same garage. Additional artists signed to their label were The Carpenters, Joe Cocker, Humble Pie, Cat Stevens, the Police, Janet Jackson, and Alpert's own album *Whipped Cream*. The hit "A Taste of Honey" from their album made A&M one of the most successful independent labels ever launched. In 1989, Alpert and

---
45 Ibid.
46 "Seagram buys PolyGram." CNNMoney. Accessed June 21, 2017. http://money.cnn.com/1998/05/21/deals/tropicana/.
47 Arango, Tim. "MCA IS HISTORY – LONG-LIVED RECORD LABEL TO BE MERGED INTO GEFFEN." New York Post. May 22, 2003. Accessed June 21, 2017. http://nypost.com/2003/05/22/mca-is-history-long-lived-record-label-to-be-merged-into-geffen/.

Moss sold their $200 investment label to PolyGram (owned at that time by Philips Electronics of Holland) for half a billion dollars.[48]

What a great lesson for people who want to form their own labels today! An investment of $200 dollars by Herb Albert and Jerry Moss to form a music company that is later sold for $500 million. With inflation of about 2.5%, that is about **$1,001,792,531.12** in today's money (2017). Anyone want to start a record label?

INVENTIONS & TECHNOLOGY AS A COMMODITY

It was the investors and business entrepreneurs who took the inventions and used them to turn music into a commodity for profits. The same process was used by investors to turn Edison's invention of the camera into the billion-dollar film and movie industry which led to movie theaters and the television networks including NBC, (originally called the red and blue networks), and ABC (which was originally the NBC blue network, but was forced into new ownership by a Federal Communication decision) and CBS.[49]

As exciting as the profits of the entertainment companies are, it is vital to remember that it's the songs, music, iconic artists, movies, shows, and programming that are drawing the audiences. The technology is just being used to create and deliver the entertainment products to the consumers and the entrepreneurs and venture capitalists. The money the industry generates is only as good as the business structures (called business models) that make it happen. One thing often leads to another. Successful business ventures create new and additional types of supporting businesses, such as radio stations and television networks. They, in turn, encourage other business opportunities including cable TV, the Internet, cell phones, microwave communications, and Wi-Fi.

---

48 "A&M Records Confirms Sale." The New York Times. September 24, 1989. Accessed June 20, 2017. http://www.nytimes.com/1989/09/25/business/a-m-records-confirms-sale.html.
49 Erickson, Harold L. "American Broadcasting Company (ABC)." Encyclopædia Britannica. Accessed June 05, 2017. https://www.britannica.com/topic/American-Broadcasting-Company#ref167749.

Terrestrial Radio & Television

The invention of radio is closely related to the invention of the telephone by Alexander Graham Bell (1847–1922), and the telegraph by Samuel Morse (1791–1872). The story goes like this:

> During the 1860s, Scottish physicist, James Clerk Maxwell (1831–1889), predicted the existence of radio waves; and in 1886, German physicist Heinrich Rudolph Hertz (1851–1894) demonstrated that rapid variations of electric current could be projected into space in the form of radio waves similar to those of light and heat . . . In 1866, Mahlon Loomis, (1826–1886), an American dentist, successfully demonstrated "wireless telegraphy". Loomis was able to make a meter connected to one kite cause another one to move, marking the first known instance of wireless aerial communication . . . Guglielmo Marconi (1874–1937), an Italian inventor, . . . sent and received his first radio signal in Italy in 1895 . . . By 1899 he flashed the first wireless signal across the English Channel . . . Nikola Tesla (1856–1943) is now credited with being the first person to patent radio technology; the Supreme Court overturned Marconi's patent in 1943 in favor of Tesla.[50]

Radio stations have never been in the music business, as they make their profits from selling "air time", better known to us as commercials. Boring! Yet, it is a great business if you can get enough listeners, as the cost of the commercials is based on the number of people listening to the radio signals. Radio uses recordings provided free from the labels to create an audience they charge advertisers to deliver their messages to. Little did Marconi know when he sent the first radio communication signal over the English Channel in 1899[51] that his invention was another opportunity to create a billion-dollar business using music as a commodity.

The "mass media" is the common term used to describe the 15,330 radio stations in the United States and the other 15,030 licensed broadcast out-

---
50 Bellis, Mary. "The Invention of Radio - Wireless Telegraphy." About.com Inventors. October 21, 2015. Accessed June 25, 2016. http://inventors.about.com/od/rstartinventions/a/radio.htm.
51 Bellis, Mary. "Everything You Need to Know about the Invention of Radio." ThoughtCo. March 26, 2017. Accessed June 05, 2017. https://www.thoughtco.com/invention-of-radio-1992382.

lets a few of which are the television networks, low power, and private communication services.⁵² The broadcast stations are referred to as *terrestrial* meaning they broadcast different types and amounts of AM (amplitude based), FM (frequency based), radio signals and VHF (very high frequencies) and UHF (ultra-high frequencies) television signals through the air. AM signals are more powerful but have a very limited dynamic range which simply means consumers can't hear much of the base or high qualities of the instruments and vocals in a recording or live broadcast. Listen to a full-range of musical recording on FM and AM and you'll quickly hear the difference.

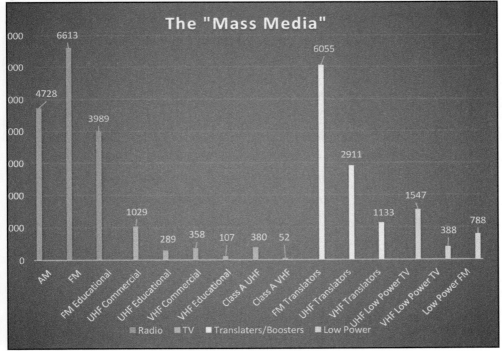

Figure 2.2: The mass media is made up of different types of terrestrial radio and television stations that broadcast entertainment products and shows over various types of networks. Currently in the United States, there are about 4728 AM radio stations, 6631 FM stations, and about 3989 FM educational radio stations. For television programming, there are 1029 UHF, 358 VHF, 396 educational and 432 Class A stations. In addition, there are 1,935 low power stations and 788 low power FM stations. To boost and send television station signal to remote areas there are an additional 10,099 FM translators and boosters.⁵³

---

52 "There Are 15,330 U.S. Radio Stations, But How Many Matter?" Hypebot. Accessed June 05, 2017. http://www.hypebot.com/hypebot/2013/10/there-are-15330-us-radio-stations-how-many-of-the-matter-to-you.html.
53 Ibid.

That is also why a lot of the hit recordings from the 1950s-1960s do not have much bass and treble in the recordings. The producers in the mix session knew the radio stations signal could not broadcast them. Compare that to a FM station signal, which broadcasts the full range of music. They also have a weak signal, and, therefore, are only used in highly densely populated areas. Television stations have UHF for *ultra-high* frequency signals and VHF for *very high* frequency signals. The difference once again is related to the quality and power of the signal being broadcast through the air. In the past in the U.S. and still today in many third world countries, we'll often see communities with antennae on the rooftops that are used to capture these types of signals.

ABC Radio	Beasley Broadcasting	Infinity Broadcasting (CBS)	Clear Channel	Cox Radio	Cumulus
73 Stations	42 Stations	179 Stations	240 Stations	80 Stations	306 Stations

Figure 2.3: Six companies own the majority of radio stations in the top 50 markets in the U.S.A. For record labels, it's often important to place their latest artists and their recordings on these networks for promotion or in order to give the public a chance to "discover" the new recordings. Stations pay performance royalties to the songwriters and music publishers through one of the three PROs in the U.S.A., ASCAP, BMI, or SESAC. Recording artists do not receive any performance royalties over terrestrial radio in this country.

Six major companies own and operate "towers" in the top fifty markets where the majority of people in the U.S.A. live. In addition, most of the six companies actually determine their programming (selection of recordings to air, if playing music) at one location and then feed the signal by satellite or Internet directly to the location (metro area) for broadcast. The mergers of the radio stations, owned by a small group of six companies, has made it more difficult for labels to break new acts and recordings.

Radio promotion is still one of the best career options in the industry. Despite the changes in the entertainment industry, it's vital for labels to place their newest releases on mass media, in order for consumers to "discover" and get excited about the music and the acts.

Getting radio stations to play an artist's new recordings is a different matter, as the stations are in the "selling advertisement business" and would rather play only the "hits" that will give them the largest audience. The size of the audience or number of people listening determines the amount of money stations charge advertisers for their commercial spots.

GE	News Corp	Disney	Viacom	Time Warner	CBS
Properties Include	Properties Include	Properties Include	Properties Include	Properties Include	Properties Include
Comcast NBC Universal Pictures Focus Features	Fox Wall Street Journal New York Post Also owns the papers in other parts of the world	ABC ESPS PIXAR Miramax Marvel Studios	MTV Nick Jr. BET CMT Paramount Pictures	CNN HBO Time Warner Bros.	Showtime Smithsonian Channel NFL.com Jeopardy 60 Minutes

Figure 2.4: The labels and music publishers promoting acts and recordings through Sync and Master licensing (songs used in film and TV production) know who owns the networks.

Publicity works with promotion to sell and enhance the artist's image through TV shows and interviews to increase and drive the popularity of the act and revenue generating products and services. This time, the labels are using the mass media to monetize the recordings of the songs and the acts to consumers and their emotions. The mass media is using the free recordings to sell advertisements and pay the bills. Both are using music as a commercial commodity. A career in publicity is one way to make your mark in the entertainment and music industry. Six seems to be the magic number in media as six major companies also own 90% of the other traditional media in the U.S.A. including (newspapers, film companies, TV networks, and cable production and systems in the United States.[54]

Now, let's take a look at one more invention, the personal computer, as you think about the countless opportunities for investors to once again monetize music into a commodity. And, in today's 360 music business, there are many opportunities for promotion and publicity careers in computer based social media.

COMPUTERS

World War II provided the first serious opportunity for the design of electronic computers developed to "break" the unbreakable secret codes used by the Germans in the war. It took the intrepid intelligence and courage of mathematician Alan Turing (1912-1954) and the help of many brilliant men and women to accomplish the task. Turing is considered the first to break the Enigma Code, the key to modern computers, algorithms, and artificial intelligence. Forget the personal computer of today or the "chips" that bring our cell phones and devices into existence. Early computers were amazingly huge, bulky, and costly. As an example, the *Electronic Numerical Integrator Analyzer and Computer (ENIAC)* was built at the University of Pennsylvania to do ballistics calculations for the U.S. military during World War II.[55] Two thousand square feet of floor space is the size of a three to four-bedroom house!

> *The ENIAC cost $500,000, weighed 30 tons and took up nearly 2,000 square feet of floor space. On the outside, ENIAC was covered in a tangle of cables, hundreds of blinking lights and nearly 6,000 mechanical switches that its operators used to tell it what to do. On the inside, almost 18,000 vacuum tubes carried electrical signals from one part of the machine to another.*[56]

The personal computer developed as the components that are used to make

54 Lutz, Ashley. "These 6 Corporations Control 90% Of The Media In America." Business Insider. June 14, 2012. Accessed June 24, 2017. http://www.businessinsider.com/these-6-corporations-control-90-of-the-media-in-america-2012-6.
55 History.com Staff. "Invention of the PC." History.com. 2011. Accessed June 25, 2016. http://www.history.com/topics/inventions/invention-of-the-pc.
56 Ibid.

computers got a lot smaller.

> In 1948, Bell Labs introduced the transistor, an electronic device that carried and amplified electrical current but was much smaller than the cumbersome vacuum tube. Ten years later, scientists at Texas Instruments and Fairchild Semiconductor came up with the integrated circuit, an invention that incorporated all of the computer's electrical parts—transistors, capacitors, resistors and diodes—into a single silicon chip . . . But one of the most significant of the inventions that paved the way for the PC revolution was the microprocessor . . . They could run the computer's programs, remember information and manage data all by themselves.[57]

If musicians can bang on something they will in an attempt to compose and create new sounds they call music. The first known computer to record music was in 1951,[58]

> . . . Ferranti Mark 1 computer at the University of Manchester - it played God Save The Queen, Baa Baa Black Sheep and In the Mood . . . Lots of great development work was done in the 1960s and 70s, but it was when Commodore launched the C64 that home computer music making really got going. It was notable for the inclusion of its SID sound chip, which enabled users to create music using a whopping three channels of synthesis.[59]

The computer, the computer chip, and its related software were the first shoe to drop in the creative destruction process forcing the industry to reinvent its business models. Even the power of creating the music shifted from labels to anyone with a laptop computer or modern personal digital device. Consumers used the software as a "tool" to reproduce copyrighted recordings without paying the songwriters, music publishers, and record labels, which are also the copyright holders. Congress did not help the situation by passing the *Audio Home Recording Act* in 1992 (also known as the DART Act). The DART Act, for the first-time, allowed consumers to make copies of the recordings they had purchased and they could also

---
[57] History.com Staff. "Invention of the PC." History.com. 2011. Accessed June 25, 2016. http://www.history.com/topics/inventions/invention-of-the-pc.
[58] Specials, Computer Music. "A brief history of computer music." MusicRadar. October 13, 2008. Accessed June 06, 2017. http://www.musicradar.com/news/tech/a-brief-history-of-computer-music-177299.
[59] Ibid.

"share" them with relatives and friends. We'll read more about this as we cover copyrights later.

THE INTERNET

Consumer use of the Internet has disrupted the old established marketing, distribution, and economy of scale in almost every industry from buying a car to getting a doctor's appointment:

> *The first workable prototype of the Internet came in the late 1960s with the creation of ARPANET, or the Advanced Research Projects Agency Network. Originally funded by the U.S. Department of Defense, AR-PANET used packet switching to allow multiple computers to communicate on a single network. The technology continued to grow in the 1970s after scientists Robert Kahn and Vinton Cerf developed Transmission Control Protocol and Internet Protocol, or TCP/IP, a communications model that set standards for how data could be transmitted between multiple net- works. ARPANET adopted TCP/IP on January 1, 1983, and from there researchers began to assemble the "network of networks" that became the modern Internet. The online world then took on a more recognizable form in 1990, when computer scientist Tim Berners-Lee invented the World Wide Web. While it's often confused with the Internet itself, the web is actually just the most common means of accessing data online in the form of websites and hyperlinks.*[60]

Providing access to the Internet has been a wonderful opportunity for people around the globe to connect and start new businesses. However, in the case of the music business it was the "other shoe" that dropped and basically destroyed the financial base of the traditional industry. Shawn Fanning was a student at Northeastern University in Boston when he invented what became Napster, which started the free file sharing system that would become the invention that started to dismantle the traditional business model and economy of the music industry.[61] With the development of his software, venture capitalist Eileen Richardson was provided

60 Andrews, Evan. "Who Invented the Internet?" History.com. 2013. Accessed June 25, 2016. http://www.history.com/news/ask- history/who-invented-the-internet.
61 Nieva, Richard. "Ashes to Ashes, Peer to Peer: An Oral History of Napster." Fortune. September 5, 2013. Accessed

a copy to try. Her review for *Fortune* magazine's website states (2013):

> *"So, I went home that night and downloaded it. And holy shit. I remember at that time, folks started saying that people didn't want to download anything onto their computers anymore, because it was all getting to be web-based. But anybody would download that, easily. I just remember shaking, thinking: Oh, my god, oh my god".*

Napster started the creative destruction process of the industry as 60 million users quickly acquired millions of copyrighted recordings worth billions of dollars, resulting in a financial loss to both labels and the creative community of songwriters, music publishers, and others. But Napster had a plan to license their software to the major labels that would connect them to their 60 million users. There was only one problem; they could not explain how anyone would make any money!

DIGITAL TRANSMISSIONS

Communication requires an originating source such as a person speaking, or in this case, a computer that has been used to create an email, voice message, or let's say a reproduced copy of a downloaded hit song, such as *Stairway to Heaven*. The message (sound created in the form of data) is carried by a medium such as air molecules, electronic and magnetic pulses, or light pulses, through the air, wires, or as high frequency radio signals (Wi-Fi) to the receiver. When two of us have a conversation, one person is creating the sounds (we hear as a language) caused by the vibration of our vocal chords that are carried as soundwaves through the air to other person's ears.

Throw a rock into a smooth lake and watch the waves form. Imagine the same thing except this time the rock is the pressure caused by the first person's vocal chords, which push the surrounding air molecules to form waves in the air. Conversely, an email, voice, or our stolen copy of *Stair-*

June 15, 2015. http://fortune.com/2013/09/05/ashes-to-ashes-peer-to-peer-an-oral-history-of-napster/.

way to Heaven must first be converted into data (binary codes of zeros and ones), which are then transmitted through the wires and air as electronic, magnetic, or light pulse beams to a receiver. If our receiver is the human ear (consisting of the drum, movable bones, etc.), the pressure causes movement that creates an electronic signal that is sent to the brain and converted into sounds.

Our brains do the rest of the work and we acknowledge the sounds as a message and then often as an emotion. If the receiver is a computer, iPhone, or some other device, the computer chip inside the device converts the data back into audio and visual frequencies we can hear and see and then our brain finish the job. In the case of the music industry a way to code and decode the music had to be invented.

MP3

Karlheinz Brandenburg, as a graduate student in Germany, led a team of software developers in the 1980's to figure out a way to digitize and transmit audio music recordings between computers through a telephone line. The main problem was then how to transmit and receive recorded music through a traditional telephone wire (which does not have the proper bandwidth) and compress and expand a distorted signal. The team used the singer Suzanne Vega's recording of *Tom's Diner* for the control base reference in the research because of the distortion in the final mix. According to Jack Ewing (2007),[62]

> *Brandenburg's involvement in digital music compression began in the early 1980s when he was a doctoral student at Germany's University of Erlangen-Nuremberg. A professor urged Brandenburg to work on the problem of how to transmit music over a digital ISDN phone line. It wasn't just a computer-coding problem. Brandenburg had to immerse himself in the science behind how people perceive music . . . When MP3 developers refined the technology to the point where Tom's Din-*

[62] Ewing, Jack. "How MP3 Was Born." Bloomberg.com. March 05, 2007. Accessed June 07, 2017. https://www.bloomberg.com/news/articles/2007-03-05/how-mp3-was-bornbusinessweek-business-news-stock-market-and-financial-advice.

er sounded true to the original, they had made a major breakthrough.[63]

The smaller and more effective the components (that make up the device), the more convenient they are for us to use. In addition, quality of the sound, picture, etc., are also much enhanced. However, it has also opened up communication connections to people, schemers, crooks, and businesses that clog our emails and text messages with unwanted advertisements. In addition, using digital personal devices allows the government and others to know where we are at all times. If you use Amazon, you know the "people who bought x also bought" formula that is based in data analytics used to build a profile of our personalities and interests for marketing purposes. When we agree to use the devices we often give away some of our personal freedoms which seems to be a combination of positive and questionable deeds.

PERSONAL DIGITAL DEVICES

Our cell phones and tablets are the next step in the technological revolution that forced the entertainment industry to shift its business model from selling albums to streaming. Essential to these devices is the digital signal that encodes the sounds and images we see displayed on our screens. Very briefly, a digital signal is simply a row of numbers called a binary code. The code in the computer software is usually a 0 and 1. The 0 is the no magnetic recorded pulse or pit (hole) in the CD disc. The 1 is the present signal on tape or disc or the pit that allows the laser beam to be reflected back to a sensor in the CD player. These are then converted into a "sound" by the computer. In this process, the computer chip is actually creating the sound from the binary code that represents the original sound.

We receive the digital signals broadcast and transmitted to our TVs, radios, cell phones from digital radio, TV stations, cable, and satellites that are converted into the recordings, movies, computer games, phone conversations, texts, whatever, by the computer chips in our devices. There

63 Ibid.

are several advantages in using digital signal as opposed to analog as they are less expense to transmit; sound and visuals are reproducing perfectly without any distortion and noise; and, the devices that take the signals, as noted above, are small and portable. Yet, the good in high quality recording and portable entertainment is also the problem. Anyone can make a perfect copy of the music and other entertainment products and upload them to the world where consumers may acquire them free. From a professional standpoint, you should be concerned, as when that upload happened the songwriters, artists, and labels did not receive any money.

SOCIAL MEDIA

Entertainment-focused venture capital companies quickly developed, and continue to launch software for people to connect interactively. Social media, as most call it, is simple a way for all of us to connect. Few think about how social media is closely tied to personal egos. With the traditional media, only a handful of people would ever become a famous "personality" known by millions of people. Social media changed all of that by giving consumers the opportunity to "spread the word" about themselves including silly things such as what you're having for lunch. However, the ability to say anything about yourself, share your opinions, or sell stuff to a little over a billion people is a very powerful tool.

Labels know the only way to profit from their investments in artists and recordings is to "get the word out" about new acts or recordings to as many people as possible. The traditional label industry gave their newest recordings to radio stations and usually provided legal payola (a slang term for providing a consulting lunch, etc.,) to encourage them to "air" the recordings. Labels hire regional promotion men and women who acted as consultants to wine and dine radio station music directors and programmers and offer them free concert tickets (among other things) to encourage them to play the new acts and releases.

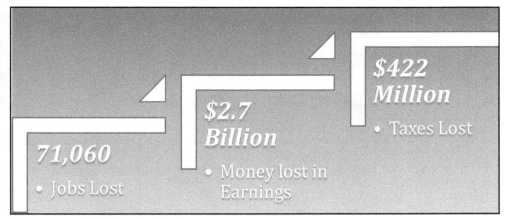

Figure 2.5: The cost of Internet illegal downloads and the shift to streaming has cost the traditional music business over 71,000 jobs, $2.7 Billion in earnings, and $422 million in taxes.[64]

The reason for this song and dance is straightforward- to get exposure for the newly signed acts and recordings. Without airplay or some type of major exposure (called promotion and publicity), the recordings usually fail to be discovered. This kind of promotion is of inestimable importance as nobody's going to hire a local band no one has heard of and nightclub owners, concert promoters, and others are no different.

Of course, traditional forms of promotion and publicity used to be easier when most of the radio stations were owned by lots of different people and companies, but now that six holding companies control the majority of the market, it's much more difficult.[65]

---

64 "MP3Skull: A Site Dedicated To Ripping Off Music." RIAA. October 07, 2015. Accessed October 06, 2017. https://www.riaa.com/mp3skull-a-site-dedicated-to-ripping-off-music/.
65 "Help for Broadcasting Schools grads." Who owns America's Radio Stations | AirTalents.com. Accessed June 24, 2017. http://airtalents.com/broadcasting-schools.html.

Social Network	Niche	Members Users per Month
Facebook	Messaging Setting up & Joining groups	2 billion (1 billion daily)
Twitter	Microblogging Twitter Card Integration Sports, News, Music Entertainment, & Lifestyle topics	320 million
LinkedIn	Business professionals social networking Resumes, job seeking network Marketing	500 million members
Google+	Communities and Collections	Google+ has 112 million active use
YouTube	Videos & search engine for entertainment products Vlogs YouTube Red	1 billion active users per month
Instagram	Photo sharing of real time photos and videos	600 million members
Pinterest	Social shopping online	10 million unique a month
Tumblr	Visual blogging Reblogging links Provides Analytics of views to your site	811,402 followers
Snapchat	Mobile based instant messaging Self-destructing "snaps" Considers itself to be a camera company	166 million daily
Reddit	Community communication	250 million members

Figure 2.6: Sources [66] [67] [68]

The other disadvantage of the traditional media is that consumers can't select the recordings, movies, or TV shows they want to listen to or watch.

[66] Morrison, Kimberly. "How Many Google Members Are Actually Active?" – Adweek. May 4, 2015. Accessed June 24, 2017. http://www.adweek.com/digital/how-many-google-members-are-actually-active/.
[67] Kleinman, Alexis. "YouTube Stats: Site Has 1 Billion Active Users Each Month." The Huffington Post. March 21, 2013. Accessed June 24, 2017. http://www.huffingtonpost.com/2013/03/21/youtube-stats_n_2922543.html.
[68] Vollero, Andrew. "SEC filings." SEC-Show. March 41, 2017. Accessed June 24, 2017. https://otp.tools.investis.com/clients/us/snap_inc/SEC/sec-show.aspx?Type=html&FilingId=12056447&Cik=0001564408.

They have to be by a radio or TV, and must passively wait until the station or source provides the entertainment program they want on the "air". And of course, we get to watch or listen to all the commercials while waiting also.

Social media's biggest advantage is often ignored. We have gotten used to the interactive quality provided through our devices and the Internet. Netflix and Spotify are great examples of selecting what we want to watch or listen to, anytime, anyplace, and anywhere. Getting consumers to "spread the word" about available programming and sources through the social media has also become vital to the music industry's success.

The other advantage is that most of the Internet content is free, or offered at a very low monthly subscription rate. The result of the passive to interactive war is that consumers are switching from traditional broadcast radio and TV to Internet sources. Labels and other entertainment companies have to "go where the audience is" for promotional and publicity purposes. In addition, the major labels and film companies are finding they also have to place their products with various Internet entities in order for consumers to find, use, or buy them.

WORD OF MOUTH

The social media buzz process has helped the label bypass traditional media or still break new acts and recordings the traditional media have passed on. The top social media sites have evolved into sites that dominate a niche for different types of consumers. As an example, MySpace is not even listed in the top ten sites anymore. What is important from a label's and a recording artist's perspective is the number of monthly members and views they have, which is often in the millions to billions.[69]

---

69 Moreau, Elise. "The Top Social Networks People Are Using Today." Lifewire. Accessed June 24, 2017. https://www.lifewire.com/top-social-networking-sites-people-are-using-3486554.

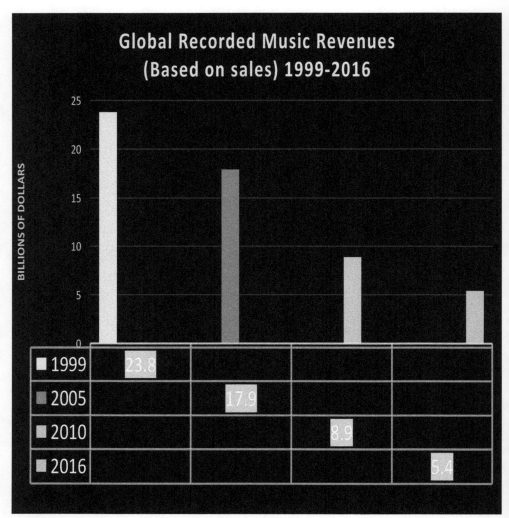

Figure 2.7: According to the GRM 2017, recorded music sales have declined from $23.8 billion in 1999 to $5.4 billion in 2016. Trend lines indicate recorded music sales will continue to decline to close to zero except for vinyl records. Sadly, vinyl records, which are included in the above figure, will not make much of a difference in financial revenues to the major labels.

MUSIC AS A COMMODITY

Access to recorded music has changed with technology over the last few centuries. Before the technology of making copies in a recording studio, music was only available through live performance. Musicians and singers often performed in exchange for room and board and were rarely praised for having a talent others found enjoyable. But with the advent of the recording studio came record labels and their investments in popular singers who they marketed as recording artists.

Consumers had to buy the record player and the disc. About 80 years ago things changed a little as music fans could also drop a coin in a machine called a jukebox. (Juke means disorderly in Gullah, a dialect language associated with some African- American population living along the coasts of South Carolina, Georgia, and Northern Atlantic Coast of Florida). With the invention of radio signals, and development of radio stations as a business, labels provided their latest recordings free (seen as promotion) to the stations.

What Happened

For the last 125 years, the conglomerates and earlier enterprising business ventures have controlled between 80 and 90% of the audio recordings, films, and mass media entertainment products in various world markets. Now, due to consumer use of p2p, and other forms of digital technology, such as the Cloud, labels have shifted their basic business models toward attracting an interactive consumer.

Some of the conglomerates have replaced their labels with intellectual property rights management. Instead of producing and selling recordings, they simply manage the use of their copyrights of songs and recordings for financial gain. Others use 360 deals, and diverse forms of contractual reversions to recoup their investments faster through revenue streams previously controlled by artists, such as merchandise sales, concert tickets, and corporate sponsorships.

Equity Loss

Now, all that stuff is out there available free on the Internet. It's almost as if 1 billion people in the world stole a few bucks out of five banks. There used to be five major labels, now the three that remain are struggling to build a new business model. So many people stealing a few bucks would empty the vaults of our mythical banks driving them all out of business.

Well, the vaults of the entertainment companies have also been emptied, as the inventory of classic film and music companies (most of the great copyrights in the films, computer games, and recorded music) have been "lifted" and are available free online. That means if the labels and entertainment companies want to stay in business, they need to create new products. To do this, they have to be prepared to invest an average of $1-2 million into newly signed recording artists, and $10-$40 million into each new movie and TV series.

Illegal downloads limit the potential size of the consumer base and market, financially crippling returns on the industries' millions of dollars in investments, and they still have to balance their profit and loss statements. Try staying in the recorded music business when about 30 billion songs have been illegally downloaded and 95% of downloads weren't purchased.

THE FIRST BOMBSHELL-EMI

EMI Group, PLC of England was the first major label to die a slow death caused by consumer use of p2p downloading and the change to digital streaming sources. It was the world's leading music publisher with over one million titles in its publishing catalogs. In 1962, EMI made history with *The Beatles*, and in 1998, EMI succeeded again with *Garth Brooks*, who has sold over 70 million albums worldwide.[70]

EMI was started in 1898, as the Gramophone Company. It merged with Columbia Graphophone in 1931 to form *Electric and Musical Industries*, better known as EMI. It had acquired many labels, including Capitol Records, United Artists Records, The Sparrow Corporation, Charisma Re-

[70] EMI, "History of EMI," Emigroup.com, http://www.emimusic.com/, (accessed 1998).

cords, and Priority Records. EMI bought Richard Branson's Virgin Music Group in 1992 for $834 million. It celebrated its first 100 years in business in 1997 and was later bought by Terra Firma, a private investment company. In their 2009 *Annual Review*, Terra Firma claimed (2009),

> *Terra Firma is busy creating value in essential businesses throughout the world in an extremely difficult environment. . . . .EMI, earnings increased from approximately £165 million to nearly £300 million over the first full fiscal year of Terra Firma's ownership. ...On the creative side, in the last 18 months, EMI has signed new agreements with over 200 artists and has continued to win numerous artistic accolades including 24 awards at the 2010 Grammys. While we are proud of our operational accomplishments at EMI, its capital structure has proven challenging.*[71]

It looked good; however, in the spring of 2011 file sharing had taken its toll as the financial walls caved in on the company and its £3.4 billion debt owed to Citi (Citibank). According to a letter written by Roger Faxon, head of EMI, to his employees (2011):

> *First off, I'd like to explain exactly what has happened. When a company's value is less than its debts, one solution is to go through an administration procedure, which allows the sale of the business in partial satisfaction of those debts. In our case, it is not hard to see that our parent company would never be able to repay the £3.4 billion it owed to Citi. With that being the case, it appointed an administrator empowered to sell EMI Group to Citi (Citibank). This is sometimes called a 'pre-pack' because it can be done in a matter of hours – and that's exactly what happened here. This was followed by an immediate recapitalization of EMI, reducing the debt by 65% to £1.2 billion.*[72]

It did not work. Later in 2011, the label that had the Beatles and Garth Brooks was sold off for $4.1 billion dollars in two separate deals. *Universal Music Group* (UMG) paid $1.9 billion for all of the recorded music master copyrights and *Sony Music* paid $2.2 billion for the music publish-

---

71 Terrafirma, "Terrafirma Annual Review 2009," http://www.terrafirma.com/ar09/AR09.pdf, (accessed July 21, 2010).
72 Roger Faxon as reported by David M. Ross, "Faxon's Note to EMI Staff," http://www.musicrow.com/2011/02/citigroup-acquires-emi/, (accessed February 4, 2011).

ing copyrights.[73] This is simply a lesson we need to understand and then use the information to move onto the new 360 business model which are starting to show growth and financial success.

SUMMARY

All of the inventions, technology, innovations, and copyright violations have forced the music business to change its way of doing business. *Creative destruction* is a business term that describes the process of innovation tied to creativity and business. Joseph Schumpeter first used the term in his book *Capitalism, Socialism, and Democracy* (1942), in which he described the process of "an industrial mutation that incessantly revolutionizes the economic structure from within incessantly destroys the old one, incessantly (creating) a new one".[74]

And that's exactly what happened to the music business and what is also in the process of taking place in the entertainment industry. Lots of jobs and money have been lost, but new and different types of jobs and revenue sources are being developed. Focus on acquiring the knowledge and skills you'll need to be successful in the 360-deal music industry. Learn about the traditional music business, because there are a lot of people still active for whom this is their business model, and, their experience in the industry. How will we make money in the music business today? Looking back and longing for the old ways of doing business is no pathway for the future.

Now that we've reviewed how consumers value music in Chapter One and how entrepreneurs made millions to billions of dollars using invention and new technologies to launch record labels in this chapter, let's take a look at the current state of the music industry. The surprise is that things are improving in many ways, including revenue generation and in emerging

---

73 Pham, Alex. "EMI Group sold as two separate pieces to Universal Music and Sony." Los Angeles Times. November 12, 2011. Accessed June 20, 2017. http://articles.latimes.com/2011/nov/12/business/la-fi-ct-emi-sold-20111112-68.
74 Schumpeter, Joseph A. "Can Capitalism Survive." In Capitalism and Democracy, 81. 6th Ed. New York, NY: Routledge, 2006.

career opportunities.

The music business is built on inventions, technology, innovation and the very smart people who have converted those ideas and innovations into a related business. They have used the technology to create music and entertainment products, and then marketed and delivered them to consumers using media and other inventions for a profit. Digital recordings, YouTube, and streaming are just the next step in the process of innovation tied to creativity and business. Take a look at this "block of knowledge" and the corresponding layers and make sure you understand the importance of innovation, inventions, and technology to the continued success of the music industry.

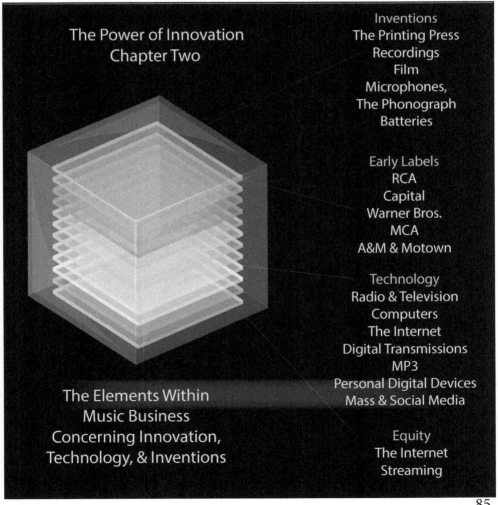

The music business is a business that has learned the art of putting in a recorded form a song by an artist which combines the singer's voice, the song, and the musicians on the recording session- which includes the recording studios, engineers, and arrangers.

The art of mixing the recording is to manipulate the levels of sound from each instrument and voice so that it sounds blended when played back on a car radio or home stereo.

If the recording is a 'hit,' that means a customer will want to listen to it again and, hopefully, purchase it.

The record business is an art that is marketed in an open market economy and only those who understand the art in the context of this market can succeed.

- Mike Curb[75]

---

75 Mike Curb, with Don Cusic, Living the Business. Nashville, TN: Brackish Publishing, 2017: 296-297.

Chapter 3

The Value of Creativity

The purpose of business is to make a profit. The music and entertainment business is certainly no exception. As we saw in Chapter Two, the decline in album sales, the increase in illegal downloads and streaming have forced the traditional industry through the "creative destruction" process. Steven Witt opens his book *How Music Got Free: The End of an Industry, The Turn of the Century and The Patient Zero of Piracy* with his own admission stating,

> *I am a member of the pirate generation. When I arrived at college in 1997, I had never heard of an mp3. By the end of my first term I had filled my 2-gigabyte hard drive with hundreds of bootlegged songs. By graduation, I had six 20 gigabyte drives of music, nearly 15,000 albums worth . . . I pirated on an industrial scale, but told no one . . . The files were procured in chat channels, and through Napster and Bittorrent; I haven't purchased an album with my own money since the turn of the millennium.*[76]

And that is the problem in a nutshell; consumers now believe that music should be free. Sounds good to me, except I know many in the industry who are giving it up because they simply are tired of working hard all of their life to be creative songwriters, musicians, singers, recording and performing artists, and industry executives. However, what appears to be dying isn't! It's just a different way for the business to operate and function. Most of the creative side is the same; it's the businesses that had to change, and, of course, that affects the budgets, strategic management decisions, and who gets paid. Let's take a look at the past, the present, and future.

---

76 Witt, Stephen. "Introduction." In *How Music Got Free: The End of an Industry, The Turn of the Century and The Patient Zero of Piracy*, 1. First Ed. New York, NY: Viking/Penguin Random House LLC, 2015.

THE TRADITIONAL MUSIC BUSINESS MODEL

The traditional business model for the music industry was based on the labels being able to sell and profit from album sales. Thus, they would sign acts, invest in the recordings and the artists, and then, sell the albums at low breakeven points that were advantageous to the label though not very supportive of the artists. However, acts that signed the traditional recoupment types of deals (artists are not paid until their royalties pay off the label debts) never had to pay the debt off out of their own pockets. At the same time, the artists had a shot at making millions as the labels' investments in their recordings, promotion, publicity, distribution, and sales often made them very famous. Label artists rarely made any money from their record deals, but made millions from the tours, merchandise, and corporate sponsorships and endorsements because they were now famous and they didn't have to pay a cent to get there.

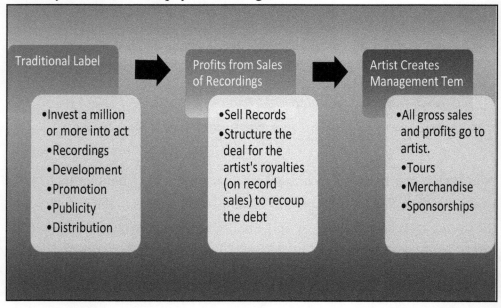

Figure 3.1: In traditional record deals the acts were signed and given an advance, plus additional monies were spent on development, promotion, publicity, marketing, and distribution. The recoupment deals were structured so that the label would often profit a million dollars or more before the act made any money. However, using the fame from the recordings released by the labels, the acts could profit million from tours, etc.

The Creative System

There are two basic systems of organization in the music industry that create and sell entertainment products. The making and selling of music is a process that usually starts with a great or wow song, which is really a three-minute (or so) short story. The next step usually belongs to the music publishers whose job it is to "exploit" (a good word in this business) the song to companies who need them.

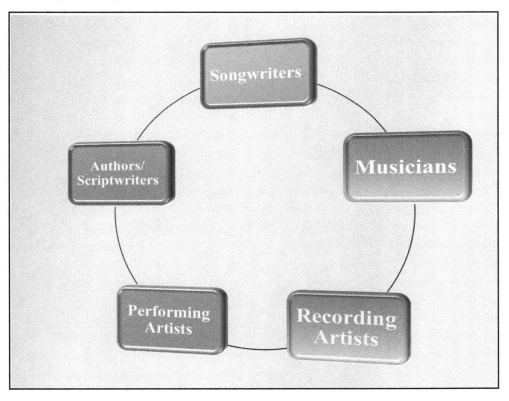

Figure 3.2: Displayed here is an example of the creative system. In this case, songwriters who write the potential "hit" songs, authors, and scriptwriters who write the plays and movies the songs might be used in, the performing artists (musicians, singers, and others), and the recording artists who perform the songs for recordings and live performances, all come together to make money on entertainment products.

This group may include some or all of the following- recording artists and their personal managers, record producers, labels, film and TV production companies, theater, advertisers, musicians, singers/performers, music therapists, and others in need of songs. Without the labels' investments in the development of recording artists and recorded products, we'd be left with only the live performance as it was centuries ago. But with the technology of recordings in the studio or on computer software, the size of the industry and potential gross revenues have skyrocketed.

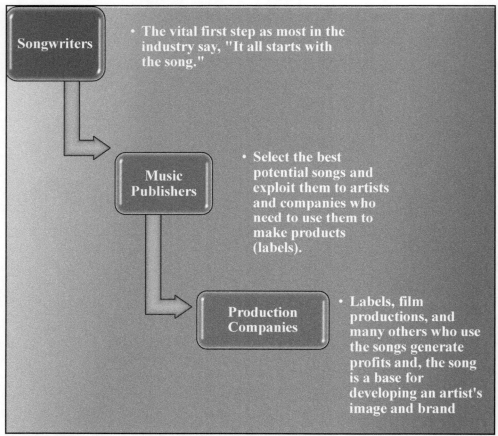

Figure 3.3: Once a song has been written, and the claim of copyright registered, the songwriter will need a music publisher to place the song with the various industry company's seeking new wow songs for their products.

The production or use of music (both live and recorded) becomes a commodity or a product that can be sold or used by the media and other forms of businesses including everything from radio stations, streaming, restaurants, stores, malls, to its use in elevators. Music is everywhere because we enjoy hearing it. It allows us to psychologically help ourselves "experience the moment" and feel something better, as we discussed in the previous chapter. Given we tend to place higher personal value on music that speaks to our emotions, we "adopt" the major artists, performers, musicians and personalities, seeing them as the most gifted. Once so valued, consumers seem willing to pay outrageous amounts of money to see acts perform live at concerts and other events.

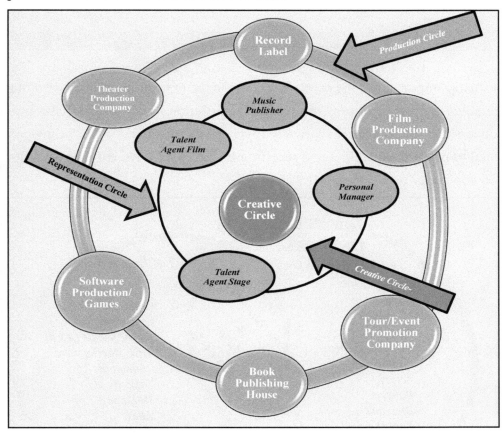

Figure 3.4: The process of creating copyrightable works such as songs, scripts for plays, recordings for labels etc. is represented by the center circle. It consists of the songwriters, authors, and others who create the songs, movie scripts and other products. They usually own what they have created (copyright), but need to get it "placed" with labels and production companies. The next circle consists of the music publishers, agents, and even personal managers who represent recording artists and other personalities. They are the "middle men and women" who pitch the copyrighted products (songs etc.) to labels, production companies and others (the outer circle), who invest into the entertainment products they will market, promote, sell, or stream for a profit.

The main components in the creative system for music apply to everything and everyone, from the local garage band playing a high school gig or a musical performance by a local singer and musicians at a wedding to the superstars on a world tour. It's surprising how many different career options are available if you have the passion, skills, and knowledge to learn what is needed, so you may want to check out the information on careers at the end of this chapter.

THE BUSINESS SYSTEM

Equally important to the creative system is the entrepreneurial system that enables writers, authors, songwriters, musicians, recording artists, producers and others who may own (copyright) the original "works" they created to profit from selling and reselling the product, thus, earning royalties on consumer uses.

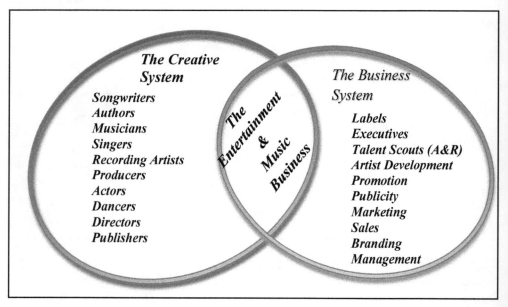

Figure 3.5: This is how we can see the creative systems -the songwriters, musicians, recordings artists and others- intersecting the business systems of labels among others who work together financing the production, promotion, marketing, and sale of entertainment products to generate profits.

For instance, songwriters sell or license their creative works to another entertainment-based company, such as a music publisher who will attempt to place the creative work with artists, labels, film and media production companies. They are also creating products and services for consumers to buy or use.

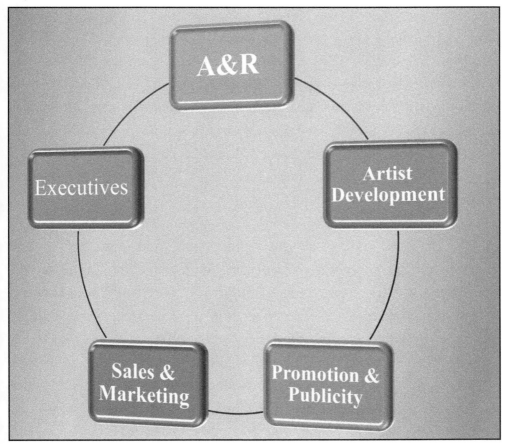

Figure 3.6: This is the business system at a typical record label. The Artist and Recording staff (Department of A&R) find and sign recording and performing artists. The Artist Development staff work on the songwriting, media skills, and performance abilities of the newly signed act. The Department of Promotion & Publicity staff promote and provide publicity to social and traditional media about the acts, recordings, tours, and representative "brands". The Sales& Marketing Department then distribute and market the recordings to retail and streaming providers, and acts on tours. An important part of it all is the executives, presidents and vice presidents who administer and finance the operations.

But don't forget our problem from Chapter One - what if consumers could now acquire or access the albums, films, and other entertainment products free?

360 ECONOMIES OF SCALE

The label business is the first of the entertainment segments to suffer the financial slide of the creative destruction process caused by the advances in technology, negative consumer behaviors, and the lack of enforcement of the copyright laws. And the transition from the recoupment album sales business to the 360-multiple right business model has been difficult. The traditional business model has been damaged beyond repair unless the government eliminates safe harbors and starts to enforce copyright laws against illegal downloads.

Labels struggle to stay in business selling albums and singles as consumers started using computers, the Internet, and personal devices to acquire their music. First, consumers just stole it from illegal websites and then they moved toward the freemium market of streaming. Many still rip the tracks without payment, but others are starting to see the wisdom in acquiring their music where acts and label are paid, on over 400 legal streaming sites. Labels shifted their business models to 360 deals which gave them additional multiple licensing rights for branding, streaming fees, merchandise fulfillment, and about 10-15% of their signed artist's gross revenues from touring, merchandise sales, endorsements, and other related sources.[77] In rare cases, the labels may get up to 30% of the artist's gross revenues, which leaves very little money for the act after paying the personal manager 15%-20%, the booking agent 10%, and the business manager 3%-5%. Add it up and the figures get crazy; 30% to the label and another possible 35% to the management team. And that's before taxes. My advice. . . don't go there!

---

77 Wacholtz, Larry E. Monetizing entertainment: an insiders handbook for careers in the entertainment & music industry. New York: Routledge, 2017.

Find & Sign Talent

- Labels request showcases, investigate acts, analyze market costs of imaging and branding, and assess the size of the potential market

Creates Recordings

- Labels know most "units" will not sell, yet they still need to have a wow song, tied to a wow recordings to market, brand & sell the act. The the recording budget covers (1) types of sessions, (2) stages of the recording sessions, & (3) cost of the recording team and studio.

Promotion

- Provides a "sample" of the recordings through YouTube, radio, media, and streaming. The exposure gained through promotion is designed to increase sales of albums, tickets, merchandise, corporate sponsorships, and promoting branded products tie-ins.

Publicity

- The artist's backstory is key to the connecting the fans to the song. The backstory is based on the image and brand crafted for use on TV talk shows, award shows, in stories planted in the popular press and on social media. Most acts have seven images based on different psychographic lifestyles, which enhance the consumer's emotional connection to the act, which improves profits.

Distribution

- In the old days this was easy and meant selling units of recordings as CDs at Mass Merchandisers, (Best Buy), Rack Jobbers (Kmart, Wal-Mart & Target), One-Stops (Mom & pop stores and chain stores), Record Clubs & PI Advertisements (per inquiry) on late night TV. Now, instead of album sales, which have lost up to 80% of its market, labels revenues are generated by access to the music through streaming such as Spotify, Apple, & Amazon's Prime, plus master recordings placed in films, branding, concert ticket & merchandise sales, and corporate sponsorships.

Figure 3.7: Labels use a step- by- step process to find and sign talent, create recordings and to provide promotion, publicity, and placement (distribution) of their products. Investment in the acts and their products (red) have increased from the one million-dollar range to around two million due to the changes and addition of branding, touring, merchandise as labels new revenue streams. Distribution of the products (green) create the opportunities to profit on the financial investments.

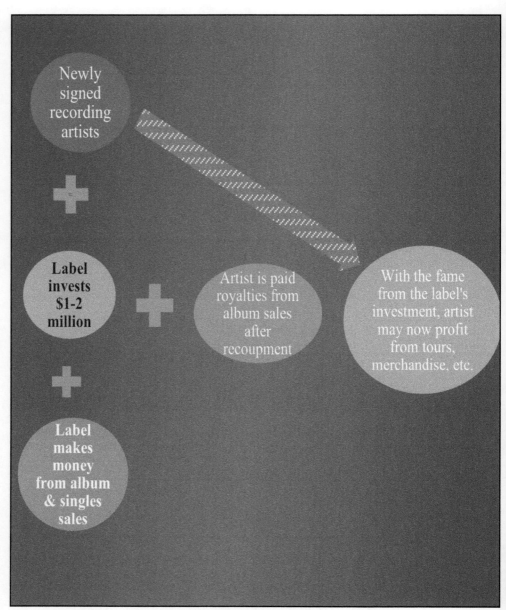

Figures 3.8: The acts rarely made much money, as their royalties were used to recoup the total debt. However, artists who became famous on the label's dime were then able to make millions of dollars off their own businesses, which included touring, merchandise sales, and other revenue streams.

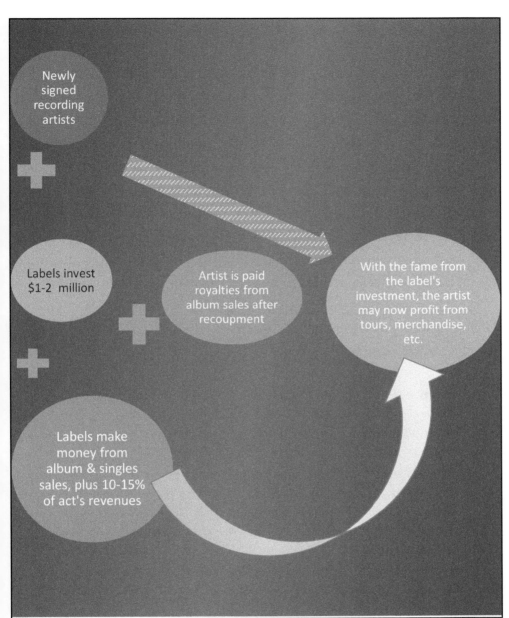

Figure 3.9: With the 360 and other types of deals, labels have gained access to the revenues that were once the artist's sole business profits. Labels often receive 10%-15% of all the gross profits from the artist's business ventures. In some cases, the figure can be as high as 30% of the act's gross. However, in that case, other limits are placed on the percentages paid in personal management and booking agents.

Now, new artists are usually required to sign a 360 deal. This means they "share" a percentage of the profits from their concert ticket sales, merchandise, and corporate sponsorship revenues with the labels who "funded" their albums and corresponding marketing. The labels and their umbrella conglomerates changed to a 360-business model to avoid possible bankruptcy. The innovations in technology have forced the industry to change the way it makes money. The power and future success of the industry is in the consumer's fingers (social click media), who are able to interactively select almost any entertainment product, ranging from a deeply discounted priced digital album to free streaming, whenever and wherever they want!

Time Warner's (2009) annual report lets us see just how much the labels saw the change coming,

> *Technology, particularly digital technology used in the entertainment industry, continues to evolve rapidly, and advances in that technology have led to alternative methods for the delivery and storage of digital content. These technological changes have driven and reinforced changes in consumer behavior, as consumers increasingly seek control over when, where and how they consume digital content. For example, content owners are increasingly delivering their content directly to consumers over the Internet, often without charge, and consumer electronics innovations have enabled consumers to view such Internet-delivered content on televisions and portable devices. Further, the current economic conditions could have the effect of accelerating the migration to digital technologies among both providers and consumers of content, with companies seeking greater efficiencies and consumers seeking more value and lower cost alternatives.*[78]

Between 1996 and 2017, the music industry lost about 74% of the old record based retail sales of vinyl, CDs, and digital downloads as consumers have changed from "buying" their music products to streaming. Sadly, the increase in vinyl is not significant enough to close the "value gap" from pur-

---
78 Time Warner, "Corporate Report," http://phx.corporate-ir.net/External.File?item=UGFyZW50SUQ9MzkxN-TR8Q2hpbGRJRD0tMXxUeXBlPTM=&t=1 (July 21, 2010)

chasing to streaming. Now 1,500 streams is considered equal to one album sold, but the payments to the labels and acts are not the same. The labels receive about 40% of the Suggest Retail List Price ($16.95) or about $6.85 before distribution of albums to brick and mortar retail. They also get about 70% of the Suggested Wholesale price on digital downloads such as iTunes. In the old recoupment deals, labels would pay off the artist's account using the artist royalties per-album sold, which are always negotiated. Let's assume a packaging fee of 15% plus, artist's royalties of 15%, minus 3% to the producer. Don't worry about this as we'll be covering it all in our chapter on labels. The problem is simple, with the new technology, album and digital sales are falling off the edge of the planet. In other words, labels can't sell many albums or singles anymore and each year the numbers keep dropping!

In addition, streaming is a different form of business as consumers do not purchase the recordings. The recording artists, who make about $1.72 per-album sold in our example, often make zip from the streaming of their master recordings. YouTube only pays about .00069¢ per-stream, which means the label makes about $1.03 cents for the 1,500 streams (equaling the sale of one album). In a brick and mortar retail store or on iTunes, artists might make over $5.00 on the sale of one album.

The traditional label business model required the label, not the artist, to invest $1 to $2 million in the unknown acts which provided them with an advance, recording costs- 50-100% of the marketing, promotion, and publicity expenses (100% when run through tour support) and tour support. Some of those recoupment types of labels still exist. They are limited to making their profits off of album sales. Of course, the labels skewed the deals in their favor so that they would often profit millions before the artist would make any money. However, the signed artists received two very important advantages, a free shot at fame and tons of money if they were smart enough to hire the right team members. By the way, if the deal failed, the artists didn't own the label a dime. As you can see, streaming has significantly changed the structure of the economics of the industry. Recoupment deals do not work for the major labels anymore. Thus, they sign all new artists to 360 deals. Labels have had to become very innovative to survive and the artists have been forced to share profits from the touring and other generated sources. The surprise is that when the label executives and artist's management team members work together, amazing things happen and the money (more than ever) starts to roll into everyone's pockets. Let's take a look at each section of the industry next starting with the laws that protect creativity . . . copyrights.

Summary

In all honesty, what the entertainment and music industry accomplishes every day is taking risks on the potential that creative works may or may not be worth something in the long term. They have to spend millions on their hunch to determine if consumers will buy or use them. This is an industry of deep pockets from the labels. The very best songs, musicians, and singers from the creative system take nothing and turn it into something that might be worth millions or even billions of dollars. Good is simply not good enough to warrant the investments, hard work, and time required to test the waters.

As you may remember, we have a situation where the success of the entrepreneurs, artist musicians, songwriters in one system and executives and experts in the other systems depends on each other for financial success. In reality, the two are like a mixture of oil and water, which honestly is difficult to mix. But it's the overlapping of the creative system and the business systems that makes the industry successful. They may not like each other and they definitely think differently, but they also know they need each other if either is to succeed. Everyone helps everyone to make a buck. Can you see why even successful indie artists may wish they had a major label deal? However, this cooperation runs deeper than just within the business or creative system.

Many wannabe (that is, amateur) recording artists still think they can become successful on their own. Usually, about ten years later, they start to understand that they'll never be successful in this industry without the help of others. Therefore, in each system, different people help each other become successful. As an example, songwriters co-write with other writers. Who needs a "wow" song, that is, one that people never get tired of? Recording artists who need to launch or revive their professional careers. Where can the artist find the perfect song? The answer, of course, is from the songwriters or the music publishers who own wow songs (or, songs that will keep making money). Now let's take a look at the corresponding "block of knowledge" for chapter three. Do you understand the reasons for the changes between the traditional and the 360 label business models? What are the advantages of the 360 business model for the label? What advantages are there for the recording artists?

The Value of Creativity
Chapter Three

Traditional Business Model
The Creative System
The Business System
Overlapping of the two systems

Economics of Scale
Traditional
Investment
Product-Recording to sell

Economics of Scale
Multiple Rights
360, 270, 180
Investment
Products-Recordings to sell
Streaming
Branding
Merchandise fulfillment
Live Ticket

The Elements Within
Music Business
Concerning the Value
Of Creativity

Labels'
Step-by Step Process
Find & Sign Talent
Create Recordings
Promotion & Publicity
Distribution

Chapter 4

Copyright Law-
The Legal Foundation of Creativity

Most of the profits from the creative efforts, investments, and business executives' administration and strategic management decisions are buoyed by the US Copyright Law, and other legal agreements between nations of the world. To understand the business of entertainment, we also need to have a basic understanding of the laws and agreements that grant ownership and property values to creative entertainment products.

Figure 4.1: Great ideas are not protected. Nobody owns an idea unless it is original, finished, and placed into a physical tangible form such as writing it on paper, on a computer disc drive, or it is recorded onto a flash drive.

The value or potential profitability of entertainment products is directly related to consumer's enjoyment and use of them. However, it's the copyright laws that provide the fundamental ownership rights (called property rights) to the creators of the entertainment products. Reading the law to me is boring, and at times, difficult to understand. So, instead, let's take a look at the important parts of the law that pertain to the music business. What is a copyright might be a good place to start. Think about this for a moment, when a songwriter composes a new song who owns it? Who is the legal author? What rights does the owner have and how can they monetize their song, musical recording, book, script, or video into a profitable career?

A Very Brief History of Copyrights

What you are about to read is somewhat familiar to you; yet, the level of detail in this overview is also an important foundation, one worth studying for your career in the entertainment and music business. It is essential to remember that because something is on the Cloud, or on YouTube, it still belongs to someone who created it or was involved in the creative process, or both. Indeed, whatever it is may look and be free, but it may be an illegal post and the copyright owners may not be receiving their fair share of royalties. The basic legal definition of a copyright is "a limited duration monopoly".[79] What does that mean, might be the question to ask yourself.

How Copyright Laws Began

Most modern copyright laws are related to the invention of the Gutenberg printing press with movable type, which we reviewed in the second chapter. Its invention reinvented the book and printing business, which led to the possibility of mass distribution of printed information, which in Europe and Great Britain had been controlled by the Church and respective political leaders. There was a fear at

---

[79] Passman, Donald S., and Randy Glass. All you need to know about the music business up-to-date information on new business models, including music streaming services ; the latest developments in digital rights ; updated numbers and statistics for the traditional industry. P. 225., 9th ed. New York, NY: Simon & Schuster, 2015.

the time that if the ability to read was widespread some people might start to question the "why" of their countries' governments and laws.

Censorship laws were tied to a larger idea of social order. There were some leaders in both the churches and the governments that perceived the invention of movable type as a possible threat to their "positions of authority", and, therefore, they tried to ban its use by businesses. Does this situation remind you of some of the controversy surrounding the use of the Internet and digital downloading? Political leaders were concerned about citizen's ability to share ideas and communicate with each other and so, back then, the politicians simply restricted the used of the printing press to companies who were "licensed" to use it. The licenses were only granted to the printers whose books were approved by the political leaders.

THE STATUTE OF ANNE

However, after a couple of hundred years, the English government passed The Statute of Anne, which is considered to be the first modern copyright law. The law defined creative works such books as property, owned by the author. The law also empowered authors with ownership property rights including control of copies and distribution. The statute's design was to "encourage learning by vesting the copies of printed books in the author or purchasers of such copies".

If you didn't pay for the book, you'd be fined and the book illegally copied would be destroyed. Think about what that would mean in today's world if everyone who had downloaded entertainment products illegally (without paying for them) were fined, and then, if they wanted new copies would be required to pay for them? According to The Avalon Project of the Yale Law School, Lillian Goldman Law Library (2008), the statute established the following fines or penalties:

> *Whereas printers, booksellers, and other persons have of late frequently taken the liberty of printing, reprinting, and publishing, or causing to be*

> *printed, reprinted, and published, books and other writings, without the consent of the authors or proprietors of such books and writings, to their very great detriment, and too often to the ruin of them and their families: for preventing therefore such practices for the future, and for the encouragement of learned men to compose and write useful books; may it please your Majesty, that it may be enacted... That the author of any book or books already composed, and not printed and published, or that shall hereafter be composed, and his assignee or assigns, shall have the sole liberty of printing and reprinting such book and books for the term of fourteen years... and That if any other bookseller, printer or other person whatsoever... print, reprint, or import, or cause to be printed, reprinted, or imported, ... the proprietor or proprietors ... shall forfeit such book or books, and all and every sheet or sheets, to the proprietor or proprietors (and)... That every such offender or offenders shall forfeit one penny for every sheet.*[80]

The Statue of Anne supported authors and publisher's ownership rights and required a fine and destruction of illegal copies. With inflation, the one-cent per-page fine would be about 40 cents per-page today. Therefore, those involved in an illegal reprinting of 300-page book in 1710 would be fined $3.00 or about $120.00 in today's money. Using the same analysis for a 10-song album with a suggested retail list price of $12.00, the fine may be as high as $960.00. That's using a formula of 1¢ per-second, for a total of 2,400 seconds on a 40-minute, 10 song-album, times the 40¢ per-page (now per-second) inflation rate totaling $960.00. Or, we could look at the ratio between the 1¢ fine to a 40¢ fine.

The average price for a book in the 1700s was about ½ guinea, which in today's money is about £50 (English pounds).[81] With an exchange rate of £1 equal to about 80¢, the cost of the book/album is something few of us could afford if we were buying it back then, as it would cost about $40 in today money.[82] If we ripped it off, the fine in today's money would be just

---

[80] "The Statute of Anne April 10, 1710." The Avalon Project, Document in Law, History and Diplomacy. 2008. Web. 8 June 2015. <http://avalon.law.yale.edu/18th_century/anne_1710.asp>.
[81] "Great Britain:Prices and Wages." Great Britain:Prices and Wages - Marteau. Accessed June 22, 2017. http://pierre-marteau.com/wiki/index.php?title=Prices_and_Wages_%28Great_Britain%29#Books_.26_Prints.
[82] Revolistic.com. Currency-Converter.net - CUEX. Accessed June 22, 2017. https://currency-converter.net/en/usd-gbp?gclid=CJHmueGc0tQCFYY7gQodGe8Ajg.

over $760.00 (80% of the book fine). The point is that if fines were issued to today's illegal Internet down loaders, and the fines were at the rate of the Statute of Anne rates in England in the 1700s when adjusted for inflation, the fines would be significant. That's not going to happen of course, but it might shed some light of the "value" of entertainment product from a historical perspective and make us wonder about how much current illegal downloading is costing the copyright owners. The Statute of Anne was used by our Founding Fathers to define and write copyright laws into our Constitution.

THE UNITED STATES CONSTITUTION

The discussion below will guide you through the connections between the Copyright Law as stated and amended in the US Constitution and how that impacts the music industry. I have broken the relevant parts of the law into sections for you to review, and then suggested ways the law is linked to the music industry. As you read, you may think about other ways the Copyright Law may need to be changed, or updated, to reflect how we consume entertainment products now and in the future. We begin with what the Law covers, as Article 1, Section 8 of the United States Constitution (2015),

> *. . . gives Congress the right to legislate copyright statute to promote the Progress of Science and Useful Arts, by securing for Limited Times to Authors and Inventors, the Exclusive Right to their respective Writings and Discoveries.*[83]

What does all this mean to the songwriters, labels, and consumers? The term "Promoting the Progress of Science and Useful Arts" means copyright (ownership protection, and rights) may only be claimed by individuals and companies that provide products and services related to the progress of science and useful arts.

---
[83] Copyright Law of the United States and Related Laws Contained in Title 17 of the United States Code. 1 Dec. 2011. Web. 6 June 2015. http://copyright.gov/title17/circ92.pdf.

Acquiring a Copyright

The government does NOT issue copyrights to anyone. A copyright simply means the right to make copies is determined by the owner of the copyright or the person who created the corresponding song, recording, book, film script or whatever else it might be under the definition of the law. What the law is really saying (in my opinion) is that the United States government will support a person or companies' "claim" of ownership if it (whatever was created) meets the requirements and standards.

The definition of the standard is also not difficult to understand as it clearly means the song, script, etc., must be original, in a tangible (physical form) and be complete (finished). Therefore, an idea in our head is not protected, as it's not in a tangible or physical form. Tell someone about a great idea you have for a movie script or a song and if they are the first to write it down, then they own it and have the right to the copyright. At that point, they control distribution (and some other things) and they will be paid (if they can sell or license it), not you.

Copyright protection exists from the time the work is created in a fixed form. The copyright immediately becomes the property of the author who created the work. The copyright is instant and in reality, when you register your claim of copyright all you are doing is registering your "claim" that you own it. The government registers the time and date of your claim.

What is a Copyright?

Copyrights are a "proof of ownership" of what you or the company has created. The value of the "copyright" is based on how in demand it will be with consumers and what they are willing to pay for it. The purpose of providing the concept of "ownership" to the creator of the scientific discovery or useful artistic expression (a song, as an example) is to improve the quality of life for all of us. Thus, the people who spend years trying to develop a new medicine or write a wow song are rewarded through the ownership of whatever it is they created. The amount of money they are paid is determined by the businesses that spring out of the creative works and the amount of money consumers or businesses will pay to have or use it.

DURATION

The legal term by securing for limited times found in Article 1, Section 8 of the U.S. Constitution means the ownership is not forever. The first duration for a copyright was for 14 years, renewable for another 14 years for a total of 28 years. Currently, a new copyright is valid for the life of the creator plus 70 years. Once the duration of copyright protection has expired, then the "creative or scientific work" falls into the public domain, which means anyone can use it without payment to the original owners (as they no longer have any rights to it). In the Figure 3.6, thick black borders are placed around the information related to duration and music copyright laws. Double lines are used to highlight acts about movies and computer software and dash lines relate to international treaties.

The first part of the Copyright Acts Chart shows the first copyright issued in 1790 which was for charts and maps. Remember Lewis & Clark? Over the next couple of pages, we'll be seeing how the laws have continued to change the nature of copyrights. Two things to consider are the duration of the copyright, listed under the "Time" heading and the "Result" which describes how the acts changed as new technologies were developed. In 1909, the duration of the copyright law was changed from the 14 years plus a renewal for another 14 years (28 total) to fifty-six years as people were living longer (28 renewable for another 28 years). Remember, the Titanic sunk in 1912 as a timeframe of events. Take a look at what also happened in 1976 and in 1998 under the Sonny Bono Act! Also, note the additional years provided for *transitional copyrights* under the 1909 act that got an additional 19 years in 1976 and an additional 20 years under

Date	Purpose	Time	Results
1790	This law provided a term of fourteen years with the option of renewing the registration for another fourteen-year term.	28 Years	Maps. Charts, and books ownership to authors and proprietors
1831	Music added to works protected against unauthorized printing and vending.	42 Years	The business of music and entertainment is now legal
1870	The law added "works of art" to the list of protected works and reserved to authors the right to create certain derivative works, including translations and dramatizations	42 Years	Allowed derivative works to be created and owned.
1895	Congress mandates that U.S. government works be not subject to copyright protection.	Zero	All government documents are non- copyrightable.
1897	Congress enacts a law to protect music against unauthorized public performance.	N/A	Legal foundation for collect of performance royalties for songwriters and music publishers.
1909	Certain class of unpublished works now eligible for registration. Term of statutory protection for a work copyrighted in published form measured from the date of publication of the work. Renewal term extended from fourteen to twenty-eight	56 Years	Widen the definition of unpublished works that could be registered. Duration for "published works" started with the date of publication not creation, Extended the duration of a copyright.
1912	Motion pictures, previously allowed to be registered only as a series of still photographs, now protected works.	56 Years	Motion pictures, film, etc., copyrightable
1914	U.S. adherence to the Buenos Aires Copyright Convention of 1910.	56 years	Established copyright protection between the United States and certain Latin American nations.

Date	Purpose	Time	Results
1953	Recording and performing rights extended to nondramatic literary works.	56 Years	Copyright of recorded versions of books, plays, etc.
1955	United States becomes party to the 1952 Universal Copyright Convention as revised in Geneva, Switzerland	56 Years	United States Copyrights extended to other agreeing nations and theirs to our country.
1972	Effective date of the act extending limited copyright protection to sound recordings fixed and first published on or after this date.	56 Years	Sound recordings provided limited copyright protection
1974	United States becomes party to the 1971 revision of the Universal Copyright Convention at Paris, France	56 years	Extended world copyright protection in agreeing nations.
1976	The 1976 Act replaced the 1909 Copyright Act and changed much of how copyright law operates, including as following:	Life of the author(s) plus 50 years	Extended the duration of the copyright and ended state registration of non-published works. Added 19 years to duration of copyrights still valid under 1909 act. Congress added exception and Fair Use rights.
1980	Copyright law amended to include computer programs	Life plus 50 to 95 years based on type of registration	Software copyrightable
1989	The effective date of United States adherence to the Berne Convention for the Protection of Literary and Artistic Works, as revised in Paris, France in 1971.	N/A	United States joins agreement at Berne (Switzerland) Convention to expend copyright protections in world territories. U.S. required to drop mandatory use of Copyright Notice ©.

Date	Purpose	Time	Results
1992	Renewal registration becomes optional on a prospective basis.	Additional duration to 75 years	As such, all works initially copyrighted between January 1, 1964 and December 31, 1977 were renewed automatically.
1992	Effective date of the Audio Home Recording Act.	N/A	The Act requires the placement of serial copy management systems in digital audio recorders and imposes royalties (DART royalties) on the sale of digital audio recording devices and media that are distributed to the copyright owners.
1993	Copyright Royalty Tribunal Reform Act of 1993	N/A	Eliminates the existing Copyright Royalty Tribunal and replaces it with (CARP) Copyright Arbitration Royalty Panels to recommend to Congress statutory license rates
1997	The No Electronic Theft (NET) Act	N/A	Defines "financial gain" in relation to copyright infringement, sets penalties for willfully infringing a copyright either for the purposes of commercial advantage or private financial gain or by reproducing or distributing (including by electronic means) phonorecords of a certain value.

Date	Purpose	Time	Results
	The Sonny Bono Copyright Term Extension Act	Life plus 70 years for 1978 and later copyrights and 95 years for current valid pre-1978 copyrights	Extends the term of copyright for most works by twenty years.
1998	The Digital Millennium Copyright Act of 1998 ("DMCA") adds provisions to the Copyright Act including:	N/A	World digital copyright rights and protections through the World Intellectual Property Organization (WIPO)
2004	The Copyright Royalty and Distribution Reform Act	N/A	Phases out the Copyright Arbitration Royalty Panel (CARP) and replaces it with the Copyright Royalty Board.

Figure 4.2: Copyright acts or laws have change dramatically over the years. Duration or ownership was originally 14 years, renewable for another 14 years for a total of 28. Currently, it's life of the surviving creator, plus 70 years. The first copyrights only covered maps, but now literary works, musical works, including any accompanying words, dramatic works, including any accompanying music (as an example, stage plays), pantomimes and choreographic works, pictorial, graphic, and sculptural works, motion pictures and other audiovisual works, sound recordings, and architectural works are protected.[84] The Digital Millennium Copyright Act in 1998 is the United States acceptance of the World Intellectual Property Organization (WIPO) to support global copyrights, trademark and intellectual properties. WIPO is a part of the United Nations and was passed "to encourage creative activity to promote and protect IP".[85]

84 "Copyright Basics." Copyrights.gov/circs/circ01.pdf. Accessed June 27, 2017. https://www.copyright.gov/circs/circ01.pdf.
85 "About Us." Inside WIPO. Accessed August 22, 2017. http://www.wipo.int/about-wipo/en/.

THE EXCLUSIVE RIGHTS OF OWNERSHIP

The last part of Article 1, Section 8 is vital in understanding the creator's Exclusive Rights to their respective writings and discoveries. Now we are addressing the "rights of owning" whatever was created.

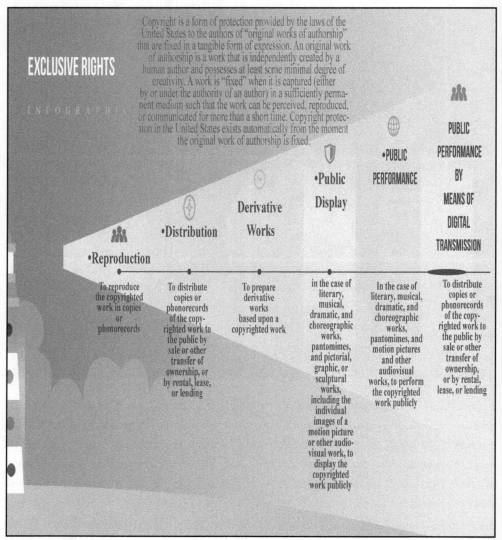

Figure 4.3: Once a copyrightable work is created, the copyright is instant as long as the work is original, fixed into a tangible (physical) form, and complete. The creator of the work is the author and owner and has six exclusive rights including reproduction, distribution, public performance and display, public performance by means of digital transmission and derivative rights.

Congress has over the years defined the exclusive rights as the right

- To *reproduce* the copyrighted work in copies or phonorecords;

- To prepare *derivative works* based upon the copyrighted work;

- To *distribute* copies or phonorecords of the copyrighted work to the public by sale or other transfer of ownership, or by rental, lease, or lending;

- in the case of literary, musical, dramatic, and choreographic works, pantomimes, and motion pictures and other audiovisual works, to *perform* the copyrighted work publicly;

- In the case of literary, musical, dramatic, and choreographic works, pantomimes, and pictorial, graphic, or sculptural works, including the individual images of a motion picture or other audiovisual work, to *display* the copyrighted work publicly; and

- In the case of sound recordings, to *perform the copyrighted work publicly by means of a digital audio transmission.*[86]

FAIR USE RIGHT-AN EXCEPTION TO THE EXCLUSIVE RIGHTS

One exception to the copyright owner's exclusive rights is "fair use" rights. Fair use is provided as part of the copyright law to allow the use of copyrighted information and products such as books and other resources for educational and commentary purposes. The amount of information used must be limited and the source must be cited. Four factors are used to determine what and if materials and entertainment products may be used without payment under the "fair use" rules. According to a letter from the Office of the Register of Copyrights (2011), when analyzing the fair use defense, courts review the four non-exhaustive factors set forth in Section 107 of the Copyright Act:

---

[86] "Copyright Basics." Copyrights.gov/circs/circ01.pdf. Accessed June 27, 2017. https://www.copyright.gov/circs/circ01.pdf.

- *The purpose and character of the use, including whether such use is of a commercial nature or is for nonprofit educational purposes;*

- *The nature of the copyrighted work;*

- *The amount and substantially of the portion used in relation to the copyrighted work as a whole; and*

- *The effect of the use upon the potential market for or value of the copyrighted work.*[87]

THE COMPULSORY LICENSES-ANOTHER EXCEPTION

Another exception to copyright ownership rights are Compulsory Licenses. Notice the plural as this types of licenses cover a variety of entertainment products when musical recordings are embedded into the programming. Examples include Jukeboxes, Public Broadcasting (PBS), cable television rebroadcast programming, digital radio programming and master recordings. Let me explain this in simple terms. Once a song has been recorded for the first times (called first use rights), it's a non-dramatic musical work (meaning non-stage or theater), it's the same basic melody as the original recording, and the new recording is release as a phonorecord, than anyone can recording the song themselves without permission. However, you'll still need to register your intention with the copyright office and pay Mechanical Licenses fees.

SAFE HARBORS

"Safe harbors" have been allowed by Congress to help with the development of digital technologies, however, they have been used by Internet businesses (such as YouTube), to profit from the invention and use of digital technologies by consumers to actively disrupt the financial foundations of the entertainment industry. Congress was placed in a difficult situation by the development of the new inventions and technology. Of course, it

---

[87] Office, U.S. Copyright. "More Information on Fair Use | U.S. Copyright Office." Copyright. Accessed August 12, 2017. https://www.copyright.gov/fair-use/more-info.html.

wanted to protect one of our nation's largest industries (the entertainment business), and, at the same time, it did not want to stop the possible advancements the new technologies might provide citizens. As is often the case, Congress created a "gray area" for companies to work in by making an exception to some of the copyright laws.

Why are YouTube and other services like them that serve as outlets for free downloading or free viewing of copyrighted materials allowed to exist? A couple of reasons, first they are "allowed" to operate as long as they pay a major percent of their income to copyright holders, such as labels. Second, they are currently considered a legal safe harbor. Think of it this way, if you are out on the water in your boat and a huge storm starts whipping the waves out of control, you'd probably want to find a "safe harbor" to anchor until after the storm. The Internet, Napster and most of the other services are the "storm" that opened innovative and many would say, illegal distribution of entertainment products most users now consider free.

INTELLECTUAL PROPERTIES

To make things a little more confusing (but not badly), there are three different types of Intellectual Properties of which copyrights are one. You should have a good understanding of what a copyright is by now, but let's look at the others so that you may better understand how to protect the name of an act, symbol, or products (Trademarks) and how you or your lawyer may protect a device you've invented (Patent).

COPYRIGHTS (©)

Copyrights provided by the laws of the United States (Title 17 U. S. Code) and similar laws in other countries provide protection (ownership of their creative properties) to the authors of original works of authorship, including literary, dramatic, musical, artistic, and other intellectual works. Copyrights encourage artistic and creative people (often using the inventions and discoveries) to make, own, and control the reproduction and distribution of what they've created.

Trademarks (TM, SM, & ®)

How do we understand the difference between a Coke and a Pepsi? By the trademark logo on the container before we open it and take a drink. It's the same with a cup of coffee at Starbucks or McDonalds. Major recording artists, band names, labels, and even the Rolling Stones red licking tongue are trademarked logos registered with governments around the world so that others may not use or infringe the corresponding products and public personalities. According to the United States Patent and Trademark Office release, *Protecting Your Trademark: Enhancing Your Rights Through Federal Registration* (2015):

> *A trademark is generally a word, phrase, symbol, or design, or a combination thereof, that identifies and distinguishes the source of the goods of one party from those of others... A service mark is the same as a trademark, except that it identifies and distinguishes the source of a service rather than goods.*[88]

Patents

Patents are issued by the government to protect ownership (property) in an original invention by preventing others from making, using or selling it as their own. The United States Patent and Trademark Office (2014) defines a patent as:

> *"the right to exclude others from making, using, offering for sale, or selling" the invention in the United States or "importing" the invention into the United States. What is granted is not the right to make, use, offer for sale, sell, or import, but the right to exclude others from making, using, offering for sale, selling or importing the invention.*[89]

---

[88] "Protecting Your Trademarks: Enhancing Your Rights Through Federal Registration." USPTO.gov. Basic Facts about Trademarks. 2015. Accessed June 6, 2015. http://www.uspto.gov/sites/default/files/BasicFacts.pdf.
[89] "Circular 40: Copyright Registration for Pictorial, Graphic, and Sculptural Works." Copyright Registration for Pictorial, Graphic and Sculptural Works. 2013. Web. 7 June 2015. <http://copyright.gov/circs/circ40.pdf>.

COPYRIGHTABLE PROTECTED WORKS

Not everything is copyrightable! The Copyright Office suggests that each of the categories be "viewed broadly" for registration. As an example, computer programs and certain "compilations" can be registered as "literary works"; maps and technical drawings can be registered as "pictorial, graphic, and sculptural works."[90] The detailed list is below-

- Literary works

- Musical works, including any accompanying words

- Dramatic works, including any accompanying music

- Pantomimes and choreographic works

- Pictorial, graphic, and sculptural works

- Motion pictures and other audiovisual works

- Architectural works

- Sound recordings, which are works that result from the fixation of a series of musical, spoken, or other sounds

Legally, companies and consumers must pay or get a license to use a copyrighted creative work in order to make copies, distribute, use it in a public performance (such as playing a song on radio or in a bar), public display, public performance by means of a digital transmission (listening to a song being streamed or watching a movie on the Internet). Plus, a new work based on another person's or companies' work (copyright), called a derivative work, must also be licensed. Most of the time consumers are not aware of the licenses fees as they are covered by labels, channels, cable companies, and streaming companies who are using and profiting from the creative works such as songs, recordings, and both when placed into movies and visual presentations. That's where a significant amount of the money paid to songwriters, recording artists, and music publisher orig-

[90] "What Works are Protected." Library of congress.gov. Accessed October 7, 2017. https://www.copyright.gov/circs/circ01.pdf.

inates, from licensing fees for the use of copyrighted original works in commercial and private businesses. Now, how important it is to register your claim of ownership of an original work you've created?

AUTHORSHIP & OWNERSHIP

There are several ways to register a creative work for a claim of copyright. But first we need to understand the difference between *authorship* and *ownership*. The word *authorship* is limited to the person or persons who created the song or recordings. They are, of course, usually also the *owner* of what they have created, which is defined as your personal property. However, songwriters, scriptwriters, and sometimes labels sell their *ownership* in the creative works they've created and yet retain authorship.

The key is *authorship and ownership* are two different things. One describes who created the work and the other describes who owns the work. Authorship of a song, recording, or other creative work brings industry fame, royalties, and additional potential successful career opportunities. Ownership may be valuable, depending on the creative work's success and use by related media and other types of public businesses, such as bars, nightclubs, radio, malls, and others who play or use the creative work repeatedly.

How valuable is it? That is determined by public demand and usage if the industry and potential consumers desire it. However, at this point, it is important to remember what you're claiming. If you created it yourself, you claim authorship. And since you're the only one who created it, you should also claim ownership of the copyright. If two wrote a song, then both are considered authors and share ownership. If the creative work fails to achieve commercial or consumer support, then there's really no need to register it. However, if it is successful, you can now see why you should register your claim of copyright. Let's look at the registration process.

COPYRIGHT REGISTRATION

Now you know the rules of the game which are- if you create it, you own it (for a limited time), and you've got six exclusive rights you can use to give away or profit from whatever you've created. However, it is very wise to register your claim of ownership for what you have created to keep others from stealing it or using it without your permission. Notice please that the Copyright Office does not issue copyrights. It simply registers the date and time you claim to own your original creation. That is powerful if you find someone is using and profiting from your creative work such as a song or a recording without your permission. This, as noted above, is called infringement of copyright and is legally actionable.

Most of these types of infringement cases are handled in lawsuits settled in court as the first person or company to register a claim of a copyright (song or recording in this case) is considered by the federal government to be the legal owner of the creative work. Therefore, if someone else registers your creative work before you, the government considers them as the true owner and that shifts the burden of proof of ownership onto you.

REGISTRATION OF COPYRIGHT- eCO

The two most popular ways to register your claim of copyright with the Library of Congress are the electronic (eCo) upload and the old snail mail paper forms, including TX, VA, PA, SR, SE and CON.[91] The Internet is full of companies who'll charge you a hundred dollars or more to register your copyright. But you can do it yourself using the eCo site in three steps:

- Complete an application

- Pay the associated fee (Pay online with credit/debit card or ACH transfer via Pay.gov, or with a deposit account)

---

[91] "ECO Registration System." Copyright.gov, United States Copyright Office, a Department of the Library of Congress. 2015. Accessed June 7, 2015. http://copyright.gov/eco/.

- Submit your work

Please note what is copyrightable and what's not and you may need to disable your browser's pop-up blocker. According to the Copyright Office (2017),

> *Anyone can use eCO to register basic claims to copyright, even those who intend to submit a hard copy(ies) of the work(s) being registered. Basic claims include literary works, visual arts work, performing arts works, sound recordings, motion pictures, single serial issues, groups of serial issues and groups of newspaper/newsletter issues. At this time, the following types of registration are not available in eCO: renewals, corrections, mask works, vessel hulls, groups of database updates, and groups of contributions to periodicals . . . Currently eCO accepts registrations for (a) any single work or (b) a collection of unpublished works by the same author and owned by the same claimant, or (c) multiple published works contained in the same unit of publication and owned by the same claimant. (Examples. A compact disk containing 10 songs; a book of poems) or (d) groups of serial issues and groups of newspaper/newsletter issues).*[92]

The eCo Internet registration is highly recommended by the Copyright Office. However, if you still want to mail in your registration, you can contact the Copyright Office and they will send you the following forms. The disadvantage is that it takes longer and there is also a higher registration fee.

---

92 Office, U.S. Copyright. "ECO Frequently Asked Questions." Copyright. Accessed June 26, 2017. https://www.copyright.gov/eco/faq.html.

TYPE	USE OF PAPER FORMS	LINK TO WEBSITE
TX Literary Works	Registration of published or unpublished nondramatic literary works, such as fiction, nonfiction, poetry, textbooks, reference works, directories, catalogs, advertising copy, compilations of information, and computer programs.	http://copyright.gov /forms/formtx.pdf.
VA Visual Arts	Registration of published or unpublished works of the visual arts. This category consists of "pictorial, graphic, or sculptural works".	http://copyright.gov /forms/formva.pdf.
PA Performance Arts	Registration of published or unpublished works of the performing arts. This class includes works prepared for the purpose of being "performed" directly before an audience or indirectly "by means of any device or process". Works include: (1) musical works, including any accompanying words; (2) dramatic works, including any accompanying music; (3) pantomimes and choreographic works; and (4) motion pictures and other audiovisual works.	http://copyright.gov /forms/formpa.pdf.
SR Sound Recordings	Registration of published or unpublished sound recordings. Form SR should be used when the copyright claim is limited to the sound recording itself, and it may also be used where the same copyright claimant is seeking simultaneous registration of the underlying musical, dramatic, or literary work embodied in the phonorecord.	http://copyright.g ov/forms/formsr. pdf
SE Serial	Registration of each individual issue of a serial. A serial is defined as a work issued or intended to be issued in successive parts bearing numerical or chronological designations and intended to be continued indefinitely.	http://copyright.gov /forms/formse.pdf.

Figure 4.4: The old snail mail registration process is still used today by the Copyright Office. You may want to consider the eCO process that is quicker and cost less money.[93]

CERTIFICATE OF REGISTRATION

At the end of an evaluation process, the Copyright Office either refuses or provides a Certificate of Registration containing a registration number.

---

93 "Copyright Basics." Copyrights.gov/circs/circ01.pdf. Accessed June 27, 2017. https://www.copyright.gov/circs/circ01.pdf.

The process is described in the Compendium as (2014):

> The U.S. Copyright Office examines applications for registering claims to copyright and any accompanying deposit copy(ies) to determine whether they satisfy the statutory requirements for registrability, including copyright ability, and otherwise comply with the Office's regulations. Based on its findings, the Office then either registers or refuses to register the claims.[94]

CERTIFICATE OF RECORDATION

What happens when you sell your copyright (ownership) in a song, or recording to a major entertainment company, such as a music publisher or record label? Usually, the new owner(s) will file a request to change the name of the "owners" at the Copyright Office. The same Certificate of Registration number issued by the Copyright Office originally is still used. The writers usually retain authorship, as the only change is who owns the creative work. Once the name of the owners is switched, a Certificate of Recordation is provided. The Compendium states (2014):

> ... any transfer of copyright ownership or other document relating to copyright may be recorded in the U.S. Copyright Office, subject to certain conditions. The recordation of documents pertaining to transfers or other ownership matters is voluntary, but recommended because: (i) it provides constructive notice of the facts stated in the recorded document if certain conditions have been met; (ii) when a transfer of copyright is timely recorded (within one month of its execution in the United States or two months of its execution outside of the United States, or any time before a conflicting transfer is recorded), the recorded transfer prevails over a later executed transfer; and (iii) a complete public record may mitigate problems related to orphan works.[95]

---

94 "COMPENDIUM: Chapter 100 U.S. Copyright Office and the Copyright Law: General Background." Copyright.gov, United States Copyright Office, a Department of the Library of Congress. December 22, 2014. Accessed June 10, 2015. http://copyright.gov/comp3/chap100/ch100-general-background.pdf.
95 "COMPENDIUM: Chapter 200 Overview of the Registration Process." Copyright.gov, United States Copyright Office a Department of the Library of Congress. December 22, 2014. Accessed June 10, 2015. http://copyright.gov/comp3/chapter200.html.

Deposit Copies

To complete the registration process, a copy or copies of your work must also be submitted by mail or uploaded using the eCo registration process. Also, detailed in the Compendium (2015):

> As a general rule, the applicant must submit a complete copy or copies of the work to register a claim to copyright. . . In specific instances, the deposit copy (ies) may be submitted in digital or physical format. The deposit copy (ies) must conform to certain requirements depending on the type of work, the deposit requirements, and whether the work is published or unpublished.[96]

Once you have established your claim to your creative work, you are ready to start to get it noticed by the industry. You can do this yourself, or hire representation to do it for you. If you are working in the industry, you want to know the artist has registered their claim of copyrighted legally before you get involved in investing as you can lose a lot of money if the process is not complete or you end up in court with an infringement issue. But, let's be positive and get the ball rolling to get that wow creative work noticed!

"Pitching" Creative Works

The entertainment industry, and the music business, is really a small community of experts who specialize in specific areas of the industry. This network of small businesses accomplishes the daily work in the industry. Songwriters, as an example, need representation to "pitch" their songs (called by the industry, "material") to the artists, labels, film production companies, media, and other who are seeking wow new songs. Who knows the right people and how to connect the new songs to the right people in the business? Music publishers. Artists need to connect with major record

---

[96] "COMPENDIUM: Chapter 200 Overview of the Registration Process." Copyright.gov, United States Copyright Office a Department of the Library of Congress. December 22, 2014. Accessed June 10, 2015. http://copyright.gov/comp3/chapter200.html.

labels and that's where well-connected personal managers and attorneys enter the picture. Artists also need gigs to earn money performing in clubs and tours, so they usually sign a deal with a booking agent.

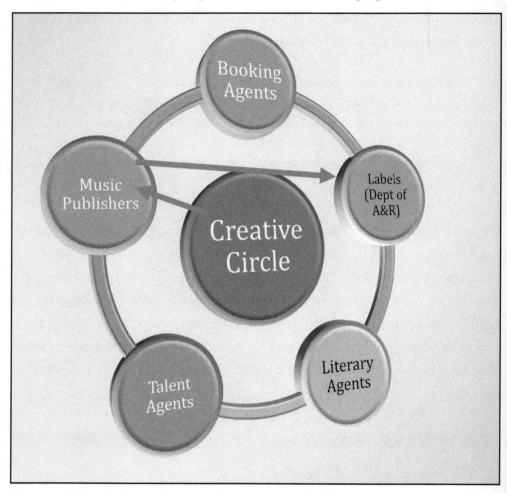

Figure 4.5: Once the song, recording, etc., is created and hopefully registered with the Copyright Office, it's time to make some money by pitching it to the people in the industry who can "place" it with song and music users such as record labels, major recording artists, advertisement, and computer game companies, and film music supervisors. By the way, notice that a copyright symbol for a song is © and a (P) inside a circle for the recording of a song. The songwriter or music publisher own the song and the record label owns the recording of the song.

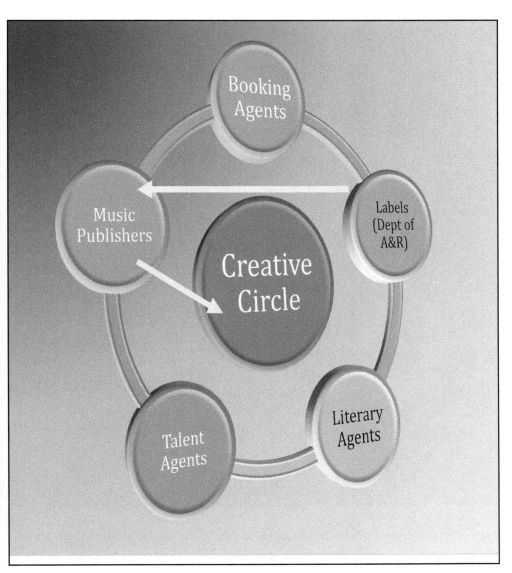

Figure 4.6: Creative works are property and must be paid for when downloading, copying or used by labels, film production companies, and consumers. As an example, the exclusive rights payments include license fees collected and paid to the copyright creators and owners. In this case, the label secures a Mechanical License from The Harry Fox Agency or directly from the music publisher and then pays a Statutory Rate fee to the music publisher. The music publisher, in turn, and depending on the deal with the songwriter, pays the songwriter a share of the fees collected. The Mechanical License fees are collected and then paid as royalties owed the music publisher and songwriters.

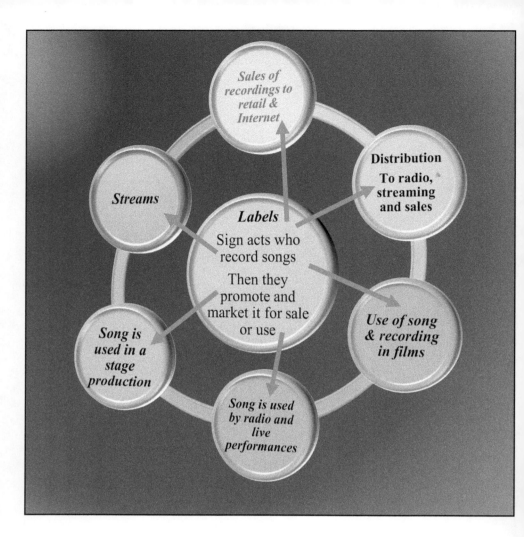

Figure 4.7: A record label's recording and distribution of a song provides multiple revenue streams for the label, music publisher, and the songwriter. The label receives royalties from the sale, use, licensing, streaming, and other uses of the recording. The music publisher and songwriter receive royalties from the use of the song in the recording because of the six exclusive rights such as reproduction, distribution, public performance, public display, and public performance by means of digital transmission. It's the multiple revenues streams from the different licenses that make publishers and songwriters rich. However, also notice that if the label had not licensed the song to record, none of the revenue streams would have generated much money.

Once the deals between the person or company who created the song, recordings, etc., and the music publisher, artists, agents, or personal managers are completed, then they pitch the creative works to the labels, film companies, concert promoters and others who will license or purchase the creative work. Most creative people tend to see this as a "little matter" until they realize that what is negotiated in a deal will determine how much they will receive in payments. Bargaining is a hard lesson to learn; yet, understanding the business and how contracts work plays a significant role in sustaining a career. In all honesty, your choices will directly determine your level of financial success. Percentage deals are not often your best choice as most major corporations are hesitant to share their actual financial records. On the other hand, as you'll soon see, percentage deals are standard in the music publishing business.

The Texas Two-Step

To summarize what's happened to the industry, over the last few years, consumers found they could use BitTorrent or some other software and steal almost any song or movie they wanted over the Internet. Nobody came and arrested them. Sure, the RIAA (Recording Industry Association of America) might have used some data mining software and discovered recordings illegally stored on personal computers and took a few to court. Making examples of a few individual and slapping their hands failed to stop the crime wave. It was simply too easy and few receive any mail or emails telling them to legally "cease and desist". We can gain a better understanding of the purpose of a cease and desist letter from *The Legal Dictionary* (2015),

> *An official order handed down by a government agency or court directing a person or entity to stop doing something immediately is called a "cease and desist order". Such an order effectively places an injunction on the person or entity that prohibits the named activity as suspicious or illegal*

> *... An individual or entity may ask the court to issue a cease and desist order for any number of reasons. Such an order often serves as a temporary injunction to suspend a party's activity until a trial can be held to*

> *determine whether or not it should be allowed to continue . . .*
>
> Copyright Infringement – An individual or entity that suspects someone else is using their copyrighted works without permission may take the first step to protecting their works by sending a cease and desist letter. The letter should contain details about the copyrighted work, proof of ownership of the copyright, and an account of how the copyright has been infringed upon . . .
>
> Trademark Infringement – While written works are assumed copyrighted when written, a trademark must be registered with the government, making it easier to enforce. A cease and desist letter should include a description of the logo or design that has been infringed upon, the date used, and what actions the recipient should take.[97]

Congress passed the Safe Harbor laws, which allow companies who use copyrighted products to provide products and services free to consumers. Of course, they had no intention of destroying the traditional music industry in the process. They were just trying to provide a time and opportunity for digital technology to mature into a better and more interactive form of communication for businesses for consumers.

The labels may be one of the temporary victims of the situation, but it's Silicon Valley who's profited. Google's YouTube is a great example of a company that receives songs, recordings, films, etc., copied and uploaded illegally by consumers, and then, makes them available free to consumers. Safe harbors put the burden of catching and requesting the violation be taken down quickly on the *copyright owner* instead of the company who is providing them as a "service" to consumers. In the past, companies such as YouTube would be shut down for the violation and the executives would be responsible for fines and probably serve time in jail. They would be in violation of the six exclusive rights of the copyright owners.

Google claims that it is trying to comply with the law as it is processing

---

[97] "Cease and Desist Order - Definition, Examples, Cases, Processes." Legal Dictionary. August 07, 2015. Accessed June 23, 2017. https://legaldictionary.net/cease-and-desist-order/.

over 75 million copyright infringements request every month.⁹⁸ It takes between 2-12 days to process the request and sadly, the copyright holders often discover their infringed copyrights products show up on other services just as quickly. The sad part, of course, is that these types of "providers" get rich while the copyright owners have to spend their time and money trying to catch the bad guys. According to IP Watchdog (2017), copyright owners must provide the following to "request" a take-down order:

- *A physical or electronic signature (i.e., /s/NAME) of a person authorized to act on behalf of the owner of the copyright that is allegedly infringed.*

- *Identification of the copyrighted work claimed to have been infringed.*

- *Identification of the material that is claimed to be infringing and information reasonably sufficient to permit the service provider to locate the material.*

- *Information reasonably sufficient to permit the service provider to contact the complaining party, such as an address, telephone number, and, if available, an electronic mail address at which the complaining party may be contacted.*

- *A statement that the complaining party has a good faith belief that use of the material in the manner complained of is not authorized by the copyright owner.*

- *A statement that the information in the notification is accurate, and under penalty of perjury, that the complaining party is authorized to act on behalf of the owner of the copyright that is allegedly infringed.*⁹⁹

In addition, Google, through YouTube, pays an average $0.00069 per play and totals only 3.8% of the market share revenues.¹⁰⁰ Most views are not

---

98 Welch, Chris. "Google received over 75 million copyright takedown requests in February." The Verge. March 07, 2016. Accessed April 25, 2017. http://www.theverge.com/2016/3/7/11172516/google-takedown-requests-75-million.
99 Quinn, Gene. "Sample DMCA Take Down Letter." IP Watchdog. Accessed April 25, 2017. http://www.ipwatchdog.com/2009/07/06/sample-dmca-take-down-letter/id=4501/.
100 "Updated! Streaming Price Bible w/ 2016 Rates : Spotify, Apple Music, YouTube, Tidal, Amazon, Pandora, Etc." The Trichordist. January 16, 2017. Accessed June 23, 2017. https://thetrichordist.com/2017/01/16/updated-stream-

monetized. Google appears to pay on average a whopping $0.00175 per play.[101] That means that a million plays (hits) on YouTube, if you own all the legal rights, will earn the copyright owner a royalty check of $1,750. Don't spend it all in one place! Just kidding. That's a loss of serious money compared to what someone could make on a single and an album, of usually ten songs.

What is Congress doing about the safe harbor problem they created? They have passed a law making the Director of the Copyright Office someone appointed by the Presidents who will also serve directly under Congress. Sadly, labels have had to threaten to shut down the steaming services (to make them pay) for using their "master" recordings. And recording artists who use to receive "royalties" on albums sold are not often paid from the streaming money paid to the labels. The bottom line is that streaming revenues simply do not cover the losses caused by the decline in album sales caused by the illegal downloads and the safe harbor streaming. All of these issues have contributed to the "creative destruction" of the traditional music industry, generating a need for the new business models and new models for financial forecasting as well as profit distribution systems.

Summary

As you can see from this chapter, the value of creativity in the music and entertainment industry has been placed into question by safe harbors. Consumers still perceive music as inspirational and highly motivating. But digital technology, the lack of enforcement in copyright laws, and the protections accorded to safe harbors have simply provided a way for consumers to access entertainment products in a system that does not compensate legal copyright owners fairly. The combination of these three elements placed the "value" of music and other entertainment products into question as a viable business opportunity compared to the past.

ing-price-bible-w-2016-rates-spotify-apple-music-youtube-tidal-amazon-pandora-etc/.
101 "The Streaming Price Bible – Spotify, YouTube and What 1 Million Plays Means to You!" The Trichordist. November 16, 2014. Accessed June 23, 2017. https://thetrichordist.com/2014/11/12/the-streaming-price-bible-spotify-youtube-and-what-1-million-plays-means-to-you/.

Safe harbors have forced the industry to change business models to take into account the new realities of trying to profit on free. What that also means is that almost everything from the way artists are signed to deals at labels to how revenues are now generated has also changed. Instead of estimating the perceived value of an act or recording, now labels have to take into account branding, the live ticket, merchandise sales, corporate endorsements, and other possible revenue streams. Here are some key copyright word definitions that you may find helpful.

An "anonymous work" is a work on the copies or phonorecords of which no natural person is identified as author.

A "collective work" is a work, such as a periodical issue, anthology, or encyclopedia, in which a number of contributions, constituting separate and independent works in themselves, are assembled into a collective whole.

A "compilation" is a work formed by the collection and assembling of preexisting materials or of data that are selected, coordinated, or arranged in such a way that the resulting work as a whole constitutes an original work of authorship. The term "compilation" includes collective works.

A "computer program" is a set of statements or instructions to be used directly or indirectly in a computer in order to bring about a certain result.

"Copies" are material objects, other than phonorecords, in which a work is fixed by any method now known or later developed, and from which the work can be perceived, reproduced, or otherwise communicated, either directly or with the aid of a machine or device. The term "copies" includes the material object, other than a phonorecord, in which the work is first fixed.

"Copyright owner", with respect to any one of the exclusive rights comprised in a copyright, refers to the owner of that particular right.

A work is "created" when it is fixed in a copy or phonorecord for the first time; where a work is prepared over a period of time, the portion of it that has been fixed at any particular time constitutes the work as of that time, and where the work has been prepared in different versions, each version constitutes a separate work.

A "derivative work" is a work based upon one or more preexisting works, such as a translation, musical arrangement, dramatization, fictionalization, motion picture version, sound recording, art reproduction, abridgment, condensation, or any other form in which a work may be recast, transformed, or adapted. A work consisting of editorial revisions, annotations, elaborations, or other modifications, which, as a whole, represent an original work of authorship, is a "derivative work".

To "display" a work means to show a copy of it, either directly or by means of a film, slide, television image, or any other device or process or, in the case of a motion picture or other audiovisual work, to show individual images nonsequentially.

A work is "fixed" in a tangible medium of expression when its embodiment in a copy or phonorecord, by or under the authority of the author, is sufficiently permanent or stable to permit it to be perceived, reproduced, or otherwise communicated for a period of more than transitory duration. A work consisting of sounds, images, or both, that are being transmitted, is "fixed" for purposes of this title if a fixation of the work is being made simultaneously with its transmission.

"Literary works" are works, other than audiovisual works, expressed in words, numbers, or other verbal or numerical symbols or indicia, regardless of the nature of the material objects, such as books, periodicals, manuscripts, phonorecords, film, tapes, disks, or cards, in which they are embodied.

"Publication" is the distribution of copies or phonorecords of a work to the public by sale or other transfer of ownership, or by rental, lease, or lending. The offering to distribute copies or phonorecords to a group of persons for purposes of further distribution, public performance, or public display, constitutes publication. A public performance or display of a work does not of itself constitute publication.

Take the empty cube below and fill in the important layers. If you need to look at the preceeding pages. What's important about the layer of information and how does one layer relate to another?

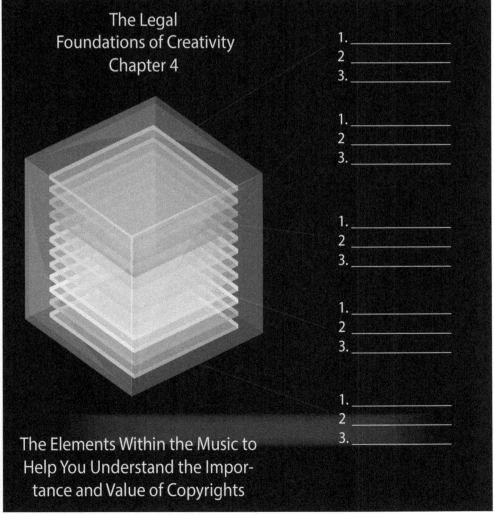

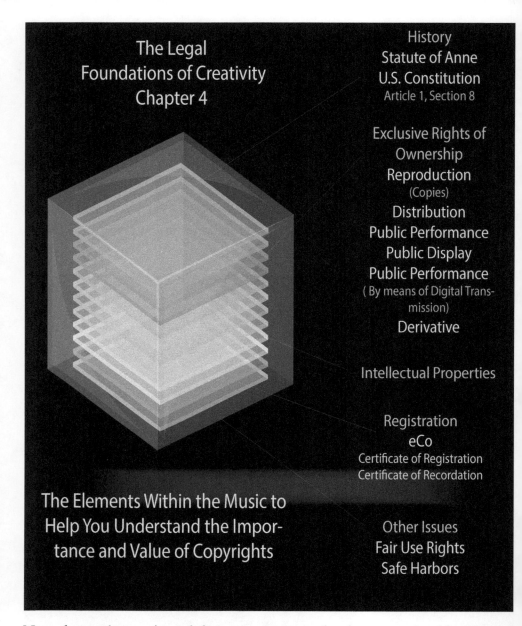

Now that we've reviewed the consumers need to be entertained in Chapter One; how innovations and technology have changed the business in Chapter Two; and here, how the tensions between copyright protection and safe harbor laws have challenged the music industry's business models, we will turn our attention to how the 360-music industry looks at its products.

Chapter 5

Songwriting & Music Publishing

It doesn't matter if we're talking about the traditional or new (360) music industry, it all starts with a wow song. There is little doubt the quality of a song's message, tied to the performance of a great singer, and the recording musicians must all come together to touch the emotions of various types of listeners. It doesn't matter if it's recorded in the studio, on a computer, or live, the glue has to be there. But it starts with a songwriter and the great or wow song. Whether you are or see yourself as songwriter or singer songwriter or you are planning on a business career in the industry, it is important that you know how great songs are made, and how they become part of the catalog at a music publishing company.

Songwriter creates song and registers claim of copyright → Songwriter (who owns the song-copyright) finds & then signs a deal with a music publisher → Music publisher pitches the song (songcasting) to major artists, labels, film production companies, and others

Figure 5.1 Songwriters are usually responsible for registering their claim of copyright with the Library of Congress' Copyright Office (use eCo for registration). Then, as the author and owner of the "creative work", they network and find the right music publishing company who may act as their "agent" to place the creative work (song) with industry related companies. The writer will first have to sign a single song contract (deal) of which there are several different types. Once the song is placed with a company, the publisher will usually "license" the use of the songs and the writer will be paid a "share."

Song Formulas

Mark Volman (2008) of the superstar group The Turtles suggests the following ten principles for writing great songs: "simplicity, clarity, compression, emphasis, consistency, coherence, specificity, reputation, unity, and genuine feeling".[102] His themes of love include feeling the need, I think I've just found her or him, the big come on, this is it, I'm in love, the honeymoon is over, cheating, leaving, remember how it used to be. His shape and form for a hit song goes "verse, pre-chorus, chorus (the hook), and the bridge".[103] Both Mark and I know there's not any formula that guarantees a hit song, but his guidelines may be helpful in suggesting to you that there is a formula or a pattern that most people are attracted to when it comes to making the emotional connection with a specific song. Mark's experience as a singer and songwriter should remind you of what you learned in Chapter One from Langer, Levitin, and others who study the emotional connection that music has with an individual's sense of self.

Connecting Lyrics & Emotions

The songwriters' abilities to describe social and personal situations and the ability to interpret the social consciousness artistically is important. Their ability to convey thoughts and observations emotionally through music and lyrics is equally paramount. Being able to play an instrument in tune is one thing; being able to create and convey emotional messages is clearly another.

Formal education in music, literature, business, psychology, sociology, and world history is enriching. However, great writers often see simple things differently and when they tie them to their own life experiences, they invite you to share these, as you listen to their song or read their book. To be successful, songwriters need to accomplish a lot more than

---
102 Volman, Mark. "Ten Principles for Writing a Great Song." Lecture, EIS 1220 The Entertainment Industry from Belmont University, Nashville, January 1, 2012.
103 Volman, Mark. "Ten Principles for Writing a Great Song." Lecture, EIS 1220 The Entertainment Industry from Belmont University, Nashville, January 1, 2012.

just writing songs. They also have to get them sold or licensed to companies who can then get them to major artists, labels, film production companies, and others.

Take the story of L. Russell Brown, whose songs have sold millions of hits, recorded by many different artists. As a kid growing up Jewish in a Newark housing project, he had to steal to eat, at times. He read *The Reader's Digest* and listened to music to escape the anguish he felt against his brutal, abusive father. He knew the only way out of the neighborhood was to fall into a life of crime, enlist in the military, or to do something really creative and crazy like write songs. After trying the first two, he returned from the military determined to give the music business a shot. After lots of hard work, and some deals he was too naïve to know were bad, he went on to a career that included writing a song that is associated with love, patriotism, and courage, "Tie a Yellow 'Round the Ole Oak Tree".[104]

CREATIVE NETWORKING

Of course, the ability to write songs that potentially connect with millions of fans is fundamental. Attitude, networking, and making things happen are also vital. However, getting songs sold to music publishers is the other side of the songwriter's success equation. It's a step-by-step process. For Brown it meant meeting people who could introduce him to others who might introduce him to still others in the industry. According to Brown (2015), "he and a co-writer friend wrote every day and were turned down more often than a cheap motel bed". "This ain't what we're looking for", became their theme song. But he didn't give up. A friend of his introduced him to one of his friends, who was dating the sister of a known songwriter. He gave Brown the phone number of the co-writer's friend, Nevel Nader.[105] They started writing together. He had a friend who invested in a demo recording. Check out the process in following figure 5.2.

---

104 Brown, L. Russell, Sandy Linzer, and Larry Wacholtz. *The Quintessential Hit Man*, Nashville, TN: Thumbs Up Publishing, 2017.
105 Brown, L. Russell. "Lunch with L." Interview by author. February 12, 2015.

```
Brown pitches his song to
• A friend of his, who . . .
```

```
Introduces him to one of his friends,
• Who was dating the sister of a known songwriter,
  who . . .
```

```
He gives Brown the phone number of the
co-writer friend, Nevel Nader
```

```
Brown visits and meets Nevel
• Brown, another writer, and Nevel co-write together.
  Nevel then, gives the demo to a friend who . . .
```

```
Nevel's friend invests money in a demo
recording
```

```
The arranger at the recording session gives
a copy of the recording to his friend
(Bobby Darin's publicist), who . . .
```

```
She gives her copy to producer Bob Crewe
who . . .
```

```
Offers Brown a major music publishing
deal with Bob Crewe's company
```

The arranger of the music on the session liked the recording so much that he gave a copy of it to his friend, who was Bobby Darin's (a famous recording artist at the time) publicist. She liked it so much she gave a copy to her friend, a famous songwriter/producer, Bob Crewe, who also owned a very successful music publishing company. Crewe was also the producer of The Four Seasons, who had just scored three number one hits on the *Billboard* charts.[106 & 107]

That's the way it usually works, one person tells another, and so on, until the right person gets a copy and then the monetizing process begins. Count the number of people and contacts Brown had to acquire, get excited, and pass a copy of the recording on to before he was able to get his first song sold to a professional music publishing company. Songwriters today have to use the same process. However, once you have a hit recording that becomes your calling card, and the doors are usually open, waiting for you (the known songwriter) to walk through it.

THE FILTERING SYSTEM

For songwriters, rejection is the name of the game and the concept of "thriving on rejection" must become your personal anthem. Everyone goes through this process also. People meeting people who know people who know others who can make things happen has always been used as a "filtering" system to eliminated most of the amateur songwriters and singers who lack the talent to make it.

Until the introduction of the Internet, the really bad stuff was rarely heard by many at the top executives who had the money and power to mold a songwriter or recording artist's career. At the same time, everyone has an opinion about what's a hit. Many people will tell stories about how they passed on songs that later won the Grammy for Song of the

---

[106] Brown, L. Russell. "Lunch with L." Interview by author. February 12, 2015.
[107] Brown, L. Russell, Sandy Linzer, and Larry Wacholtz. "Non-formated." In *I'M L. RUSSELL BROWN and I Wrote.... "TIE A YELLOW RIBBON ROUND THE OLE OAK TREE".and This Is My Story... & Smash*. Unpublished ed. Vol. First. Nashville, TN: Non-Published, 2015.

Year. With the advent of computers, the Internet, and digital technology, anyone who wants to take a shot at being a songwriter can record and upload the finished product to one of the thousands of Internet sites.

Two problems are created when the social media route to production and publicity is taken. The first is a lot a really bad stuff is out on the Internet and second, if the song or the recording is a wow or great, you've already given it away, which destroys any incentive labels had to offer you a deal. However, millions of hits on the Internet will get you a shot at pitching whatever else you have to industry executives. This is complicated part of the new business model in the music industry. The new industry is difficult, as if a new act uses the Internet, they are giving away their recordings. Yet if they generate enough "hits"; then, the label may become interested in signing them. As a part of A&R, label personnel know the motivation behind an artists' choices to break themselves, as they now judge steams and live ticket revenues over Internet hits on a website. It's the same situation for songwriters and music publishers as labels consider who wrote the songs for the breaking acts as a way to determine the potential strength of the writers and publisher's creativity.

THE PRODUCTION MATRIX

Songwriters often have to learn the hard way that their financial success is determined by how well consumers connect emotionally to the acts using their songs. Writing a wow song doesn't mean much until it's recorded and performed by "a great", that is, known, recording artist and musicians. That means that marrying the right artist to the right song is one of the most important qualities of a producer. Then, the labels must also deliver the recordings to consumer's eyes and ears, so they may discover the song. Almost anyone can sit on top of a mountain and write songs. However, if you want to make a living at it, you'll need the industry (producers, artists, labels, promoters, etc.) to invest their time, money, and careers into selecting your song for their next recording project, event, film, or computer game. As you read this book, I hope you are realizing that in knowing the creative and entrepreneurial dimensions of the music industry, you will be honing your skills in both developing new entertainment products and in the business of the music business.

THE FIRST STEP

If you want to be a successful songwriter don't post or give away your songs. Instead, join professional songwriters organizations, meet others, and co-write like crazy. There are many such organizations across the country where songwriters encourage each other, co-write, and get advice from the experts.

Co-write with someone who is better than you. Writing with others helps you see a lyric and hear music from a different perspective and often improves your songwriting. The goal is to get a song you and others strongly believe has potential, and then, start connecting with music publishers in the industry. At times, music publishers, on hearing your demo, will like what you are doing, but feel it needs some sort of improvement. They may recommend co-writers to improve your skills. This is not an insult; it is an effort on their part to invite you to show commitment to your career as an artist, and it is a test or measure of your willingness to work within the industry.

REFERRALS

Most music publishers will not accept unsolicited songs. So, how can you get past the armed guards to submit your material? Look for referrals, that is, someone who knows someone established and respected in the industry whose who's referral may get you an appointment. Do not lie or use someone's name as a referral without permission. Performing Rights Organizations (called PROs) such as ASCAP, BMI, and SESAC usually provide a few minutes to listen to new writers' material. If the writer has great potential, they'll want to sign them to their organization for representation with public performance royalties, such as radio station airplay. Let them listen to your work and if they like what they hear, they will often refer you to established music publishers they think might click with your type and style of songs.

WHAT PUBLISHERS DO FOR SONGWRITERS

Find a music publisher who is well connected to the most successful people in the industry. They should be a pro-active mentor between the songwriter (you) and the labels, producers, artist managers, and recording artists, who are looking for wow songs. Such a publisher will help you become a better songwriter by offering you constructive criticism. Make sure they are honest business people who have a good reputation and passion for your success, beyond their own.

Music publishers administrate the owner's copyrights. That's one of the reasons they want to own your song which is the first thing to know about music publishing/songwriting deals. Once they acquire your ownership in the song (the copyright) then they rework the song, evaluate which company to pitch it to (called songcasting), and then often rerecord it into a demo before giving it to a songplugger to get it "placed" in the industry.

THE FREE INTERNET MARKETPLACE

We've already talked about egos and trying to leap frog the established industry by DYI. If you do put your creative works on the Internet it's already been released. If it doesn't generate several million real hits, the labels are less inclined to consider listening to your material later. It's already failed. However, nobody knows where the next big thing, whatever that might be, is coming from, and even a blind squirrel finds a nut sometimes, so go for it. Think about what you'll learn from the experience.

Be aware that the industry has lots of interns and lower level employees scanning the Internet all the time seeking new acts, songs, recordings, that labels could develop into the next money machine (you). So, if they don't see a great buzz, see a burst of fans digging it, they're going to pass, and it may be harder for you to get your foot in the door the next time.

Wow Songs

Everyone, and I really do mean everyone, is looking for the next "wow" song. As you've probably already guessed, nobody really knows what it is until they've heard it. This makes it even harder to get the attention of the industry executives when you're trying to sell it to major music publishers. The reason is that it's just so darn rare to hear a new song that rocks you, gives you goosebumps, and that you feel deep in your gut, it's a hit.

Remember the first job of the music publishers and label executives? To find the next big thing (in this case a song) they can then use to launch a new act or save an existing fading act and at the same time, turn a huge profit. Predicting success only looks like a mystery. If the act has already had some success, the odds are better than launching someone who has no visibility with the consumers. But, there's still no guarantee. Take a look at the following chart to see how industry executives perceive "value" in the different areas of the entertainment and music industry.

Projected Values

The bottom line is that most of the "songs" pitched are good, but they need to be really great or a wow and that's rare. Why does it need to be a wow? Because the executives will probably spend one million dollars or more to turn your song and others into an album, and create and fund a marketing plan to launch an act. Sometimes it comes down to a gut reaction between two or three potential wow songs that determine which creative work is finally selected for production. Even at that point, the executives' final decision is often based on which one might be more profitable. Maybe only two people out of three think it's a wow, as we all think differently, which can be a challenge as most major labels want a unanimous decision on new songs in the A&R Department and all board members on signing a new act. Each part of the industry is then built on the wow song as you'll see on the next page in figure 5.3!

TYPES OF MUSIC PUBLISHERS

There are different types of music publishers to be aware of before pitching your wow songs as the amount of money you make relates to the usage of your song in products consumers enjoy.

> *Major music publishers* are often affiliated with or owned by a major record label or entertainment based company. Therefore, they are powerful and can quickly connect your songs to the most famous recording artists and music supervisors who select your material for films being produced by their host company such as Universal, Time Warner, Sony Entertainment, or Disney.
>
> *Genre based music publishers* focus to niche formats such as children's music, media and advertisement production companies and computer game soundtracks.

Size is relevant as small independently owned publishers who are connected to powerful industry executives may use their ownership as bargaining chips in Co-Pub and Administrative Deals. Yet, the songwriter/music publishers who are not connected to the major music publishers usually fail to get their songs distribute to the global market, and can't issue or process licenses, which leaves them struggling financially. In the end it really comes down to (a) how great is the song, and (b) who do you know that can get the wow song to the right music publishers who are connected.

Industry Entity	Value	Benefits ties to Value
Song Writers	Value	Wow songs are the foundation of the industry. Royalties (From sales and licensing of songs)
Music Publishers	Value	Royalties (From sales and licensing of songs) and The company's value is based on owning copyright's that currently and in the future, may generate potential additional royalties and licensing fees)
Recording Artists	Value	Royalties from a percentage of gross from sales, use of, or by product of- • Recordings • Streaming • Live ticket shows • Merchandise • Corporate sponsorship • Branding • Endorsements • Other sources
Musicians & Backup Singers	Value	Team members who create the excellent musical tracks for recordings artists, film sound tracks and other media. Wages from independent contractors, artistic support from producers, and union representation provide world class entertainment
Labels	Value	Labels provide the funding to support the artistic careers of artists, musicians, and others in the creative systems, plus the employees in the business system. Artist recordings provides many businesses with their foundation products including the film industry, mass media, social media, and Internet providers, plus it provides environmental background music for restaurants, and many other businesses. The success of the artist's recordings also provides live ticket event opportunities for promoters, merchandise and branding.
Artist Performance Agencies	Value	Provide representation to musicians, singers, film and stage actors and other types of creative people. Unions and guilds include • AF of M (The American Federation of Musicians) • SAG-AFTRA (The Screen Actors Guild &The American Federation of Television and Radio Artists) • Equity (Stage and theater actors) • AES (Audio Engineering Society) Not a union, however, a helpful organization to support audio engineers and their craft. Agents are paid a percentage of the artist's income such as 10% of gross for booking agents, 15% to 20% of gross for personal management, 5% of gross for business management and other sources. Booking agents are paid on 10% of the gross (show price for the acts performance), such as 10% of gross
Promoters Touring	Value	Fund the live ticket events such as concerts, computer game events and others. Profits depend on the type of deal and breakeven points after all expenses are paid from sponsorships and ticket sales

SONGWRITER/MUSIC PUBLISHING DEALS

Let's say you did it! You've written a wow song and you're pitching it to a major music publisher. They love it and decide to offer you a deal. What are you going to do now? What do you need to know when you are offered a music publishing deal? Here's where you've got to think about what is in your best interest first! Of course, you want a music publisher representing you and your songs who will be supportive, aggressive in the placement of the material (your songs), and support you with great demos. You also want good co-writers, and choices among co-writers. Whatever you get in the final deal is what you negotiate, so forget your ego, get down to business, and start to build a great partnership and respectful relationship with a major music publisher.

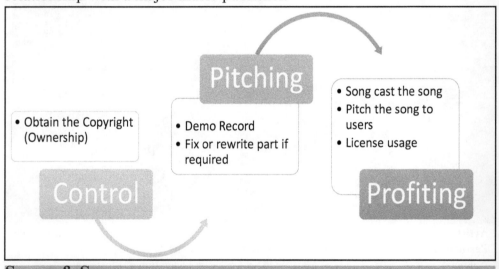

SPLITS & SHARES

Three things are negotiated in every deal. These are- (a) the songwriter's royalties, which are a percentage of the total income (called the songwriter's share); (b) the music publisher's royalties that are a percentage of the total income (called the music publisher's share); and, (c) the ownership of the copyright, which may be a valuable and a sellable property based on how many companies want to use the song and how many consumers want to buy or listen to it in the future.

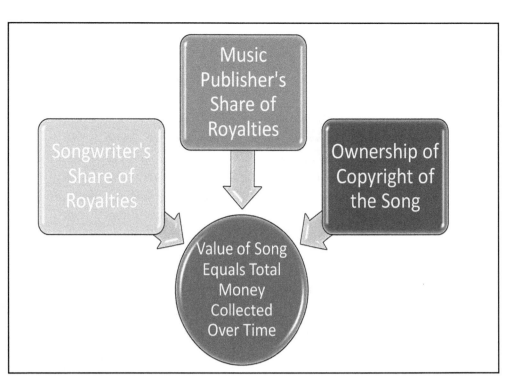

Figure 5.4: The total value of a song depends on how much it is used in recordings, films, movies, computer games, live performances, and other licensing opportunities. How much money the songwriters receive (usually 50%) and music publishers receive (the remaining 50%) of licensing fees which become royalties is determined by consumer purchases and streaming, and businesses such as concerts, radio and other media and entertainment products. The third source of revenue is ownership of the copyright (which by law is a legal form of property which may be sold, given away, or handed down to others in an estate).

At the same time, music publishers know the value of the song is often determined over a long period of time. If the song is used in cuts by other acts, movies, computer games, etc., music publishers can sell it for millions to other music publishers who are increasing the value of their catalog.

Think of it this way, if you buy a house (property) and keep it many years, it's probably going to double or triple in value. As an example, Bluejay claims (2009),

> *Appreciation matters because it can make the difference between whether it's better to buy a home or continue renting. And even small changes in the appreciation rate can change the long-term value of buying considerably. A $235k home becomes worth $485k at 3% appreciation after 30 years, but it becomes worth a whopping $649k at 4% appreciation.*[108]

And remember, a song is also a piece of "property", just as the house is in our example. The value of the song is determined by license fees collected for the use of the song by labels, film production companies, media, businesses, and consumers. Business and media gain the right to use a song in the form of their business products (recordings or films, as examples) or services they provide (radio broadcast, nightclubs, or streaming sites, as examples), through buying the correct license.

Ask Questions

Let's say you are selling your song to music publishers and they offer you a 50% share deal. Fifty/fifty sounds fair as you wrote the song and you're expecting the music publishing company to license it whenever and wherever possible. Shouldn't you receive at least half of the royalties generated? Should you go with the deal or ask another question? If you answered YES to my question and took my offer, you just got zapped, as you'll only get 25% of the royalties. But you thought it was a 50/50 deal! The key word you always want to hear is "share" and then are we talking about my share as the writer or your share as the music publisher?

The royalties collected from licensing are usually divided into two shares, the songwriter's share and the music publisher's share. Something that

---
108 Bluejay, Michael. "How to Buy a House." Historical real estate appreciation rate in the United States. 2009. Accessed June 29, 2017. http://michaelbluejay.com/house/appreciation.html.

is a little difficult to understand as the industry refers to each "share" as 100%, when it is really only 50% of the royalties collected. In other words, 50% of the money generated for the use of a song is equal to 100% of the share. Many in the industry say a song is worth 200%, which of course, is impossible. Just remember that in most music publishing deals, the songwriter's share is worth 50% of the total money generated. The music publisher's share is worth the remaining 50% of the total revenue generated. The important thing to remember is anytime you see or hear the word "share", you're only talking about half of the generated revenues. As an example, a 100% share of the songwriter's royalties is really only 50% of the total royalties being generated. So, if someone says we'll split the money 50/50, what are you going to ask? How about what share are we talking about, songwriter's, music publisher's, or the total money being generated? Never be afraid to ask the question, 100% of what?

Songwriters and music publishers are paid for the use of their creative works, so who do you think they want to record or use their songs (called material in the industry)? The answer is the biggest and most famous artist on the planet. In both systems, knowing the right people and having the right connections leads to success. People within the systems use each other to create the types of products and business marketing campaigns that make everyone successful. As a famous songwriter once told me, "when the tide comes in, all the boats are raised in the water". In other words, when an artist or recording becomes very successful all the people who worked on creating and selling it make a profit including the songwriter and the music publisher.

TYPES OF MUSIC PUBLISHING DEALS

The five most common types of music publisher/songwriter deals are (a) Work-Made-for-Hire, (b) Single Song Contract, (c) Staff Publishing Deal, (d) Co-publishing deal, (e) an Administration Deal, and, (f) the Shark Deal.

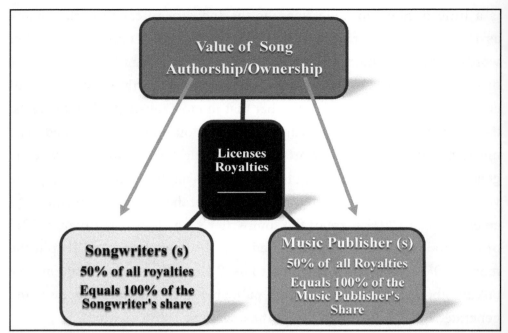

Figure 5.5: The typical songwriter-music publisher deal gives the music publisher the ownership of the copyright (song) in exchange for 50% (royalties) of all the money generated from licensing the song. The downside of the deal is the music publisher will own the song until it falls into public domain, which is the life of the creator plus 70 years. The first time an author/creator may request the copyright be returned is after 35 to 40 years of ownership.

WORK-MADE-FOR-HIRE DEAL

In professional songwriting, Work-Made-for-Hire returns us to when songwriters were paid a lump sum of money for their songs and the rights to use them. Much of that type of deal was structured around the development of New York's Tin Pan Alley. Traditionally, writers and music publishers split all royalties generated from licensing 50/50. But this is different. Examples of a Work-made-for-Hire arrangement include specific one-time jobs, such as writing jingles or music beds for commercials for radio or TV. The employer (person who hired you to write the song) is usually considered the author and copyright owner of the song, unless you put it in writing that you are to be credited as the author. Which by the way, you should be. All the money you, as the songwriter, will be paid is a one time, upfront fee, which means that you'll never see any additional royalties, even if the song become a smash hit later.

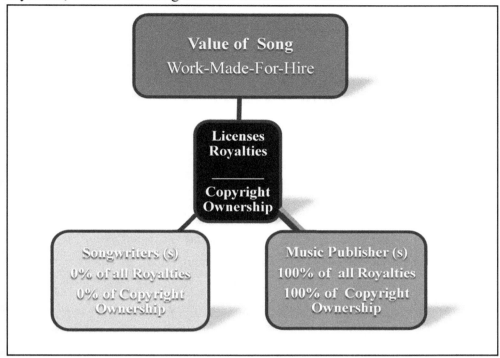

Figure 5.6: If you work as an independent contractor and someone hires you to write a song, book, or paint a figure on the wall, who owns the copyrighted "creative works?" It is usually the person or company who hired you and all you receive is the money paid upfront to complete the work. The hiring company or person owns the copyright and will be paid all royalties for the licensing of the work. The exception is a Work-Made-for-Hire arrangement when the artist hired has a clause written into the contract allowing him/her to retain the copyright. A quick search of the Internet will give you some sample Work-Made-for-Hire agreement templates to use as reference. These should be used to help you have a good, informed discussion with an entertainment lawyer, and not to encourage you to do this yourself.

The statutory definition of a Work-Made-for-Hire, according to The U.S Copyright Office (2013) is

> . . . A work prepared by an employee within the scope of his or her employment, or A work specially ordered or commissioned for use as a contribution to a collective work, as a part of a motion picture or other audiovisual work, as a translation, as a supplementary work, as a

compilation, as an instructional text, as a test, as answer material for a test, or as an atlas, if the parties expressly agree in a written instrument signed by them that the work shall be considered a work made for hire... A supplementary work is defined as a work prepared for publication as a secondary adjunct to a work by another author for the purpose of introducing, concluding, illustrating, explaining, revising, commenting upon, or assisting in the use of the other work, such as forewords, afterword, pictorial illustrations, maps, charts, tables, editorial notes, musical arrangements, answer material for tests, bibliographies, appendices and indexes.[109]

INDIE DEAL

Independent writers are offered a single song contract when a music publisher wants to make a deal for the one song. In most Indie Deals, the songwriter receives no advance, but may earn 100% of the songwriter's share of royalties (equal to 50% of the total royalties generated), if they know how to negotiate for it. What you're doing once again is giving up 100% ownership in the copyright of the song (ownership) in exchange for the 50% of the total royalties generated by the use of the song as it's placed with major artists, labels, film and movie production companies, and so on.

STAFF DEALS

Staff writer deals provide songwriters an advance on their royalties, plus the opportunity to co-write with other major writers. A Staff Deal is similar to the Indie Deal except the music publisher provides advance money in exchange for exclusivity. That means the songwriter may only write songs for the publisher who they are signed with and who's providing the money. Staff Deals are considered a step up from the Work-Made-for-Hire Deal as the business relationship is now a long-term arrangement (if the writer can supply enough hits).

---

109 "U.S. Copyright Office - Help: Author." U.S. Copyright Office - Help: Author. April 4, 2013. Accessed July 14, 2015.

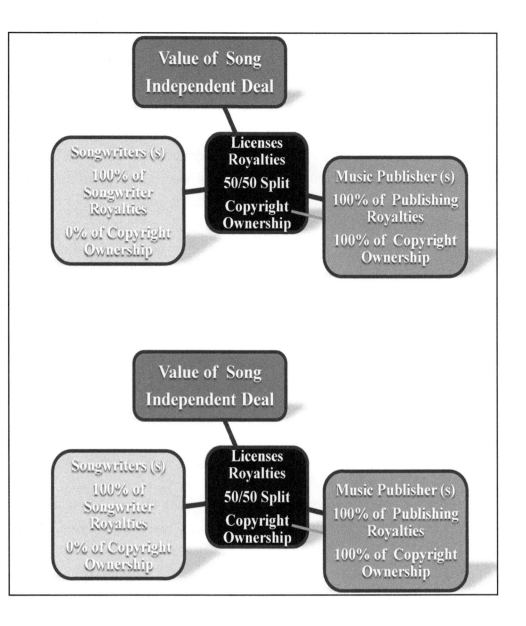

Figure 5.7: An independent deal is when the songwriter or creative artist is offered a single song contract (if we're talking about songwriters) in exchange for 50% of the royalties which are called (crazy as this is) 100% of the songwriting share. Staff deals are an indication the writer has arrived at a professional level in the industry as the music publisher pays a small annual stipend of $18-$24,000 a year (paid quarterly) for the writer to write. The royalties and copyright ownership is the same in both the indie and staff deals.

To summarize, a Staff Deal occurs when (a) the writer and the music publisher usually share the royalties generated, (b) the writer is provided with a financial advance, (c) the publisher is able to recoup their financial advances out of the songwriters share of the royalties, (d) and, if the song makes enough money, both profit. As you already know, in the Work-Made-for-Hire Deal, all of the money generated (excluding the money paid in a one-time fee) and the ownership of the copyright go to the person or company who hired the songwriter to write the song. Copyright ownership of the song is the same in most Indie Deals and Staff Deals. Thus, in the Indie Deals and Staff Deals, the amount of money made by both is determined by the media, businesses, and consumers use and buying of the entertainment products the song is used in and the license fees generated from businesses that use the song or recording in their businesses. However, it also depends on the negotiated terms in the deal, which is why both music publishers and songwriters need to understand how the 360-music industry works. It's important that both understand what their options are and how to negotiate a reasonable deal.

QUOTAS

Co-writing provides opportunities to improve songwriting skills, make industry contacts, network with others and make a reasonable living instead of flipping hamburger to earn a living. Staff writers are paid the advance which is sometimes called a draw in exchange for a quota of acceptable songs (usually 8-12 annually). Remember, that all songs written under staff writer deals are often owned by the music publisher, and, all the advances are recoupable from the songwriter's share of royalties, if generated. However, the music publisher is taking a risk as, if the deal fails to generate enough royalties, the staff writer does not owe any money to the music publisher who provided the advances.

CO-PUBLISHING DEAL

Co-Publishing Deals help songwriters capture more of the song's equity or potential value by establishing co-ownership of the copyright. Co-Publishing Deals are negotiated between the writer and music publisher during the acquisition of the song when more than one publisher is involved. In this case, the songwriter is also a music publisher meaning that the writer has one company to write songs and another to publish them. The problem is that most of these one-person companies do not have the connections or time to actually pitch the songs (material) to the labels, artists, film, and movie production companies, etc., who in turn, license them to use in their entertainment products.

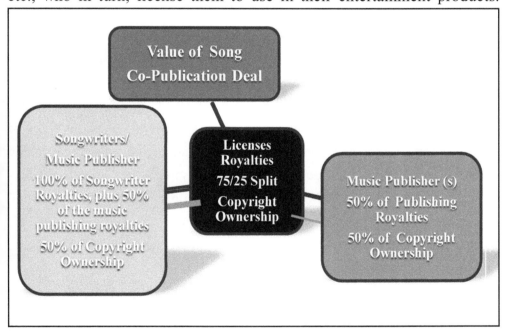

Figure 5.8: Once you've written a few hits and maybe a wow or two, then you as the songwriter have more power to negotiate a better deal. Most famous writers declare themselves a music publisher as well as a songwriter. They own two businesses that give them the power to seek additional royalties from the music publisher who wants to make a deal. The Co-publication deal enables the writer/publisher to gain half of the music publisher's royalties and 50% of the copyright ownership. Thus, in reality the language may be a little confusing, but the split is now 75%-25% in favor of the songwriter/publisher. In addition, they will now own 50% of the song's copyright.

Therefore, songwriters, music producers, and recording artist-owned music publishing companies make Co-publishing Deals with the major publishers. These deals focus on world distribution and administration of paperwork, such as licenses and royalty collections, in exchange for a percentage of the music publisher's share of the royalties and 50% of the copyright ownership. On the other hand, the songwriter, producer, label, or recording artist (whoever owns the song) gives up half of their copyright of the song. Now, the total royalties are split 75/25, with 75% of the total generated revenues going to the original songwriter/co-publisher (100% of the songwriter's share and 50% of the publisher's share) and the remaining half of the music publisher's share (25% of the total) going to the other music publisher.

To summarize, Co-Publishing deals work to the advantage of both the songwriter, who is also a publisher, and the established industry music publisher, but only when you've got a wow song. The music publisher receives a share of the copyright ownership, which increases the value of their catalog. At the same time, they collect half of the music publishing share of royalties (which equals 25% of the song's total generated revenues). The songwriter, who is also functioning as the music publisher, also wins, as they receive distribution and industry connections, plus half of the music publishers' share, in addition to the full songwriting share.

If the co-publisher is located in a foreign country, then this type of deal is often called a Sub-Publishing Deal, as it recognizes that the overseas publisher is getting part of the royalties in exchange for collecting royalties in their territory of the world. Thus, the songwriter is pitching a song to an established music publishers who can generate the connections and licenses fees the songwriter is not able to accomplish themselves. Yet, the songwriter who also has their own music publishing company may want to increase the amount of money they earn from the deal. To accomplish that they have to retain part of the ownership of the song, which you already know is called a copyright. The terms of the co-publishing deal depend on (a) the songwriter owning their own music publishing company, (b) the established music publisher's willingness to receive only half of the music publishing share in exchange for the other half based on the strength of the song's potential for generating licensed royalties, and (c) the songwriter's ability negotiate this type of deal.

ADMINISTRATIVE MUSIC PUBLISHING DEAL

An Administrative Music Publishing Deal is the same as the Co-pub, except the songwriter (who is also publisher) retains 100% ownership of the copyright. This tactic allows songwriters who own their own publishing companies to keep absolute ownership of their song's copyright. The royalty splits are the same as in the Co-pub Deal. The established music publisher acts only as an administrator placing the song with music and entertainment production companies, and issues mechanical licenses, registers songs with the corresponding performance rights organizations, and commonly collects royalties in exchange for 50% of the publisher's share of the revenues. In other words, they administrate the use of the copyright (song) and then share 50/50 in the music publishers share, but they do not retain any ownership of the copyright. Why would they do it?

Administrative deals are rare, but when they occur, it's usually between a very successful and well-known writer, who is also a publisher, and a major label music publisher. The major label music publisher may easily exploit the song's potential equity worldwide. Remember, the money from the revenue streams are the same as in the Co-Publishing deal, so once again the question is why would they do it? Think about the value of the song once recorded by a major artist, streamed by consumers and licensed by businesses around the world. Consider the royalties generated from multiple sources, and you'll see that it's still very profitable.

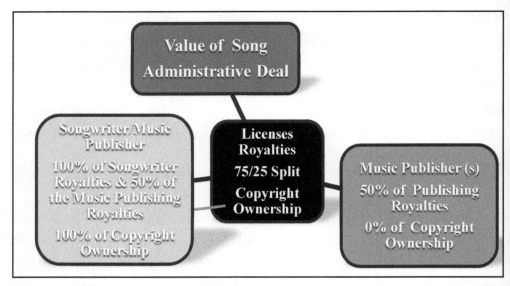

Figure 5.9: The administrative deal is the best as a songwriter, who is also a music publisher, can hope wish to achieve. It's really how famous songwriters often retire, as they own 100% of the copyrights of the songs they have written. They can either have the world music publisher distribute and take care of all licensing and collections or they can sell their entire song catalog (since they own the copyrights) for 5%-15% of the five-year average income, which may add up to millions. And if they decide to sell their copyrights, they still collect their share of the songwriting royalties on all future royalties generated that may be passed down to the next generation.

SHARK DEAL

Whenever a publisher compliments your song and then asks you to put money into the deal to share the expenses, you are being cheated. Just remember, you don't pay them; they pay you! It is your song, your property, not theirs. There are many examples of songs being sold to music publishers (mostly in the 1950s and early 60s) for a few thousand to hundreds of dollars or less. The only money shark publishers usually make is what the songwriter paid them to publish your song. In most cases, they do not have the industry contacts to place songs with a major artist, producer, or label, and correspondingly, writers almost never receive any royalties. Unethical music publishers, who offer Shark Deals, are considered rip-off artists, as they are in the business of making money off of the songwriter, not the songs.

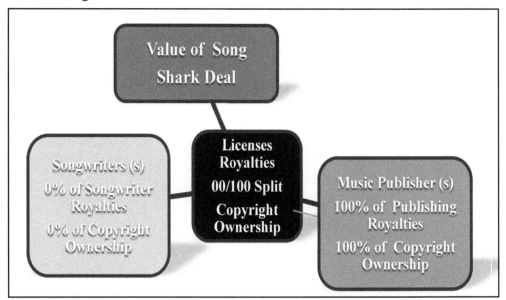

Figure 5.10: This is easy -if you pay them money you're getting taken to the cleaners. Publishers pay you; you do not pay them. You can run around telling friends you've got a publishing deal, but don't expect to make any money.

LICENSING PUBLISHED SONGS

Once music publishers have contracted potential wow songs through the various types of music publishing/songwriting deals, it's time to rework them, demo record, and then pitch them to labels, music supervisors (films), advertising agencies, and many other companies who use songs in their businesses. This is how they make their money and depending on the deal the songwriter made, it's how they make their money also. Music publishers offer mechanical licenses directly or through The Harry Fox Agency, and Sync Licensing directly for use of the songs they own in commercials, film, and visual media. ASCAP, BMI, and SESAC acts as "agents" representing songwriters and music publishers to collect licensing fees, which are turned into royalties for songwriters and music publishers after they take out an administrative fee. Print licenses are issued to music or book companies who use the print versions of the songs and lyrics as lyrics sheets, sheet music and folios.

TYPES OF LICENSES

The five major types of license are:

- **Reproduction (Mechanical) Licenses:** Songs distributed in physical and digital form. The royalties are generally collected and paid by the Harry Fox Agency, who in turn pays the music publisher and then who may or may not (depending on the deal) pay the songwriters. This is complicated as now more than recorded products purchased at retail and on-line are considered mechanicals. As examples, ring tones, permanent digital downloads (called a DPD or digital phonorecord delivery), and interactive steams from locker-based and bundled music Internet streaming services (considered an electronic transmission royalty) require a mechanical license.

- **Public Performance Licenses:** Songs broadcast on radio (terrestrial and satellite), streaming, in live venues, and other public places require a Public Performance License that is often call a blanket license. The royalties are collected and paid by public performance societies (ASCAP, BMI, and SESAC and GMR which is a new copy called Global Music Rights). Each broadcaster receives a blanket license from each performing rights society, in exchange for a royalty fee. Fees are converted into "royalties" and then paid directly to the music publishers and songwriters. There are about another 200 PRO's in foreign countries most of which have only one or two per-country. As examples, SOCAN is in Canada, OSA in the Czech Republic, SACEM collects the money in France, GEMA in Germany, and ACUM in Israel.[110]

---

[110] "International Performance Rights Organizations." International Performance Rights Organizations. Accessed December 29, 2017. https://www.audiosparx.com/info/international-performance-rights-organizations.cfm.

- **Synchronization Licenses:** songs used in film, television, commercials, music videos, etc. Publishers enter into direct license deal with users, who may or may not pay songwriters depending on the deal.

- **Master License:** This one is different as a master license is required by a film or movie production company (visual presentations including YouTube) for THE RECORDING OF THE SONG from the record label who owns the copyright of the recording of the song. Thus, two licenses are required for the use of a recording of a song in a visual presentation. The production company is required to acquire a sync license for the use of the song from the music publisher and a master license from the label who owns the recording of the song. Music publishers enter into direct license deals for both.

- **Folio Licenses:** Music published in written form as lyrics and music notation either as bound music folios or on-line lyric and tablature websites. Publishers enter into direct license deals with users.[111]

The more successful the song is the more licensing fees are generated and the potential future licensing will determine the copyright's value. If you own a song, such as the holiday hit "Silver Bells", played year after year during the holidays, or an oldie but goodie hit recording (say, "Lyin' Eyes" by the Eagles) played on radio for decades; or, a song placed into a TV show or movie that becomes a classic hit around the world, then it's probably worth millions of dollars. How much of that generated money is going to be yours depends on your ability to negotiate the shares and ownership in your best interest when you first made the deal. Once that's done, the money will keep coming in as long as the song is being

111 "Music Publishing 101." NMPA.org. 2014. Accessed July 19, 2015. http://nmpa.org/about/#music_publishing.

purchased or used in the media and within businesses. That is until it falls into public domain!

Therefore, songwriting deals are negotiations between the songwriter (s) and music publisher (s) to determine how much money each will receive from their share of the royalties and who is going to own all or a percentage of the copyright of the song. Royalties are paid quarterly or every three-months (January, March, June, and September) based on the amount of money collected the previous three months.

THE NATIONAL MUSIC PUBLISHERS ASSOCIATION OF AMERICA (NMPA)

The National Music Publishers Association (NMPA) is the trade organization that represents music publishers in the United States. Similar organizations are found in other parts of the world. According to the NMPA (2016):

> *Founded in 1917, the NMPA is the trade association representing all music publishers and their songwriting partners. The NMPA's mandate is to protect and advance the interests of music publishers and songwriters in matters relating to the domestic and global protection of music copyrights. The goal of the NMPA is to protect its members' property rights on the legislative, litigation and regulatory fronts. Most of the major and independent music publishing companies are members of the NMPA, including top execs from Sony/ATV Music, Universal Music Publishing Group, Warner/Chappell Music, Kobalt Music Group, BMG Rights Management, Peermusic, SONGS Music and Disney Music Group.*[112]

MECHANICAL LICENSES

Let's take a look at the various types of licenses in detail. Mechanical Licenses still generate royalties from the sale of albums and singles that are

---
112 Kawashima, Dale. "NMPA President David Israelite Discusses The Latest Issues In The Battle For Songwriters & Publishers To Be Paid Higher Royalties." NMPA. May 4, 2016. Accessed June 30, 2017. http://nmpa.org/sound_off/nmpa-president-david-israelite-discusses-the-latest-issues-in-the-battle-for-songwriters-publish-

paid to songwriters through their music publisher. There's just one small problem with that concept now and it's streaming! If consumers can acquire the music they want to listen to anytime, anyplace, for free, why buy albums and singles? In 2016, streaming actually generated more money for the labels than album sales and therefore, with the significant reduction of retail and digital sales comes a reduction in music publisher and songwriter royalties. Accordingly, the definition of "mechanicals" was recently expanded to including streaming. At first, the term digital mechanical was used, now all of the various mechanical licenses sources are simply titled "mechanicals". According to The Harry Fox Agency (2017),

> *A mechanical license grants the rights to reproduce and distribute copyrighted musical compositions (songs) on CDs, records, tapes, ringtones, permanent digital downloads, interactive streams and other digital configurations supporting various business models, including locker-based music services and bundled music offerings. If you want to record and distribute a song that you don't own or control, or if your business requires the distribution of music that was written by others, you need to obtain a mechanical license. A mechanical license doesn't include the use of a song in a video. That use requires a synchronization license which you will need to obtain by contacting the publisher(s) directly.*[113]

THE HARRY FOX AGENCY (SESAC)

Most American music publishers use The Harry Fox Agency (HFA) to issue mechanical licenses and collect royalties, primarily from the record labels, for the use of their songs (recall the publishers own the copyright) on labels' recordings. HFA originated in 1927 and used to represent about 48,000 music publishers in the United States.[114] However in 2014, as consumers switched from buying albums and singles to streaming they sold the com-

---

ers-to-be-paid-higher-royalties/.
113 S.E.S.A.C. "What is a Mechanical License?" What is a Mechanical License? Accessed December 23, 2017. https://www.harryfox.com/license_music/what_is_mechanical_license.html.
114 Christman, Ed. "SESAC Buys the Harry Fox Agency." Billbaord.com. July 7, 2015. Accessed July 26, 2015. http://www.billboard.com/articles/news/6620210/sesac-buys-the-harry-fox-agency.

pany to SESAC for about $20 million dollars.[115] As *Billboard* reported in July 2015,

> ... "Licensing is fragmented across both multiple types of rights, as well as multiple territories for the streaming services that represent the future growth opportunity of the music industry," SESAC chairman and CEO John Josephson said in a statement. "The result is a complex, opaque and currently inefficient licensing regime that fails to deliver the best outcomes for creators and publishers, as well as end users. What excites us about this transaction is the ability it provides to make the licensing process both simpler and more efficient, and in so doing create additional value for music creators and publishers, as well as the digital music platforms".[116]

Record labels are required to pay a statutory rate (set by the government) for the use of a song in a recording. Set by the Copyright Royalty Board and then approved by Congress, the rate is currently a little over 9¢. The Mechanical License got its name initially from the mechanical action of the player pianos, which used punched paper cylinders, known as piano rolls, to generate music for the musician. This how the player piano worked,

> In 1863, the Frenchman Fourneaux invented the player piano. He called it, "Pianista", the first pneumatic piano mechanism, which was introduced at the Philadelphia Centennial Exhibition in 1876. In 1887, a year after Votey invented the Pianola; Edwin Welte introduced the perforated paper roll in Germany. The perforated roll mechanism to make music was based on the Jacquard punch cards used to weave designs into cloth . . . Punched paper rolls also drove the first 88-note player pianos. Their music is created when the operator or "pianoist" pumps foot pedals that operate a vacuum motor. An 88-note piano roll tracking mechanism, powered by an air motor, transports the punched roll across the tracker bar. Each piano key is connected to the tracker bar, one hole per key. On 88-note player pianos, by varying the pressure applied to the foot pedals and manipulating levers mounted below the keyboard, the operator manually adds color and expression to the music.[117]

---
115 Ibid.
116 Ibid.
117 Kochanny, Thaddeus. "Origins of the player piano." Player Piano History. February 11, 2017. Accessed June 30,

If you bought a player piano, musicians could play it the norm with fingers on the keys, or if they couldn't play it, the piano wo' itself" by using paper roles full of perforated holes that would a. piano to play itself with the air pressure built up from the foot pedals. But how would the songwriter get paid? The answer is the companies who created and sold the paper rolls had to get a license from the music publishers to be able to make the "holy paper" rolls.

Ever heard of "grooves in a recording of an old album, or "pits" in a CD disc, or "magnetic binary codes" in computer recordings? It's all the same principle as using a product on or in devices that allow us to hear someone's great song created by a songwriter (who should receive payment for the creative work) and the music publisher (who owns the copyright). Is this starting to make sense yet? Can you also see how the paper roll companies are associated with today's record labels and how the perforated holes in the piano rolls are similar to the pits (holes) in CDs and DVDs?

THE STATUTORY RATE, COMPENSATION, AND LICENSING

The statutory rate is currently 9.1¢ per-song ($.091) for a song at or under 5 minutes multiplied by the number of units pressed, shipped, downloaded, or sold. Thus, if a label presses or downloads a combination of 1,000,000 units, the cost for the license is 9.1¢ times 1,000,000 or $91,000 per-song paid by the label to the music publisher(s) who may then pay or not pay the songwriter depending on the deal between the two. A ten-song album (with all songs under 5 minutes in length) cost the label $910,000 with once again the money being sent to the music publisher, usually through The Harry Fox Agency who acts as the middleman.

If the song's recorded time is over five minutes, then the Statutory Rate shifts to a per-minute rate of 01.75¢ per-minute ($.0175) times the total number of minutes. Each minute is "rounded" up to the next minute even if the song is just one second over. Thus, as an example, if the recorded
2017. http://www.amica.org/Live/Instruments/Player_Pianos/Player_Piano_History.htm.

ength of the song is 5:01 (1 second over the limit), then the entire rate shifts to a per-minute rate of 01.75¢ per-minute, times 6 minutes. As an example, a song with the recorded time of 8:01 is considered a nine-minute song, so the mechanical license fee is 01.75¢ times 9 minutes for a total of $0.1575 cents per-unit pressed, ship, downloaded, or sold. The Statutory Rate (amount) is usually locked in at the time the recording is released for the first time.

The amount of money being collected for "mechanicals" is declining as fewer consumers are buying singles and albums. This first started with iTunes as consumers by-passed the albums and bought only their favorite singles. Now, they buy less as streaming becomes more and more popular. Mechanicals are now also defined as interactive streaming, but the royalties are less than if the consumers had purchased the music at retail.

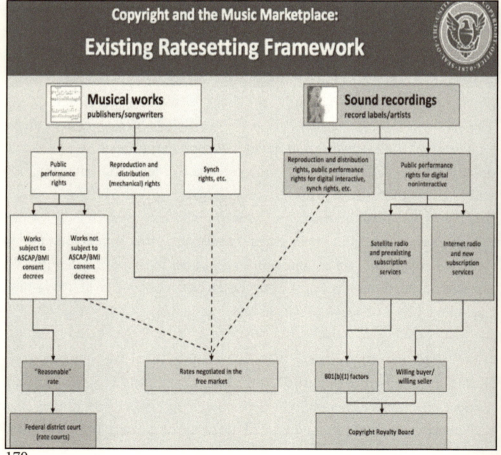

Figure 5.11: The current licensing systems for songwriters and music publishers, plus labels and sound recordings use the six exclusive rights of the copyright holder to establish a licensing process. The Harry Fox Agency collects royalties for Mechanical Licenses (reproduction and distribution), The PROs, ASCAP, BMI, and SESAC, collect for public performances, music publishers usually negotiate directly with the industry related companies who want to use the song in a visual presentation, lyrics in books, and other types of use licenses.

THE CONTROLLED COMPOSITION CLAUSE (CCC)

Labels, of course, complained about the cost of the Mechanical License so Congress provided an exception to the rule. To qualify, the main recording artist (a) has to own a publishing company with all or part of the publishing share of the song; (b) is the songwriter; or, (c) is one of the co-writers of the song (receiving part of the songwriter share); or, (d) is the first to record and release the song which means controlling first use rights. If any of these criteria are met, the label can declare the song a controlled composition, and pays 75% of the statutory rate for the mechanical licenses instead of the full rate.

At the current full statutory rate of $.091 per-song, per-unit sold, the music publisher and the songwriter each receive $.045 or a little less than a nickel per-song sold or downloaded. Under the CCC, the rate is reduced to 75% of the $0.091 or $0.06825, a little less than three and a half cents ($0.034125) per-unit sold. However, the recording artist is now also considered a songwriter, so the original songwriter usually takes the financial hit (as there are now two songwriters instead of one), and split the $.034125 payment to the songwriters share to $.0170625 or a little less than two cents per-unit sold. Can you understand how the songwriter might be a little upset as he or she thought their mechanical royalties would be about four and a half cents per-unit sold and instead it ends up being less than two cents? Why do labels usually use the CCC exception? On a million selling song and depending on the type of deal, the writer is usually paid half of the statutory rate or $45,000 ($.045 times 1,000,000 units sold). However, if the CCC is used, then the shares are reduced to

75% or $.034125 per-unit sold and the pennies add up fast. Look at the math! Remember the Statutory Rate per-song, 5 minutes and under equals $.091 statutory rate (x) 10 songs or 91¢ per-album. The Controlled Composition Rate per-song, 5 minutes and under equals $.0685 statutory rate (x) 10 songs or 68.25¢ per album.

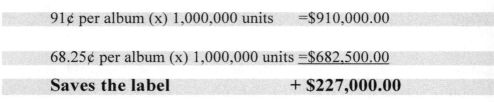

91¢ per album (x) 1,000,000 units =$910,000.00

68.25¢ per album (x) 1,000,000 units =$682,500.00

Saves the label   + $227,000.00

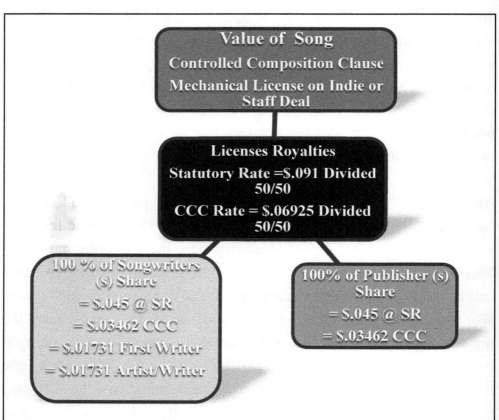

Figure 5.12: The Controlled Composition Clause is an exception to the statutory rate of the Mechanical License. Labels were upset about the rapid increase in the statutory rate and they wanted an exception. If the royalty artist signed to the label meets one these four qualifiers- songwriter, co-writer, owner of some of the publishing, or, controls the first use rights- then the labels only pay 75% of the statutory rate for the Mechanical Licenses. La-

bels love it- publishers hate it. *Instead of making 4.5 cents per unit sold, the writer's share is reduced to 3.4 cents. If the artist is declared a "co-writer," then the writer's royalties are reduced to only 1.73 cents per unit. That is about a 62% reduction in the royalties paid.*

INDIE RECORDINGS OF COVER SONGS

Before you can record and sell a cover song yourself, you have to file a Notice of Intent to Obtain a Compulsory License with the music publisher, which you may acquire from The Harry Fox Agency. According to section §201.18 of the Copyright Law,

> *. . . (1) A "Notice of Intention" is a Notice identified in section 115(b) of title 17 of the United States Code, and required by that section to be served on a copyright owner or, in certain cases, to be filed in the Copyright Office, before or within thirty days after making, and before distributing any phonorecords of the work, in order to obtain a compulsory license..*[118]

You will still also need a Mechanical License, which can be obtained from the Harry Fox Agency online, (if you're selling 2,500 copies or less) to consumers. The payment of the license is only for the song and not the original recording. And of course, it is not legal to make copies of any label's original recordings (owned by the label) without written permission.

INTERACTIVE STREAMS & DIGITAL CONFIGURATION MECHANICALS

Streaming in various forms now requires a mechanical licenses. However, the fees vary and are completed as you'll see on charts (figures 5.13), and the next few pages. The following rates will rise over the next 5 years due to the Copyright Royalty Board's ruling of January 2018 which increases the 10.5% percentage songwriters and music publishers receive from streaming to 15.1%.[119]

---
118 "Notice of Intention to Obtain a Compulsory License for Making and Distributing Phonorecords of Nondramatic Musical Works." Copyright.com. July 23, 2015. Accessed July 27, 2015.
119 BuzzAngle Music 2017 US Year End Report." BuzzAngle Music. Accessed January 26, 2018. http://www.buzzanglemusic.com/us-2017-ytd-report/.

Mechanical License-Use	Type	Example	Statutory Rate	All in's Pool (Greater of)	Calculate Royalty Pool Payment
CDs, LPs, Cassettes, & Other songs/etc., embodied in physical mediums	Physical Sales	Songs or Copyrighted materials embedded in various physical mediums.	.091¢ for recordings of 5 minutes or less		
			.0175¢ per minute for recording over 5 minutes (rounded up)		
Bundled Subscription Services	Streaming sales	Subscription service sold with another product (Mobile phone)		10.5% of music service revenues	1. Take Performance Royalties out of pool to determine Mechanicals
				21% of service payment to labels	2 Take the greater of Mechanical All in's or 25¢ per subscriber
				17.36% of service payment to labels if pass through	2. Divide the number of plays into the payable royalty pool of total Mechanicals
Music Bundles	Streaming, and sales	Sale of two or more physical recordings. Permanent digital download or ringtones for one price		11.35% of music service revenues	1. Take Performance Royalties out of pool to determine Mechanicals
				21% of service payment to labels	2. Separate royalty pool by device
				17.36% of service payment to labels if pass through	3. Divide the number of plays BY EACH DEVICE TYPE into the payable royalty pool of total Mechanicals
Purchased Content Locker	Streaming and sales	Services for free to purchaser of paid downloads or CDs.		12% of music service revenues	1. Take Performance Royalties out of pool to determine Mechanicals
				22% of service payment to labels (PDDS)	2. Divide the number of plays into the payable royalty pool of total Mechanicals to determine royalty-per-play
				18% of service payment to labels	

Figure 5.13: The amount of royalties paid as mechanicals for interactive streams and digital Internet and related devices such as iPads and cellphones is complex. Congress has been wording to change the mechanical licensing process and royalty streams paid to music publishers and songwriters fairer and more efficient.[120] The Copyright Royalty Board's ruling of January 2018 provides a 43% increase on DPD licenses to music publishers and songwriters over the next five years. Thus, the rates listed will be changing from a bottom figure of 10.5% to 15.1% over the next few years.[121]

Mechanical License-Use	Type	Example	Statutory Rate	All in's Pool (Greater of)	Calculate Royalty Pool Payment
Free Non-Subscription (Spotify as example)	Streaming	Streaming offered for free		10.5% of music service revenues	1. Take Performance Royalties out of pool to determine Mechanicals
				22% of service payment to labels (if not pass through)	2. Divide the number of plays into the payable royalty pool of total Mechanicals
				18% of service payment to labels if pass through	
Mixed Service Bundle	Streaming and sales	Sale of music service with non-music products (Internet service)-one price		11.35% of music service revenues	1. Take Performance Royalties out of pool to determine Mechanicals
				21% of service payment to labels	2. Divide the number of plays into the payable royalty pool of total Mechanicals
				17.36% of service payment to labels if pass through	

SAMPLING

Sampling is a different story as the recordings are owned by labels and

---

120 Christman, Ed. "Music Modernization Act Introduced In the House of Representatives, With Major Music Licensing Reform At Stake." Billboard. December 12, 2017. Accessed December 24, 2017. https://www.billboard.com/articles/business/8078543/music-modernization-act-house-of-representatives-licensing-reform.
121 BuzzAngle Music 2017 US Year End Report." BuzzAngle Music. Accessed January 26, 2018. http://www.buzzanglemusic.com/us-2017-ytd-report/.

therefore, you must get permission to use even a small part of one note. Honestly, most labels will not allow any of their recordings (they own them and control the copyrights), to be used for sampling without providing permission, being given credit on the new products, and receiving a usually sizable payment from the person or company using the samples in products for sale.

PUBLIC PERFORMANCE OR "BLANKET" LICENSES

The American Society of Composers, Authors, and Publishers (ASCAP), Broadcast Music, Incorporated (BMI), and SESAC are the three performance rights organizations who represent songwriters and music publisher in the United States. If you remember, one of the Exclusive Rights of owning a song (copyright) covers "public performance", which simply means, in most cases, the use of a song by a business. The song may be in a recording, movie, live performance, digital stream or in many other formats. Businesses using music sometimes do not realize the songs (music) being used or played in their bar or establishment is actually owned (copyrighted) and that the songwriters and music publishers must be paid. Some don't like the law until ASCAP, BMI, and SESAC explain the situation, and, then note they are actually providing a service to them at a much lower cost than if they tried doing it themselves. In addition, businesses gain legal access to millions of songs in recordings, etc., to use in their businesses once the license fees have been submitted.

ASCAP, BMI, and SESAC in the United States, SOCAN in Canada, and many others in the rest of the world, act as agents to collect public performance royalties from the establishments who use songs in their daily business operations. They provided Blanket Licenses to settle the account and the amount paid by the business owners which depends on the size of the establishment, type of business, number of seats, tables, etc., and other variables determined by the PROs and by court order. The PROs collect Blanket License fees from the users of songs (music) in a public performance. The PROs then pay the money, minus about 10% or so for administration, directly to their affiliated writers and publishers as public performance royalties. Foreign royalties collected by agencies and PROs in foreign territories are often delayed more than six months. Advances, which are pre-payments of anticipated royalties, may be provided by performing rights agencies such as ASCAP, BMI, and SESAC, if the song is doing well and royalties are expected to be collected. Let's take a closer look at ASCAP, BMI, and SESAC.

ASCAP

The American Society of Composers, Authors and Publishers (ASCAP) was formed in 1914 to help music publishers and songwriters collect their public performance royalties. It is a nonprofit organization owned and operated by its 600,000 songwriters and music publisher members, with the main function to collect performance royalties on a catalog of over 10 million songs.[122] ASCAP's membership agreement defines a "public performance" as,

> *The term "public performance" shall be construed to mean vocal, instrumental and/ or mechanical renditions and representations in any manner or by any method whatsoever, including transmissions by radio and television broadcasting stations, transmission by telephony and/or "wired wireless"; and/or reproductions of performances and renditions by means of devices for reproducing sound recorded in synchronism or timed relation with the taking of motion pictures.*[123]

And it defines a "musical work" as anything that ". . . shall be construed to mean musical compositions and dramatic co-musical compositions, the words and music . . . and the respective arrangements".[124] ASCAP monitors over half a billion performances annually in order to provide correct

---

122 "About ASCAP." Www.ascap.com. Accessed July 01, 2017. https://www.ascap.com/about-us.
123 "ASCAP Writers Agreement." ASCAP Writers Agreement. Accessed July 1, 2017. https://www.ascap.com/-/media/files/pdf/join/ascap-writer-agreement.pdf?la=en.
124 "ASACP Publishers Agreement." ASCAP.com. Accessed July 1, 2017. https://www.ascap.com/-/media/files/pdf/join/ascap-publisher-agreement.pdf?la=en.

licensing to establishments such as radio stations TV and cable networks, websites, concert halls and venues, sports arenas, clubs, bars, malls, skating rinks, and many other types of businesses. According to the ASCAP website (2017) to apply for membership writers must have,

> ... written or co-written a musical work or song that has been performed publicly in any venue licensable by ASCAP (club, live concert, symphonic concert or recital venue, college or university, etc.), performed in an audio visual or electronic medium (film, website, television program, radio station, etc.), commercially recorded, or published as sheet music, a score, or folio which is available for sale or rental.[125]

To apply as a music publisher, members must have,

> ... engaged in the music publishing business, and has assumed the financial risk involved in the normal publication of musical works, or owns compositions regularly performed by ASCAP's licensees. Applicant further represents that Applicant is the publisher of at least one musical work or song that has been performed publicly in any venue licensable by ASCAP (club, live concert, symphonic concert or recital venue, college or university, etc.), performed in an audio visual or electronic medium (film, website, television program, radio station, etc.), commercially recorded, or published as sheet music, a score, or folio which is available for sale or rental. Additionally, applicant warrants that at least one work it publishes is a domestic or foreign copyrighted musical composition owned by applicant; and if it is a foreign copyright, performing rights for the United States and Canada are owned or controlled by Applicant.[126]

Money collected and the rates charged are based on over 100 different types of licenses including live, recorded, or audio only or audio/visual and the size of the establishment or potential audience. Rates for restaurants, nightclubs, bars and similar establishments depend on whether the music is live or recorded, whether it's audio only or audio and visual, the number of nights per-week music is offered, whether admission is charged

---

[125] "ASCAP Writers Agreement." ASCAP Writers Agreement. Accessed July 1, 2017. https://www.ascap.com/-/media/files/pdf/join/ascap-writer-agreement.pdf?la=en.
[126] "ASACP Publishers Agreement." ASCAP.com. Accessed July 1, 2017. https://www.ascap.com/-/media/files/pdf/join/ascap-publisher-agreement.pdf?la=en.

and several other factors. Concert rates are based on the ticket revenue and seating capacity of the facility. Rates for music used by corporations are based upon the number of employees. College and university rates are based upon the number of full time students; retail store rates depend on the number of speakers and square footage. Hotel rates are based on a percentage of entertainment expenses for live music and an additional charge if recorded music is used.[127] ASCAP's monitoring and payment system has evolved over the last few years. It uses Media Monitors and Media Base to provide digital fingerprinting of broadcast performances in addition to the ones mentioned in the previous paragraph. Then, it uses its own Audio Performance Management (APM) system to quickly analyze the data and pay its members.[128]

BMI

Broadcast Music, Incorporated (BMI) has about 750,000 affiliate songwriters, composers, and music publishers they represent. Their catalog is nearly 12 million songs. BMI was formed as a non-profit organization in 1939 by 600 plus radio stations in order to provide all music users with an option to leave ASCAP, who had recently raised its rates. It collects about $1 billion dollars a year from its licensed business establishments in the United States and from the fees collected by about 90 performing rights organizations around the world.[129] According to BMI.com (2017),

> *BMI is the bridge between songwriters and the businesses and organizations that want to play their music publicly. As a global leader in music rights management . . . Since it's the business or organization that's benefiting from the performance of music, management is responsible for ensuring that the organization is properly licensed. This responsibility cannot be passed on to anyone else even if the musicians hired are independent contractors . . . BMI supports its songwriters, composers and publishers by taking care of an important aspect of their careers – getting*

127 "Why ASCAP Licenses Bars, Restaurants and Music Venues." Www.ascap.com. Accessed July 01, 2017. https://www.ascap.com/help/ascap-licensing/why-ascap-licenses-bars-restaurants-music-venues.
128 "Turning Performances Into Dollars." Www.ascap.com. Accessed July 01, 2017. https://www.ascap.com/help/royalties-and-payment/payment/dollars.
129 "About." BMI.com. Accessed June 30, 2017. https://www.bmi.com/about.

> paid ... We also have an enduring commitment to innovation that brings our copyright owners and licensees new technologies to manage their music and their music use.

BMI considers payment of a single "unit" or performance equal to 200%, which you recognize as similar to the language found in some songwriter/music publishing deals.[130] Then, they divide the royalties into 100% to the music publishers and the other 100% to the songwriters and pay each directly.[131] BMI's performance must be 60 seconds or longer, and they require radio stations to complete written logs in addition to digital recognition technology to assure accuracy. Royalties are based on the number of plays on the total number of stations. Songs that are played over 95,000 times in one quarter qualify for a "hit song bonus". Songs that are played over 2.5 million times and have at least 15,000 plays in one quarter receive the "standard hit bonus".[132] Theme credits are given to songs that are identified with a TV show and are used in the opening and closing credits.[133]

SESAC

SESAC is a different story. Much smaller than ASCAP or BMI, it is a privately owned for-profit business. Paul Heinecke formed SESAC in 1930 to represent European publishers and religious works. According to SESAC.com (2010),

> SESAC was founded in New York in 1930 by German immigrant Paul Heinecke, who, to help European publishers with their American performance royalties, established SESAC as the Society of European Stage Authors and Composers[134]

---

[130] "U.S. Radio Royalties." BMI.com. 2013. Accessed June 30, 2017. http://www.bmi.com/creators/royalty/us_radio_royalties/detail.
[131] "U.S. Radio Royalties." BMI.com. 2013. Accessed June 30, 2017. http://www.bmi.com/creators/royalty/us_radio_royalties/detail.
[132] "General Royalty Information." BMI.com. 2013. Accessed June 30, 2017. http://www.bmi.com/creators/royalty/general_information/detail.
[133] "General Royalty Information." BMI.com. 2017. Accessed June 30, 2017. https://www.bmi.com/creators/royalty/general_information.
[134] "SESAC was established in 1930 and built on service, tradition and innovation." Our History :: SESAC. Accessed

Recently, it dropped its formal name, and is now SESAC. [illegible] when they signed their first songwriters, SESAC represented on[illegible] publishers. In 1993, the family owned company was sold to Stephen S[illegible] Freddie Gershon, and Ira Smith, and they signed Bob Dylan and Neil Diamond as writers.[135] In addition, during the last several years, SESAC has been the leading technology innovator of the performance rights organizations by using BDS (Broadcast Data Systems) and watermark technology for performance tracking and royalty distribution.[136]

SESAC is the only American company that controls both mechanical and performance rights licensing with its recent purchase of The Harry Fox Agency. In addition, its recent purchase of Rumblefish as a subsidiary was merged with The Harry Fox Agency to make it easy for consumers who want to license uploaded material to YouTube and other sites through its Slingshot licensing process. According to the SESAC website (2017),

> *SESAC Holdings is unique in its ability to offer singular licenses for the works of its affiliated writers and publishers that aggregate both performance and mechanical rights in order to drive greater efficiency in licensing for music users, as well as enhanced value for music creators and publishers. Its businesses operate on a sophisticated information technology and data platform to provide timely, efficient royalty collection and distribution . . . SESAC Holdings' acquisition of The Harry Fox Agency (HFA) accelerated its transition to a "multi-rights" organization with HFA's deep publisher relations and mechanical licensing history. Following the HFA acquisition, SESAC's Rumblefish subsidiary was merged with HFA's Slingshot business unit under the Rumblefish brand.*[137]

SESAC also collects royalties from radio, TV stations, cable, new media, concerts, bars, clubs, the same places as ASCAP and BMI. It also helps build songwriters' careers, gather licensing information, and host award shows, just as the other performance rights organizations. SESAC prides

June 30, 2017. https://www.sesac.com/About/History.aspx.

135 "SESAC was established in 1930 and built on service, tradition and innovation." Our History :: SESAC. Accessed June 30, 2017. https://www.sesac.com/About/History.aspx.

136 "Songwriting and Music Business Basics." SESAC EDU: FAQs :: SESAC. Accessed June 30, 2017. https://www.sesac.com/EDU/faqs.aspx.

137 About Us :: SESAC. Accessed June 30, 2017. https://www.sesac.com/About/About.aspx.

...all and powerful as they focus on the success of their ...nd music publishers.[138] In other words, while they pay ... of royalties to their affiliate writers and publishers, they ... standards for membership. Therefore, the majority of ... publishers are making money, while only a small percent ...BMI's are financially successful. According to the SESAC website (2017), their general royalty formula is:

$$Performances \times Affiliate\ Share \times Bonus\ Factor\ (if\ app) = Credits$$
$$License\ Fees\ Available\ for\ Distribution\ /\ Total\ Credits = Value\ Factor$$
$$Credits \times Value\ Factor = Royalty\ Payment^{139}$$

Consent Decree

Both ASCAP and BMI, which are non-profit organizations, must follow the Consent Decree first issued by the United States District Court, Southern District of New York (White Plains), February 26, 1941, and recently upheld in a second amended final judgment. SESAC, which is a for-profit company, is not required to follow the decree. The decree established the rule under which ASCAP and BMI are allowed to operate representing songwriters and music publishers for public performances. According to the decree (1941 second amended final judgment) still in effect,

> (Section E) A "blanket License" means a non-exclusive license that authorizes a music user to perform ASCAP (BMI) music, . . . (Section F) Broadcaster means any person who transmits audio or audio-visual content substantially similar to content that is transmitted by over the air or cable radio or television station or networks as they exit . . . or that transmits the signal of another broadcaster (1) over the air, (2) via cable television or direct broadcast satellite, or (3) via other existing or yet

---

138 "Radio." Radio :: SESAC. Accessed July 01, 2017. https://www.sesac.com/WritersPublishers/HowWePay/Radio.aspx.
139 "Other Sources." Other Sources :: SESAC. Accessed June 30, 2017. https://www.sesac.com/WritersPublishers/HowWePay/Other.aspx.

> to be developed transmission technologies, to audiences using radios, televisions sets, computers, or other receiving or playing devices . . . (Section H) "On-line music user" means a person that publicly performs works in the ASCAP repertory (same for BMI) via the Internet or similar transmission facility.[140]

In addition, the decree states what ASCAP and BMI are not allowed to become MROs or multiple rights organizations. Recently, both ASCAP and BMI have wanted to become MROs instead of the PROs. The court has rejected their request, as you'll see in these excerpts from Section Four of the decree, which clearly states (1941, second amended final judgment),

> (Section A) Holding, acquiring, licensing enforcing, or negotiating concerning any foreign or domestic right in copyrighted musical compositions other than rights of public performance . . . (Section D) Granting any license to any music user for right of public performance in excel of five years' duration . . . (Section E) Granting to, enforcing against, collecting any monies from, or negotiating with any motion picture theater exhibitor concerning the right of public performance for using synchronized with motion pictures[141]

SYNCHRONIZATION LICENSES

Synchronization Licenses (better known in the industry as a Sync License) permit movie, film, computer game companies and many others to "sync" a song to their visual production. When we think of all of the songs and recordings that have been copied and uploaded with some funky video to YouTube, the number of copyright violations is mind blowing. According to Heather McDonald (2017),

> When a director or producer wants to use a particular song in his work, he must contact the owner of that piece. The owner typically offers the music at a particular fee for one-time use. The cost will be depen-

---

140 "Second Amended Final Decree." ASCAP.com. February 26, 1941. Accessed July 1, 2017. https://www.ascap.com/-/media/files/pdf/members/governing-documents/ascapafj2.pdf.
141 "Second Amended Final Decree." ASCAP.com. February 26, 1941. Accessed July 1, 2017. https://www.ascap.com/-/media/files/pdf/members/governing-documents/ascapafj2.pdf.

dent on the prominence of the piece, how it will be used, how much of the song will be used in the piece and whether or not the piece will be used in its original form or covered by another artist. Depending on the song, the cost can range from a small fee for a relatively unknown piece to hundreds of thousands of dollars for a well-known song.[142]

The key is to obtain the license before the release of the project. That's why the deal is usually negotiated before production is completed. Think of it this way, when a musician or singer on a live TV show starts to sing or play a song without the producer already having cleared the songs use with a license, a lawsuit is sure to follow. Revenue generated may or may not be shared with the songwriter depending on the music publishing/songwriters deal.

MASTER LICENSE

While the Sync License is required for the use of a song in a visual production, a master license is required to use the recording of the song. Remember, the song is owned by the music publisher; so, the Sync License is obtained form them. But the recording of the song is owned by record label that recorded it and thus, the Master License must also be negotiated if the producer plans on using the original recording in the film, movie or other type of entertainment product.

FOLIO AND PRINT SHEET MUSIC

Print, folio, and sheet music used to drive the industry. But as we know, technology and personal devices have changed all of that. Still, musicians, students, arrangers, conductors, and others use sheet music when performing and recording. Sheet music may be sold in a brick and mortar instrument store, or websites that allow consumers to download sheet music directly to their own computers and printers. Sheet music royalties for songwriters and music publisher are a small percentage (often 10-20

---
142 McDonald, Heather. "What is a Sync License and How Can You Sell One?" The Balance. Accessed July 01, 2017. https://www.thebalance.com/what-is-a-sync-license-2460940.

percent) of the suggested retail list price, as most publishers turn the work over to a book printing company. Once again, the amount of money paid to the songwriters by the music publisher depends on the deal between the two of them.

OTHER LICENSES

A Transcription License is used to combine a mechanical recording of a song with a public performance which is often used in malls, stores, and elevators. Yes, we're talking about boring background or elevator music which is often supplied by a third party company such as Muzak to large chain stores and mall operators who what to control the mood, song selection, and musical experience of the consumers. Dramatic Licenses are for songs used in theatrical productions from Broadway to your local high school play. The songs in a play are licensed as a Dramatic or Grand license which means ownership is controlled by the owners of the play. The key thing for us to know is that the songs do not fall under the Compulsory License which means it may not be recorded by others unless direct permission from the owner is granted.

SELLING COPYRIGHTS/SELLING THE MUSIC PUBLISHING COMPANY

Remember that a song is considered property, which means it may increase it's value expressed in currency terms. When it comes to selling copyrights or song catalogs (a listing of all the songs owned by one person or company), the price is often based on the average gross generated revenue over five years, multiplied by 5, 10, or 15. The 5, 10, and 15 are the number of years it would take for the song to generate enough revenues to pay itself off. Therefore, if the song or catalog grossed an average $100,000 annually, the low bid would be $500,000, the middle bid $1,000,000, and the high bid, $1,500,000. In addition, if the seller of the copyright is also the songwriter, then they have only sold their ownership of the song or catalog and they will still receive their songwriter's share of the revenues generated for their life plus seventy years. That's why owning all or part of a copyright is important and as you can see, it's how people get rich. Music publishers, like songwriters, have their own professional organization. One of the main functions of the NMPA, as noted, is to protect copyrights.

PROFESSIONAL ORGANIZATIONS

The Songwriters Guild of America (SGA) was formed in 1931 by songwriters Billy Rose, George M. Meyer, and Edgar Leslie.[143] As a voluntary songwriters association run by and for its members, it provides services and activities songwriters may need to be successful in the business. The SGA offers workshops, critique sessions, pitch opportunities, access to catalogs, award events, publishing company audits, catalog administration, financial evaluations, medical and life insurance, and legislative and legal support. The Guild's support provided several important legal provisions in the 1976 Copyright Act.[144]

NSAI & OTHER OPPORTUNITIES

The Nashville Songwriters Association International (NSAI) is a good example of a non-profit organization for members who are interested in networking with other writers. The NSAI sponsors regional workshops in various locations in the U.S. and Europe. NSAI also offers a song evaluation service to its members. Songs submitted are evaluated for their commercial appeal based on the theme, lyrics, melody, and overall impact. Once a year, the NSAI also sponsors Tin Pan Alley South, which is a series of shows, workshops, and opportunities for members to network and write with professional writers.

---

143 Songwriter's Guild of America, "SGA Provides 75 Years of Advocacy, Education to Songwriters," http://www.songwritersguild.com/history.htm, (accessed July 15, 2010).
144 Ibid.

Type of License	Use of License	Purchaser of License	How/Who collects the license fees	Licenses fees paid as royalties
Mechanicals	Song used in the production of an audio	Labels- Music Companies	Harry Fox Agency	Copyright Owner- Music Publisher & Writers depending on the deal
Synchronization "Sync"	Song used in the production of a visual presentation	Film, movie & visual production companies	Direct	Copyright Owner- Music Publisher & Writers depending on the deal
Master	Audio recording owned by record label	Film, movie & visual production companies	Direct	Record label
Blanket (Public Performance)	Song performed live or on a recording used by a business	Mass Media radio, TV, clubs, restaurants, businesses, churches, and venues.	ASCAP BMI SESAC	Royalties collected and split paid directly to Music Publisher(s) & Songwriter(s)
Digital Public Performance	Song performed live or on a recording used by a business digitally transmitted by satellite	Satellite, Digital Providers & Broadcast radio, (passively transmitted over the Internet or microwave)	Sound Exchange	Recording Artist, Labels, and Recording Musicians
Print	Song lyric and written music sold in sheet music and other printed forms	Book publishing companies	Direct	Copyright Owner- Music Publisher & Writers depending on the deal
Transcription	Combination of a Mechanical and Blanket License	Audio Productions (resale to chain stores) & production for audio commercials	Direct	Copyright Owner- Music Publisher & Writers depending on the deal
Dramatic	Stage Performance of a song written as part of a theatrical presentation	Theater Production Company	Direct	Copyright owner

Figure 5.14: Here's a review of the different types of licenses music publisher offer industry- related song users who want to create new entertainment products. The same licenses are also offered to businesses using songs in their daily operations.

Summary

Songwriters have to create the magic, which turns out to be the foundation of the music industry, by creating great or wow songs. But that's only the beginning, as they need to find the right type of music publisher (agent) who will aggressively attempt to "place" their songs with industry labels, artists, movie producers, and others. Music publishers offer different types of deals to songwriters to obtain the copyright (ownership) of their songs before trying to place them with the industry. Deals include:

- **Work-Made-for-Hire**
- **Independent or Staff deals**
- **Co-publication deal**
- **Administrative deal**
- **Shark deal**

Songwriters usually have to negotiate their own deals, before they have an attorney look at it, so it's important to understand the detail offered in the various types of deals.

The better music publishers are proactive in selecting songs they think artists will want to record or others in the industry will want to use for commercial purposes. Contracts customarily state that music publishers have satisfied their contractual obligations when they have, to the best of their ability, attempted to place (called song pitching) a song with music users. It is very difficult for a songwriter or their attorney to define and prove what that really means, so it's important to have a trusting and partnership type of relationship between the writers and music publishers. In addition, publishers can usually provide a stack of invoices and paid statements as proof of their attempt to place songs with record labels, recording artists, and other types of music users. Sometimes the marriage between the songwriter and music publisher succeed for a lifetime, others often fail.

If the song the music publisher attempts to place with song users turns out to be less than a wow, the deal may be in jeopardy, even if it is signed and looks good to all parties. Publishers may default in their contractual obligations if they fail to provide licenses to music users including major recording artists; provide sheet music (of the song) to music stores; or, fail to place the song in radio and TV commercials, advertisements, and movie soundtracks. However, they own your song for life plus 70, or, minimum of 35-40 years before you can recapture your copyrights. Now, you can try to put in reversion clauses, which you return the song to you earlier, but they are rare, unless you are well-known in the industry and have a track record of smash hits.

Music publishers offer several different types of licenses. Recall that Mechanical Licenses are required by labels before they can record, distribute, and sell recordings of a song owned by a music publisher. SESAC, ASCAP and BMI are PROs that represent songwriters and music publishers by providing "Blanket" licenses to businesses that use songs in their daily business activities.

The Harry Fox Agency controls about 80% of the mechanical licensing in the United States. It was recently purchased by SESAC, which is one of the performing rights organizations. Sync licenses are secured from the music publisher before a song may be used in a visual presentation such as a film, TV show, or YouTube stream. If the producers want to use the actual label's recording of the song, then a Master license is also required. Printed sheet music is usually provided through a book company or printing company by a "Print" license between the music publisher. Sheet music is sold in instrument stores, online, and through other venues. In the next chapter, we'll be combining what we've learned so far about the Copyright Laws, licensing, deals, and the roles of the music publisher as if you were going to start your own 360 music industry related business.

Once again, let's look at the cube for this chapter and ask yourself if we know and understand how each layer of information relates to each other. The key to understanding music publishing is to focus on (a) the types of deals music publishers make with songwriters, (b) how much money becomes the songwriters share and the music publishers share, (c) the types of licenses music publishers provide to the companies and individuals who want to use or license their copyrighted songs, (d) the agent companies who work for the music publishers such as The Harry Fox Agency and the companies who represent both the music publishers and the songwriters such as ASCAP, BMI, and SESAC.

Also, make sure you know which license each company represents and offers. Do you know the difference between a Sync and Master License? Why are both often required when a music supervisor wants to use a song in a movie? What is the NMPA and who do they represent? Think along the line of answering the questions and how the answers from one questions may also be part of another question or "layer".

There is serious money in public performances, especially when your song is promoted on radio stations. A number one song on Top Forty or Country radio stations totals about half a million dollars collected and paid. It's usually split 50/50 with the writers getting about $250,000 and the music publisher also receiving about $250,000, minus administrative fees. What if the same song and recording is also used in a movie. More money, that's what we like! What license or licenses are required and how much additional money might the songwriters and music publisher receive. How is the money collected for the Sync and Master Licenses? Now what if a clothing manufacture wants to use some of the song lyrics on a T-shirt? What happens if the mechanicals draw more money due to album sales and single stream in the millions. That's more money and that's how songwriters and music publishers get rich, when they start receiving mail box money (quarterly) from multiple revenue streams.

The Songwriting & Music Publishing Block
Chapter Five

Connecting Music & Emotion
Wow Songs
Pitching to Music Publishers

Types of Music Publishers
Administration

Types of Deals
Work-for-Hire
Indie & Staff Deals
Co-Pub Deals
Administrative Deals
Shark Deals

Types of Licenses
Reproduction/Audio-Mechanical
(Statutory Rate & The CCC)
Public Performance-Blanket
Synchronization-Audio to Visual Media
Print-Book & Sheet Music
Master License-Recording of Song (Labels)

Elements Within
The Music Business/
Songwriting &
Music Publishing

Licensing Companies
The Harry Fox Agency
ASCAP, BMI, & SESAC

N.M.P.A.

I believe that having a niche and a five-year plan are essential to succeed with an independent record company.

Because I started a record company with my own money, I soon realized I was going to be working from record to record, living from meal to meal and leasing my office from week to week.

I'm not sure I would recommend this to anyone, but that's what I did. In fact, that's all I did. During the first five years (1964-1968) of my first record distribution agreement, we worked constantly, creating records and soundtracks so that we could justify having our own record company.

We worked hard during that period, day after day, and at night I dreamed about the record business.

- Mike Curb[1]

---

1 Mike Curb, with Don Cusic, Living the Business. Nashville, TN: Brackish Publishing, 2017: 77-78.

Chapter 6

Breaking In-Career Entrepreneurship

If we want to travel from one part of town to another most of us might jump into our cars or a local bus, subway, tram, or train to take us there. What if combustion engines didn't exist? We'd be walking from place to place. We may be the most creative, talented person around; yet, if we can't get where we need to go, we'll miss most of the opportunities we could have had or we'll just have to do what we can ourselves. In our example, it means walking everywhere which is probably a lot healthier, though time consuming and very limiting.

The purpose of this chapter is to provide you with the hard facts about what it really takes to get your shot as an artist seeking a career in this industry. Non-artist career opportunities require the same knowledge and experience, so helping a local act get started iniates you as a future industry executive at the same time. This chapter includes three career timeline check sheets and suggestions on how to organize your band into a legal form of business. If you're serious about your passion to become involved in this amazing industry, start today in your local community.

In the music industry, record labels have solved our travel problems as they help artists travel the road to success from nowhere to affluence and big bucks. They provide recordings that help the mass media and thousands of other businesses travel a road from silence to enjoyable environments, and for consumers, it's often a road from boring to inspiration. So, let's start thinking of labels as a music business "engine" that moves the industry's products (recordings) and services (acts and live ticket events). Let's also consider the label employees as parts of the engine vital to its horsepower and success. One bad part (employee) and the engine blows up. Believe it or not, so does the label's latest album project, act, and sometimes jobs and careers.

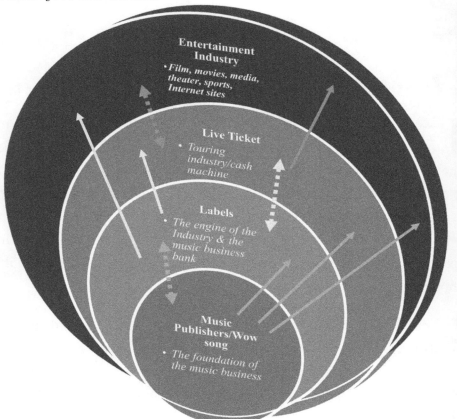

Figure 6.1: Record labels are often considered the "engine and the banks" of the music industry, as they spend the money on acts and their recordings that are used by other entertainment industry entities. Music publishers place their songs with labels (Mechanical License) and other products, such as films, TV shows and mass media (Sync License) and the recordings of the songs from the labels may also be used in movies and mass media visual products, (Master Licenses). The songs are often used in live performances, in clubs and concert tours, and sporting events (Public Performance/Blanket License). Without the labels acting as banks, making all of this production flow happen (the engine), other parts of the industry would suffer financially, and, some would not exist. The interactive orange and yellow dotted lines indicate licensing deals between the different types of entertainment companies (business to business). The solid lines represent the domino effect of how one industry entity relies on the others to create products and services for consumers and other businesses. Your job as a breaking act is to become one consumers want to spend money on which then inserts you into this business system where other companies also profit off your fame and success.

In addition, don't forget the members of the team (producers, musicians, singers, etc.,) who create in the studio and on stage live ticket products, and shows the labels are financing. Teamwork! And what makes this all hang together? Money! From the previous chapters, we know that wow songs are the foundation of the industry, now we know that labels are the banks and engine who commence the process once an act is successful in their local market.

CREATING RECORDING ARTISTS

In the previous chapter, we discussed what makes music publishers successful. The answer is a wow song! If they don't have that, all the industry connections, pitches, and licensing is a waste of time. So, let's ask the question again, but this time, what makes labels successful? The answer is a wow recording artist!

Sure, there's much to accomplish after you've signed the act and probably spent $500,000 to two million dollars on the recordings, marketing, promotion, publicity, branding and distribution, but it's all a waste of time, if you don't have the great act found and signed. First, let's look at the other side of the equation, the musicians and singers who want to have a public career.

ARTIST'S CAREER TIMELINE-BEGINNINGS

Very few have the passion, drive, guts, music business knowledge and saneness of mind to take a serious shot at becoming a recording artist. It's easy to dream of being one, but it takes much more than singing in tune and playing an instrument to become one. In the beginning, determine if you're into performing for the shear enjoyment of it or to perform for a career, making enough for a decent living, or to become a famous, glamorous, rich, world renown musician or rock star.

THE DIGITAL ADVANTAGE

Digital products have become the wannabe recording artist's best friend. With auto tuning and various types of computer software, almost anyone is able to upload tracks to YouTube, SoundCloud, CD baby, iTunes, or thousands of other sites. There are currently over 1.2 billion websites[2] with about six being added every second.

Artist's Career Timeline- Beginnings	
	DISCOVER MUSICAL PREFERENCES (GENRE)
	SHAPE YOUR ABILITIES THROUGH PRIVATE LESSONS AND GIGGING
	DISCOVER PERFORMANCE ABILITIES (INSTRUMENTS & VOCALS WITH OTHERS)
	DEVELOP MUSICAL STYLE (BASED ON YOUR OWN CREATIVE PERSONALITY)
	FIND OTHER ARTISTS WITH SIMILAR STYLES, CREATIVITY, TALENT & ABILITIES
	PERFORMANCE WITH OTHERS IN CHOIR OR BAND TO DISCOVER JOY OF PERFORMING WITH OTHERS
	LEARN TO BE THE BEST YOU CAN BE (WHAT MAKES YOU UNIQUE AS A VOCALISTS, MUSICIANS OR BOTH)
	BE A SOLO & A PERFORMING GROUP/BAND
	EVALUATE CROWD REACTION OF YOUR PERFORMANCE (QUALITY OF TALENT, SHOWMANSHIP OF YOURSELF AS A SOLO ACT & MEMBER OF PERFORMANCE GROUP MEMBER)
	EVALUATE CROWD REACTION OF BAND OR GROUP (QUALITY OF TALENT, SHOWMANSHIP OF ACT/SHOW)
	EVALUATE PERFORMING AS ENJOYMENT VS. POSSIBILITY OF MAKING IT A BUSINESS AND CAREER
	DECIDE IF YOU WANT TO TURN FUN/HOBBIES INTO A BUSINESS

Figure 6.2: Artist's Career Timeline-Beginnings-Playing a musical instrument, singing are fun and very satisfying, but turning your creativity into something consumers will pay to hear or watch is often another story. [3]

[2] "Total number of Websites." Total number of Websites - Internet Live Stats. Accessed July 04, 2017. http://www.internetlivestats.com/total-number-of-websites/.
[3] Wacholtz, Larry E. Monetizing entertainment: an insider's handbook for careers in the entertainment & music industry. New York: Routledge, 2017.

Artist's Career Timeline (Turning Professional in the Business)	DECIDE IF YOU WANT TO TURN FUN/HOBBIES INTO A BUSINESS	
	FORM THE PROFESSIONAL ACT- EITHER AS A SOLO OR BAND	
	DECIDE ON YOUR LEGAL FORM OF BUSINESS BY MAKING THE FOLLOWING DECISIONS, AND THEN, FILE THE PAPERWORK WITH THE LOCAL, STATE, AND NATIONAL AUTHORITIES	WHO OWNS THE BUSINESS OF THE BAND?
		WHO OWNS THE NAME OF THE BAND?
		WHO IS THE BOSS, OR, IS IT SHARED (WHICH WILL NOT WORK IN THE LONG RUN)?
		WHO WILL CONTROL THE BOOKS AND PAY THE BILLS?
		HOW WILL YOU PAY BILLS?
	NEXT, DEVELOP THE UNIQUE QUALITIES OF THE BAND (WHAT WILL MAKE IT SELLABLE TO NIGHTCLUB OWNERS, PROMOTERS, AND BOOKING AGENTS). CONSIDER THE FOLLOWING-	SOUND
		VISUAL PERFORMANCE
		MATERIAL TO BE PERFORMED
		SONGS TO BE WRITTEN
		VOCAL BLEND AND PERFORMANCE
	TIME TO GET SERIOUS ABOUT THE BAND AS A CAREER & PROFESSION. ALL MEMBERS OF THE BAND SHOULD SIGN A PARTNERSHIP, LLC OR CORPORATION AGREEMENT SETTING OUT IN WRITING THE DECISIONS MADE EARLIER ABOUT YOUR LEGAL FORM OF BUSINESS.	

Figure 6.3: Artist's Career Timeline -Turning professional is difficult, as various types of sounds and performances may or may not predict success or what will connect with consumers emotionally. That's when the wallets come out and the dollars start to indicate just how much consumers are willing to spend on you.[4]

---

[4] Wacholtz, Larry E. Monetizing entertainment: an insider's handbook for careers in the entertainment & music industry. New York: Routledge, 2017.

With over three hundred hours of video uploaded per minute to YouTube alone, it may take up to thirty years before your video even makes it onto an active channel. Wannabes, in particular, should rethink YouTube as the best way to get noticed in the industry. And industry executives have told me that acts that perform in local markets have a better chance of creating a buzz, as live shows, local and broadcast media, as we discussed earlier, are helpful in creating interest in you or your act. In fact, neither a YouTube video nor the live show will be any good to you (or the act you may be managing) without a solid business plan to help you know where you are headed in the entertainment business.

BUSINESS PLAN

Sometimes it's difficult for new acts and bands to realize the music business is really a business. The best way to educate yourselves about the realities of business is to complete a business plan. It's a great method to determine the expenses, personal time, marketing, promotion, and other legal filings you'll need to consider before you can think about profits and making it a career. In the 360 deal music industry, the business plan needs to outline your understanding of professional networking and how revenue and shares will be managed.

GETTING DISCOVERED

If you're trying to compete in the major leagues, you'll need live show performances, songs, recordings, that have the potential of being a wow. You can't be everywhere at the same time, but your recordings and videos can! Having recordings (which is a product) and a live ticket show (which is a service) both good enough to get the attention of consumers and labels is the first step in career entrepreneurship. In general, if you're a college graduate who wants to be a professional musician, recording artist or an iconic superstar performer, there's no place for you to "get a job". Therefore, consider forming your own company as an entrepreneur to become successful.

Remember, major recording artists are not employees of a label. They are independent contractors hired as a work-for-hire and everything they contribute in the recording studio is owned by the label. They are not full- time employees. Therefore, most artists who want to become successful discover that first they have to become career entrepreneurs with a fundamental understanding of business. This is what a friend of mine (Beverly) calls career entrepreneurship and suggests as the first steps you'll need to take to become successful in this business.

Building your fan base, who will want your products and attend your shows, is part of detemining if what you have is something consumers will buy. It's also the start of the buzz, as in getting discovered and spreading the word. Deciding on a label and your representation team are the next major steps in building your career as an artist, if you are successful in the first step. In the new 360 business model, most of the money your entreprenuerial business generates will come from live ticket shows with recordings, merchandise, and sponsorships to follow.

It's difficult to sell albums and singles, but using a wow song and its recording as promotion often leads to a growing fan base, and then, eventually streaming royalties and larger live ticket venues. And remember that "Streaming is now the dominant platform for music consumption, and it's growing rapidly--up 76% year-over-year, according to Nielsen".[5] The career timeline steps that have been provided in this chapter describe the starting processes of developing a unique sound, image, live show, and fan club in the local market where your goal is to dominate the niche. Once that is complete, then making the wow recordings (often tied to videos) uploaded to the most popular websites, such as YouTube and others, may provide consumers with an easy way to "discover" you, if you can just get the consumers to view the page or video.

---

5 Greenburg, Zack O'Malley. "Inside The Weeknd's $92 Million Year--And The New Streaming Economy Behind It." Forbes. June 19, 2017. Accessed July 05, 2017. https://www.forbes.com/sites/zackomalleygreenburg/2017/06/12/inside-the-weeknds-big-year-and-the-new-streaming-economy/#20e138d833c5.

Career Timeline (Turning Professional as Performers)

USE YOUR UNIQUE SOUND, VISUAL PERFORMANCE, AND MUSICIANSHIP TO DETERMINE THE FOLLOWING;	IMAGE
	BRAND
	SHOW
PRACTICE, PRACTICE, AND DO IT AGAIN, AGAIN, AND AGAIN	
PUT ON A SMALL SHOW AND EVALUATE THE RESPONSE TO EACH SONG PERFORMED BY OBSERVING THE FANS' ATTENTION AND RESPONSE TO EACH SONG. HAVE A PERSON NOBODY KNOWS MINGLE WITH PEOPLE ATTENDING AND LISTEN FOR THEIR COMMENTS. IF POSSIBLE HAVE THAT PERSON ASK PEOPLE ENJOYING IT WHAT THEY LIKED MOST ABOUT THE ACT. NOTE THE RESPONSES AND GENDER, AGE, AND OTHER POSSIBLE DEMOGRAPHICS OF THE RESPONDENTS. IF THIS IS WORKING, USE THE INFORMATION TO DETERMINE THE ACT'S POTENTIAL MARKET. THEN ONCE AGAIN, REVIEW YOUR BAND AGREEMENT AND THE FOLLOWING:	WHO OWNS THE BUSINESS OF THE BAND?
	WHO IS THE BOSS OR IS IT SHARED (WHICH WILL NOT WORK IN THE LONG RUN)?
	WHO OWNS THE NAME OF THE BAND?
	WHO WILL CONTROL THE BOOKS AND PAY THE BILLS?
	HOW WILL YOU PAY BILLS?
NEXT DEVELOP THE UNIQUE QUALITIES OF THE BAND (WHAT WILL MAKE IT SELLABLE) TO NIGHT CLUB OWNERS, PROMOTERS, AND BOOKING AGENTS BASED ON THE AUDIENCE RESPONSES AND COMMENTS. CONSIDER THE FOLLOWING:	SOUND
	VISUAL PERFORMANCE
	MATERIAL TO BE PERFORMED
	SONGS TO BE WRITTEN
	VOCAL BLEND AND PERFORMANCE
DEVELOP A BUSINESS PLAN TO DETERMINE THE FEASIBILITY OF TURNING THE BAND INTO A PROFITABLE VENTURE. COMPLETE THE FOLLOWING STEPS:	DESCRIBE YOUR COMPANY (WHAT IT OFFERS TO OTHERS)
	PRODUCTS (SHOWS, RECORDINGS, MERCHANDISE AVAILABLE)
	MARKET ANALYSIS (RESEARCH THE MARKET PLACE & THE LOCAL INDUSTRY TO DETERMINE YOUR POTENTIAL MARKET AND INCOME)
	BUILD YOUR BUSINESS TEAM MODEL ON THE MANAGEMENT STRUCTURE THAT FITS YOUR BANDS' BUSINESS
	DETERMINE YOUR MARKETING PLAN INCLUDING AN ELECTRONIC PRESS KIT, PROMOTION, PUBLICITY, WEBSITE, AGGREGATORS, DISTRIBUTION, & PARTNERS
	COMPLETE YOUR FINANCIAL PROJECTIONS TO RUN THE BUSINESS, & PROFIT AND LOSS STATEMENT.

As you can see in figure 6.4 on the previous page, there are many steips in the final steps in the process. However, after you've successfully accomplished the previous steps and developed your sound, image, brand, and fan base to the point where you dominate your niche in the local market, it's time to form your own label and capture a larger audience and fan base.

- First, write a wow song based on the fans' reactions at live performances, then register your claim of copyright.

- Record the song using a studio or a computer and register your claim of copyright of the recording of the song you wrote.

- Form a legal business and register and file the forms for a business license with local, state, and sometimes national government agencies.

- Remember, the © symbol is often used (but not required since the Berne Convention) for the song you've created.

- The "P inside a circle" is the copyright symbol for the actual recording of the song created in the studio or on your computer.

- The ® symbol provides a notice that you've registered the name of your company (your own label) with the Library of Congress patent & trademark office.

- The ™ is used to indicate the same thing on product labels, but it is not registered with the government.

If you have already built your fan base, as suggested in the previous steps, your fans will now click on your videos, or demand they be posted. This is one of the secrets of business- you build the consumer demand before you provide the products (videos and recordings). Now, you've got the products and the consumers who want to see the products. They will, through texting and messaging, increase the size of your developing fan base. The mistake that most beginning artists make is to post a video without having anybody know that it exists, and not having a fan base eager to view it.

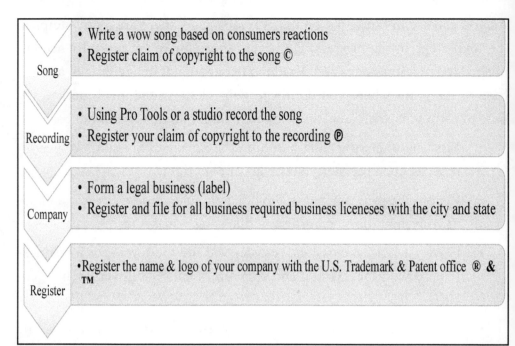

Figure 6.5: To summarize, if you're starting your own band, don't forget to plug into the business "system" by registering your claim of the copyright or the songs you've written and the recordings you've made. Also, form a legal business and register your business with the U.S. Trademark & Patent Office.

ENTREPRENEURSHIP LESSON

One summer, on a flight to Berlin, I sat next to a tall attractive woman in her late twenties. I was surprised to discover she was flying to Germany to sing as the featured artist with the Berlin Opera. As we exchanged pleasantries, she was surprised to learn that I teach classes about the music business. As I congratulated her on her success, she explained how her college professors had taught her how to sing, but not how to make a living as an artist in the business. That she had to learn herself. She taught herself about networking, the legal, marketing, promotion, management, and accounting aspects of the business. In the end, she found out that nobody was coming to "discover her", and she realized that to be a financially successful artist, she first had to become an entrepreneur, own her business, and learn how to manage and market herself. It was a hard lesson to learn and it took many years away from her singing career.

It is often a substantial head adjustment to think in business terms for creative people such as songwriters, musicians, vocalists, audio engineers, graphic artists, and others. But you've got to do it if you want to work in this industry. Where are you going to find a job as a musician, singer, audio engineer, or producer? Let's put it a different way, who is going to hire you? The studio musicians better have a connection with producers, because that's who hires them for a session, just as personal managers hire on-the-road-musicians to back up the famous recording artists on the tour. One of the hardest lessons in this business to learn is that jobs are usually only acquired through networking and the connections you make with other creative individual and businesses who hire creative talents as independent contractors. There's lot of work and careers opportunities available, but you've got to make the connections.

TYPES OF BUSINESSES

Smart creative talents become entrepreneurs, business owners, and sometime even employers. Forming a business as a working vocalist, musician, producer or audio engineer will lead to meeting other business executives who need to hire great people with your talents. Forming a business, or let's say in our example, a record label as a legal entity often requires filing forms with the city or state you live in. There are four different types of businesses each with their own advantages and disadvantages for you to consider. According to attorney Wesley Jones (2013) these are,

- **Sole Proprietorship** – *This is the simplest business entity there is. As the name implies, the establishment has just one owner. That owner may choose to use his or her own name or "d/b/a", which means, "doing business as". The requirements are minimal – just a social security number and the necessary permits and licenses . . . Benefits include the fact that income is taxed once. . . are not subjected to as much government involvement and taxation*

- *... it is very easy to dissolve. (However) the owner's personal assets ... may be negatively affected.*

- **Partnership** – *... two or more individuals form a written agreement to operate a business together. Partnerships can also be established between other businesses ... fairly simple and inexpensive to establish. However, (there are a) unique set of tax and liability issues... this type of business allows for shared responsibilities ... unresolved issues can endanger the business.*

- **Corporation** – *... the most flexible type of company... state-chartered and have a number of legal rights... owners have limited liability because the corporation has separate legal standing. However, corporations undergo a great deal of scrutiny and are held accountable for their actions at a higher level... government oversees the operations... requires them to appoint a board of directors, hold regular meetings, record and publish meeting minutes. Income is also subject to taxation as both personal and business revenue.*

- **Limited Liability Corporation -LLC** – *... have many of the same built-in advantages as corporations. Along with their limited liability, LLCs can be owned by a variety of entities, including individuals, trusts, other LLCs, and corporations. When it is set up under the proper guidelines, an LLC can be taxed like a partnership, which is an advantage. However, ... paperwork required to form and operate an LLC to ensure that it will not be taxed as a corporation.*[6]

WHY START A LABEL?

Why form a record label as a business? There are several advantages including tax benefits, including write offs, in some cases legal pro-

[6] Jones, Wesley. "Four Major Business Formation Types." The Law Office of Wesley Scott Jones, P.C. June 5, 2013. Accessed July 05, 2017. http://wsjlaw.com/2013/06/four-major-business-formation-types/.

tection. But most importantly, streaming services pay their fees to labels for the use of their master recordings including yours! Additionally, if you become financially successful, owning your own label may put you into a much more powerful position if a major label wants to sign you as an act or buy out your label. Remember, you own it, so if someone or another business wants to buy it, you will set the price.

INDIE LABELS

You may be tempted to form your own independent label, or to sign with one. Here are some things to know about indies, as they are commonly called. About 18-20% of the music industry is the independent market (on a global basis) and once you've got a solid fan base in the local market it's time to create and monetize a wow recording to a larger market.

You can't loose by trying to start your own business as an artist and another business as a label. Wisdom comes from experience, success grows out of failure. But as most of us know, failure is a sure thing if we don't take a shot. Acquire the education, experience, knowledge, contacts, and everything else you need to create the best recordings and shows possible. To start a successful label, you'll need to consider the following. Think about the genre, sound, feel of the total recording from your fans' perspective. Make it uniquely yours, so that you've got something special that sticks out from all the rest of the wannabes. Create opportunities for the band's image and branding.

Try to create something exciting, as people are not interested in something that already exists. Another business concept that is true for the music business is that the most successful acts create a sound, live performance, that allows consumers to get excited about what they are feeling. It's the rebels, the people who are rejected all the time, but who have something people want, that set the new trends and define popular culture in entertainment.

Consider the African-American acts of early rock 'n roll, who merged the blues with country to make a new sound. Consider Bill Haley and the Comets, the Beach Boys, Bob Dylan, Cyndi Lauper, and others. Consider The Weeknd, Arianna Grande, The Black Keys, Imagine Dragons, and you're next in line, if you are as talented in business as you are behind the mic.

If you are going to be something similar to a cover band, most people will not be interested as they already have the original. Be an artist, but think like an entrepreneur, who is going to solve a problem for consumers. Their problem is they are bored; the solution is your talent and the way you present it through the products and shows you create and sell to promoters, nightclub owners, and others. You need to be special in a way that major labels will want to partner with you as a business. And remember, most of the planet will discover you because of your recordings, not by seeing you in person, live on a stage. That comes later.

TIMING

If you've got a product and a fan base that knows who you are, who want to hear and see more of what you've got, then, you're in the right place at the right time. This is called *consumer demand,* and that's what you're really trying to accomplish as a new artist. Placing your recordings on Spotify, and other providers, who have artist friendly options, allows you to follow the numbers of streams and locations of the consumers who choose to listen to your recordings. The information you receive will empower you as an artist to understand what you're doing well and what you need to improve or change.

INDIE LABEL ENTREPRENEURSHIP

In the 360 music business world, ideally, you want to have your label, as a successful artist, so you're not depending on a major label for distribution. Then, if a major label still wants to sign you or buy your label to acquire you as an act, they may have to buy out part or all of your label and that means you'll make a lot more money. Two examples of successful musicians who started their own labels are Drake and The Weeknd. According to Zack O'Malley Greenburg in a *Forbes* article (2017),

> The Weeknd knows as well as anyone that streaming isn't the future of music--it's the present. As digital downloads and physical sales plummet, streaming is increasing overall music consumption-- Drake (No. 4 on {Forbes} list at $94 million) and The Weeknd (No. 6, $92 million) have clocked a combined 17.5 billion streams--and that creates other kinds of monetization, including touring revenue. Abel "the Weeknd" Tesfaye parlayed his play count--5.5 billion streams in the past two years--into an estimated $75 million touring advance. To him it's all part of the model he's been following throughout his rapid rise, one that applies to all sorts of businesses: Create an excellent product, make it widely available and flip the monetization switch when the timing is right. "I really wanted people who had no idea who I was to hear my project," he says. "You don't do that by asking for money."[7]

However, at the end of the day, creating your own career and having your own label is difficult as 70% of independent artists appear to still want a major label deal.[8] Why? Because they've discovered the major label's financial investments, promotion, publicity, and marketing are often the best and quickest ways to succeed in the music business.

PERCEIVED VALUES OF ACTS

How do labels know which acts to sign? They research consumers in order to consider the perceived "value" of an act and their products (recordings, live shows, and branding) before signing on the dotted line. It's not easy to determine the potential "value", or how much money a song, recording, artist, music video, or stage show may generate. But the majors use metadata, analytics, and multiple research companies to help determine

---

[7] Greenburg, Zack O'Malley. "Inside The Weeknd's $92 Million Year--And The New Streaming Economy Behind It." Forbes. June 19, 2017. Accessed July 05, 2017. https://www.forbes.com/sites/zackomalleygreenburg/2017/06/12/inside-the-weeknds-big-year-and-the-new-streaming-economy/#20e138d833c5.
[8] "News." 'Investing in Music' report shows record labels invest US$4.3 billion in A&R and marketing. November 25, 2014. Accessed July 06, 2017. http://www.ifpi.org/news/record-labels-invest-us-4-3-billion-in-AR-and-marketing.

the available music market. Once they've found an act to consider signing, they often conduct psychographic analysis research to determine the act's market potential (lifestyle analysis) of how many millions of people might buy the recordings, stream recordings, attend the concerts, buy the merchandise, and emotionally connect with a specific brand. Then, they consider the cost of creating the act, artist development, the recording budget, marketing plan including promotion and publicity, distribution, and tour support. Finally, an accountant looks over the numbers and calculates the financial risk of the investment into the act compared to the possible gross profits. It's also difficult for promoters and managers to guess a consumer's emotional connection to the products and acts. Why do you think personal managers and promoters wait until an artist is already successful or has a label deal in the "works" before signing a new act to a management deal? Here's a clue, how do you think managers get paid?

SUMMARY

Have you ever heard of someone who started on top? As an example, have you ever heard of a college graduate who is entering the workforce being hired to run a multi-million-dollar company? Probably not! Yet, many prospective artists often assume they are the "next big thing" and should be offered millions of dollars because they've got a few people back home who told them they're great.

The executives in the leather chairs, quite honestly, hope the wannabe is correct and that they are beyond great! But most of the prospective artists seeking a major label deal simply do not have a clue about what the industry is or how it operates. Most do not even know who to hire, fire, or how the money is made. Most do not understand entrepreneurship, psychographics, analytics, market shares, recoupment, shameless self-promotion, consumer bases, corporate structures, networking, copyrights, and the list goes on and on. That's the reason most industry artists and executives suggest artists start in the local market.

Career entrepreneurship is a way of understanding how to prepare for a career in the entertainment industry. As this chapter has indicated, you have choices to make about how you launch your career, the type of business entity that will fit you or the act the best, and whether or not, after completing your business plan, you will be better off pursuing a deal with a major label or staying as an indie. You will always want a good career, deal, a loyal fan base, and great products, but you want to move from being discovered to becoming that established local or superstar act, if you are able. In Chapters 7 and 8, we focus on the economics of the 360 deal and how to monetize your creativity.

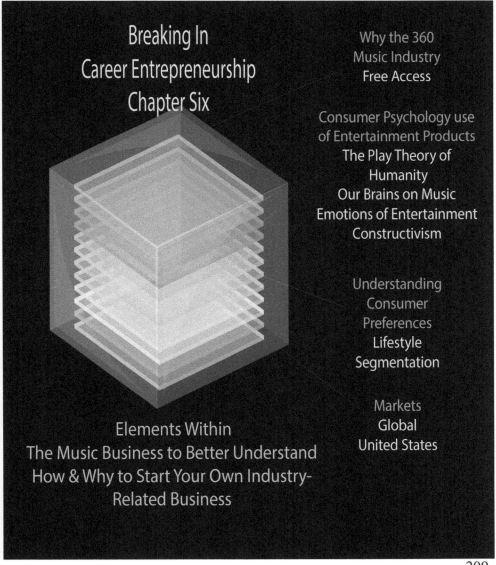

Chapter 7

Labels (Multiple Rights Organizations)

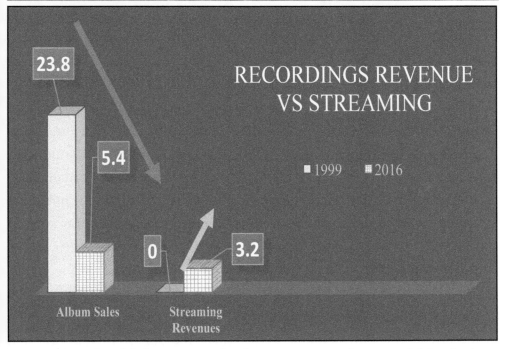

Figure 7.1: Before labels sign acts, they have to compare the costs of doing business, (signing, recording, marketing, distributing the act) to projected revenues. As you can see, the loss of album and single sales at retail have contributed to the decrease in revenues from $23.8 billion in 1999 to only $5.4 billion in 2016 (reported in 2017). The decrease in revenues has forced the label to find other sources of revenue, often called multiple rights (from the artists) now found in 360 artists' contracts.

The key to music industry success for labels in the past was selling large numbers of recordings. It's still the same today for many independent labels who offer limited budgets of $25,000 to $100,000 instead of the $500,000 to two million dollar budgets offered by Sony Music, WMG, or UMG. Labels would often recoup their expenses out of the act's royalties (breakeven point) with 75,000 to slightly over 225,000 units sold. The breakeven points depend on the total cost of the project compared to the number of units sold, which often vary from act to act. The recording artist rarely received any royalties until the labels sold more than 450,000 to 500,000 units. The difference between the two figures usually gave the label's profits of a million dollars or more before the act was paid anything.

Traditional Market Economies of Scale

The arrangement I described above is called the recoupment deal. As frustrating as this was for most new artists, there were two wonderful benefits to most recoupment deals. The first was the act got a shot at fame and financial success, as all the money they'd earned from touring, merchandise sales, endorsements, (minus tour expenses) went directly into their bank accounts. They didn't have to pay a penny for their career launch as the labels paid all the bills through the recordings, promotion, publicity, and marketing schemes to sell records. Labels even supplied tour support funds (and still do) to help the acts rehearse, hire personal, and tour. In addition, if the album failed, acts walked away, oweing zip to the labels. In other words, it was the label's spending on the acts and the promotion of their recordings that resulted (if the recordings connected with fans) in the artists becoming famous giving them the opportunity to tour and become wealthy.

Some will argue that vinyl records are going to save the record business. Trends appear to indicate that's not the case, as most vinyl releases only sell about 50,000 albums which is not enough to make up for the significant decrease in CD sales. In addition, in 2016 vinyl recording even with the expressive increases in sales only totaled 5% of recorded music sales (about $416 million).[145]   If we compare the number of vinyl recordings sold in 2016 with the 1999 figures of recorded unit sales of $23 billion, the total of vinyl sales would be less than on percent.

Recoupable Label Budgets

---

145 Morris, Chris. "Vinyl Sales Are Not Just a Hipster Thing Anymore." Vinyl Record Sales At A 28 Year High | Fortune.com. April 16, 2016. Accessed July 06, 2017. http://fortune.com/2016/04/16/vinyl-sales-record-store-day/.

The cost of doing business, or the amount of money labels invest in acts to launch their recordings and careers, often averages between $500,000 to $2,000,0000 per artist per album.

Label Steps	Title	Expense	Purpose	All In's	Recoup-able	Total
Find and sign act	Advance	$50,000-$300,000	Acquire act (Exclusively)	Yes	100%	$100,000
Record an Album	Recording Budget	$50,000-$200,000	Sales & Promotion	Yes	100%	$200,000
Album/ Singles Licensing	Mechanicals *As an example, on 150,000 ten song albums sold	Statutory $136,500	Acquired Right to record, Sell, & license recordings	Yes	100%	($136,500) not used in this example
		Controlled Composition Clause @ $0.06825	Reduce Mechanical payments (pressed 150,000)	Yes	100%	$102,375 used in this example
All-Ins Total						$402,375
Marketing/ Promotion	Radio Airplay Music Videos Advertisements *Trade Magazines *Popular Press * Media Website Street Promotion Social Media	100%-200% of the All-Ins	Exposure Key word **(Sample)**	No	50%	
		100%-200% of the All-Ins------ *If declared part of Tour Support	Give consumers a way to discover act and songs	Yes	100%	$400,000
Marketing/ Publicity	Interviews Talk Show *Radio & TV Social Media Print/Magazines Award Shows	50%-100% of the All-Ins	Exposure Key word **(Backstory)**	No	50%	
		100% recoupable *If declared part of Tour Support	Gives consumers a way to emotionally connect with act's life story-Leads to **Image** & **Branding**	Yes	100%	$200,000
Tour Support	Start Up Funds	$50,000-$125,000	Support act on road & label receives 10-15% of act's gross revenues	Yes	100%	$100,000
Label Investment						$1,102,375

Figure 7.2: The cost of launching an album and act depends on the projected and estimated gross revenues the label predicts the project will make, minus the cost of the project.

According to the IFPI (2014, the latest figures), labels spend between $500,000 to $2,000,000 on each act.[146] The three major labels in 2014 spent about $4.3 billion on their signed artists including $50,000 to $350,000 for Advances; $150,000 to $500,000 for the Recording Budget; $25,000 to $300,000 for the Music Videos; $50,0000-$150,000 for Tour Support; and, $200,000 to $700,000 on Marketing and Promotion.[147]

As you can see from *figure 7.2*, all of the financial investment by a label into an act's career are based on projected profits. In the example, the label invested a little more than $1,100,000 into the act and their career. The budget lines are about average for new acts with labels under the old recoupable business system and also with new acts signed to 360 deals. The All-Ins are 100% recoupable under the traditional model meaning that the label will recoup all of the invested money out of the artist royalties if they can sell enough albums and singles to break-even. The marketing, promotion and publicity, and other expenses, such as artist development, are recouped out of the artist's royalties on album and single sales at 50%; unless, the label runs the numbers though tour support which they often do. The promotion and publicity budget were often based on a percentage of the total all-ins consisting of the advance payment to the act for signing the deal, the recording budget for the album and the mechanical license fees. Tour support funds were and still are provided as the labels want the acts out touring.

Figure 7.3 is an example of the recoupable financials from the label selling albums and singles and using the artist's royalties to break-even and make a profit. Notice how the label profits before the artist makes any money. Yet, the act did not have to invest any money and has a shot at making millions off of the label's promotion and publicity for tours.

---

[146] "News." 'Investing in Music' report shows record labels invest US$4.3 billion in A&R and marketing. November 25, 2014. Accessed July 06, 2017. http://www.ifpi.org/news/record-labels-invest-us-4-3-billion-in-AR-and-marketing.

[147] "News." 'Investing in Music' report shows record labels invest US$4.3 billion in A&R and marketing. November 25, 2014. Accessed July 06, 2017. http://www.ifpi.org/news/record-labels-invest-us-4-3-billion-in-AR-and-marketing.

Label	Investment	Unit Revenues	Act's Account	Debt	Profits
Initial Investment	$1,102,375		Account at Label	$1,102,375	
Suggested Retail List Price (SLRP)	$16.95	$6.78 (40% of SLRP) Retail stores $6.78 (-) 2.01 $4.77 (Label earning)	Artist Royalties Per-Unit Sold paid to the debt $2.01	*Note-Artist receives 17 points (percent) with a package fee of 15% and 3 points paid to the producer. $16.95 SLRP (-)2.54 Package Fee $14.41 Royalty Base 17 points (-)3 points to producer 14 points to artist $14.41 Royalty Base (x) 14 points $2.01 per- unit sold	The label, which earns $4.77 per retail sale, takes the artist's royalty of $2.01 and applies it to their investment balance.
Suggested Wholesale List Price (SWLP) for Digital Download	$10.00	$7.00 (70% of SWLP) iTunes, etc. $7.00 (-) $1.40 $5.60 (Label earning)	Artist Royalties Per-Unit Sold paid to the debt $1.40	*Note-Artist receives 17 points (percent), with no package fee and 3 points being paid to the producer. $10.00 SWLP 17 points (-)3 points to producer 14 points to artist $10.00 Royalty Base (x) 14 points $1.40 per-unit sold	If they sell the number of units for the act to break even, the labels profit in the millions of dollars
	Per-Unit	Total Debt	Break Even	Difference	Profit
Artist's Royalties	$2.01 CDs	$1,102,375	548,445 units	----------------------	Zero Payout
Label-SLRP	$4.77	$1,102,375	231,305 units	317,140 units	$1,512,757
Artist's Royalties	$1.40 Digital	$1,102,375	787,410 units	----------------------	Zero Payout
Label-SWLP Download	$5.60	$1,102,375	196,825 units	590,585 units	$3,307,276

215

Three-sixty deals are defined as Multiple Rights, which simply means the label is acquiring additional rights and revenues from the recording artist which used to be controlled by and belong to the artist only. In the past, record deals were tied to recoupment of the debt out of the artist's royalties, based on album and singles sales only. Once the full debt at the label in the artist's name was satisfied, the artist was paid royalties instead of it being applied to the debt.

Now, the record labels are no longer in the record business only, because they can't survive when consumers don't buy recordings. Think about how things change and become obsolete- what happened to the buggy whip business once the auto industry became prominent? Guess where the record business is headed now that we have streaming and consumers no longer need to buy recordings? Recordings are still going to be produced in studios for promotional purposes and released to streaming sites to generate money, but the decline in record sales will continue in a devasting manner.

The benefit of the creative destruction process is that companies who want to survive need to innovate. The record labels changed their business model to the 360 model to survive, which means they are thriving and so are the artists who need their industry and financial expertise to build their careers. Through this transition, the labels have appeared to save their businesses, though the foundation is far from solid. The purpose of multiple rights contracts (360 deals) with artists is to provide additional products and services consumers will use, buy, and enjoy by helping them to psychologically connect their construed emotions and pocketbooks to the artist's image and iconic brands. The bottom line is additional revenues.

There has been a major shift in distribution of recorded music from specialty shops to online digital retailers in recent years. According to the R.I.A.A., record stores (brick and mortar) share of U.S. music sales has declined to 28% of sales in calendar year 2008. The last eight years has been far worse, as the numbers are almost invisible. Many stores now sell CDs and related items as a niche stock item, while their main inventory is bigger ticket merchandise, fashions, beverages and food, or all the above.

PHYSICAL SALES

In calendar year 2015, according to IFPI's latest figures, the music industry grossed $15 billion in trade value of sales. The difference between the $10.2 billion generated by the three major labels and the $15 billion is the impact of the independent labels and other types of related businesses worldwide, such as the concert business. Over time, major labels have built significant recorded music catalogs, which are long-lived assets that are exploited year after year. The sale of catalog material is typically more profitable than that of new releases, given lower development costs and more limited marketing costs. Through the end of the third calendar quarter of 2016 (i.e., the week ending September 29, 2016), according to SoundScan, 56% of all calendar year-to-date U.S. album unit sales, excluding streaming sales, were from recordings more than 18 months old, with 48% from recordings more than three years old.[148]

DIGITAL DOWNLOADS

Mass-market retailers accounted for 15% of total industry unit sales calculated on a total album plus digital track equivalent (ten tracks per album) unit basis in the U.S. in calendar year 2015, according to SoundScan data.[149] Online sales of physical products, as well as digital downloads, have

---

148 Levin, Eric, comp. SEC Filings - Warner Music Group Corp. Commission File Number 001-32502. Vol. ANNUAL REPORT PURSUANT TO SECTION 13 OR 15(d) OF THE SECURITIES EXCHANGE ACT OF 1934. For the fiscal year ended September 30, 2016. Washington, DC: Warner Music Group, 2016.

149 Levin, Eric, comp. SEC Filings - Warner Music Group Corp. Commission File Number 001-32502. Vol. ANNUAL REPORT PURSUANT TO SECTION 13 OR 15(d) OF THE SECURITIES EXCHANGE ACT OF 1934. For the fiscal year ended September 30, 2016. Washington, DC: Warner Music Group, 2016.

grown to represent an increasing share of U.S. unit sales and combined they accounted for 71% of total industry unit sales (meaning recordings only) in calendar year 2015. In addition, revenues resulting from music streaming services now represent a significant share of the overall recorded music market in the United States. Streaming continues to cause the decline in physical and digital download sales and revenues.

Freemium

In spite of this weird situation, where consumers have access to music free, labels are making more money than ever. They have been quickly changing their business models to adapt to the situation. By understanding the concept of creativity, business principles, entrepreneurship, intellectual properties consumer behavior, demographics, psychographics, metadata analysis, and how the industry works, labels have converted themselves into Entertainment Multiple Rights Management Companies (EMRMC). Therefore, labels have been innovatively developing other areas in the industry such as branding, interactive streaming, management of digital content, digital access distribution, rights management, act merchandise fulfillment, and other sources of revenue.

Multiple Rights Revenues

Streaming is about ACCESS to our favorite music, film, computer games, etc., and that is the wave of the future. Even with the new models of distribution, many creative people and businesses are not being paid much money. The problem has been to find an economic solution that will infuse the use of digital technologies with consumers' perceptions of value. Though some of the entertainment services will remain free, we still have to watch or listen to the commercials. Buying a CD or DVD simply gives us access to the entertainment products we want to hear or watch. The same holds true with streaming, except the amount of money (revenues) going to the recording artists, songwriters, and music publishers (due to the loss of Mechanical License royalties tied to the decrease in album and single sells), is dramatic.

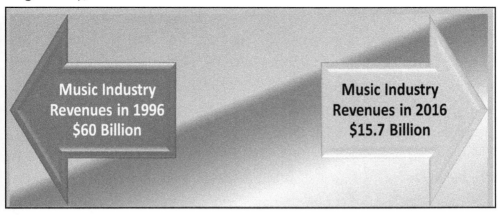

Figure 7.4: The music industry has dropped from a gross of about $60 billion in 1999 down to about $15.7 billion in 2016 (adjusted for inflation as reported in 2017). The labels are recovering, yet, the recording artists, songwriters, and music publishers are not yet receiving similar royalties, as streaming is a different form of delivery. The traditional systems based artist's royalties, music publisher's, and songwriter's royalties on retail sales (Mechanicals and artist royalties from sales) and radio station airplay (Blanket licenses). However, with the switch to streaming by consumers, the labels are collecting significant money, but the recording artists, songwriters, and music publishers have not yet received payments equivalent to their creative efforts.

STREAMING

The innovative technologies of audio and video streaming have not yet generated enough revenue to pay all the copyright holders, recording artists, and songwriters, who formerly benefited from CD and DVD sales. However, the goal of the labels has remained unchanged, as they continue to discover and promote products consumers perceive as an emotional experience. Streaming revenues have simply not closed the "value gap" or the money lost due to the decline in album and single sales now that consumers obtain their music free.

Where does money from streaming come from? To get the answer, we have to once again look at who owns what. Record labels spend millions of dollars breaking a new act and of course, that includes the recording, marketing, promotion, publicity, and distribution of the recordings and act. There are several ways (called revenue streams) labels generate money from the artists in today world. However, we already know that selling albums is not one of them as 78% of that market has dried up and the future trend is continual shrinkage. Sadly, the sales of vinyl records don't even make a dent in solving the problem.

The facing *Figure 7.5* published in *TheTrichordist.com* (2013) again shows how many streams an act has to have before any serious money is paid to the rights' holders, such as labels. Remember, that in 1999, world revenues for album and single sales were a little over $23 billion dollars. In the United States, it was about $14.3 billion dollars. Note, this chart indicates that the labels had an annual difference in revenues generated between 1999 and 2009 of a negative $8.3 billion dollars (yearly reduction annually) or a reduction of 56% of their previous revenues. With streaming, the three major labels receive about 70% of the above figures. For example, if YouTube transmits a song one million times, the total pay to the label is $2,500 ($0.0025) X a million streams, X 70% paid to the labels, which equals $1,750. The R.I.A.A considers 1,500 streams equal to one album sale and 150 streams equal to one single unit sold. [150] Audio streaming provides part of the solution as the record labels, who own the master recordings, now demand millions and billions of dollars for the use of their products. Spotify, Amazon Prime, Apple Music, Tidal, and Google Play are forced into a situation where they either pay the money or the labels can shut them down. The *TheTrichordist.com* (2017) provides us with an example of how much each of the most popular streaming sites pays.

---

150 "Music Streaming Math, Can It All Add Up?" The Trichordist. February 07, 2013. Accessed July 03, 2017. https://thetrichordist.com/2013/02/08/music-streaming-math-will-it-all-add-up/.

	DSP / STORE	Stream Quantity % of Total	Stream Revenue % of Total	Avg Amount Per Steam	Streams Per Song	Streams Per Album	Marketshare Quantity	Marketshare Revenue
1	Spotify	62.97%	69.57%	0.00437	139	1,394	62.97%	69.57%
2	Apple iTunes	7.18%	13.35%	0.00735	83	828	7.18%	13.35%
3	Google	2.36%	4.03%	0.00676	90	901	2.36%	4.03%
4	YouTube	21.70%	3.81%	0.00069	876	8,764	21.70%	3.81%
5	Deezer	2.19%	3.54%	0.00640	95	952	2.19%	3.54%
6	Rhapsody	0.52%	2.52%	0.01900	32	321	0.52%	2.52%
7	Xbox Music	0.12%	0.97%	0.03060	20	199	0.12%	0.97%
8	Amazon	0.63%	0.64%	0.00402	151	1,515	0.63%	0.64%
9	Tidal	0.10%	0.33%	0.01250	49	487	0.10%	0.33%
10	Telecom Italia	0.04%	0.25%	0.02189	28	278	0.04%	0.25%
11	24-7 Entertainment	0.07%	0.19%	0.00993	61	613	97.82%	99.00%
12	PlayNetwork	0.74%	0.12%	0.00065	943	9,429		
13	KKBOX	0.13%	0.12%	0.00358	170	1,701		
14	NMusic	0.04%	0.07%	0.00740	82	823		
15	AMI	0.03%	0.07%	0.00877	69	695		
16	RDIO	0.04%	0.07%	0.00690	88	882		
17	Nokia	0.17%	0.06%	0.00138	440	4,399		
18	Touchtunes	0.02%	0.05%	0.01150	53	530		
19	Cricket	0.01%	0.04%	0.01593	38	382		
20	Beats Music	0.01%	0.03%	0.01731	35	352		
21	Yandex LLC	0.77%	0.03%	0.00016	3,744	37,444		
22	Slacker	0.02%	0.03%	0.00442	138	1,379		
23	Qobuz	0.00%	0.02%	0.02940	21	207		
24	Pandora	0.07%	0.02%	0.00133	456	4,565		
25	Music Unlimited	0.00%	0.02%	0.02399	25	254		
26	PCM Technologies	0.01%	0.02%	0.00564	108	1,079		
27	Saavn	0.03%	0.01%	0.00146	417	4,168		
28	Akazoo	0.00%	0.01%	0.37847	2	16		
29	AWA	0.00%	0.01%	0.00801	76	760		
30	Medianet	0.01%	0.01%	0.00272	224	2,241		
	TOP 30 TOTALS :	100.00%	100.00%	0.00395	154	1,540		

Figure 7.5: Details the streaming rates paid by streaming providers to the copyright holder of the recordings which are the labels. Labels are not required to share the fees collected with their recording artists as they previously did with album and single sales.[151]

[151] "Music Streaming Math, Can It All Add Up?" The Trichordist. February 07, 2013. Accessed

The low per-stream rates paid places the labels in the unique situation of demanding all the money possible up front (70% of gross revenues), while at the same time, keeping the providers afloat to continue generating more money. YouTube and other video streaming services are also in the same situation. As you may remember, the three major labels lost 78% of the $23.8 billion they generated in 1999 compared to the only $5.4 billion generated from album sales in 2016. How much of $18.4 billion lost have the three major labels recaptured through streaming?

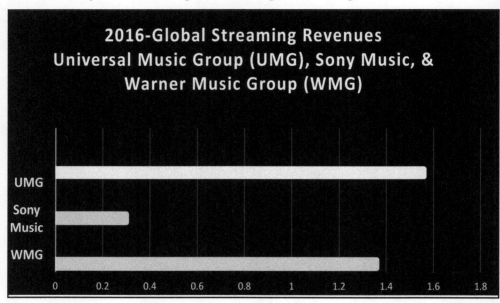

Figure 7.6: Universal Music Group (UMG) was paid $1.56 billion for streams in 2016. Sony Music made only $299 million, and Warner Music Group (WMG) totaled only $1.36 billion. The major labels combined streaming revenues was only $3.219 billion which is only 17.5% of the total money lost by the decline of recorded music sales.

The three major labels in 2016 totaled only $3.219 billion which is only 17.5% of the revenues lost by the decline in album and single sales from 1999 (adjusted for inflation). But the parts of a penny do add up to some serious money being generated. Not as much as album and singles use to, but the trend toward streaming is not the wave of the future, it's the way

July 03, 2017. https://thetrichordist.com/2013/02/08/music-streaming-math-will-it-all-add-up/.

it is right now.[152] [153] [154] Remember, that 1,500 streams is considered equal (somewhat) to the same money labels received on the sale of one album. Also, 150 streams is considered equal to the amount of money labels received on the sale on one single.

	1999 Rev	2009 Rev	Difference	Percentage
	$14.6 B	$6.3 B	$8.3 B	56%
Spotify Paid Subs		Sub Per Yr	Total Gross Rev	Paid @ 70%
1,000,000	$	120.00 $	120,000,000.00 $	84,000,000.00
30,000,000	$	120.00 $	3,600,000,000.00 $	2,520,000,000.00
90,000,000	$	120.00 $	10,800,000,000.00 $	7,560,000,000.00
Service		Plays	Per Play	Gross Paid
YouTube		1,000,000	0.0025 $	2,500.00
YouTube		10,000,000	0.0025 $	25,000.00
YouTube		100,000,000	0.0025 $	250,000.00
YouTube		1,000,000,000	0.0025 $	2,500,000.00
YouTube		10,000,000,000	0.0025 $	25,000,000.00
YouTube		100,000,000,000	0.0025 $	250,000,000.00
YouTube		1,000,000,000,000	0.0025 $	2,500,000,000.00
Service		Plays	Per Play	Gross Paid
Spotify		1,000,000	0.00515 $	5,150.00
Spotify		10,000,000	0.00515 $	51,500.00
Spotify		100,000,000	0.00515 $	515,000.00
Spotify		1,000,000,000	0.00515 $	5,150,000.00
Spotify		10,000,000,000	0.00515 $	51,500,000.00
Spotify		100,000,000,000	0.00515 $	515,000,000.00
Spotify		1,000,000,000,000	0.00515 $	5,150,000,000.00

Figure 7.7: Spotify has almost 70% of the market but they only pay now $0.00437 compared to the $0.00521 in 2014. A close reading of the table appears to indicate the piddling amount of revenues generated by streaming in the industry. Notice also that YouTube owned almost 22% of the video market share but only generated 3.81% of the revenue paying only $0.00069 per stream. Here's another surprise, the top ten streaming companies control 97.82% of the market and generate 99% of the revenue, leaving other sites such as Beats Music, Pandora, and MediaNet to fight over the last percent.[155]

152 Levin, Eric, comp. SEC Filings - Warner Music Group Corp. Commission File Number 001-32502. Vol. ANNUAL REPORT PURSUANT TO SECTION 13 OR 15(d) OF THE SECURITIES EXCHANGE ACT OF 1934. For the fiscal year ended September 30, 2016. Washington, DC: Warner Music Group, 2016.
153 "Investor Relations." SONY. Accessed May 16, 2017. https://www.sony.net/SonyInfo/IR/library/ar/Archive.html.
154 "Universal Music 2016 Earnings: Streaming Drove Revenue Growth for Recordings, Publishing." Billboard. February 24, 2017. Accessed May16, 2017. http://www.billboard.com/articles/business/7701980/universal-music-group-2016-earnings-streaming.
155 "Updated! Streaming Price Bible w/ 2016 Rates : Spotify, Apple Music, YouTube, Tidal, Amazon, Pando-

Music Publishing

As we already know from the previous chapters, music publishing is a very profitable business for several reasons. Traditionally, labels have also owned publishing companies, keeping everything in house which kept the costs of doing business controlled and manageable. In 360 deals, depending on how the contract is negotiated, labels may expand their revenues by exploiting some in other types of music entities, which also helps the artists who are also co-writers.

Labels want to profit any way possible, so when a new act is signed, often the first thing they will do is listen to all the material (songs) in the label's publishing companies. If the act records one of them, the labels save tons of money in licensing fees. Second, if the act records one of the labels music publishing songs, then the label can use the CCC (Controlled Composition Clause) if any fees are required, once again saving money. In addition, songs generate many licensing opportunities labels will use in combination with acts, their images, and branding.

Image and Branding

Consumers connect to the music industry through their emotional connection to specific artists and their recordings. Their emotional connection is driven by the image they have of the artists that seems to fulfill a soulful, emotional desire or need they may have in their lives. It's a "who they think the act is" constructed by themselves (often in the subconscious) that seems to allow fans to feel totally loved, inspired, and motivated. Through psychographic research, we've often found acts may have as many as seven different images held by different types of consumers.

---

ra, Etc." The Trichordist. January 16, 2017. Accessed July 03, 2017. https://thetrichordist.com/2017/01/16/updated-streaming-price-bible-w-2016-rates-spotify-apple-music-youtube-tidal-amazon-pandora-etc/.

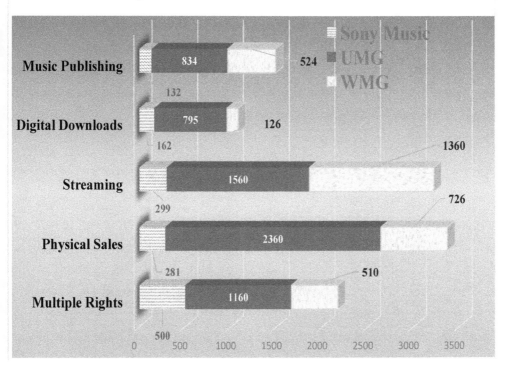

Figure 7.8: In 2016, the three major labels' (Sony Music, Warner Music Group, and Universal Music Group) gross revenue streams, as reported in 2017, were music publishing, digital downloads, streaming, physical sales, and multiple rights management. Threethings to consider, multiple rights, streaming, and branding are connected to 360 deals. The future trends in revenues point toward significant decreases in physical and digital download sales and increases in streaming. Already in early 2017, streaming revenues had passed physical sales revenues indicating how quickly the revenue figures are changing.[156][157][158]

Branding falls under *multiple rights* in the artist's agreement. It is the process of connecting consumer's positive constructs and emotions from the act's image to commercial products, which the act endorses by plac-

---

156 Levin, Eric, comp. SEC Filings - Warner Music Group Corp. Commission File Number 001-32502. Vol. ANNUAL REPORT PURSUANT TO SECTION 13 OR 15(d) OF THE SECURITIES EXCHANGE ACT OF 1934. For the fiscal year ended September 30, 2016. Washington, DC: Warner Music Group, 2016.
157 "Investor Relations." SONY. Accessed May 16, 2017. https://www.sony.net/SonyInfo/IR/library/ar/Archive.html.
158 "Universal Music 2016 Earnings: Streaming Drove Revenue Growth for Recordings, Publishing." Billboard. February 24, 2017. Accessed May16, 2017. http://www.billboard.com/articles/business/7701980/universal-music-group-2016-earnings-streaming.

ing their name or image on it to increase the perceived value of the item to the consumer. When consumers make the mental connection of the act (and their emotions from the recordings and shows) to certain available products, they are more likely to pay a higher price for it due to the enjoyment of being associated with it or its use. *This is called lifestyle marketing.* Both the labels and the act receive additional royalties for allowing branded products to be associated with and use the artist name, image, and likeness with their products and services.

Merchandise Fulfillment

Labels also profit in the multiple rights of providing merchandise to the acts for their concerts, live events, and website management. Controlling the websites lets the labels maintain the content and also profit form the on-site stores where consumers may purchase additional merchandise. The labels buy merchandise in larger quantities, which gives them a price break on the cost and operational expenses. The savings are often passed along to the acts through their personal manager, so that both may share in the increased profits.

360 Deal Strategic Management

The labels have always been the drivers of the other industry related businesses such as music publishing, touring, and representation (personal managers, talents agents, booking agents and business managers). So, it's been very important to the survival of the industry that labels reinvented their business models. The changes in the business models have also provided entrepreneurial opportunities for both the artists and business executives. According to an article in *Forbes Magazine* (2017),[159] label operations are changing in six substantial ways, as they evolve into multiple rights management companies:

---

[159] Hu, Cherie. "The Record Labels of The Future Are Already Here." Forbes. October 18, 2016. Accessed May 29, 2017.https://www.forbes.com/sites/cheriehu/2016/10/15/the-record-labels-of-the-future-are-already-here/#7b1a2a-5d872a.

More Artist Run

Many record labels today act as a "music bank"—providing base-level funding and infrastructure for musical careers in exchange for equity, while leaving long-term financial and creative decisions to the artists themselves.

Brand-driven

Aside from thought leadership . . . strategy involves native branding on social media sites, perhaps at the expense of immediate incremental revenue . . . pages direct followers to external links (Spotify, YouTube, Apple Music) (and) creating native Facebook videos, photos and other media will make it easier for users to engage . . .

Price-flexible

Most record labels now receive as much as 80% of their revenues from streaming . . . revenues from Universal Music Group's streaming business skyrocketed by 62.4 percent year-over-year as of August 2016, . . . Sony Music saw a 38.4% year-over-year increase in streaming revenue in the quarter ending June 30 . . . the three majors are cumulatively turning over just under $10m every 24 hours from streaming . . . streaming users, however, are listening to music for free (e.g. at least 60 million, of Spotify's 100+ million users are only on the free tier, and fewer than 5% of Pandora users pay for its ad-free services).

Cross-promotional

. . . emerging independent labels, especially in the electronic sphere, are allowing artists to sign and partner with multiple additional labels . . ."In 2016, it's not about being on a label," claims Gramatik. "It's about exposing your music to as many people as possible as quickly as possible, so you can build a following, start touring, become financially independent and finally be able to fully focus on your art." [160]

---

160 Hu, Cherie. "The Record Labels of The Future Are Already Here." Forbes. October 18, 2016. Accessed May 29, 2017.https://www.forbes.com/sites/cheriehu/2016/10/15/the-record-labels-of-the-future-are-already-here/#7b1a2a-5d872a.

More able to connect artists with technologists

> *. . . levels of sophistication—and subsequent confusion—continue to rise in music marketing and distribution, especially around issues of monetization and ownership. . . The present challenge is to bridge the gap between the languages of art and business. A new business model is not the same thing as a new song."*

More diversified into live events and culture

> *. . . Live event revenues are already compensating for the decline in recorded revenues in the wider music industry, a trend that will likely be replicated on the individual label level. . . Major labels and artists are already launching their own alcohol brands that cater more to concert-going crowds, and could take a step further into hands-on event planning and promotion.*[161]

The changes in the technology that have forced the labels into multiple rights management have also opened up the opportunity for them to play the role of consultants to the act's business interest. Both now realize the industry is much more than selling albums and working together as partners to increase the financial success of both.

THE GLUE

The other surprise to many consumers, students, and even career professionals is the degree to which different segments of the industry must work together if any are to be financially successful. Let me say it again, without the great songwriters, the musicians, artists, labels, radio, and other forms of media, the music business is basically dead in the water. On the other hand, without initial and long-term financial support and industry connections, songwriters and their music publishers usually fail to sell or license any of their material. Thus, if you really want a great gig

---

161 Hu, Cherie. "The Record Labels of The Future Are Already Here." Forbes. October 18, 2016. Accessed May 29, 2017. https://www.forbes.com/sites/cheriehu/2016/10/15/the-record-labels-of-the-future-are-already-here/#7b1a2a5d872a.

in this business, start by understanding the big picture of how it all works together.

When we combine digital streaming with live music ticket sales, sponsorships, CDs, digital downloads, and music publishing royalties, the industry generates about $54 billion, with a predicted increase of 2.1% to about $59 billion in 2020.[162] Labels create the recordings which provide revenues for songwriters and music publishers.

Five Territories

The world's major financial markets for labels is restricted to five territories- the United States, Japan/Korea, Germany, France, and the United Kingdom. According to IFPI, these collectively accounted for 72% of the related sales in the recorded music market in calendar year 2015.

Country	% of local acts in the national top 10 albums of 2013	Country	% of local acts in the national top 10 albums of 2013
Japan	100%	Netherlands	80%
Italy	90%	Denmark	78%
Sweden	90%	France	75%
US	90%	UK	71%
Brazil	90%	Germany	70%
Spain	86%	Norway	56%

Figure 7.9: Many artists think that when they sign with a major label, they are going to be famous everywhere. But recent label investment data into A&R and Marketing indicate that's not the case, as the majority of albums sold in 10 of the 12 of the largest music markets are local talent.

The U.S., which is the most significant exporter of music, is also the largest territory for recorded music sales, constituting 33% of total calendar year 2015 recorded music sales on a trade value basis. The U.S. and Japan

---
162 PricewaterhouseCoopers. "Global entertainment and media outlook: 2016-2020." PwC. 2017. Accessed May 27, 2017.,https://www.pwc.com/us/en/industry/entertainment-media/publications/global-entertainment-media-outlook.html.

are largely local music markets, with 93% and 87%, respectively, of their calendar year 2015 physical music sales consisting of domestic repertoire. In contrast, markets like the U.K. have higher percentages of international sales, with international repertoire in that territory constituting 42% of physical music sales.[163]

LOCAL REPERTOIRE

Over the past five years (2014, latest figures), labels have invested more than $20 billion dollars into A&R and the marketing of signing artists and selling their products.[164] Most of us may never hear many of the newly signed acts, as they are considered "local repertoire" and they have "sold 70% of the top 10 albums in 10 of the leading 12 major and secondary world music markets."[165] Notice that many of the countries such as Japan to the Netherlands sell 80% to 100% of the recorded and related products in their homeland.

In addition, some global consumers have shifted from American products to local acts such as the K-pop (South Korean) and J-pop (Japan) markets. The evidence for this is

> According to IFPI, the top five territories (the U.S., Japan, the U.K., Germany, and France) collectively accounted for 72% of the related sales in the recorded music market in calendar year 2015. The U.S., which is the most significant exporter of music, is also the largest territory for recorded music sales, constituting 33% of total calendar year 2015 recorded music sales on a trade value basis. The U.S. and Japan are largely local music markets, with 93% and 87% of their calendar year 2015 physical music sales consisting of domestic repertoire, respectively. In contrast, markets like the U.K. have higher percentages of international sales, with internation-

---

163 Wacholtz, Larry E. Monetizing entertainment: an insiders handbook for careers in the entertainment & music industry. New York: Routledge, 2017.
164 "News." 'Investing in Music' report shows record labels invest US$4.3 billion in A&R and marketing. November 25, 2014. Accessed July 06, 2017. http://www.ifpi.org/news/record-labels-invest-us-4-3-billion-in-AR-and-marketing.
165 "News." 'Investing in Music' report shows record labels invest US$4.3 billion in A&R and marketing. November 25, 2014. Accessed July 06, 2017. http://www.ifpi.org/news/record-labels-invest-us-4-3-billion-in-AR-and-marketing.

al repertoire in that territory constituting 42% of physical music sales.[166]

Music Business' Connection to Entertainment Media

Labels record albums to generate streaming, branding and live ticket opportunities for the acts they signed. Film companies purchase film rights from major book publishing to create major films out of successful books. The music industry then licenses the use of the songs and master recordings to be used in the production of the films, computer games, advertisements, and other media.

The "big picture" is that the entertainment and media (both traditional and social) generate about $1.8 trillion annually.[167] All the segments on a global scale generate revenues in the billions of dollars. When we break it down into additional subsections, we'll often find the numbers are in the billions to hundreds of millions of dollars.

Additionally, most of the areas described by PricewaterhouseCoopers (PwC) are also directly tied in one way or another to the music industry. PwC describes the industries as thirteen segments including book publishing, business to business, cinema, Internet access, Internet advertising, magazine publishing, music, newspaper publishing, out of home advertising, radio, TV advertising, TV and video and video games. Other research companies combine different types of industry- related businesses making the final numbers hard to crunch. Thus, there are many ways to figure the estimated "value" of the entertainment industry. Yet, using many sources, we can still find variations in what to count as part of these industries and some rather conservative estimates of the value of different sectors. No matter what is on "the list," it appears to represent revenue of about $1.8

---

166 "News." 'Investing in Music' report shows record labels invest US$4.3 billion in A&R and marketing. November 25, 2014. Accessed July 06, 2017. http://www.ifpi.org/news/record-labels-invest-us-4-3-billion-in-AR-and-marketing.
167 PricewaterhouseCoopers. "Global entertainment and media outlook: 2016-2020." PwC. 2017. Accessed May 27, 2017.   https://www.pwc.com/us/en/industry/entertainment-media/publications/global-entertainment-media-outlook.html.

trillion in 2016 with an expected increase to about $2.1 trillion by 2020.[168]

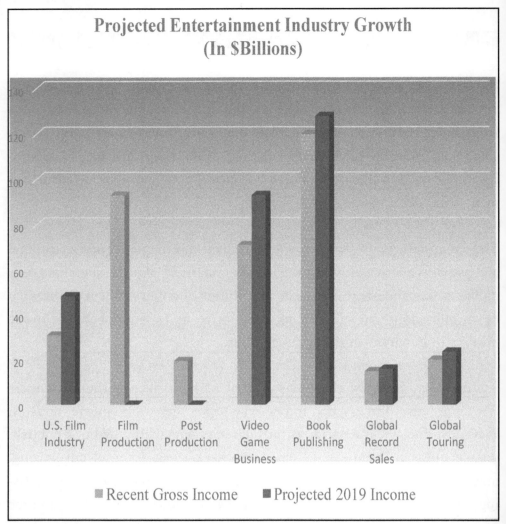

Figure 7.10: PriceWaterhouseCoopers (2015) projects growth in various segments of the entertainment industry, including global music and touring, will rise to roughly $29 billion by 2019. Source: Global Entertainment and Media Outlook 2015–2019.[169]

---

168 PricewaterhouseCoopers. "Global entertainment and media outlook: 2016-2020." PwC. 2017. Accessed May 27, 2017. https://www.pwc.com/us/en/industry/entertainment-media/publications/global-entertainment-media-outlook.html.
169 PricewaterhouseCoopers. "Global entertainment and media outlook: 2016-2020." PwC. 2017. Accessed May 27, 2017. https://www.pwc.com/us/en/industry/entertainment-media/publications/global-entertainment-media-outlook.html.

CINEMA REVENUES

Cinema revenue is defined somewhat narrowly by PwC (2016) as box office and advertising gross revenues. Cinema revenue has a global impact of about $26 billion. And if we add in subscription TV (in many countries of the world TV broadcast is licensed), plus production, video-on-demand, and many other film based or related sources for entertainment, the value of the cinema business jumps to about $564 billion US dollars.[170]

BOOK & OTHER PUBLISHING REVENUES

PricewaterhouseCoopers (2016) claims publishing revenues (defined as all types of consumer and educational printed books and eBooks) total about $147 billion annually. They also estimate the publishing segment will slow for printed books, but because of the 11.7% increase expected in the revenues of eBooks, the entire publishing industry will increase about 1.7% until 2020. The popular media has been saying books are dying- that seems not to be the case. What is important is that the delivery method for reading is changing and eBooks, considered "new" a few years ago, have stabilized as an entertainment media revenue source in more ways than you probably knew.[171]

ADVERTISING REVENUES

Advertising is the big enchilada with revenue in the neighborhood of $600 billion in 2016. Entertainment advertising on TV, radio, the Internet, print and other types of social and traditional media currently gross about $272 billion. The figure is estimated to rise significantly to over $350 billion by 2020.[172]

---
170 PricewaterhouseCoopers. "Global entertainment and media outlook: 2016-2020." PwC. 2017. Accessed May 27, 2017. https://www.pwc.com/us/en/industry/entertainment-media/publications/global-entertainment-media-outlook.html.
171 PricewaterhouseCoopers. "Global entertainment and media outlook: 2016-2020." PwC. 2017. Accessed May 27, 2017. https://www.pwc.com/us/en/industry/entertainment-media/publications/global-entertainment-media-outlook.html.
172 PricewaterhouseCoopers. "Global entertainment and media outlook: 2016-2020." PwC. 2017. Accessed May 27, 2017. https://www.pwc.com/us/en/industry/entertainment-media/publications/global-entertainment-media-out-

COMPUTER AND DIGITAL GAMES REVENUES

Computer and digital games account for about $52.4 billion now but revenues are expected to rise to over $66 billion by 2020. The global Internet access market rocks at about $510 billion being generated now and around $634 billion in 2020. The growth in revenue appears to correlate with the improvement in the availability of faster downloading speeds, which will also help the streaming of movies, music, and games. The North American (U.S.A. and Canada) professional sports markets total about $67 billion currently from ticket sales, media rights licensing, sponsorship, and merchandise receipts. The world market tops out at about $145 billion with the addition of football (soccer), the Olympics, and other types of professional sports. [173]

SUMMARY

The music industry is the first of the entertainment segments to suffer the financial slide of the creative destruction process caused by the advances in technology, negative consumer behaviors, and the lack of enforcement of the copyright laws. And the transition from the recoupment album sales business to the 360-multiple right business model has been difficult. The traditional business model has been damaged beyond repair unless the government eliminates safe harbors and start to enforce copyright laws against illegal downloads. While consumers are happy that technology has developed now to the point where if you buy a device (personal computer, tablet, cell phone or etc.), then, lots of music and entertainment products may be listened to, viewed or obtain anytime, anyplace, and usually free. Most businesses (including non-profits) are based on the concept of investing time and money to develop products (albums, streams, recordings, live shows in our case), and services (radio, accountants, charities, etc.,)

---

look.html.
173 PricewaterhouseCoopers. "Global entertainment and media outlook: 2016-2020." PwC. 2017. Accessed May 27, 2017. https://www.pwc.com/us/en/industry/entertainment-media/publications/global-entertainment-media-outlook.html.

consumers may pay to own or use. Almost everyone loves some genre of music, but now that it may be acquired "free" most of the creative artists, labels, investors, and others, who created it, are having a difficult time receiving the same amount of money (the way they use to) from their creative products.

Still, labels are making money again by reinventing their business models. The 360 deals convert the music industry point of purchase of recorded products (which is a product) to a service (which is an amenity or benefit). The money adds up as Warner Music Group, Sony Music, and Universal Music combine grossed $3.2 billion in 2016. That's still a long way away from the $23 billion labels grossed in 1999. But, if we also add multiple rights revenues, which include live ticket percentages of 10-15% into the label's gross, then that adds another $2.17 billion.

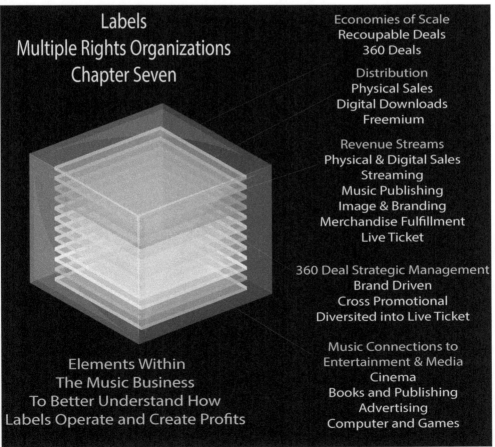

Chapter 8

Creating Profits Out of Creativity

Labels have a five-step process to find, sign, create recordings, promote, distribute and then sell or license the recordings in exchange for profits on their million dollar investments.

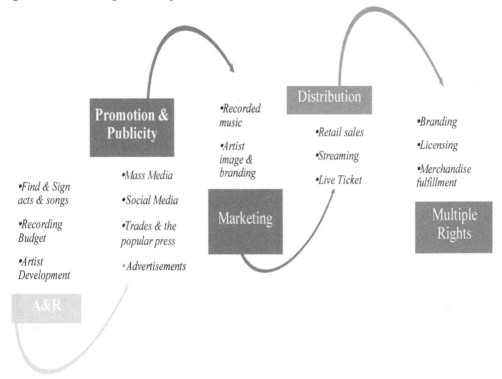

Figure 8.1: Each of the label departments is headed by a Vice President who guides a team of unique employees with the knowledge, skills, communication abilities, and business savvy required to accomplish their specific tasks for both the artists and label executives.

To accomplish this, the labels are divided into several departments each with a specific task to accomplish in the step-by-step process. The departments have their own separate, but interlinked responsibilities, controlled by a Vice-President in each department.

The key concept is that the artist is now the investment, instead of the recordings. Labels, as you've already discovered, make the majority of their profits from the artist's live ticket, merchandise, corporate sponsorships, and streaming, which are all tied to the artist's image and brand. Thus, their investments are now more directly into the act, instead of in the recordings as in earlier forms of deals.

Administration

A Chief Executive Officer (CEO) heads the labels and the external operations and communications with the holding companies such as Sony, Warner Music, or Universal Music Group. The President of the label usually serves under the CEO, and, administers the internal operations of the label.

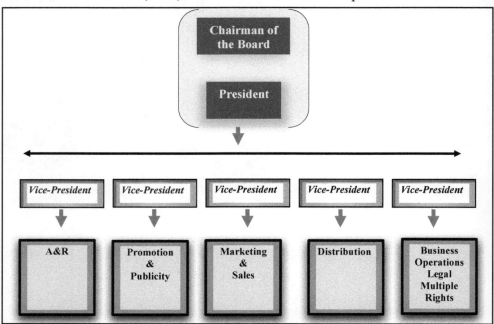

Figure 8.2: The Chairman of the Board (CEO) and the President meet to determine the strategic management plan for the operation and administration of the label. The President and Vice Presidents of each department meet weekly to accomplish the goals outlined in the strategic plan. Each act is analyzed to determine how successfully they are meeting their financial formula marker and contributing to the label achieving the goals outlined in the strategic management plan. The arrow shows how the Vice Presidents communicate between each other to determine how each department is accomplishing their tasks.

Weekly Meeting

Most labels have a weekly meeting run by the President with the respective department Vice-Presidents to review their artists' progress with the label, and, to consider various marketing strategies that might increase their success. Each roster artist is analyzed for record sales, streams, and gross revenues generated by live ticket (touring) events, of which the labels will receive 10-15% (and sometimes as high as 30% with restrictions), on a 360-deal contract. Some of the artists may also be songwriters. If that's the case, music publishing royalties paid to the label's music publishing companies may be added to the totals.

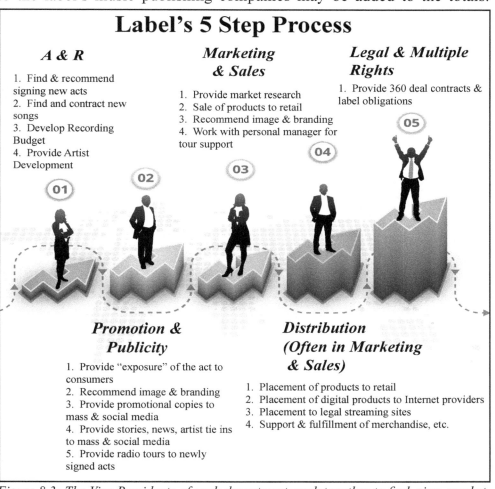

Figure 8.3: *The Vice Presidents of each department work together to find, sign, market, promote, provide publicity, and strategies for each act to increase profits at the label.*

The Financial Formula

As mentioned previously, labels invest anywhere from $500,000 to $2,000,0000 per artist per album (average of 10 songs). All of the financial numbers need to hit a required "formula financial figure" pre-determined by the label's executives and accountants. The formula is a projected percentage of gross revenues required to satisfy (recoup) the label's total investment in the act over a specific period of time. The formula goal is at least double to three times the money the labels might would have earned though other "safe" investments. The label tends to lean toward financial strategy operations similar to venture capitalists, who invest in "risky" opportunities that may pay immense profits. As expected, the nature of doing business as a record label is high pressure, and should be considered risker than most other types of businesses associated with the entertainment industry.

Expenditure	Purpose	Low Payment	High Payment
Advance to Artist	Signing the Deal	$50,000	$350,000
Recording Budget	Recording Album	$150,000	$500,000
Marketing Plan	Promotion	$150,000	$500,000
	Publicity	$50,000	$200,000
	Music Video's	$50,000	$300,000
	Tour Support	$50,000	$150,000
Total		$500,000	$2,000,000

Figure 8.4: Each department at a label is full of people with the expertise, knowledge, and experience to help launch an artist in a 360 deal. A&R's job includes understanding consumers' wants and desires in order to find and recommend signing the acts who have the potential to become financially successful. Promotion & Publicity's job is to have a deep understanding of consumers' musical and entertainment preferences and tie that knowledge to their understanding of the mass and social media analytics. Sales & Marketing need to understand retail outlets from unique entrepreneurial to corporate business structures. As you can see it cost a lot of money, with the act receiving an advance between $50,000 to $350,000. The recording budgets range from $150-$500,000 for superstars. The Marketing Plan often takes most of the money for promotion, publicity, and tour support. [174]

---

[174] "News." 'Investing in Music' report shows record labels invest US$4.3 billion in A&R and marketing. November 25, 2014. Accessed July 06, 2017. http://www.ifpi.org/news/record-labels-invest-us-4-3-billion-in-AR-and-

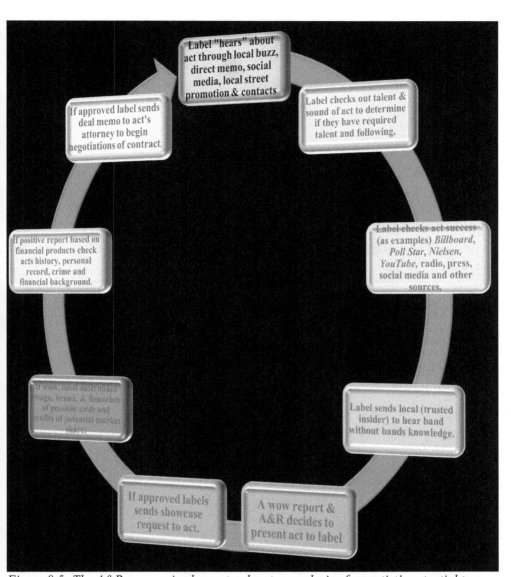

Figure 8.5: The A&R process is also a step-by-step analysis of an artist's potential to generate significant revenues for the label. In the digital world tied to 360 deals, artists are responsible for creating their own unique sound, image, fan base, and an exciting buzz in their local markets. When they have reached the point they need a major label's money, guidance, promotion, publicity, and marketing to increase their success, they may contact the label through a "pitch memo". In response, labels may send a request for the act to showcase their talent live. If, and that's a big if, the label executives decide to sign the act, then a "deal memo" is sent to them or their attorney to determine if the act is interested in pursuing an agreement.[175]

marketing.
175 Wacholtz, Larry E. Monetizing entertainment: an insiders handbook for creers in the entertainment & music

DEPARTMENT OF ARTISTS & REPERTOIRE (A&R)

Better known as A&R, the Department of Artists and Repertoire is the link between the label's creative and business executives. The department is sometimes divided into two sections, creative and administrative, as is the case at Sony Music. Creative A&R are the "ears" of the label, always searching for a new artists and songs that will help make the label become more profitable.

The Vice President of A&R runs the operations. It's vital to the success of the label to sign the types of talent and songs that will help the label achieve its financial goals. The VP most often has been a producer of successful acts in the past and also understands or has been a part of the executive operations at other labels. A&R has to filter through many acts and songs to find what they hope will be "the next big thing". The business side of A&R develops the recording budget and often provides artist development for the act which might include songwriters, media training, and perfecting their live show performances. If the label and act are in agreement then a contact is offered between the act's attorney and the labels. The A&R process for finding and signing a new act is step-by-step with each level discussed at the weekly meeting. A typical search includes the following steps:

- The label "hears" about act through local buzz, a direct memo from the act or someone connected to the label or through social media, local street promotion & contacts.
- The label checks out the talent & sound of act to determine if they have the required talent and following.
- The label checks the act's track record of success (as examples) *Billboard, Poll Star, Nielsen, YouTube,* radio, press, social media and other sources.
- Label sends a local (trusted insider) to hear the band without the band's knowledge.
- A wow report may help A&R to present the act to label executives.

industry. New York: Routledge, 2017.

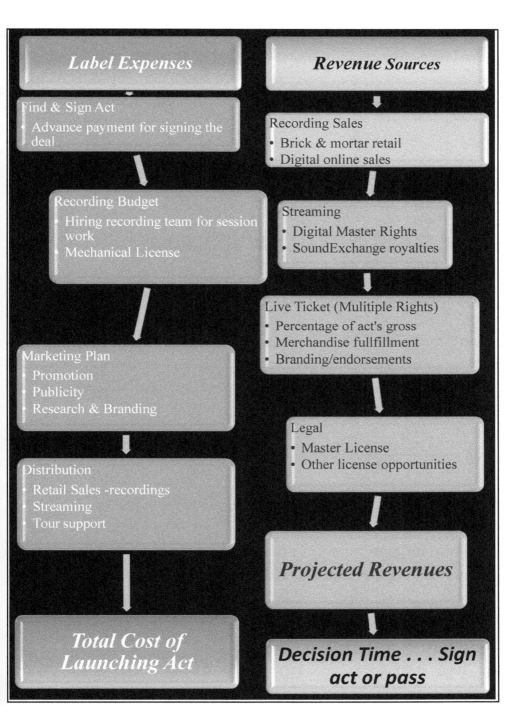

Figure 8.6: The most difficult decision to make in the music business is to sign an act. The decision usually is determined after the financial projects of the cost of signing, developing, and marketing the act are compared to the potential profits.

- If approved, the labels sends showcase request to act. If a wow performance, the label will determine if the image, brand, & financials of costs vs profits "fit" into a sizable potential market share.
- If positive report based on financial projections suggest significant potential profits, then the label checks into the acts history, personal record, crime and financial background.
- If approved, label may send a deal memo to the act's attorney to begin negotiations of contract.

Signing Acts & Songs-Deal Points

Major label deals are usually 70 to 150 page contracts covering just about everything you could ever imagine. What's really in the deal the artist's attorney and label's attorney have negotiated? Obviously, the act is thrilled to be offered a major label deal but before they sign it, they'll need to know what's in it. What both need to know and understand is what the artist's and the label are committing to accomplish. It's important, as deals can be seven years long, which means you could be tied up to that label for the next seven years for your life. Take the time at the outset to be sure the deal is "good" and that you understand it before you sign.

Labels offer contracts reflecting the steps they plan to take to pay up front money (called an advance), recordings, development, administrative branding, promotion, publicity, and tour support. The total expenditures are then listed as a deficit in the artist's name on the label's accounting books. The advances, recordings, licensing, and tour support are 100% recoupable. That means (depending on the deal), the label's expenditures will be recoupable from all revenue streams, including the sale of recordings, streaming licensing fees, and the multiple rights revenues from touring, branding, merchandise fulfillment sales, corporate endorsements, and other sources. Promotion, publicity, special consumers research is 50% recoupable unless tied to tour support advances (which they often are) making them also 100% recoupable.

In exchange, labels own 100% of the master recordings, and usually 10%-12% of all the money (gross) from the act's complementary products, shows, and revenues.[176] These typically include touring, merchandise, album sales, corporate sponsorships, and branding. Because the labels own 100% of the master recordings, many are currently keeping 100% of the streaming fee paid from Spotify and the other providers. However, in the future, this may change, but it all depends on what's negotiated in the deal. Let's take a look at some of the important contract terms each is agreeing to provide.

EXCLUSIVE RECORDING AGREEMENT-

Exclusive Recording Agreements require the artist signing the deal may only record for the label offering the deal. If they want to record with another artists at another label they must have permission from their label. Additional terms include,

- **Description of Services**-explains what each party is responsible for including the artist and the label. The most important words in most contracts are "you will cause" which means the artist is responsible to complete any specific items listed, including hiring the producer (with the label's approval), securing mechanical licenses, and the hiring of all other third parties including the audio engineer, musicians, and background singers.

- **The Term of the Agreement**-usually requires a commitment from the act for up to seven years. However, it is usually divided into an initial period of one year, one album (or less) and then six option years with an additional album or less. Artist usually give up their right to option out of the deal when they sign it, which means the label will make the decision to extended the year by year or drop the act.

- **Commitment Album & Other Expenses**-means the label is only committed to pay for the first recordings during the initial period, not the full seven years of recordings, tour support, etc. They only pay year to year based on how successful the act is generating reve-

---
176 Complementary products is a term used by Bharat Anand in *The Content Trap. A Strategist's Guide to Digital Change*. New York: Random Business, 2016.

nue. If the first album and other revenues from touring, merchandise, etc., hit the formula amounts, then the label will pick up the option and then all the second-year expenses are defined as commitment responsibilities of the label.

- **Recording Elements**-The label pays all the recording bills based on approved budget the artists often have to create themselves. Dates and times of the sessions must also be approved by A&R before any sessions, as well as the songs selected to be recorded. Once the album is completed, the artist delivers the master tapes to A&R for approval. If rejected, the label usually pays the bills, but the artist is then required to create an acceptable album out of their own pocket. The major labels are signatories to the musicians and vocalist unions, which means that any royalty artist with that label who also plays an instrument or who sings on the album must belong to the AF of M and/or SAG-AFTRA.

- **Material**- These are typically songs the artist brings to the label. Selecting the right ones is the producer's job, who also controls the recording budget, and will produce the actual session. Songs must be non-published (new and never released) in any media prior to the recording (first use rights). Greatest hit albums will not count as a commitment album.

- **Royalties**-Artist royalties are called "points" on album deals and percentages on all the other act's revenues. New royalty artists make 12-15 points (percentage of the suggested retail list price) on a 40/20/40 split of CDs and vinyl sold through brick and mortar retail. Internet downloads are a 70/30 split with the labels receiving the 70%. Artist royalties are still considered points, but this time it is figured from the wholesale or discounted Internet list price. Superstars are often paid 20 points or more.

- **Accounting**-Artists usually receive a semi-annual or quarterly statement informing them of the financials tied to their deals. It is sent to their business manager who control the act's financial records. Royalty artists usually have the right to have an accountant review their label's "books" once a year but most request the audit in advance and in writing.

- **Independent Contractors**-The royalty artist signing the recording deal is a not full- time employee. They are hired as a work-for-hire, which means the label will retain the copyright of the vocal and music performances in the master recordings for the length of the life of the artist plus 70 years. Remember our chapter on copyrights?

- **Image/Brand**-The artist's stage name, identification, likeness, bio, and photos of the artist are copyrighted and trademarked. The artist usually grants a global exclusive right to the label to use for sub-licensing logos, likeness, and stage names for the manufacturing and exploitation of their merchandise, branded products, and endorsements.

A&R's job, in addition to finding great acts, is to find wow songs. Labels usually have affiliated music publishing companies. New acts usually search the catalog of songs owned by the labels' publishing companies to determine if there's any they might want to record.

EXECUTIVE EXPERIENCE

The entertainment and music industry, as you have seen, is complex and made up of many moving parts. How labels operate, how to derive profits out of creativity, and, the decisions that need to be made often come from the executive's previous failures and successes. For students who want a job in the industry, an internship is obviously a great way to start meeting the right people and begin to learn the business of the business by watching and listening to the experienced industry leaders.

So the question then is, how do you get your first break in the industry? The answers are through networking and through internships. Through these you gain knowledge that becomes part of your value to the industry; or, said differently, how you might get your first job in the business. Let's take a look at the various departments in the record label, so you get an understanding of how they operate.

Recording Budget

The big surprise for many newly signed artists to label deals is that they will have to develop and present to the label a recording budget. The purpose, of course, is to educate the artist about the cost of master recording sessions and to reduce the conflicts and communication about the number of songs, producers, musicians, and background vocalists will be hire. In the deal with the label, the artist usually also agrees to submit all the paperwork for licensing the songs (mechanicals), and hiring the producer. Both the budget and producer must be approved by the Vice-President of A&R before any sessions can commence. In addition, once the album or tracks are completed, the artist is required to present the final master recordings to the VP for final approval. At which point, the label will pay all the master recording expenses. Budgets for album master recordings often range from $150,000 for newly signed acts to $500,000 for major superstars.

Artist Development

Labels seek recording artists who have been able to capture the imagination of the consumers in a local market by building their own fan base, and a local buzz. Labels view success in a local market as an indication that if the act is developed, recorded, and exploited (marketed), they may become very profitable. According to record producer Jimmy Bowen, whose artists included Frank Sinatra, Dean Martin, to Hank Williams, Jr., (1984),

> You should always strive to work with an artist who is a one-of-a-kind. They are the only ones that really break through. You can record an artist who's a copy of an artist, you can have success with them, but it's not really worth the effort. Anytime you have an artist who's like somebody else, you're starting off in second place, no matter how well you produce it. If you're producing a one-of-a-kind artist, you're doing something

new. ...Sometimes a one-of-a-kind is not obvious when you first start with them. Usually, there will be a little something, you'll hear, just four bars somewhere, you'll see them in person, you'll hear them with a guitar or piano someplace, and you'll catch that little moment of magic. You've got to hunt it, look for it. You're always hunting that gold, that one-of-a-kind. And when you see it, it may be 4 years away; 6 month away; that's your problem. You've got to figure out when it is, see if you can get it into a point where it's valuable before you lose the opportunity to work with it.[177]

Artist Development may be its own department or part of A&R or even Marketing within a label. However, while marketing in the traditional business model was usually tied to sales and distribution of unit sales, in 360 deals the role of artist development has been expanded into branding, touring, and live show presentations. Psychographic research or lifestyle research comparing the global music markets determines image behaviors and branding products that may generate additional profits for the act and label. In general, for new acts artist development usually includes,[178]

- **Image Development** includes acting, speech, appearance, demeanor, and social manners. The artist's image frequently has to be enhanced. Trainers are hired to help the artist control a weight and/or drug problem, dentists to improve the smile, and stylists to suggest various types of cosmetics, clothing, and hairstyles for concert, stage, TV, and/or movie appearances. Image consultants are hired to suggest methods to help the act appear comfortable and confident on stage and with the media.

- **Creative Development** focuses on songwriting, music publishing, and the ability to promote the artist through shameless self-promotion. They may also (if interested) learn how to contribute to video script treatments, productions, and audio interviews for promotion and publicity.

---

177 Jimmy Bowen (as quoted by Larry Wacholtz) Inside Country Music, Billboard Books, (New York: Watson-Guptil Publishers, 1986) & Larry Wacholtz, Lights, Glitter and Business Sense, Thumbs Up Publishing, (Washington: Cheney, 1984) 184-198.
178 Wacholtz, Larry E. Monetizing entertainment: an insiders handbook for careers in the entertainment & music industry. New York: Routledge, 2017.

- **Branding** has become very important, as album sales have decreased. The marketing plan, promotion, publicity, and street date launch are usually based on the act's image tied to various consumer types discovered through the label's psychographic research. Branding is tied to the products, and endorsements of products, that will appeal to the consumers, as defined by their lifestyles, through the psychographic research and other resources. Remember this is the emotion business and it's the consumer's reactions to the act's image and recordings that open up the merchandise, branding, and touring opportunities. Under 360 deals, labels profit from the complete package, not just the recordings.

Department of Promotion & Publicity

Promotion is the "exposure" of the iconic artists and their recordings to radio stations, mass and social media, music videos, and other outlets. The purpose is to give customers a chance to "discover" the recordings and the corresponding recording artists. Publicity strengthens promotion by providing the back story of the act, which is really the artist's life-story, beliefs, and positive world view. The labels often hire independent promoters to motivate radio station airplay, as well as to create the buzz for local retail sales. Professional publicists place stories in the trade magazines and popular press. They also book the acts for interviews on TV and radio.

The all-in budget, which is discussed in detail later, represents the combined expenses the label's incur for advances paid to the act for signing the deal; recording sessions costs; pressings; and, the mechanical licenses. Budgets for promotion are expensive- usually in a range of 100% to 200% of the all-ins. Publicity is often budgeted at 50% to 100% of the all-ins. There is one exception to this policy. Major superstars usually require less in the promotional budgets, as they are already famous; yet, they usually want more money in their advances or recording budgets. The traditional recoupment business model had three levels of promotion national, regional, and local, all of which had their advantages and disadvantages.

In 360 deals, the labels have advanced psychographic research methods, and other forms of lifestyle analytics-based target marketing. Feedback analytics from streaming audio and video sites provide marketing locations tied to regions, zip codes, and in some cases, very detailed consumer personal information including devices used and Internet site visit habits.

The 360 model is actually more powerful and less expensive than buying national advertisements, as labels can focus on the types of consumers most likely to be interested and excited about specific artists. Then tours, appearances, and discount advertisements are booked and placed where the fans are physically, and, where they like to visit in cyberspace. If a fan uses a specific browser on their computer or device, then on certain pages, advertisements albums and singles information, tour dates, and discount offers magically appear featuring the acts they most likely might enjoy.

RADIO

Labels describe radio station airplay for recordings they've released as promotion; and, therefore they provide the radio stations free recordings, called promotional copies. However, stations still must pay ASCAP, BMI, and SESAC music publishers and writers for using the song in the recording in the form of a blanket license. According to the Federal Communication Commission (FCC, 2015), there are 15,470 full power radio stations in the United States of which 11,380 are commercial AM and FM stations and the remaining 4,090 are FM educational stations usually tied to PBS and universities.[179] There are also UHF commercials and educational TV stations, FM translators and boosters, low-power TV stations that bring the total uses of the airwaves to over 31,000.[180]

---

[179] "FCC News, BROADCAST STATION TOTALS AS OF SEPTEMBER 30, 2015." FCC.gov. October 9, 2015. Accessed November 5, 2015. http://transition.fcc.gov/Daily_Releases/Daily_Business/2015/db1009/DOC-335798A1.pdf.
[180] "FCC News, BROADCAST STATION TOTALS AS OF SEPTEMBER 30, 2015." FCC.gov. October 9, 2015. Accessed November 5, 2015. http://transition.fcc.gov/Daily_Releases/Daily_Business/2015/db1009/DOC-335798A1.

Radio Programming

Radio stations have varying degrees of importance to labels for promotion, depending on the station location, signal power, audience size, and broadcasting hours of operation. Some stations are only 1,000 watts AM and others 50,000 watt AM. The quality of the broadcast signal on AM is poor, yet the signal is strong compared to a higher quality, but weaker signal on FM. Digital signals are mandatory on TV, satellites, and cable. There are a few radio stations that are starting to use digital signals, and newer cars can pick up these digital signals for a higher quality sound. However, not all the cars and homes have digital radio receivers in them, so it will take a few years to the complete change to digital radio.

Radio Tours

Newly signed recording artists may be required to take a "radio tour" to visit the program and music directors at radio station networks and independent smaller stations around the country. The purpose is to introduce the new acts and their music to the people who can help get their music on the air. Then it is up to them to construe how the new recordings may fit into their music formats or stations programming.

Promotional Copies

Recordings sent to radio stations and networks for broadcasting still cost the label money, as they have to pay for the creation of the master tape, copies to be pressed and shipped or sent digitally through emails to program directors. Artist royalties are not paid on promotional copies played on radio stations in the United States, but they are in most of the rest of the world.

Mass Media-Passive Communication

The term "mass media" is used to describe the 15,348 radio stations, the 4,938 TV stations at various powers, plus the 10,099 translators and boosters licensed to broadcast outlets in the United States.[181] Nev-

---
[181] "There Are 15,330 U.S. Radio Stations, But How Many Matter?" Hypebot. Accessed June 05, 2017. http://www.pdf.

ertheless, I'd like you to consider mass media as any means of communication that reaches a significant number of people at the same time. Therefore, the term mass media traditionally alludes to (a) delivery systems; (b) the type of communicative message; or, entertainment programming being delivered; and, (c) the hundreds to millions of people who are receiving the same message simultaneously.

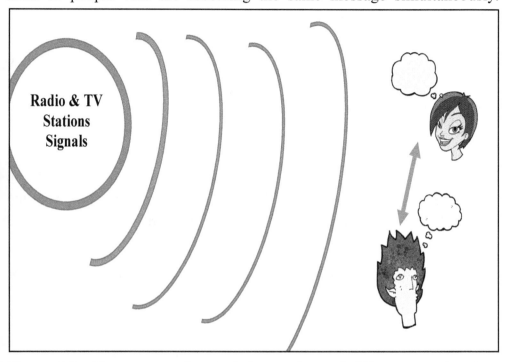

Figure 8.7: The mass media, including radio and TV stations, broadcast one signal to all who are passively watching and listening. The programming (the communication message, advertisement, TV show, or recording being played) is controlled by the station, print media, or other mass media source.

The key point about all mass media is that it is a passive signal or message, as in a book, newspaper, radio station airplay, or television broadcast. For the television networks, the same time means a three hour delay between the east coast to the west coast through the different time zones. For radio broadcasts and satellite programming, it's often simultaneous to all consumers. For books and magazines, the time period for sales is stretched over a few days to a month. All mass media programming is passive, meaning that it's a one-way signal, or message in print, sent to the listen-

hypebot.com/hypebot/2013/10/there-are-15330-us-radio-stations-how-many-of-the-matter-to-you.html.

ers, viewers, or readers who all receive the same communicative message. In other words, the viewer, or listener has to wait for the programing they want instead of clicking for it on a streaming channel such as Spotify.

Day Parts

Radio listeners are divided into average listeners per-hour (quarter of an hour by Nielsen Research) and ages such as 18 or older, 55 or older, etc. As an example, in May of 2015 nationally on all radio there were 35,600,000 Americans listening to radio stations at 7 a.m. in the morning compared to only 5,663,300 listening at 11 p.m. in the evening.[182] The majority of people listening to radio on all devices is the highest during what the industry likes to call "drive time" or when people are in their cars driving to work. Thus, the cost of advertising at that time in the morning (6 a.m. to 9 a.m.) is much more expensive than 9 p.m. to midnight as the amount of people listening is only about 16% of the drive time audience.[183]

Social Media

In the music industry, every successful artist today is texting, Tweeting, and doing everything else they can think of to connect with their fan base. Social media takes the traditional mass media "middleman" out of the connection process. Live appearances on national TV shows are still important, but everything has changed in the last few years as fewer people are watching those late-night shows and more are connected to their devices.

Social Media-Interactive Communication

Social media provides interactive signals between the customers, businesses, and providers unlike the passive delivery system found in the traditional mass media. The advantages are beyond significant as Internet social media sites and Internet providers provide an experience similar to

---
182 "Insights." The Total Audience Report: Q2 2015. May 1, 2015. Accessed November 11, 2015. http://www.nielsen.com/us/en/insights/reports/2015/the-total-audience-report-q2-2015.html.
183 Loynes, A. (2015). 2014 NIELSEN MUSIC U.S. REPORT. Retrieved November 13, 2015, from http://www.nielsen.com/content/dam/corporate/us/en/public factsheets/Soundscan/nielsen-2014-year-end-music-report-us.pdf

talking to a person face-to-face.

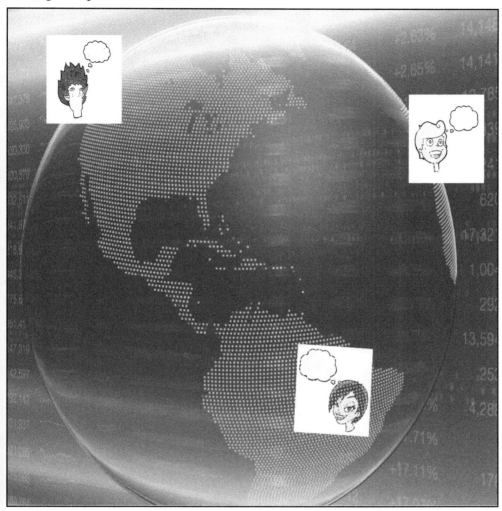

Figure 8.8: Here we can see the advantage of social media in creating the buzz, as one person who discovers a song that inspires them, sells another, and then, that person tells another. In no time, the streamed recording has a million or more hits. Notice the control of the song selected is now in the hands of the consumers and that the communication is interactive.

The communication is much quicker, less expensive, and often, more fun and engaging. As an example, if a fan wants to catch an interview with their favorite recording artist, watching a TV show and listening to a radio interview places the fan in the role of an outside observer. Boring! But, on the Internet fans can actually ask questions and receive a quick response. Social media sites also provide Tweets, Facetime, and many other ways for consumers to establish cyberspace communities, new relationships locally or with "friends" in distant countries.

Successful artists go where the fans are and the potential new fans are in cyberspace on social media sites. Once again, time is money, and the direct approach in the industry now is social media in 360 deals, because it's quicker, cheaper, and works much better. In addition, the fans seem to sense a "closer connection" to their favorite acts which tends to increase their excitement and the buzzing support they provide the artists and their labels by spreading the word. In addition, consumers can interactively select the types of programs and recordings the want to watch or hear anytime, any place, and anywhere with their devices. It makes me wonder how much of the traditional mass media will survive over the next few years.

Industry insiders and the wannabes also use social media to network with others in the business. As an example, *Billboard Magazine* has a weekly subscription of only 17,000; an online readership of 115,000, but it has 15.2 million fans (views monthly) and music industry insiders who read the .com and .biz sites. *Billboard Mobile* has 6.7 million hits a month from insiders and consumers connecting with the website and charts, 12.9 million a month who use the networks for social connections, and it also sponsors 20 plus event every year to help target industry insiders with fan based information[184].

MARKETING AND SALES DEPARTMENT

Industry executives use media as promotional opportunities to break new acts and products to the consumer market. Remember, the label's job at this stage of the game is to help the public "discover" and "get excited" about their entertainment products and acts. The labels rely on the Four Ps of marketing to get their acts' products into retail stores, onto digital sites, and in front of live audiences. The Four Ps are product (the recordings); promo-

---

184 "There Are 15,330 U.S. Radio Stations, But How Many Matter?" Hypebot. Accessed June 05, 2017. http://www.hypebot.com/hypebot/2013/10/there-are-15330-us-radio-stations-how-many-of-the-matter-to-you.html.

tion (process of creating and nurturing the target consumer market); price (what the products will sell for, with profits considered in the pricing); and, position (distribution). Marketing and Sales consider the Four Ps in determining the suggested retail list price (SLRP) for the album, and work closely with their research team to create the right price point for the consumer.

Market Research

Marketing uses 360 promotion and publicity analytics from many sources to determine the best marketplace for the label's products and acts. At the weekly meeting, the Vice President of Marketing and Sales reports all income sources on each signed artist with the label in order for the President and VPs to make informed decisions (related to the marketing plan) that may help the act become more successful. It costs the labels less to place stories and ads where social media users can discover them. Using analytics and other consumer research information provided to the labels, labels purchase focused ads directed towards specific fan bases, instead of buying very expensive national ads in a shotgun approach. Why advertise to 300 million when for a lot less money you can advertise to the few million fans who are most likely to respond?

Nielsen Marketing is one of the top research companies in the industry. Major labels use them and others to provide facts and figures the executives need to develop promotional, publicity, and marketing plans for launching an act and their recordings.[185] Some of the research Nielsen (2017), provides includes

- Broadcast Data Services (BDS) which reports the actual radio station airplay of every artist. As as example, let's say the recording artists Imagine Dragons have a total of 325,000 airplays of their last single on radio stations. The Nielsen report to the labels will often list the number of plays by each station and where they are in the country. In addition, it will provide the number of listeners

---

[185] "Insights." The Total Audience Report: Q2 2015. May 1, 2015. Accessed November 11, 2015. http://www.nielsen.com/us/en/insights/reports/2015/the-total-audience-report-q2-2015.html.

who actually heard the recording (depending on the location, power of the tower, and time of day) which in this case could be over 12 million. That's powerful information that will help the label and personal manager decide where the act may want to tour and where the label may want to throw more money into promotion.

- Streaming is also reported to the labels from Spotify, Slacker, MediaNet, Veno, YouTube, AOL Radio and others. Remember, 1,500 streams equals about the same amount of money to the label as one album sold and 150 streams equal about the same amount as one single sold at retail.

- Album and singles sold by chain stores, mass merchandisers and digital download from the Internet.

- The weekly number of units sold by genre, region, territory, and formats including everything from rock to world music and the format platform they were purchased on such as CDs, LPs (vinyl), DVDs, and Digital.

- The weekly, monthly, and annual reports of all streaming, airplay, retail sales of recordings and live touring grosses and merchandise for WMG (Warner Music Group), UMG (Universal Music Group), and Sony Entertainment, plus all independent labels.[186]

Once the target consumer base audience is discovered, then the timing and the media to be used become very important. It's a little like a multiple level target practice game, as the labels are trying to connect the target consumers with the advertisements, publicity, social media interviews, news items, and recordings the consumers might most enjoy. The real questions are where's the target audience at a specific time; what are they doing; what devices are they using; and, what media or social media programming or sites are they connected to?

As you can see, the game is to figure out where the audience is so that

---

186 "Nielsen Broadcast Data Encore/Nielsen Soundscan", Nielsen. Accessed December 31, 2017. http://www.nielsen.com/bds.html.

you can save money by connecting directly with the fans and spending less on advertising. If this works, the promotion and publicity are connecting with the target consumers, then the odds of an act "catching on" and the corresponding profits collected by the label are considerably enhanced. That is, if the consumers connect and enjoy them. And that is only known after the audience have found them through traditional and/or social media or a buzz message from a friend.

Media/Device	Total Number of Users	Total Medium Monthly Time in Hours/Minutes per user
Traditional TV	284,817,000	151:33
DVD's/ Blu-Ray Devices	182,725,000	5:36
Game Consoles	98,664.000	9:15
Multimedia Devices	53,236,000	4:42
Internet on Computer	192,875,000	30:36
Watching Video on the Internet	138,502,000	12:13
Web Application on a Smartphone	170,303,000	44:32
Watching Video on a Smartphone	128,432,000	1:53
Listening to AM/FM Radio	260,099,000	58:10

Figure 8.9: Before consumers buy or use music products, they've got to "discover" the recordings and acts. The average use of media by consumers is over 11 hours per-day in the United States. Which traditional or social media is being used depends on demographics and psychographic lifestyle choices. Label executives use information and research supplied by various companies to determine products placement, advertisements, publicity, and promotion plans. Source: Nielsen 2015.

Cyberspace advertisements drive sales, streams, and concert attendance. In cooperation with the act's personal manager, marketing personnel discuss options, and usually approve Internet and social media advertising campaigns, if the numbers indicate reasonable returns on expenditures. The labels then find more sources for the money needed to pay the licensing fees. And usually approve if the numbers indicate additional potential revenues.

Devices	7.a.m.	Noon	8.p.m.	Midnight	5.a.m.
TV	36.3%	35.7%	62%	66.7%	49.4%
Radio	39.8%	33.4%	9.6%	4.8%	27%
TV Connected Devices	1.5%	3.2%	6.4%	8.3%	3.3%
Computers	6.5%	10.6%	7.3%	6.3%	5%
Smartphones	12.3%	14%	11%	10.1%	10.7%
Tablets	3.5%	3%	3.8%	3.8%	4.6%

Figure 8.10: The size of the audience may be changing and so are the devices consumers use to connect to various types of traditional and social media. Source: Nielsen 2015.

DISTRIBUTION DEPARTMENT

At many labels, the Distribution Department is part of the Sales and Marketing Department. Yet, they have distinct roles. Distribution's purpose is the placement of CDs and vinyl into brick and mortar retail (what's left of them) stores, recordings to streaming sites (so the labels can license their use). They also assist with the act's tour management by fulfilling merchandise and other obligations, if that is part of the artist's deal with the label. They have to get the product into the market place; whereas, Marketing and Sales develop the marketing plans and sales strategies before analyzing the results.

RECORDED MUSIC AND DISTRIBUTION

Distribution provides the mechanics behind the executive's decisions on where, when, and how to place recordings into retail markets for sales, on broadcast radio, and on the streaming sites. In the 360 deals, distribution is also connected to supporting the live ticket events with fulfillments (as negotiated in the contract and determined by the act's personal manager) of merchandise and branded products. In addition, labels often control the act's website, and, in some cases, this department may also be involved with sourcing the information and sales of related artist's products (if contracted).

Retail Sales

As previously stated, retail outlets in the traditional business models are related to the sales of the recordings tagged as "units." It may be a CD, vinyl, or other format, but as far as sales are concerned, it's a unit. Traditional retail unit sales, as we've already mentioned several times, are declining fast, and, so are the retail outlets- One-Stops, Mass Merchandisers, Rack Jobbers, P.I. (Per-inquire advertising), and digital downloads at sites including iTunes and Amazon.com. In the past, *BMG Direct* and *Columbia House* were used to unload overstock recordings for a huge profit. The CDs were sold at higher prices, as a heavy discount offer hyped membership, but then the required additional monthly purchases were at the SRLP or offered with a small discount. Columbia House has shifted to DVDs and has stopped selling CDs. BMG Direct ended all sales of music in 2009.[187] Labels still make money from the sale of the recordings they place into retail, yet it easy to see the downward trends caused by streaming.

Free Goods

How can labels and distributors motivate retail outlets to stock unheard of entertainment products and recordings, including newly signed acts? Labels provide free goods (free units that can be sold) to retail outlets to stimulate sales. Retailers usually want some guarantee from distributors that they will not lose money or be stuck with albums they can't sell. Thus, the labels (through the distributors) usually give a certain amount

---

[187] Kreps, Daniel. ""12 For One" CD Deals No More: BMG Music Service Ends In June." Rolling Stone. March 10, 2009. Accessed July 08, 2017. http://www.rollingstone.com/music/news/12-for-one-cd-deals-no-more-bmg-music-service-ends-in-june-20090310.

of new and unknown artist releases to the retail outlet (as much as 25%) when they buy and stock a minimum inventory. Additionally, retail will usually demand 100% return on the unsold units. Thus, should the retail store agree to stock and sell the new release, it can sell or give away free units it did not pay for, as the label will accept returns on all the units bought that didn't sell. In addition, remember that mechanical royalties are not paid on free goods to the music publishers and songwriters.

Location	Chain Stores	Independent	Mass Merchandisers	Digital Download
City	3.2%	4.3%	7.4%	16.9%
Sub	3.8%	4.6%	10.5%	18.9%
Rural	1.7%	3.0%	7.8%	17.4%
Totals	8.7%	11.9%	25.7%	53.2%

Figure 8.11: The Nielsen figures for unit sales indicates two items we should be aware of in the new 360 industry. Recording are purchased most in suburbs instead of the city or rural stores and consumers purchase almost 53% of their recordings on-line.[188]

ISRC Codes

The International Standard Recording Code (ISRC) is used to identify each recorded audio and music video track (audio only) in the world. It's a 12-digit alphanumeric code labels apply and pay for (about $2.00 per-single song) that allows the recordings to be tracked for sales, airplay, digital transmissions, and streams. It's also used by the trade magazines including *Billboard* to track plays, streams, and sales.[189][190]

UPC Codes

Universal Product Codes (UPC Codes) are a 12-digit number that is represented by the bar codes required to sell products in retail and for distribution. SoundScan and other companies use the codes to determine the

188 "Nielsen Broadcast Data Encore/Nielsen Soundscan", Nielsen. Accessed December 31, 2017. http://www.nielsen.com/bds.html.
189 Department, Simply Barcodes – ISRC. "Frequently Asked Questions about ISRC Codes." ISRC Codes :: Register ISRC Codes for Music and Video @ Simply Barcodes - Global ISRC Experts. Accessed July 13, 2017. http://www.isrc.net/general-faq.html?keyword=isrc code&matchtype=e&position=1t1&gclid=CKTrvKiohtUCFdgIgQodLnUEEw.
190 Department, Simply Barcodes – ISRC. "Frequently Asked Questions about ISRC Codes." ISRC Codes :: Register ISRC Codes for Music and Video @ Simply Barcodes - Global ISRC Experts. Accessed July 13, 2017. http://www.isrc.net/general-faq.html?keyword=isrc code&matchtype=e&position=1t1&gclid=CKTrvKiohtUCFdgIgQodLnUEEw.

number of units sold for reports used by the labels, managers, music publishers, and others.[191]

DIGITAL DOWNLOADS

Digital downloads are still sold by iTunes, Amazon.com, and others, but are declining quickly as consumers move to free streaming. Under the traditional business model, the economic ratio was a benefit to the label and the consumers, as the consumer paid less for the recordings and the labels made slightly more money per unit.

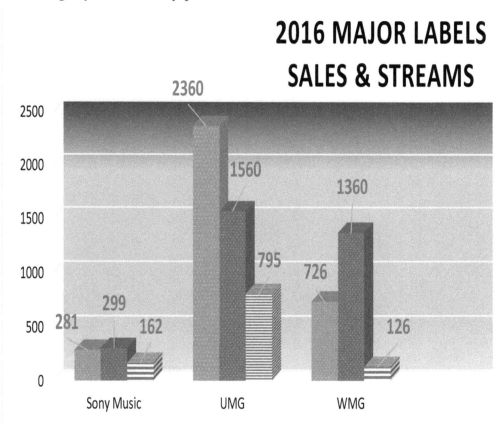

Figure 8.12: The three major labels' revenues are quickly moving away from albums and single sales into streaming. Physical sales in 2016 were $281 million for Sony Music, $2.3 billion for Universal Music Group (UMG), and $726 million for Warner Music Group (WMG). Digital downloads totaled $162 million for Sony Music; $795 million for UMG; and, $126 million for WMG. Streaming added $299 million to Sony's bottom line and $1.56

---

[191] "How to Get a UPC Barcode | The Label Experts." Electronic Imaging Materials. Accessed July 13, 2017. http://barcode-labels.com/solutions/upc-labels/upc-info/.

billion to UMB, and $1.36 billion.

The split is 70/30 with the label receiving the 70% and saving on the expenses of pressing the units, shipping and handling, and other expenses. The middleman distributor and the brick and mortar retail outlets are eliminated in the digital download deal. However, in 2016, digital download sales started to nosedive by over 20% from 2015, as consumers continued to switch to streaming.[192]

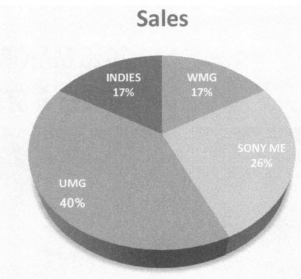

Figure 8.13: Sales of all types of units for 2017 indicated that WMG about 17% of the market, SONY Music/Entertainment 26%, UMG 40% and all the other labels (Indies) 17%.[193]

Why buy music or even steal it when we can stream it instantly free on our computers, cell phones, or mobile devices any time we want it? Consumer behavior trends in uses of cell phones and other devices to acquire entertainment products by streaming (instead of buying) is a major cognitive shift in the ways consumers "think" about obtaining products and services. The music business and its fans are not going back to the way things were before personal computers, the Internet, and devices became mainstream. That's why labels have morphed into the 360-multiple rights

---

192 "Music Downloads Post Their Worst Decline EVER." Digital Music News. March 08, 2017. Accessed July 08, 2017. https://www.digitalmusicnews.com/2016/07/07/music-downloads-worse-decline/.
193 "Nielsen Broadcast Data Encore/Nielen Soundscan", Nielsen. Accessed December 31, 2017. http://www.nielsen.com/bds.html.

business model and why it's a different business.

SPOTIFY

Streaming music sites merge the idea of acquiring music over the Internet (Rhapsody and Spotify) with social networking, tied to the labels' desire to make money and break new artists. The streaming sites (such as Spotify) sync everything on all our devices. Amazon.com offers its Prime Music and digital store with its corresponding phone app and Kindle reader. Spotify is a European model that offers music free with advertisements, or for a low monthly fee without advertisements, and millions of songs we can listen to almost instantly. It has about 20 million paying subscribers ($10 per month) and 55-60 million free users who tolerate the advertisements. However, the service is quickly growing its audience base as consumers change their listening habits toward streaming. The common denominator is the music. It is the glue that connects the consumers to the acts and the labels intend to profit from that connection, along with the investors in the website providers. Spotify also has a "dashboard" function that provides artists' managers and labels with analytics (algorithmic curating) about the location, demographics, and minor psychographic lifestyles of their listeners. Very cool for decisions that need to be made about touring dates and locations, ticket sales, promotion, and merchandise offers.

STREAMING REVENUES VS. SALES

Recording artists make about 75¢ to a dollar on downloaded album sales, and on CD album sales about $1.50 to $2.25. They make about 8¢ -12¢ or more for a one-song recording. Labels gross about $7.00 on an album purchase and about 70¢ on a single sale, out of which they have to pay mechanicals, artist royalties, and other administrative fees. How much do they make from one stream? Hold on to your hat, as this will give us a clue about the economics of streaming for the artist and label.

DIFFERENT ROYALTIES

Royalties earned may depend on whether the Internet Service Provider or ISP -Spotify or Pandora- is paying subscriptions or drawing down advertising based revenues. As an example, if the customer buys a single CD or digital download, the label will owe the royalty artist close to 8¢-12¢. Nonetheless, labels receive $0.0012 from Spotify on an advertising revenue stream free to the consumer and $0.0059 on a subscription stream. Both streams pay far less than one-cent and the artist may be paid zero depending on the deal with the label. To counter the loss of revenue, the major labels receive 70% of all of Spotify's generated revenues. The R.I.A.A. recently determined that 1,500 streams will equal one album sale and 150 stream is equal to one single song sold. The key revenue stream for the labels is streaming as, for the first time, streaming generated more money than album and single physical sales in 2016.

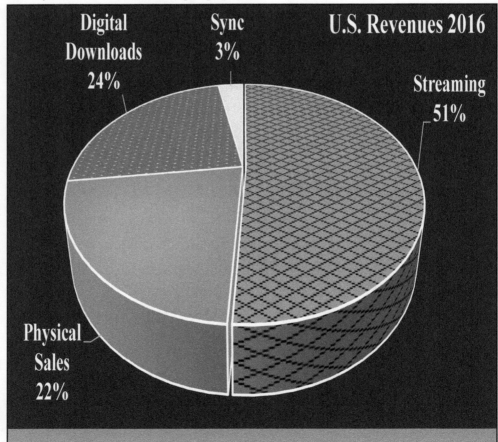

Figure 8.14: In 2016 in the United States, the labels' revenues in streaming moved over the 50% mark for the first time. Trends indicate continued downward sales for both physical and digital downloads and significant increases in streaming. Note, the digital downloads also include ringtones.[194]

Another way labels make a small amount of money is to force provides who accept non legal uploads of their recordings by consumers to pay them for their use. One view or listen to a copy (audio) is a violation. On the other side, You Tube and others are often seen by the industry as promotion. Nevertheless, labels then threaten them for money or shut them down. Sort of a sleazy way of doing business, as the labels would rather be paid for their copyrights, but since that hasn't happened yet, they have been forced to "do their best" in this unregulated vacuum. What would happen if the legal shoe drops on YouTube? According to a January 2015 article on *PollStar*, industry insider Irving Azoff is getting ready for that to happen,

> . . . mogul Irving Azoff formed performing rights organization Global Rights Services and ended the new year rattling his formidable sword at the online video service over 20,000 songs, for which he figures YouTube owes $1 billion.[195]

LEGAL/MULTIPLE RIGHTS

Multiple rights refer to the legal side of the 360 deals. Labels now make multiple revenues that used to only be paid to the artist. As an example, labels now provide and are part of tour support money, branding, merchandise fulfillment, and corporate sponsorships. Notice this list does not mention selling recordings! So the labels have had to bridge the traditional recoupment business model and the artist personal management business model to generate enough revenues to remain close to profitable. Attorneys draw up contracts that connect licensing of the act's branding opportunities, merch fulfillment, and other revenue generating opportunities.

---

194 Friedlander, Joshua P. "News and Notes on 2016 RIAA shipment and Revenue Statistics." RIAA 2016 Year End News Notes. 2017. Accessed July 8, 2017. http://www.riaa.com/wp-content/uploads/2017/03/RIAA-2016-Year-End-News-Notes.pdf.
195 Speer, Deborah. "2014 IN REVIEW." Pollstarpro.com. January 9, 2015. Accessed November 25, 2015. http://www.

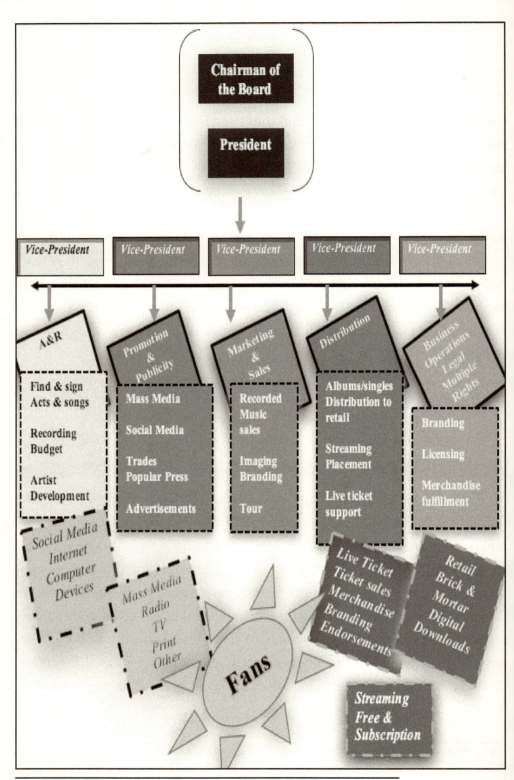

pollstarpro.com/NewsContent.aspx?cat=&com=1&ArticleID=815796.

The labels then receive a percentage of the gross revenues from merchandise, corporate sponsorships, and endorsements and the acts gross revenues (sometimes depending on which is greater). The branding side of the industry is estimated at $2.1 billion annually.[196] On the previous page note the label's process for signing the act to the point of launching their career and corresponding products. Connect the various label departments with each other and how they work as teams to provide promotion and publicity through the mass and social media to launch the acts new products including recordings, streams, brands, merchandise, corporate sponsorships and of course, the live ticket concert tours. Remember our hard lesson, the purpose of all of this hard work and investment in talent, creativity, and people is profit. This is a business. . . a fun business, but still a business.

SUMMARY

Record labels have changed their business models from selling recordings to adopting a multiple rights business model, which extends to both the products (recordings) and the service (recording to streaming providers) while supporting, and profiting from, the live ticket events of their artists. It's the 360 deals the labels have switched into that allows them to continue to sign acts, record albums, and market, promote, and distribute recordings.

However, record sales have dropped from $23 billion in 1999 to less than $5 billion in 2017. The added revenues from the streaming and artist's gross revenues (10%-12%) have not yet made up 50% of the money lost due to the decline in album and single unit sales. Independent labels make up about 20% of the gross revenues generated by the business. This has created a great opportunity for entrepreneurs, artists, musicians, and executives to start their own labels. If they can become successful locally, then the major labels may come in and buy them out for significant amounts of money.

---

[196] "Branding." Branding | Billboard. Accessed July 12, 2017. http://www.billboard.com/biz/branding.

Many of the newly signed acts think the 360 deals are unfair until they try making it as an independent. Then, they discover how much the label's money, and the Departments of A&R, Promotion and Publicity, Marketing and Sales, Distribution, and Legal/Multiple Rights help their careers, they tend to change their minds. The major labels including Warner Music Group, Sony Music, and Universal Music Group are managed by a team of executives topped by a Chairperson of the Board or CEO.

The CEO handles the external connections and communications with the parent company or mega-entertainment corporation. CEOs are the top executives, and are responsible for establishing a strategic management plan, including financial goals to be generated by the label business. The President serves under the CEO and is responsible for the internal administration and the day-to-day operations that are designed to achieve the strategic management plan's annual goals

In the next chapter, it's time to examine what the artist is responsible for accomplishing in the first year after the deal has been signed. But, before moving to the next chapter, please review the following "Block of Knowledge" and make sure you understand the layers of information and also consider how each layer relates to the one above or below it. Put is all together and you'll start to understand how labels really operate.

Creating Profits Out of Creativity
Chapter Eight

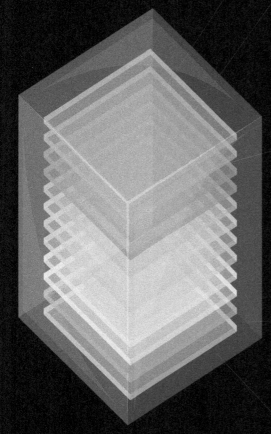

Elements Within
The Music Business
To Better Understand How
To Create Profits out of Creativity

Label Administration
  Weekly Meetings
  Financial formulas

Department of A&R
  Signing Acts & Songs
  Exclusive Recording Deals
  (Deal Points)
  Recording Budgets
  Artist Development

Department of Promotion
& Publicity
  Radio
  (Radio Programming)
  Mass Media
  (Day Parts)
  Social Media

Department of Marketing & Sales
  Market Research
  Branding

Department of Distribution
  Recorded Music
  (Retail & Digital)
  Mass Media
  (Day Parts)
  Free Goods/Promotional Copies
  ISRC & UPC Codes
  Streaming
  Sound Exchange

I believe it is important to sign the best talent, preferably an artists who can perform live as well as on record.

Often the best country stars are like rock starts who can put on a great performance and captivate an audience. If we achieve this, then a hit record can be taken to the next level and create a career for an artist who will become a star.

Records will mean more and sell more because they will be part of the body of work of a star.

- Mike Curb [197]

---

197 Mike Curb, with Don Cusic, Living the Business. Nashville, TN: Brackish Publishing, 2017: 364.

Chapter 9

The First Year

Are you starting to sense the difference between the traditional business model and the 360 model, where any entertainment products consumers want will be available anytime? Retail stores in malls are closing quickly, radio and TV stations are struggling to maintain audiences, and at the same time, Jeff Bezos (who started Amazon.com) is now the second richest man in the world. According to *USA Today* (2017),

> Jeff Bezos, Amazon (AMZN) founder and CEO, is now the second-richest person on the planet, besting Warren Buffett of Omaha-based investment conglomerate Berkshire Hathaway (BRKA). Bezos' wealth climbed to $75.6 billion on Wednesday, according to the Bloomberg Billionaires Index. As the music business continues to change, we'll see more of these types of rags to riches stories and my guess is that it will have something to do with streaming.[198]

The music industry is probably ahead of what's going to happen to other types of businesses as consumers adopt digital devices and the Internet for their purchasing of almost all products and services. The music business has been able to move through the creative destruction process that everything from politics and education are about to encounter.

THE ARTIST'S PERSPECTIVE

In Chapter Eight we examined the 360 business model from the labels perspective, in this chapter we'll look at it from the acts perspective. In the first year, newly signed acts usually start to wonder where's the money or a better way to say it; Where's my money? Good question as this is the time many of the acts' relatives start coming out of the woods (some of whom you've never known). Of course, they think that now that your

---

198 M, Laura, and Aro Network. "Jeff Bezos is now the second-richest person in the world." USA Today. March 30, 2017. Accessed July 09, 2017. https://www.usatoday.com/story/tech/talkingtech/2017/03/29/jeff-bezos-worlds-second-richest-person/99810880/.

signed to a major label deal, you must be worth millions and they just need this little loan, gift, or whatever.

Little do they know the business, let alone that you haven't really earned any money yet. But it brings up a darn good question, how does an artist in todays industry make money? We've looked in previous chapters how the label executives think, how they invest their time and money into an act and how they project profits. But how about the act? How can the artist make the labels investment of $500,000 to $2,000,000 profitable for the label and at the same time make a buck or two for themselves? Here's the reality side of the industry or the under belly where the creative artist sometimes feel as if they are a coal miner in debt to the company (the man) and they can never seem to pay back their obligated debt. Some seem to think they are working this month to pay off last months debt and they never make enough to pay off the debt and move on. If you don't get the concept watch the first few minutes of the movie *Coal Miner's Daughter*, which is the life story about artist Loretta Lynn.

Labels invest in creative artists and treat them well on the front end, yet executives have told me "we expect them to work hard and make sure that we make our profits on the back end". In reality, acts do not owe any money to the labels (if it's a legit deal), as the labels are investing in the act's creativity on a bet that the artists will become successful and everyone will generate profits. However, the labels usually take their profits first and pay their expenses or bills back out of a percentage of the artists royalties. In the old days the percentage was 100% on artists royalties paid on albums and single sales when the industry was only about selling recordings.

The break-even points were 150,000 to about 225,000 albums sold and all of the act's royalties were used to pay off the debt. However, due to the way the deals were constructed (by the label's attorney), the break-even point before the act often started making any money was about half a million units sold. The difference between the true break-even point and the act's break-even point provided the labels with a profit of roughly a million or more. Not a bad deal, a million dollar investment and a million dollar profit. The acts were paid zip but were making significant money as they got 100% of the live ticket money for their performance, merchandise, and from corporate sponsorships.

The act still use the fame labels create for them with radio airplay and album promotion to profit from the live ticket and merchandise sales. And what the heck, the labels pay all the money required to hire the best musicians, back ground sings, rent the studio, and hired a world class producer. In addition, the labels pay for the distribution, promotion of the act and the recordings and also pay for publicity. All of it didn't cost the act a dime! If it works the labels might make a profit from the sale of the recordings. If the label sells between about 500,000 units (where they didn't have pay the act royalties) and 1,000,000 units sold the act's mail box often see a check of about one million dollars as the royalties start to kick in. What happens if the label and act fail to generate consumers' excitement? The act is dropped from the deal and they do not owe the label a dime.

Well, the industry has changed with the demand for free recordings by consumers. You see where this is headed, if the labels can't make back their money on album and single recording sales they've have to go where the money is and that's the live ticket. What this really means is that acts have had to give up a percentage (10-15%) of their gross income from the live ticket and other events and revenue streams to the labels in order for the labels to stay in business. Let's be honest, even the most successful acts today still want and sometimes need the labels tour support money to stay on tour and generate needed new monies from the live ticket events.

Live Ticket

The record labels have used the 360 deal as their solution to the creative destruction of album sales. With their backs to the wall, they have been able to transform their business model in a way that supports the rest of the industry. It's true that artists have had to give up a percentage of their gross revenues that were not previously connected to the record labels. However, artists are now made to realize labels invest the money often required for a new act on the front end to break into the industry, but the labels are going to receive part of the acts gross revenues on the back end. The 360 deals are a necessary step in the sustainability process for both the act and label. The end game is everyone works more closely together, not only on breaking of the act, but also during their entire career. The label consults more with the artists, personal managers, and acts as a fulfillment company for merchandise and other items associated with branding and the live ticket. Even the songwriters and music publishers profit from the 360 deal arrangements as the money they formerly received from Mechanical Licensing has dropped dramatically from the decline in album sales, yet they now receive some money from the streaming. Now because the labels have survived, and provide recordings to streaming companies, songwriters and music publishers again find themselves profiting from this new revenue stream.

The recording artists have also had to change under 360 deals. They now have to accomplish much more than just record and perform at shows. Sure, they still need the wow vocals and songwriting skills, but now add amazing showmanship with wow live performances, acting skills for media, and iconic and charismatic branding, pitching or sales skills. Fans' money spent on live event ticketing, merchandise, and branded products drives up the artist's gross revenue. And remember, labels receive 10%-15% under multiple rights agreements. These other revenue streams added together have totaled only about half of the revenue labels made selling albums in 1999 which was $23 billion. Yet, the direction is toward full financial recovery over the next several years.

Distribution's job in the live ticket or touring marketing is the fulfillment of any label's legal obligations contracted with the artists concerning the manufacturing, placement, and sales of approved merchandise and branded products. It's often to the artist's advantage to let the label sub-contract the design, manufacturing, placement and sales of these items at a lower cost than the acts could arrange themselves. The acts simply get a check indicating their percentage of royalties from sales instead of having to put up the front money to have the items created, placed, and sold at concerts.

THE NEW ACT'S FIRST YEAR

If a band gets a major label offer and accepts it, over the next year they will be put through a step-by-step process before the label unveils the recordings and the act on a tour. Now that we have an idea of what the label is doing the first year, what is the artist supposed to accomplish? Here's an example of what the artist will need to accomplish in one year.

Representation

- Interview personal managers and hire one with the approval of the label
- Sign Personal Management Agreement after reviewing it with an independent lawyer
- On the recommendations of the personal manager, select a booking agent, and a business manager, and later, a road manager and tour support personal

Studio

- Record an album or a number of singles for release by the label
- Hire a producer with the approval of the label
- Find songs for an album and submit them to the producer for approval
- Write and submit a recording budget to label for their approval
- Secure all third parties for the album production, including musicians and singers.
- Locate the studio best- suited for the act and rent it with the approval of the label.

Label Relations

- Meet with all label personnel from executives to interns and get to know their names. Ask for their suggestions and ask what you might provide that would improve their ability to market or sell you.

Artist Development

- Set up a music publishing company co-owned with label
- Refine songwriting skills with noted songwriters
- Write new songs (if possible)
- Further define and develop personal image and branding matched to target market consumers' tastes
- Learn about your consumer base of fans (psychographics of who they are, where they live, and personal preferences), so that you know how to talk to them and greet them.
- Media trainings on how to dress, wear makeup for TV, and live shows (including the male artists)
- Develop interview and media skills for shameless self-promotion
- Take acting and, sometimes, dance lessons for stage movement and videos
- Work with a weight trainer, nutritionist, and in the gym for better physical conditioning
- Take voice lessons to learn how to perform nightly and save vocal chords.

Branding

- Attend branding meetings with label executives and independent marketing specialists to develop a brand
- Meet and participate in developing a branding marketing plan

Promotion

- Radio station tour of key radio stations and networks to meet and

- greet music directors and others who may play your recordings
- Attend photo shoots to have promotion and publicity pictures taken and approved
- Shoot a music video and submit final edit to label for approval
- Set up official website with label independent contractors
- Supply all required information to website with label's approval
- Meet with advertisers when called on by label executives

Publicity

- Meet with publicity at label and provide interviews for the trade and popular press
- Develop a social media platform and activate it with approval of label
- Meet with TV show producers to develop a talk show schedule
- Provide scaled interviews to radio stations networks
- Approve all photographs, videos, and marketing materials used in publicity
- Designate one charity for publicity and promotion purposes

Marketing

- Meet with marketing and sales to help develop and understand the marketing plan and submit to label for approval
- Be available for point of purchase retail, if needed
- Be available for meeting Internet streaming executives
- Provide all information required for website presence
- Meet with distribution, marketing with the personal manager to approve all fulfillment merchandise (including designs and logos) for tours, if in the label deal contract
- Approve all photographs
- Approve all budgets for marketing plans

Live Show & Tour

- Meet with executives and invite them to rehearsals for tour
- Make sure representation and label executives are working together on all aspects of tour fulfillment
- Meet with executives provide tour support and co-advertisement funds for sponsoring radio stations, offer your assistance to promote (when requested).

Established acts have already been through the step- by- step process and the label executives will continue to support the act and their representation to build the act's career into superstar status, if possible. Can you start to see why it takes about a year for the labels to prepare an artist for the first album release and tour? The more successful the artist becomes, the busier they will be with all of the above items to increase their fan base.

THE LABEL'S FIRST YEAR

The label is also in the touring or live ticket game, as they have provided the front money (tour support) for the acts to start their concert business and they receive 10-15% of all the artist's gross revenues. They don't want the act priced too low or too high, as that might cause most of the promoters to pass until the act gains enough fame and fans to warrant a reasonable tour. On the other hand, the purpose for being on the road and providing live shows is exposure and building the fan base. The trick is to jumpstart the act's touring business by matching the act to the venues and expected fan base, allowing the fans to connect with the act and spread the news and excitement about the performance through social media.

If you are on an independent label, then beginning acts expect to just break even on a show and start a positive buzz with the attending fans who connected with the artists and their performance. This type of buzz is just pulling their act together and they are learning the business and certainly not ready to be seen by a major label's A&R Department.

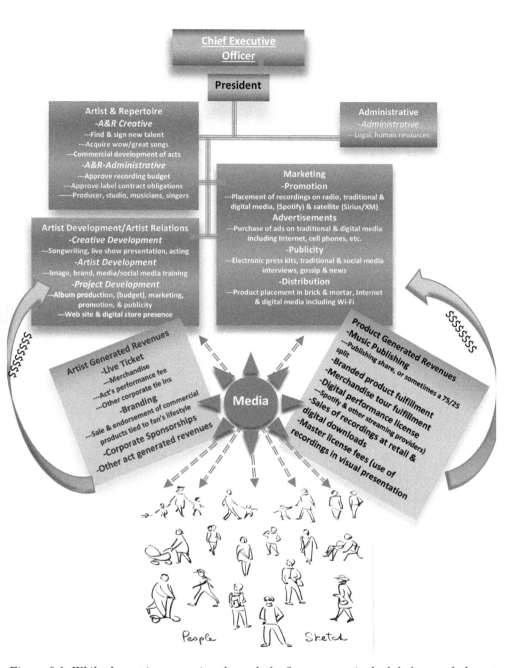

Figure 9.1: While the act is processing through the first year, so is the label as each department develops the act and their corresponding products such as recordings, show, brands, and image to "launch" through traditional, social media. The streaming media's use of the recordings, the sale of the live ticket and merchandise, plus endorsements generate funds and profits for the label.

Throw a few amps and guitars in a van and let's put on a show is the point they are at in their careers. No money is involved, and, therefore, professional representation is out of the question. The band and artists that have hit local and regional success are touring and making a decent living in the process. However, they are also stuck under the glass ceiling as they can't get the promotion and publicity needed to take them to the next level. Their budget is tied to paying the bills, and, probably supporting the family.

The regional acts who are noticed by the major labels may be invited to provide a showcase (for A&R), putting them on their way to a larger market, if they can secure a major label deal. If they fail, then an independent label may step in and sign the act hoping they can "pump them up" to a level where the major labels will want to buy out the deal.

LABEL ANALYSIS OF TOUR NUMBERS

The label executives review the numbers in their weekly meetings to see if the live ticket shows are increasing ticket sales, unit sales, streams, merchandise sales, and, if any possible branding or corporate offers have been made. Once you have achieved some success in the industry, you should be aware of the following professional organizations and research companies that will provide you and industry sources detailed information about your concert gross revenues, the numbers of times your songs have been streamed, the analytics of your tours and the best locations for you to meet and greet your fans.

COMPUTING ROYALTIES

The amount of money an act actually puts into to bank depends on many variables. But let's answer the act's question. Where's my money? In simple terms traditional record labels signed acts, funded their recording of an album (10 songs) or an EP (4 songs), then promoted the recordings to mass media who would play them for free. They also provided funding for publicity (which many people assume is free, but it isn't) in order for the fans to discover more about the acts life and beliefs or "frame of ref-

erence". Remember what you read in the Chapter One abo
think and their connection to entertainment products?

In effect, the traditional labels get radio stations to play r
er famous recordings by giving them free recordings that w
draw an audience who wanted to hear the recordings. That allowed the stations to charge businesses for their advertisements. It's called air time and in most cases, the more powerful the station with the largest number of people listening bills the highest for their advertisements. By doing this freebie for the stations, labels provided a method for the consumers who listen to the station to "discover and enjoy" their recordings. And the radio stations made a profit off of a product they got free from the labels. Remember from the previous chapters we learned that radio stations still must pay a "public performance" fee for a blanket license from ASCAP, BMI or SESAC in the United States and other PROs overseas for the right to use the songs in the recordings for their businesses. Still, getting the recordings free from the labels helps their financial bottom line.

The recording artist who now has their recordings on many radio stations is still yelling "where's my money". This is about the time the act learns they are not paid for radio station airplay of their recordings. In most of the world they are, but not in the United States as the radio stations have a powerful lobbing organization that continues to persuade Congress to leave the law as it is written. The sixth exclusive right has started to change this. Radio station signals transmitted over the Internet now pay a small royalty fee to Sound Exchange as authorized by Congress to collect fees for the label, acts, and original musicians on the session.

SOUNDEXCHANGE

SoundExchange collects royalties and fees ($3 billion plus, since it was commissioned by Congress in 1995), and pays them to directly to their 110,000 members consisting of the featured (royalty artists) and non-featured performing artists, (musicians and background singers), and the la-

owns of the copyright of the master recording.[199] Licenses are [issu]ed for companies digitally transmitting the recordings of songs over the Internet, including Sirius XM satellite, non-interactive webcaster, and cable TV music channels, who are required to pay this digital performance royalty license fee.[200] The January 1, 2018 to December 31, 2022 rates for satellite audio radio services are 15.5% of gross revenues and 7.5% of gross revenues for per-existing subscription services (Sirius XM) which are described as PSSs.[201] For commercial webcasters, the rates are $500 per-station or channel and for webcasters with over 100 stations the fee is $50,000. The monthly liability is $0.0018 per-performance for non-subscription transmissions and $0.0023 per-performance for subscription transmissions. For non-commercial webcasters, the rates are $0.0018 per excess performance.[202]

The Small Print in the Deal

As you can understand, record labels in the past made most of their money from the sale of the recordings. The artists were paid a percentage of the retail or wholesale price of the recordings depending on the deal they made with the labels. Thus, if the act signed a recoupment deal on the release of the recordings they were and still are often paid a percentage of the suggested retail or wholesale list price (SRLP or WLP). However, the deals usually have a couple of surprises build into the small print in the back of the contract.

Here's an example of what I'm talking about. Let's say you are the artists and your attorney negotiates 14 "points" on your album deal. That simply means you'll receive 14 percent of the SRLP which the label sets at $16.95. In reality, we know the album may be sold for $12.95 at most stores yet, that does not matter as the amount of artist's royalties are based on the SRLP not on what the album is sold for at retail.

---

199 Speer, Deborah. "2014 IN REVIEW." Pollstarpro.com. January 9, 2015. Accessed November 25, 2015. http://www.pollstarpro.com/NewsContent.aspx?cat=&com=1&ArticleID=815796.
200 "SoundExchange." SoundExchange. 2014. Accessed November 24, 2015. http://www.soundexchange.com/about/.
201 (https://www.crb.gov/), Copyright Royalty Board. "Current Developments." Copyright Royalty Board. December 14, 2017. Accessed January 01, 2018. https://www.crb.gov/.
202 "Noncommercial Webcasters 2018 Rates." SoundExchange. Accessed January 01, 2018. https://www.soundexchange.com/service-provider/rates/noncommercial-webcasters-rates/.

Financials	Details of Royalties
$16.95	SRLP
X .14	Times the acts royalty points
$2.37	What the act expects on each unit sold

Thus, the artist is usually assuming they will be paid about $2.37 on each album or unit sold. But now for one of the surprises, called a packaging, or breakage or digital storage fee. It's important for the personal manager and attorney to explain what this means to the act before they sign the deal; however, it's not always done or the act is so excited they just sign the deal without really reading and understanding what it means to them and their long term career.

Financials	Details of Royalties
$16.95	SRLP
X .25	Package/Breakage/Storage fee (Percentage)
$4.25	Package fee total
$12.70	Royalty base (SRLP minus the Package Fee)
X .14	Times the acts royalty points
$1.78	What the acts expects now on each unit sold

When the package/breakage/storage fee is added, a new royalty base is created which reduces the acts royalty to what appears to be $1.78 per-unit sold. That's a lose of almost 59 cents per-unit sold due to the small print in the back of the contract.

Financials	Details of Royalties
$16.95	SRLP
X .25	Package/Breakage/Storage fee (Percentage)
$4.25	Package fee total

Financials	Details of Royalties
$12.70	Royalty base (SRLP minus the Package Fee)
X .11	Times the acts royalty points. The artist who "hires" the producer pays the producer "points" out of their "points. Let's say the act pays the producer 3 points or 3% out of their 14%.
$1.40	What the acts expects now on each unit sold

But we're not done. The act who hired the producer may also have to pay 1%-3% of their royalty points to the producer. That reduces the acts royalties to $1.40 per-unit sold, a loss of 97 cents or almost 41% of the original royalty of $2.37. Now that we know how much the act might make, how much might the label make off of its' investment.

As previously stated, the labels "sell" the $16.95 SRLP album to a whole sale company for between 40% to 50% of the SRLP of $16.95 (depending on the type of distribution) or between $8.48 to $6.78. We'll use the average of the two or $7.63 per-unit the label makes. Note that the labels do not make the full SRLP of $16.95, but only 40% to 50% of that sum as the whole seller usually sells the album for an additional 20% of the SRLP, half of which goes to the major record label distribution wing or sub distributor and the other 50% to the local distributer. The wholesaler delivers and sells the album to a store (retail outlet) for between $10.17 and $11.87. We'll use the average of the two again which is $11.02 The difference between the wholesale price of $11.02 and what the store sells the album to customers for is the stores profits.

The adjusted $1.40 (artist royalties) to be paid to the artist is redirected to the artist's debt account at the label. Remember, the act does not owe any money to the label, but the label uses the artist's royalty to pay off their investment in the artist debt account at the label.

Financials	Details of Royalties
$7.63	Label receives from whole seller
(-) $1.40	Royalty paid to artist re-coupable fund at label
$6.23	Profit to the label per-unit sold
Zero	Amount paid to artist

Remember, the artist is yelling "where's my money"? Are you starting to see why the artist is not going to receiving any royalties until the full debt is paid at the label? Let's look at how many units the label will have to sell before the artist starts receiving their royalties. The label sold the album to a whole seller for an average of $7.63. They subtract the $1.40 they own the artist (per-unit royalty) and apply it to the act's debt account at the label. Thus, if there is a million dollar debt at the label and the label sell one album, the debt is reduced to $999,998.60. Now, please remember the debt is the labels, not the acts. They are just recouping their investment in the act until the artist's royalties pay off their investment (debt). Once the debt is paid off, then the $1.40 artist's royalty is paid to the artist.

Financials	Details of Royalties
$7.63	Label receives from wholesaler
(-) $1.40	Royalty paid to artist re-coupable fund at label
$6.23	Profit to the label per-unit sold
Zero	Amount paid to artist
$1,000,000	Artist debt account at label
Divided by	Total debt divided by the artist royalties ($1.40 per-unit)
$1.40	
714,285 Units	Number of units needed to be sold before the ACT breaks-even
Zero	Amount of artist royalties paid act

The numbers are in the label's favor; yet, they put their $1,000,000 or so into the act's creative efforts in hope of making a profit. If the act hits as in this case, the label receives over three million dollars in profits before the act receives any money from album sales. If the act fails, then the act walks and the label must swallow the loss from their investment. But not all is lost for the artist either as they may now be famous from the radio station airplay, promotion, and publicity. They either have or sign a personal manager who then exploits the fame of the act into profits from concerts, merchandise sales, corporate sponsorships, and other sources.

Financials	Details of Royalties
$7.63	Label receives from wholesaler
(-) $1.40	Royalty paid to artist re-coupable fund at label
$6.23	Profit to the label per-units sold
Zero	Amount paid to artist
$1,000,000	Artist debt account at label
Divided by $6.23	Total debt divided by the label's profit per-unit sold minus the artist royalties ($1.40 per-unit)
160,513	Number of units needed to be sold before the LABEL breaks- even
714,265 Units	ARTIST break-even point (units sold)
160,513 Units	Number of units needed to be sold before the LABEL breaks- even
553,752 Units	DIFFERENCE
X $6.23	Label receives per unit-sold
$3,449,874.00	Profit label makes before artist starts to receive any artist royalties
Zero	Amount of money the artist's is paid per-unit sold.

The producer's royalties are held by the label so that the artist does not have to pay the royalties out of their own pockets if the project breaks-even. Otherwise, the act would have to pay 3% of the royalty base $12.70 on every album sold after the break-even point which is $1.78 minus $1.40 or 38 cents per-unit. One additional point is to never sign a deal with the producer that make you (the artist) pay for royalties for all the albums sold from day one. In our situation that would be 714,265 units or $271,420.70.

If the album is sold at wholesale, such as an Internet sale on iTunes, then the act receives their royalties based on the albums WLP which is usually around $10.00. Now the acts' 14 points minus the 3 points held for the producer results in 11% of the ten dollar WLP or $1.10 instead of the $1.40 they were making through traditional brick and mortar retail. Another 30 cent loss to the act. Remember the act thought they were getting 14% of the SRLP of $16.95 which was $2.34. However, due to the details in the deal and the switch by consumers to digital downloads, the act only ends up with a royalty between $1.40 to $1.10 per-unit sold, which is a loss of between $1.27 to 97 cents per-unit sold.

MULTIPLE RIGHTS PAYMENTS

Multiple rights payments to the act on branding, merchandise, corporate sponsorship and other items are not really royalties. They are simply a percentage of the net after all expenses are paid by the label for the creation, manufacturing, production, advertisements, distribution, sales, and promotion of the item being marketed.

- Branding is usually determined before the new acts are signed to the label in order for a "brand" to be established for the artist and then an analysis of the potential corresponding products and profits are added to the bottom line to determine if the act is worth signing.

- Merchandise sales are analyzed base on the potential popularity of the act tied to the live ticket. It's the size of the audience of ticket buyers and their age, gender, income, and psychographic "world view" or lifestyle that are also considered before the act is signed. Remember, again what you learned about this in Chapter One. Now you can understand why it important in the 360 music industry to know the fans preferences. Low numbers on an audience draw reduces the labels opportunity to profit off the additional multiple rights granted by the artists who signs the deal as fewer branded products, merchandise, and corporate sponsorships will be sold. Once again, the label is looking at how much profit they make off of their $500,000 to $2,000,000 investment into the act. Being a fulfillment company of the merchandise is just another way the labels are making more money off the acts live ticket events.

- Corporate sponsorships are provided by companies who want to link their products to the lifestyle of the fan base of the artists. Sponsorship may be initiated by the personal management company, the label, or by a company who approaches the act directly. By linking the product to the act, corporations connect to the artist fans and their excitement for the act is connected to their products. In turn, this emotional connection may encourage the fans to "look" favorably on the products which they may than want to buy, rent, or lease which drives up the corporations profits. Typical sponsorship are priced at everything from equipment usage to millions of dollars.

- As I've said many times, the labels are now having a difficult time selling recordings to the public at the rate and amount found in the past. Thus, they demand in the 360 deals between 10% to 15% of the artist's gross revenues. In reality, it's a kickback fee to the labels for investing in the artists creative careers. The other side of the coin is that labels are receiving Master License fees from streaming companies such as Spotify in the millions of dollars; and, yet they are not paying their recording artist's (nore do they need to) any of those fees to make up for the lost artist royalties due to the decrease in album and single sales.

THE RECORDING INDUSTRY ASSOCIATION OF AMERICA

The R.I.A.A. represents the major and independent record labels in the United States. They provide research, Congressional support, and the gold, platinum, and diamond awards based on record sales. According to the R.I.A.A. website (2017),

> The Recording Industry Association of America (RIAA) is the trade organization that supports and promotes the creative and financial vitality of the major music companies. Its members comprise the most vibrant record industry in the world, investing in great artists to help them reach their potential and connect to their fans. Nearly 85% of all legitimate recorded music produced and sold in the United States is created, manufactured or distributed by RIAA members.[203]

GOLD, PLATINUM, & DIAMOND AWARDS

In the halls of many of the executive offices in major labels are the old vinyl gold records awards hanging on the walls. Success was visually hanging right in front of me as I'd walk down the halls to meetings. A gold award is for the pressing, selling, or the streaming equivalent (1,500 streams equal one sale) of 500,000 units; platinum is a million and diamond for ten million.

THE INTERNATIONAL FEDERATION OF THE PHONOGRAPHIC INDUSTRY (IFPI)

The International Federation of the Phonographic Industry is similar to the R.I.A.A. The IFPI represents 1,300 labels and industry entities in sixty countries. The organization is headquartered in London and has offices in Asia, Latin America, and Europe. They cover specific insights and analysis on recorded music sales and label operations from a global perspective. They provide excellent research, education papers, and sourcebooks that present a solid assessment of the global music industry.

NIELSEN

Remember, Nielsen is a top research firm labels use to determine sales, streaming, and consumer behavior, plus consumer confidence, retail, and TV ratings. It uses SoundScan (a company it bought many years ago) to scan bar codes of recorded music sold at retail. Concert and other unit sales may be also reported to add to the totals. Billboard uses the reports to determine sales in chart listings and labels use them to determine artist unit sales. According to Nielsen.com (2017),

---

[203] "What We Do." RIAA. Accessed July 12, 2017. https://www.riaa.com/what-we-do/.

. . . Nielsen is the authority in tracking what music people are buying both in-store and digitally. Nielsen compiles data from more than 39,000 retail outlets globally, to help record labels, publishers, artists, artist management and performance rights organizations understand what albums, singles and music videos people are buying, and where they're buying them. . . .. On a weekly basis, Nielsen collects point-of-sale (POS) data in 19 countries. . . In the U.S. and Canada, physical and digital titles from venues, mass merchants, retail chains, independent record stores and digital download providers can be viewed by UPC, ISRC, artist, market, retailer type or genre. In Europe and Oceania, digital track and song sales are available in Austria, Belgium, Denmark, Finland, France, Germany, Greece, Ireland, Italy, Luxembourg, the Netherlands, Norway, Portugal, Spain, Sweden, Switzerland, the U.K., Australia and New Zealand.[204]

BILLBOARD

Billboard Magazine reports business information about the music industry weekly in print and daily online at *Billboard.com* and *Billboard.biz*. The two most important charts are *The Hot 100* and *The Billboard 200*. *The Hot 100* analyzes radio station air plays, single sales, and streaming plays to determine the top 100 singles in the United States. *The Billboard 200* is based on sales reports and streaming as 1,500 streams equals one album/unit sale. Other charts include Pop, R&B/Hip Hop, Latin, Dance/Electronic, Rock, Country, Christian/Gospel, and International rankings in various global territories. *Billboard* also offers several educational and networking conferences, including on festivals, and annual industry meetings.

VARIETY

Variety is the weekly trade magazine that reports box office revenues and business news about the film, movie, music, theater and other areas of the entertainment industry. Industry personnel rely on *Variety* to provide them with news and announcements about upcoming films, the new TV season and other opportunities for music to be incorporated into other forms of entertainment productions. As a music publisher and a record label, you would want them to place songs and recordings in their new productions.

---

204 Music Sales Measurement. Accessed July 13, 2017. http://www.nielsen.com/us/en/solutions/measurement/music-sales-measurement.html.

Visual production music supervisors who find your marketing and promotion in *Variety* will know how to reach you, as they need to acquire a Sync License from the music publishers for the use of a song and the labels for a Master License for the use of the recording of the song.

BUZZ ANGLE

Buzz Angle provides daily reports on the chart placement, sales, and streams of major labels and many addition acts signed on independent labels. They also provide a click-able drop down list where the number of streams and sales for recorded products are available for the major markets for setting up tours in the United States. Just to let you know how much the traditional industry has continued to shift toward the 360-business model, look at the 2017 year-end results from Buzz Angle (2018).

- There were only two albums to break 1 million pure album sales during 2017: top selling album of the year, Reputation by Taylor Swift, with 1,899,772 sales and ÷ by Ed Sheeran with 1,042,255 album sales.

- The top-selling vinyl album of the year was Guardians of the Galaxy: Awesome Mix Vol. 1 with 64,175 sales.

- The top digital album of 2017 was reputation by Taylor Swift with 865,446 digital sales.

- Audio streams reached a new record high of 376.9 billion, up 50% over 2016.

- Subscription streams grew 57% and accounted for 80% of total audio streams in 2017, up from 76% of total in 2016.

- There were more than twice as many streams on any given day during 2017 (daily average of 1.67 billion) than there were song downloads for the entire year (563.7 million).

- The daily average number of audio on-demand streams in 2017 was 1,057,218,000.[205]

---

205 BuzzAngle Music 2017 US Year End Report." BuzzAngle Music. Accessed January 26, 2018. http://www.buzzanglemusic.com/us-2017-ytd-report/.

Summary

It is often a surprise to recording artists who have signed a new deal the number and variety of entrepreneurial activities they need to complete in the first year. Each label department has several monetary, imaging, branding, and marketing issues the artists contribute to and approve. Thus, under the 360 deals, the artist and their personal manager will act more like partners with the label executives in the building of the artist's successful career.

In 360 deals, the acts themselves often approve related merchandise and endorsements finalized by the legal team, who controls the multiple or expanded rights in order to increase profits. Artists need to be available to the label executives to contribute to and acknowledge the executives' decisions. Even such simple items as photograph approvals for promotion and publicity are part of the first year job of the act. At the same time, the artist needs to remember that this is a business and therefore contracts and deals are often in favor of the labels desire to profit off their investment in the recordings, merchandises, corporate sponsorships, and live tickets events they have helped fund.

Nielsen Research, Buzz Angle.com, and the trade magazines, *Billboard, PollStar,* and *Variety* provide insights into the act's success with news, numbers, and charts such as the Hot 100 singles for airplay, sales, and streams, and the *Billboard* 200 for album sales with 1,500 streams equaling one unit sold. In chapter 10, let's look at the first major accomplishment the artist will need to achieve as the success of their career is based on what happens in the recording studio.

The First Year Experience
Chapter Nine

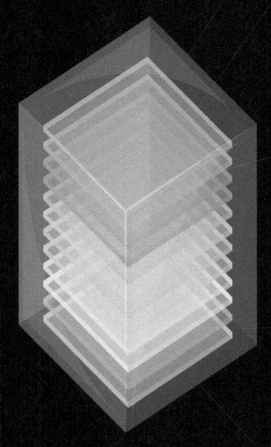

Elements Within
The Music Business
To Better Understand How
Signed Acts Use Their First Year

The First Year
Representation
(Artist Management)
Recording studio
(Creating an Album)
Label Relations
(People in Each Department)
Artist Development
(Songwriting)
(Media Training)
(Show Presentation)
Image
Branding
(Product Affiliation)
Promotion
(Radio Tour)
(Music Videos)
(Marketing Photo Shoot)
Publicity
(Press Stories)
(Trade Magazines)
(Radio & TV Interviews)
Marketing
(Advertisements)
Live Ticket/tour
(Rehearsal)
(Booking Agent to Place Tour)

Trade Magazine
Billboard
PollStar
Variety

Chapter 10
Creating Recordings

Labels create recordings in order to start the processes that lead to the promotion, publicity, marketing, distribution, streaming, and branding for the signed roster acts. The success of these steps should lead to trending unit sales, development of the live ticket revenues, and the end game in as steady a stream of profits as the label can hope to have.

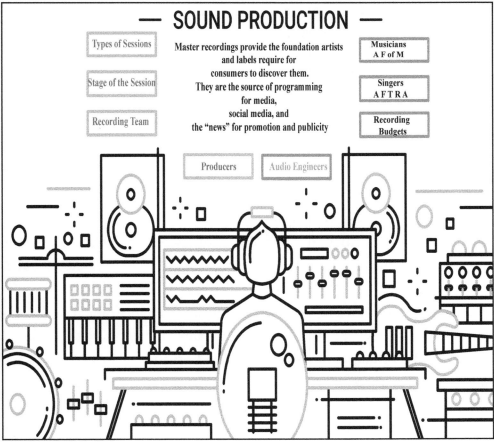

Without the recordings, nobody has a chance to discover the artists. Therefore, recordings are both an investment and a necessity in the label business. When I lay it out this way- first, you find the act, then, you develop it, and market it, it looks much easier than it is. One of the greatest record producers ever, Quincy Jones said what you're trying to do in the recording studio is *". . . to bottle lightning all the time. There's no use putting a record out unless it's got some magic on it. And magic doesn't come easy."*[206]

SHIFT OF FOCUS

Studio recordings have always been a tricky balance between money and time, which songs to select for specific artists that will be good for their sound, brand, and image, and how to monetize it all. In the entertainment business, there's an underlying philosophical conflict between the creative and business sides of the industry, especially in the recording studio. The labels want to spend less money and get the best out of their artists. The acts either think or know they will sound better if the labels will spend more! The successful industry professionals (both the creative and executives) have to accept these philosophical differences and work together to the create magic, or as Quincey Jones says, the "lightning in a bottle".

Nonetheless, when large sums of money are involved, attitudes often develop about where to draw the line between what is needed for "art" and what is affordable and will not disrupt profits for the label business. In the past, disagreements have ranged from friendly discussions to lawsuits, which sometimes defined the boundaries of conversations and long-term friendships. Some of that still exists; yet, with 360 deals and the revenues generated from album and single sales falling by almost 80% since 1999, recording budgets have had to change. Thus, the focus of the industry executives has shifted from spending the big bucks in the studio to the larger picture of the streaming, the live ticket, and branding. For producers and musicians, it a good thing to understand the economics of the industry. According to Jimmy Bowen, who has produced platinum albums and artists, including Frank Sinatra,

---

206 Quincy Jones, *The Recording Industry Career Handbook*, NARAS Foundations (NARAS: Los Angeles, CA) 1995. The phrase lightning in a bottle is used to describe something challenging, maybe impossible, that is dependent on luck more than well-laid plans.

> ...If you're going to be a record producer, you must have an overall knowledge of the music industry. From a business standpoint you must, at all times, know where the industry stands. ...for example, if you're about to meet with a label head to discuss producing an act... if you know what's going on in the state of the industry, you're not going to blow yourself out of the deal by coming in too high (asking for too much money).[207]

One of the things that "knowing what's going on" in the current music industry means is that newly signed acts are unlikely to sign a full album deal in their first contract. They will have to wait until the second or third year when their fan clubs and concert attendances numbers warrant it. Another thing this means is that only some of the tracks may be recorded in a studio with live musicians. The rest of the album and vocals may be produced using ProTools, with only the producer sitting by the artist's side. It's just much harder to create sellable tracks in a free world of streaming, so the budgets have been slimmed down whenever possible. Still, the labels want to support the acts in building their careers, so the very best producers, musicians, and vocalists are still hired for the sessions that are still being scheduled.

In the 360-deal music industry, the labels look to make recoupment deals. Though we have discussed these earlier, a recap as we start our look into the recording business is going to be helpful to get you focused on the significance of the type of deal to the recording budget. Recall that on the front end of a recording deal, the label acts as a bank, providing financial security to pay for the artists' recordings, tours, and advances and the artists never owe the label any money. It is the label that pays off the loan (to itself) by applying the artists' royalties and some of the streaming, branding, or live ticket revenues generated (depending on the detail in the contract) from each unit sold to a small percentage of the revenues generated to clear the debt.

---

[207] Jimmy Bowen (as quoted by Larry Wacholtz) *Inside Country Music*, Billboard Books, (New York: Watson-Guptil Publishers, 1986) & Larry Wacholtz, *Lights, Glitter and Business Sense*, Thumbs Up Publishing, (Washington: Cheney, 1984) 184-198

However, it's usually money the artist would receive in royalties if the debt had been paid off. It's rare for the label to contribute any of its revenues to the deal. Therefore, it is the label who signed, financed the master recordings, and marketing, promotion, etc., that pays off its own debt by using the act's royalties. What does it cost the artist? Only their talent and "best efforts" to create recordings and shows the labels may see generate some money for a profit. But, if the act is a bust, or a flop and consumers do not connect, then the act walks and does not own the label a dime. That is why it is so important for the label to make as many leveraged, or "right choices," as it can when it comes to selecting an artist or band. To help you see how that works, we are focused in this chapter on the recording process, the personnel and tools of the recording trade, and how to create recording budgets. Let's start with a tour of where we go to make that recording.

STUDIOS

To make money, labels and music companies invest capital in their signed artists and their hired recording teams, instead of financing recording studios. Traditional studios tend to be earmarked by their acoustics (sound) and "feel", as well as by equipment, cost, and reputation for the hits that were made there. In the past, these recording studios were more of an integral part of the music business than they are now, yet traditional studios fall into five categories:

- **Master Studios** – most master studios are solidly packed with the latest acoustic audio equipment and special effects toys producers use to create great tracks.

- **Project/Mini Studios** – fills the gap between the very expensive master studios and the basic demo studios. They are often filled with dated equipment and minor acoustics.

- **Post-Production Studios** – after overdubbing sessions, producers and artists often move to the special equipment in the post-production studio to mix the master tapes to computer flash drives.

- **Demo Studios** – these studios are often the older analog studios with minor special effects equipment. They are used for demos as well as vanity and limited budget recordings.

Labels still use traditional studios on some or all of the royalty artists' tracks, as the talents of the recording artists, musicians, audio engineer, and producers and the room acoustics may provide a better "feel" and sound then can be captured on software programs. Floating walls, ceilings, and floors are used to isolated sound from room to room in performance studios and control rooms. Grooves are cut into the floors, walls are mounted on rubber tubes, and ceilings are often spring-loaded. Windows between the performance rooms and control room are often made of two thick double-or triple-pane pieces of glass separated by several inches of air space. Soundproof doors complete the package. Studios are usually divided into

- **Performance rooms** where the royalty artists and musicians perform.

- **The Control room** where the producer and audio engineers supervise and control the quality and amount of the recorded signal.

- **Equipment rooms** that isolate the noise and heat generated by tape recorders, amps, computers, room equalizers, and most of the other electrical equipment needed in the traditional recording process.

- **Storage areas** where microphones, music stands headsets, cords, direct boxes, and other recording gear are stored.

These spaces are then inhabited by the recording team, the artist, and the musicians, who will work together to make the record.

THE RECORDING TEAM

Even superstars, who may like to think they are great in and of themselves, realize it's the talented studio musicians, backup singers, audio engineers, and record producers who create wow recordings that may lead to a famous and profitable career. The royalty artists (acts signed to the recording deal) job in the recording studio is to sing, plain and simple. It's the producer who is the boss, in charge of the final musical production. The audio engineer works for the producer. The engineer's job is to get the types of sound quality on the instruments and vocals that satisfy the producer. In these next paragraphs, we will take a quick look at who is in the studio and what they need to know to be valuable to the label. Whether you are an aspiring artist or you are drawn to the business of the music business, it is essential to know who is on your team, and if one of these positions interests you, how to get that job and stay in it.

PRODUCERS

The session producer is the captain of the ship, directing and stimulating the creative elements of the audio engineer, studio musicians, and recording artists through each stage of the recording. Suggested skills and knowledge include a passion for music, an understanding of music theory and sight-reading, and in some places knowledge of the "number system." Producers also need to know copyright laws, music publishing, business finance, and the music business subsystems. Musicianship skills are essential for music producers. Successful producers communicate well with others, are decisive leaders, understand basic accounting skills for controlling budgets, and have strategic management skills for administration. In addition, producers commonly have a consummate understanding of recording studio acoustics, basic electronics, equipment capabilities, and an almost magical ability to "marry" the right song to the right recording artist.

Producers know other industry professionals through networking, showcases, parties, meetings, professional organizations, industry events, award shows, etc., and the industry movers and shakers or the executives who fund the projects.[208] But in reality, everyone in the industry knows that producers usually got the act they are producing in the studio because of their last hit recording.

INDEPENDENT PRODUCERS

Independent producers begin their careers learning the trade by producing demo sessions for publishers and custom or vanity albums that are often non-label productions paid for by the recording artist or band. Demo recordings that showcase the recording artists or songs are "pitched" to a record label in order to get a publishing deal or a recording deal. Great demo recordings often lead to the next step in the career of a producer: working for a label in the A&R department, which may then bring many other opportunities.

Major independent producers are at the top of their game. They often earn $2,000-5,000 per side (per song) depending on the genre of music and the financial success of the acts they are producing. In addition, producers may receive points (usually 1-3%) of the artist's royalties on each unit sold. Major producers are highly respected for their abilities to produce hit records. Their successes make them behind-the-scenes stars within their own industry. Because major producers gain so much power and respect in the industry, they control their destiny as clever entrepreneurs by letting different labels and artists bid for their services. Sometimes, labels hire very successful producers as executives to run a label and use and protect their talents instead of competing with them.

STUDIO MUSICIANS

All musicians are creative artists, as it doesn't matter where they play or

---

208 Bruce Weber, "Jerry Wexler, A Behind-the-Scenes Force in Black Music is Dead at 91," New York Times, http://www.nytimes.com/2008/08/16/arts/music/16wexler.html?_r=2&hp=&pagewanted=all, (accessed March 19, 2011).

how much money they make. Although the royalty artists usually get the fans and fame, it is the musicians in the recordings session who recorded the tracks and the "feel" of the song in the recording who are the real heroes.

Working musicians are paid for their performances. Those who join the American Federation of Musicians union (AF of M) are properly represented in their careers. The musicians who recorded the tracks in the studio are rarely the road musicians backing the royalty artists in a live ticket event. Others may be classically trained and form smaller groups to perform at special social, political, or other types of events.

On the other hand, great studio musicians can make thousands of dollars a day, charging double or triple scale for a three-hour session. They often become true stars known only by the best producers and recording artists. Studio musicians play their instruments to highlight the marriage of the song to the vocal characteristics of the recording artist. Recording opportunities include music soundtracks for TV shows, movies, commercials, jingles, and major artists' recordings. Possessing musical talent is imperative if you want to be a recording artist or studio musician. In addition, a music education and an understanding of copyright law, music publishing, networking, and the music business are important for success.

AUDIO ENGINEERS

Audio engineers mix the creativity of music and the artistic capabilities of the artists, musicians, and background singers, usually called background vocalists (BGVs), to the technological potential of the studio's acoustics and equipment to record the best sound and performances. The successful audio engineer will want to have skills and knowledge of the business of music and entertainment, some music theory, familiarity with copyright laws, and an understanding of the systems of music publishing, marketing, management, and business finance. Knowledge of computer software programs, such as ProTools, and Logic Pro, are important, as the industry uses the less expensive software to save money on the recording projects. Audio engineers should also have a grasp of basic electronics, acoustics, and recording equipment variables. They should show a continuous desire to learn the latest technical advances in recording equipment and audio production. Communication skills and the ability to work with highly creative individuals are also helpful. They need to be able to have fun, experiment, be a little crazy and bend the rules, or do whatever it takes to get the best creative performance possible out the artists. In their 2011 book, *Come Together,* Courtney and Cassidy state,

> *George Martin (the Beatles' producer) brought a new engineer, Geoff Emerick, into the control room. ...Emerick had raised thought the EMI ranks quickly and was young enough to have a healthy disregard for the "rule, "a fact that endeared him to the Beatles. Emerick was not fazed when John Lennon told him that his voice should sound like the Dalai Lama singing from a mountaintop. Run the voice though a rotating speaker cabinet (normally used for an electronic organ). Problem solved. He thought nothing of flipping the tape around and recording a guitar solo with the tape reversed, so that when the song is played forward, the guitar solo is played backwards (this is a distinctive and now easily recognizable sound, in which each note fades in and ends with the "attach" of the plectrum). He was willing to cut a tape into little pieces, glue it all back together in random pieces, and add it to the final mix if that was what the Beatles wanted.*[209]

Entry-level audio engineers are often college students who are working in a studio as interns. At the same time, they are recording local musicians on the latest computer recording software. They are rarely paid for their efforts; however, they are given opportunities to learn the basics and to meet members of the creative team.

Second Engineers are a step up the ladder from entry-level engineers. They set up microphones, cables, headsets, the console, and alignment of the tape machines. Second Engineers may also run the tape machines,

---

[209] Richard Courtney & George Cassidy, *Come Together: The Business Wisdom of The Beatles*, (New York, NY: Turner Publishing, 2011) 101.

or computer software, keep the log sheets during the sessions, and occasionally, they will hone their audio and mixing skills by going on the road with artists.

Staff Engineers are sometimes employed at a recording studio, as they may have to record any level of session, from demo to master, with major recording artists and triple scale musicians. Major-Artist/Independent staff engineers are "on-call" for and most often to work on master sessions for label artists and known superstars. Their pay is negotiable, ranging between $1,000 a day, plus expenses, to huge per-side salaries based on their track record.

Royalty Artists

Labels sign *royalty artists* as independent contractors on a work-for-hire basis, meaning they will not own the recordings they are being paid to create. In addition, as the deal is a work-for-hire, they will not be able to "recapture" the copyright after 35-40 years, as they never were the copyright owners.

Both the royalty artists and the BGVs are required to be members of the Screen Actors Guild/American Federation of Television and Radio Artists union (SAG/AFTRA). Since the major labels are signatories to the union agreements, the singers and musician must be members of the union before they can work in a recording session.

Studio Singers

We have all seen the three to five people at the mics off to the side of the lead singers. These are the background singers provide the harmony in recording sessions and live performances. It is amazing how often background vocalists are needed to blend their voices with the main star to improve or "carry" the superstar act. Professional singers are found everywhere- on recordings, in choirs, advertisements, jingles, and movie soundtracks – you name it; they are there. Professional singers who work for studios frequently net more money than label artists, as they do not have to support an entourage of road musicians, managers, producers, and label marketing and promotion executives.

Demo singers find entry-level work at publishing companies singing demo recordings. Nonunion members and college interns may earn $10-$50 a song, which is not much money, but singing in a recording studio is different from performing in a choir or on stage. Demo sessions provide the novice studio singers with some valuable studio experience. The acoustics, lighting, and monitoring are often quite complex. So, the more experience gained in the studio, the quicker an artist may become a professional, royalty artist. There is also another advantage, as producers, A&R, and artist managers often listen to the demo tapes hoping to find a great song. Sometimes, they also find a great voice! Therefore, singing on demos is a great way to gain studio experience and be heard by many industry insiders who are seeking the "next big thing."

Now, let's take a look at the tools in the studio that create the sound which is what captures the emotion of the would-be consumer.

AESTHETICS

While musicians and vocalists create the music in the performance studio, the audio engineer and producer enhance the quality of the sound in the control room. They may use tone controls (equalizers) on the console to improve the quality of the signal. Just as colors of paint help create emotions in a piece of art, engineers use acoustics, microphones, and consoles to emphasize and match the "feel" of the song to the image, brand, and vocal characteristics of the recording artist.

MICROPHONES

Microphones convert soundwaves into electronic signals. They all sound different, have different axes, or acoustic points, for picking up sounds, and, contribute differently to the overall sound quality. Thus, engineers know which ones to select, and where to place them in the performance room, in the correct proximity to the talent and instruments. Proper selection and usage is often the difference between a "great" sounding session and something less.

Here is how the microphone system in a typical studio is made up:

- **Dynamic mics** have a coil or wire in the element (top) of the mic. Sound waves vibrate a plastic diaphragm connected to a coil of wire, moving the coil in and out of a permanent magnetic field. Electricity is created anytime you pass a wire through a magnetic force field. Thus, the movement converts the sound waves (acoustic waves) into an electronic signal.[210]

- **Ribbon mics** operate on the same principle as dynamic microphones, except they have flexible, metallic ribbons for sound waves to vibrate in and out on the permanent magnetic force field. Because the ribbon is flexible, the quality of the sound generated is often considered smoother and warmer.[211]

- **Condenser mics** have two plates that hold a static electronic charge. One is a permanent plate and the other is moveable. Sound waves move the moveable plate, changing the distance between the two plates, which generates an electrical output. Condenser microphones need batteries or a phantom power source supplied through the microphone cable.[212]

---

210 Answers.encyclopedia.com, "How Dynamic Microphones Work," Answers.encyclopedia.com, http://answers.encyclopedia.com/question/do-dynamic-microphones, (accessed August 5, 2010).
211 Answers.encyclopedia.com, "How Dynamic Microphones Work," Answers.encyclopedia.com, http://answers.encyclopedia.com/question/do-dynamic-microphones, (accessed August 5, 2010).
212 Answers.encyclopedia.com, "How Dynamic Microphones Work," Answers.encyclopedia.com, http://answers.encyclopedia.com/question/do-dynamic-microphones, (accessed August 5, 2010).

Pickup Patterns

Microphones have different pickup patterns or areas where they are most sensitive to sound. The patterns are used to acoustically isolate one instrument or vocal, excluding the leakage of sounds from other instruments or vocals into the microphone. Engineers also use pickup patterns to induce an acoustic mixture of "live" sound (omni-directional) from a very isolated single sound source. Consumers often feel the quality of the mixture of the sound as an emotion when they hear the recording. Examples include:

- **Omni-directional pickup patterns** allow sound waves to enter from all directions into the mic at approximately the same loudness level (measured in dBs).

- **Cardioid pickup patterns** cancel the sound coming from the sides and rear of the mic. Most engineers use mics with cardioid patterns to limit and avoid leakage problems that usually occur when using omni-directional mics.

- **Bidirectional pickup patterns** receive sound waves from the front and back of the mic and cancel out sound waves coming from the sides of the mic.

Consoles/Boards

Consoles act as traffic cops, dividing and directing the microphone signals and connecting instruments to various destinations, all at about 186,000 miles per-second. Each microphone is one signal controlled through one module in the console. Signal flow in the basic tracks stage of the recording session is from the mics in the studio into the console. The sound is split and sent to the 24-track tape machine or hard disk drive (computer); the monitors in the control room (speakers); the musicians' headsets (earphones); the effects (add echo, reverb, pitch control to signals); and, the two-track master tape machine or computer. Playback (to listen to the recording) reverses the signal flow from the tape machines or computer hard disk drive and allows the producer, audio engineer, musicians, and vocalists a chance to check their creative work.

Recorders/Software

Digital and analog tape machines are used to record a magnetic copy of both the amplitude (loudness) and frequency (number of vibrations per second) sent through the console (analog) or a pulse code modulation (digital) to the tape recorder.[213] The advantages of analog tape recordings for the label are a "warmer sound" at a lower price. However, there is also distortion of the signal and an unwanted tape hiss. Digital machines, on the other hand, convert the microphone electronic signals into binary codes of 0s and 1s (pulse or no pulse). They use the recording tape to store the binary code. It's the computer inside the tape machine that reproduces the sounds we hear as music. The advantages of digital recording include the lack of noise and distortion that are usually found in analog recordings. Computer software programs, such as Pro Tools and Logic Pro, are they sound great and cost very little compared to actual physical studios. Yet the quality of the music is linked directly to the ability of the engineers running the equipment.

Speakers

In the control room, the electronic signals (from the microphones to the console) are converted back into acoustic sound waves by monitors (speakers). To make sure they are providing a correct sound (flat frequency response), room equalizers are used to compensate for the "hype of the sound" created by the speakers and control room acoustics. As an example, control rooms are shot with "pink noise," which measures the frequency response to determine how to use the room equalizers to compensate for the acoustical problems. If the engineer and producer can't hear the music correctly, the final mix will be messed up as well.

---

213 Answers.encyclopedia.com, "How is Sound Recorded on an Audio Recorder," Answers.encyclopedia.com,

The electronic signals coming into the console from the microphones, tape machines, effects, and computer software programs are amplified and divided into different frequencies (bass, mid-range, and treble) by a crossover network (often in the speakers) and then sent to the corresponding bass, mid-range, and treble speakers, described below-

- **Woofer speaker** cones vibrate slowly and move a significant amount of air to reproduce bass frequencies.

- **Mid-range speakers** have smaller cones that vibrate faster which creates higher mid-range tones (frequencies).

- **Tweeters** reproduce the highest frequencies adding clarity to the quality of the music or sounds we're hearing.

The bass or lower frequencies have longer and more powerful wavelengths, while the highest tones are shorter and much more directional. Thus, room acoustics need to be correct in order for the audio engineer and producer to hear the signal correctly as they mix the tracks.

EFFECTS

Effects equipment, called "outboard gear," are devices used to improve, change, or fake the quality of the signal and overall "feel" consumers might perceive from listening to the signal (recordings). Of course, most of these "effects" are now generated within software programs. Commonly used generated effects include the following:

- **Compressions** are used to reduce the amplitude (loudness) of a signal to record a proper signal on analog tape. Compression is also used to change the quality of the sound of instruments and vocalists. Settings include compression ratios and attack and release times used to fatten or tighten the quality of sound (the sound of a kick drum or bass guitar perhaps).

- **Echo** is used to make the singer or instruments sound as if they were in a different size room than the actual recording studio. Long reflections of 50 milliseconds or greater are perceived as a repetition of a direct sound wave. Think about singing in the shower: the "echo" sound created makes everybody a singer... except me!

- **Gates** are switches set on a threshold used to stop signals based on amplitude (loudness). Gates are used to block noise (other instruments) from leaking into microphones during the actual session. They are often used on drums and overdub vocals to "tighten" the quality of the sound.

- **Harmonizers** offer hope for even me when it comes to singing. Along with changing or correcting the pitch, they can electronically double (with a slight delay) one vocalist or instrument to make it sound as if there were two. The delay settings can be varied between echo and reverberation, which differ in time settings.[214]

- **Limiters** compress the dynamic range of a signal to its maximum compression. The amplitude is "limited" to the maximum settings, which tend to make the signal sound "thinner."

- **Slap Effect** is a delayed sound perceived as a distinct echo, usually set for a delay of 35-250 milliseconds. Think of the early "rockabilly" recordings of Elvis, Carl Perkins, and Johnny Cash, and you'll know how producers used it in the 1950s.

Now that we have seen the important parts of the recording studio and learned the roles of those who work in it, let's get into the actual recording process. Coming up will be how we plan to pay for that recoupment

---

[214] Noiseaddicts.com, "First Ever Recording of Digital Music," Noiseaddicts.com, http://www.noiseaddicts.com/2008/08/first-ever-recording-of-digital-music/, (accessed August 5, 2010).

deal generate session, since as a label, it is "all on us" to make the magic happen for a reasonable cost!

Studio Schedules

In major recording cities, New York, Los Angeles, Nashville, Memphis, Miami, or Seattle, sessions are "booked" in three-hour blocks scheduled from 10 a.m., to 1 p.m., 2 to 5 p.m., 6 to 9 p.m., and 10 p.m. to 1 a.m. This allows producers, musicians, and vocalists to move from project to project during the day by going from one session to another as all the studios are working on the same hourly schedule. The hour between sessions is for tearing down the current session and setting up the next session. Let's take a look at the process of a recording session based on the experience of record producer Jimmy Bowen.

The Recording Process- Setting the Stage for Success

As we know, producers are in charge of the recording processes, budget, and material or "songs" the artist will be singing. But in the studio, they are also responsible for the creative performance of the recording team, both individually and working together to create wow tracks. Creative people can sometimes be difficult to work with, so the producer has to maintain control of the session or it may turn into something resembling of circus, costing the label thousands of dollars per-hour. In addition, producers must know the current state of the financial situation in the industry.

Pre-Production

Bowen (1984) claims there are five basic steps in preproduction for recording an act. These are: (a) finding the artist, (b) researching the artist, (c) finding the material (songs), (d) hiring the musicians, and (e) setting up the session. As he explained it to me,

You've got to have an artist to work with; that is the first thing. When

you're first getting started you will probably work with artists who you wouldn't work with later on, but more than likely, you'll both be at the same stage. ...You'll produce some artists you probably shouldn't. You'll cause some marriages to happen that aren't the ideal marriages, but you must get some experience. When this happens, make sure you always do the very best job you can. If you realize that it's a super bad marriage, get out of it as gracefully as you can. Save the artist's time, save the artist's money, save your own reputation. You always want to maintain a business approach. If it doesn't work you're sorry it didn't work, but you'd rather not waste any more money.[215]

Even though some time has passed since we spoke about this, the process remains the same. Label executives continually take chances on who might be successful, and producers work hard to make sure the artist has a chance at success once they are in the studio.

So, producers are valued for their years of experience, musical knowledge, and opinions about "what" the public wants to hear. They work with the artist and the label to produce the acts, while understanding the need for the songs and the artists' vocal performance to build their image and brand. Marrying the right song to the right artist is essential, as the song can help define the artist's image and brand. The two must fit together in a way that allow the melody and lyrics to reinforce the perceptions consumers have of the artist's image. Here is Bowen's advice on how to make that connection,

The first thing I suggest you do with an artist, when you first get involved with producing a specific artist, is to get a discography of that artist (a copy of all their recordings over their entire career, even the bad stuff). The artist has known themselves all of their life, you haven't! Don't try to come in after the artist has been singing for 12-14 years, working on their craft and hope you're going to jump on the train and ride a winner. Go at it seriously. ...There's so much you learn from researching the artist. You learn what not to do and you learn what to

---

[215] Jimmy Bowen (as quoted by Larry Wacholtz) *Inside Country Music*, Billboard Books, (New York: Watson-Guptil Publishers, 1986) & Larry Wacholtz, *Lights, Glitter and Business Sense*, Thumbs Up Publishing, (Washington: Cheney, 1984) 184-198

> do. It's like anything else. A doctor wants an x-ray to try and figure out what's wrong before shooting medicine into you, at least a good doctor does. Some of them write prescriptions over the telephone. Beware of the doctor who does that. Beware of a producer who's ready to go to the studio a week or two after he's met the artist or gets the deal. He's looking for a miracle to happen; he's hoping it will all work out.

> ...Being a producer, you've got to be a psychologist, not a psychiatrist, but a psychologist. You've got to dig into the artist's head. You've got to find out what makes an artist tick, what makes him give 100% sometimes, 80% sometimes, and 20% sometimes, or you're going to be looking for luck, hoping the night you booked the studio you're going to get 100% and you may not get it. ...Have a deep relaxed discussion with the artist, read your artist and find out what environment will let them open up, relax, and have the best place to have a rap with you. If it's in a bar over a beer or at his house, go do it. If it's at your house, do it. If it's at the studio late at night go do it. Wherever. Find a place where that artist is more comfortable, where he'll open up to you, so he or she will talk to you, so you can start to read and understand them.[216]

Producers are required to find and select the right songs for the artist to record. In Bowen's experience, this means,

> You take a hit song if it comes from an ex-wife. You take a hit song if it comes from your biggest enemy. You owe that to the artist. Your job is to make hit records. He's paying you. It's his life and his money. Go out and hunt those songs. Anywhere you get a hit song is great. The obvious place to look is publishers and you need to have a good rapport with them. We look for material all the time. ...When I say, the hunt is on, that's just what I mean. It's not going to come to you very often. You've got to create the relationships before the great songs are brought to you. You've got to go out and make yourself known. ...Thirty days before you're going to record an artist, put the word out. Then the songs flood in. The problem is that when you're going though songs (the last few weeks before a session) there's a tendency to take the best of the worst. So, have a big, long listening session for songs, cull out of 50 about 6 or 7. Get away from them until the

---
216 Jimmy Bowen (as quoted by Larry Wacholtz) *Inside Country Music*, Billboard Books, (New York: Watson-Guptil Publishers, 1986) & Larry Wacholtz, *Lights, Glitter and Business Sense*, Thumbs Up Publishing, (Washington: Cheney, 1984) 184-198

next day and then go back and listen to those 6 or 7. You'll probably throw away 3 or 4 of them. ...Then play the songs for the artist. ...With the great songs, you'll both just light up. You'll light up, the artist' will light up. The great ones, you don't miss them. If you miss the great ones, then, I'd suggest plumbing or electrical work, because you aren't going to make it. ...Also, when the hunt is on research old songs. Don't eliminate the possibility of 20 or 30 years of success.[217]

The quality of the studio musicians, the recording artist's performances, the production, and the engineering all contribute to the final sound and feel of the recording. The producer plays a key role in communicating the vision of the recording to the artist and the studio musicians and singers. Not an easy thing to do! Together, they need to create a final master recording that is far superior to the original demo. Bowen described his experience providing that vision this way,

It's like casting a movie if you put together a bad cast you're going to have a dog movie. ...Talk to the artist about the musicians that he or she likes or doesn't like. Never cast a session and have a musician on it the artist has a bad vibe with. You're just putting a negative into your music that you don't need. ... The whole trick is to figure out everything around the artist so when you go to tape, to make your record, you've got everything at max. You want the musicians at max; you want the artist at max. You want everything at its best. The ones that break through are the magical records that happen that way.[218]

The producer is also in charge of time-management and effective use of resources. Most recording sessions have a strong "on the clock" structure to them as time is money, for everyone involved.

STAGES OF A RECORDING SESSION

Recording sessions are usually accomplished in four stages, whether the

---

217 Jimmy Bowen (as quoted by Larry Wacholtz) *Inside Country Music*, Billboard Books, (New York: Watson-Guptil Publishers, 1986) & Larry Wacholtz, *Lights, Glitter and Business Sense,* Thumbs Up Publishing, (Washington: Cheney, 1984) 184-198

218 Jimmy Bowen (as quoted by Larry Wacholtz) *Inside Country Music*, Billboard Books, (New York: Watson-Guptil Publishers, 1986) & Larry Wacholtz, *Lights, Glitter and Business Sense,* Thumbs Up Publishing, (Washington: Cheney, 1984) 184-198

primary means of recording is in the studio or with computer software, or using both at the same time.

BASIC TRACKS

The first stage of a recording session in the studio is called basic tracks or tracking. The rhythm instruments and scratch (rough or practice) vocals lay the foundation for the rest of the instruments and layers of vocals, which are cut later in their sessions. Basic tracking instruments may include drums, bass guitar, piano, and electric and acoustic guitars. The recording artist adds a reference or scratch vocal for the musicians to listen to while they play. Most of the "scratch" vocals are later ignored, though sometimes they are used in the master recording final mix.

The session process involves the musicians and vocalists listening to the demo recording of the song, tuning up, and practicing the song at least a few times to prepare for the recording. Many of the studio musicians in Los Angeles, New York, and Nashville learn and contribute their musical creative performances to the essence of the song in just a few minutes.

Basic tracks are recorded once the musicians and vocalists are ready. The audio engineer will have set the microphones, monitors, and headphones for the sound capture. Then, the equalization and effects levels are set and reworked until the producer is satisfied with the quality of the sound during the practice and process of learning the song.

In basic tracks, the vocalist sings into the mic which converts the acoustic signal into an electronic signal that travels at the speed of light to the console or "board". The audio engineer then monitors the amount of signal that is sent to one of the analog or digital tracks on a tape machine or computer software program. The vocalists hear themselves and the other performers through the signal being sent back from the console to their headphones. The engineer will need to know how to manage the digital and analog sounds, which are detailed below.

DIGITAL VS ANALOG RECORDINGS

If the recording is in analog, the right amount of signal on the tape is difficult. Too much signal will distort the tape. Too little signal will cause the playback to be noisy. Digital tape recorders and computer recordings provide a larger dynamic range, which solves some of the engineer's distortion and noise problems.

If most of the musicians play poorly, the recording process is repeated. When the producer approves the basic musical tracks, the minor musical problems are usually fixed later. Logs are then completed, which are written notes about the recording of the songs. Notes include length of the song, problems that need to be corrected in the overdub stage, and equalization and effects settings. Logs are stored in the box with the master tape, or, as notes stored in the software. These are used in later recording sessions to alert the engineer and producers of necessary issues. Once the song has been recorded and the producer is satisfied then everyone listens during the playback for mistakes and opportunities to improve their performances. If recorded properly, the "take" becomes a "master."

OVERDUBBING

Overdubbing is the second stage of the typical recording session. Additional instrumental performances and vocals are added to the previously recorded master tape. The prior basic tracks are saved and the tape machine is placed into selective synchronization which turns the record heads on the previous recorded tracks into playback heads. The process was invented by guitarist Les Paul in the late 1940s.[219] This allows the new instruments and vocals to be recorded in time with the instruments and vocals that were first recorded in the basic track sessions. On Pro Tools and other software, it's just a click of the mouse that accomplishes the same steps.

---

219 Joe Cellini, "Les Paul Invented Here," Apple Pro, http://www.apple.com/pro/profiles/lespaul/, (accessed March 22, 2011).

Signal flow in overdubbing is a combination of basic tracks and playback. The signal is played off the record head in playback and sent to the console where it is split and sent to the monitors, effects, 2-track/DAT (digital audio tape recorder) or computer and through the cue system to the musicians' and recording artists' headsets. Once the musicians and singers hear the signal from the previously recorded tracks, they play or sing their new tracks. Thus, in overdubbing, the signal from a previously recorded track is sent back to the console, and, then to the headphones of the performers. One it's heard, the vocalist sings along with the previously recorded tracks. There is a slight delay between the playback head track being sent to the performers in the studio, and the new tracks being recorded, but it's so quick, we can't hear it.

MIXDOWN

The last stage in the recording process is mixdown. After all the instruments and vocals have been recorded and overdubbed, the 24, 32, or digital tape machine or computer program is used to mix all the musical and vocal tracks to 2 tracks (stereo) left and right. Producers and audio engineers mix the tracks according to the "style" of the music genre (rock, hip hop, blues, jazz), by creating stereo images (using pan pots, which are switches and faders on the console that move the signal from left to right or anywhere in between), and create a 3-D effect by acoustically positioning and pre-echo signals correlated to a dry signal.

Of course, the mixdown process is highly creative, and often depends on the perspective of the producers. Some labels use different producers to mix the same track, and then select the one they want to release. "Signal flow" in mixdown, converts the magnetic signal stored on the tape of the analog or digital tape machine or computer into electrical signals which are sent to the console and speakers in order for the producers and audio engineers to hear "what they've got." Then, using the reverb, echo, pitch, slap and equalizing the signals (instruments and vocals) and panning (stereo positioning), they build the final mixed master.

MASTERING

The mastering process for CDs is different from mp3s, as described by Harris (2010):

> *In conventional CDs, these 1s and 0s are represented by millions of tiny bumps and flat areas on the disc's reflective surface. The bumps and flats are arranged in a continuous track that measures about 0.5 microns (millionths of a meter) across and 3.5 miles (5 km) long... To read this information, the CD player passes a laser beam over the track. When the laser passes over a flat area in the track, the beam is reflected directly to an optical sensor on the laser assembly. The CD player interprets this as a 1. When the beam passes over a bump, the light is bounced away from the optical sensor. The CD player recognizes this as a 0.[220] ... CD-recordable discs, or CD-Rs, don't have any bumps or flat areas at all. Instead, they have a smooth reflective metal layer, which rests on top of a layer of photosensitive dye. When the disc is blank, the dye is translucent: Light can shine through and reflect off the metal surface. But when you heat the dye layer with concentrated light of a particular frequency and intensity, the dye turns opaque: It darkens to the point that light can't pass through.[221]*

If the recording team of musicians, recording artists, audio engineers, and producers has done its job, the creativity of the recording session has been "captured" on tape or computer and held on flash drives.

Earlier, I mentioned that to be in the recording studio, musicians needed to be AF of M or SAG-AFTRA members. Because the union determines what musicians are paid, as well as offering them representation and benefits packages, we are going to look at how the unions work before we see how recording budgets are constructed to accommodate employee costs. No matter how glamorous the music industry may seem, and how creative the team of artists and recording personnel are, they are employees working on a project who need to be paid, and from a union point of view,

---

221 Tom Harris, "How CD Burner Work," Howstuffworks.com, http://computer.howstuffworks.com/cd-burner1.htm, (accessed March 22, 2011).

whose interests need to be protected.

UNIONS

As mentioned previously, the major labels have signed union agreements, and all the musicians and singers will be members of the AF of M (musicians) or SAG-AFTRA (vocalists). This is what the unions offer their membership.

SAG-AFTRA

The Screen Actors Guild/American Federation of Television and Radio Artists (SAG-AFTRA) merged in 2012 into one super union representing actors, announcers, TV newscasters and personalities, and professional singers.[222] According to the SAG-AFTRA website (2017),

> *SAG-AFTRA represents approximately 160,000 actors, announcers, broadcast journalists, dancers, DJs, news writers, news editors, program hosts, puppeteers, recording artists, singers, stunt performers, voiceover artists and other media professionals. SAG-AFTRA members are the faces and voices that entertain and inform America and the world. With national offices in Los Angeles and New York, and local offices nationwide, SAG-AFTRA members work together to secure the strongest protections for media artists into the 21st century and beyond.*[223]

THE AF OF M

Major record labels are signatories to The American Federation of Musicians Sound Recording Labor Agreement (formerly the Phonograph Record Label Agreement) that governs the wages, benefits, and working conditions of all its members, including studio musicians.[224] According to information posted on their homepage, www.afm.org (2017),

---

[222] Nikki Finke, Deadline Hollywood, "Sag/AFTRA Merger Approved," http://www.deadline.com/2012/03/sag-aftra-merger-approved-screen-actors-guild-american-federation-television-radio-arts/, (accessed July 15, 2013).
[223] "About Us." About Us | SAG-AFTRA. Accessed July 14, 2017. https://www.sagaftra.org/content/about-us.
[224] AF of M, "Sound Recording Label Agreement," AF of M, http://www.afm.org/uploads/image, (accessed March 22, 2011).

> 80,000 musicians comprise the American Federation of Musicians of the United States and Canada (AFM). We perform in orchestras, backup bands, festivals, clubs and theaters—both on Broadway and on tour. AFM members also make music for films, TV, commercials and sound recordings. As the largest union of musicians in the world, we have the power to make the music industry work for musicians.[225]

In the days of free music, the AF of M is supporting their members by making sure all of the uses of the recorded music are accounted for and the musicians who performed on the sessions are paid accordingly. As their website claims (2017),

> Musicians working in recording and digital media have joined forces in AFM to fight for better pay, improved industry standards, healthcare, and a secure retirement. They perform on recordings—both in the studio and on live performances that are recorded. They record radio, TV and online commercials, film and video game scores, and appear on live and pre-recorded TV . . . It's not unusual for musicians to hear one of their recordings at the movies or while watching TV, prompting the question, "Am I due money for my music being used?" The answer is yes if you are a union musician. Musicians recording under a union contract usually receive "new use" fees including pension benefits when their recordings are re-used . . . New use, sometimes called re-use, is when a recording is used outside of its intended purpose. For example, music originally recorded for a CD is later used on a TV show or in a commercial triggering a new use payment. New use payments apply for all types of original recorded music, including sound recordings, TV and film scores . . . AFM musicians also receive payment when their music is licensed for use in formats outside of its intended use (e.g., theatrical film scores released to "supplemental markets" such as DVD, pay-tv, streaming, cable, and in-flight use) or when excerpts of their music are used ("clip use").[226]

State governments can also play a role in employment, especially, if as is the case in Tennessee, for example, your studio and your label are in a

---

225 Ink, Social. "About AFM." American Federation of Musicians. Accessed July 14, 2017. http://www.afm.org/about/about-afm/.
226 "Sound Recording Agreement." American Federation of Musicians. Accessed July 15, 2017. http://www.afm.org/wp-content/uploads/2016/03/Sound-Recording-Agreement.pdf.

right-to-work state.

RIGHT-TO-WORK STATES

From a business perspective, there are separate types of sessions, with the differences based on union or nonunion agreements and the recording studios locations. There are 25 right-to-work states in the union, where workers do not have to belong to a union to work in union-based jobs. That's why many Hollywood films are made outside of California and New York.[227] In the recording business, the unions (AF of M and SAG-AFTRA) represent the best musicians and singers for studio work yet, they are not allowed to record with non-union members or non-union sessions. Sadly, there's less work for these very talented artists due to the economics of the music business' decline of record sales. To survive, some record on non-union sessions anyway and the unions simply ignore the work with a "blind eye" policy, as they know people need to work for a living.

THE AF OF M SOUND RECORDING LABOR AGREEMENT

The major labels all support unions and have signed the AF of M's extended *Sound Recording Labor Agreement with the Sound Recording Special Payments Fund (SPF)* and the *Sound Recording Trust Agreement* (MPTF). The labor agreement is 130 plus pages of union rules and regulations the labels have agreed to abide by to support the musicians who have helped them create the products they need to profit in their businesses. The agreement, stated on the AF of M's website (2017) encompasses-

> *For the purposes of this Agreement, the terms "phonograph record and record" shall mean any phonograph record, digital audio file, compact disc, tape recording or any other device reproducing sound, whether now in existence or which may come into existence. For the purposes of this Agreement, the term "master record? Shall include any matrix, "mother", stamper, or other device from which another such master record or phonograph record is produced, reproduced, pressed or otherwise processed . . . This agreement shall cover and relate to members*

---
227 Sherk, James. "25 States Are Now Right-to-Work States." The Daily Signal. March 09, 2015. Accessed July 15, 2017. http://dailysignal.com/2015/03/09/25-states-now-right-work-states/.

of the Federation wherever they shall perform, as employees, services for the Company as instrumental musicians or as leaders, contractors, copyists, orchestrator's and arrangers of instrumental music (all of whom are collectively referred to as "musicians") in the recording of phonograph records or Covered Concert DVDs (as defined in Exhibit A(I)(J)), and side musicians engaged in "on-camera sideline work in Traditional Music Videos (as defined in Exhibit B), and to any other person employed as a Musician in the recording of phonograph records, Covered Concert DVDs within the United States or Canada or a present territory or possession of either (herein called "Domestic Area").[228]

In addition, major labels and others who have signed the agreement also contribute to the *Special Payments Fund* and the *Sound Recording Trust Agreement*.

THE SPECIAL PAYMENTS FUND

Basically, the labels pay 0.55% (a little over one half of one percent) of the wholesale price of $8.98 or lower, after sales of 25,000 units on CDs and other items and over 150,000 on singles.[229] Payments are to the union, and they pay the musicians who were on the session over the next four years at declining percentages. According to the agreement (2017),

> *Each musician, ... shall receive as a special payment a fraction of the total distribution which shall be determined as follows: the numerator of said fraction shall be a sum determined by adding the scale wages payable to such musician ... (i) during the immediately preceding calendar year weighted or multiplied by 100 percent, (ii) during the immediately preceding calendar year ... 80 percent, (iii) during the immediately preceding calendar year less two ... 60 percent, (iv) during the immediately preceding calendar year ... 40 percent, and (v) during the ... by 20 percent. ... In the case of arrangers and orchestrators scale wages ... shall be deemed to be 150 percent of the scale wages paid to an instrumentalist for each session on which the arranger or*

---

228 "Sound Recording Agreement." American Federation of Musicians. Accessed July 15, 2017. http://www.afm.org/wp-content/uploads/2016/03/Sound-Recording-Agreement.pdf.
229 "Sound Recording Agreement." American Federation of Musicians. Accessed July 15, 2017. http://www.afm.org/wp-content/uploads/2016/03/Sound-Recording-Agreement.pdf.

orchestrator performed services.[230]

THE SOUND RECORDING TRUST AGREEMENT

The *Sound Recording Trust Agreement* pays AF of M musicians' salaries for free live public performances in parks and other venues.[231] The labels pay into the fund at,

> ... a rate of .20475% of manufacturer's suggested retail price to a maximum suggested retail price of $8.98 for each record, wire or tape recording or other devices. In the case of compact discs, such suggested maximum retail price shall be $10.98.[232]

That's less than one percent of the SRLP for singles once they have sold over 150,000 unites and 25,000 for CDs and other types of sellable recorded products. Free goods are not included in the totals and labels may also deduct their packaging fees up to "20% on phonograph records and 30% of the suggested retail price for tapes, cartridges and compact discs."[233]

THE SAG-AFTRA NATIONAL CODE OF FAIR PRACTICE FOR SOUND RECORDINGS

The major labels and about 600 other entertainment production companies have signed the *SAG-AFTRA National Code of Fair Practice for Sound Recordings*, often referred to as "The Code." It establishes the recording session rates for royalty artist singers, back up vocalists and many other personalities involved in the media. According to the SAG-AFTRA website it (2017),

> ... covers sound recordings on CDs, digital, vinyl, etc., and includes all music formats as well as audiobooks, cast albums, and any other

---

[230] "About The Fund." Sound-recording.org. Accessed July 15, 2017. http://www.sound-recording.org/about.html?-auth_sid=d1e55a34428f9c4a18a5ad5f5834e5a4.
[231] "M.P.T.F. RECORDING INDUSTRIES MUSIC PERFORMANCE TRUST FUND." Edmonton Musicians Association - Local 390 A.F. of M. Accessed July 15, 2017. http://www.afmedmonton.ca/mptf.asp.
[232] "Sound Recording Agreement." American Federation of Musicians. Accessed July 15, 2017. http://www.afm.org/wp-content/uploads/2016/03/Sound-Recording-Agreement.pdf.
[233] "Sound Recording Agreement." American Federation of Musicians. Accessed July 15, 2017. http://www.afm.org/wp-content/uploads/2016/03/Sound-Recording-Agreement.pdf.

sound recording utilizing vocal performance. The Code not only covers singers, but announcers, actors, comedians, narrators, and sound effects artists as well. The Code applies to artists who work at scale and over scale, and who appear as both royalty and non-royalty artists. In addition, some artists may be royalty artists for their own recordings, but qualify as non-royalty artists when they appear on other artists' recordings.[234]

SAG-AFTRA also has a health and retirement fund paid on a per-song or hourly rate of 12.75% of the total amount earned by the singer on the recording session. The AF of M's pension fund rate is 12.81% and an addition health and welfare fee of $26-24.00 for the first session call and $20.00 per session for same day service.[235] The AF of M's pension fund on limited pressings and demos is 11.99%.

As an example, a backup singer is paid a basic session rate of $107.50 per-hour on a minimum of a 2-hour session call for a total of $215.00. On top of that, the labels pay the health and pension fund an additional 12.75% or an additional $27.41 for a total of $242.41. If the singer is done in five minutes, the rate is still $242.41. If it takes an additional hour, then it's another $107.50 plus the H&W at 12.75% or $13.70. Add it up for a three-hour session and the singer will be paid $363.62. Four back up singers (BGVs or background singers) for a three-hour session call will cost the label $1,454.48. One of them must be a "Contractor," and that's an additional $56.00 for the session call. Now the total for four SAG-AFTRA singers for a three-hour session is $1,510.48. By the way, to get the singer at the rate of $107.50, plus the P&W rate of 12.75%, we'd have to hire at least three.[236]

SAG-AFTRA Contingent Scales

[234] "SAG-AFTRA Sound Recording Code." SAGAFTRA.org Sound Recording Code at a Glance. Accessed July 15, 2017. https://www.sagaftra.org/files/sound_recordings_code_at_a_glance_2017.pdf.
[235] " Recording Scale Summary Sheet 7/03/2017." AF of M Recording Scale Summary Sheet 7/03/2017. July 3, 2017. Accessed July 15, 2017. http://www.nashvillemusicians.org/sites/default/files/Media%20Root/AFM%20RECORDING%20SCALE%20SUMMARY%20SHEET2018.pdf.
[236] "SAG-AFTRA Sound Recording Code." SAGAFTRA.org Sound Recording Code at a Glance. Accessed July 15, 2017. https://www.sagaftra.org/files/sound_recordings_code_at_a_glance_2017.pdf.

SAG-AFTRA non-royalty singers, that is, the talent not signed to record deals who still perform on the recordings, also receive residuals called "contingent scale" payments. According to the SAG-AFTRA *Sound Recording Code* (2017),

> "Contingent Scale" refers to additional payments made to non-royalty artists appearing on recordings that reach certain sales levels in the U.S. The term "non-royalty" refers to the artist's status on that recording. So, if a royalty artist appears as a background singer on another artist's recording, he/she is considered "non-royalty" for contingent scale purposes for that song. Contingent scale applies to recordings recorded after 1974 which have not been previously released (e.g., it does not apply to "greatest hits" albums). Recordings cease to be eligible for contingent scale treatment ten years after their original release. A contingent scale payment of a specific percentage of the applicable minimum scale is made to an artist for each side on which he/she appears on the recording, each time the album reaches one of the . . . sales plateaus.[237]

Units Sold (Plateaus)	Percentage or Original Payments Due
157,500-499,000	50%
500,000-999,000	60%
1,000,000-3,000,000	75%

Figure 10.1: Contingent scale payments are made to the singers on a recording session once the unit sales have reach various plateaus. Of course, these payment have dramatically been reduced with the decline of unit sales as consumers continue to switch to streaming.

The sales plateaus royalties last for ten years from the street date and includes audio and video downloads, master ringtones, subscription au-

---

[237] "SAG-AFTRA Sound Recording Code." SAGAFTRA.org Sound Recording Code at a Glance. Accessed July 15, 2017. https://www.sagaftra.org/files/sound_recordings_code_at_a_glance_2017.pdf.

dio and video services with royalties paid by the label distributed by the SAG-AFTRA and Industry Sound Recordings Distribution Fund.[238]

RECORDING BUDGETS

The amount of money the recording team members receive for session work is based on their fame, track record, contacts, and the kind of sessions the label authorizes. Record budgets are usually determined in advance by the label. At times, the signed royalty artists are required to submit their own budget requests. Budgets are based on many factors -union scales agreements, the purpose of the recordings, and the marketing plan. The recording scale for the five types of sessions including (a) Master session, (b) Low Budget, (c) Limited Pressings, (d) Demo, and (e) the right- to-work state indie sessions vary from thousands of dollars to a few hundred as you'll see in the following figure 10.2.

RECORDING RATE SCALES

The rate sheets of Figure 10.2 are comprised of the producer recording session fees, the audio engineer per-hour and per-day rates, AF of M union musicians, SAG-AFTRA singer scales, and additional session expenses such as cartage and per-diem. In the next example, it's your turn to determine a recording budget. *What does it cost to record a ten song album?* The answer is up to you. Assume four sessions per-song as an average per-day rate. Basic tracks and a scratch vocal by the royalty artist are recorded in the first session from 10am to 1pm. The first overdubbing session from 2pm-5pm is usually for additional musicians and a possible lead vocal. The second overdubbing session is for back-up singers and any the royalty artists, if needed. The fourth session (which is usually completed on another day) is for the three-hour mix-down session.

---

[238] "SAG-AFTRA Sound Recording Code." SAGAFTRA.org Sound Recording Code at a Glance. Accessed July 15, 2017. https://www.sagaftra.org/files/sound_recordings_code_at_a_glance_2017.pdf.

Type of Session	Master (3 Hour Call)	Low Budget (3 Hour Call)	Limited Pressing	Demo (3 Hour Call)	Indie
Producer Paid by the side	Negotiated Range $2,000-$5,000	Negotiated Range $500-$2,500	Negotiated Range $500-$2,500	Negotiated Range $50-200	Negotiated
Audio Engineer Per hour, Day, or session	Negotiated Range $100-$150	Negotiated Range $50-$100 Per-	Negotiated Range $50-$100	Negotiated Range Intern-$0.0-$50	Negotiated
Musicians Per 3 hour Session call	AF of M Side Musician $409.28	AF of M Side Musician $229.93	AF of M Side Musician $196.50	AF of M Side Musician $156.	Non-Union Side Musician Negotiated
	H&W $26.00	H&W $26.00	H&W $24.00	H&W $24.00	None
	Pension/EP $52.43 (12.81%)	Pension/EP $29.45 (12.81%)	Pension/EP $23.56 (12.81%)	Pension/EP $18.70 (12.81%)	None
	Total $487.71	Total $285.38	Total $244.06	Total $198.70	Negotiated
Cartage	$17.00-$35.00 Per-Session	$17.00-$35.00 Per-Session	$17.00-$35.00 Per-Session	$17.00-$35.00 Per-Session	
Lead Musician (Double Scale) Per 3-hour Session call	AF of M Lead Musician $818.56	AF of M Lead Musician $459.85 Per-3	AF of M Lead Musician $395.00 Per-3	AF of M Lead Musician $312.00 Per-3	Non-Union Side Musician Negotiated
	H&W $26.00	H&W $26.00	H&W $24.00	H&W $24.00	None
	Pension/EP $104.86 (12.81%)	Pension/EP $52.43 (12.81%)	Pension/EP $47.12 (11.99%)	Pension/EP $37.41 (11.99%)	None
	Total $949.42	Total $538.28	Total $466.12	Total $373.41	Negotiated

Royalty Artists (Soloists and Duos) Paid per the side or hour	AFTRA Royalty Artist (lead vocalist)	AFTRA Royalty Artist (lead vocalist)	AFTRA Royalty Artist (lead vocalist)	AFTRA Royalty Artist (lead vocalist)	Non-Union Side Artist (lead vocalist)
	$236.25	$236.25	$236.25	$236.25	Negotiated
	Health & Retirement $30.12 (12.75%)	Health & Retirement $30.12 (12.75%)	Health & Retirement $30.12 (12.75%)	Health & Retirement $30.12 (12.75%)	None
	Total $266.37	Total $266.37	Total $266.37	Total $266.37	Negotiated
Major label artist paid triple rate- Budget for scale X triple rate X 3 hours	$2,126.25	$2,126.25	$2,126.25		
Singers (3-8) Paid per the side or hour	AFTRA Royalty Artist (lead vocalist)	AFTRA Royalty Artist (lead vocalist)	AFTRA Royalty Artist (lead vocalist)	AFTRA Royalty Artist (lead vocalist)	Non-Union Vocalists
	$107.50	$107.50	$107.50	$107.50	Negotiated
	Health & Retirement $13.70 (12.75%)	Health & Retirement $13.70 (12.75%)	Health & Retirement $13.70 (12.75%)	Health & Retirement $13.70 (12.75%)	None
	Total $121.02	Total $121.02	Total $121.02	Total $121.02	Negotiated
Singer Contractor Per session	AFTRA Contractor $56.00	AFTRA Contractor $56.00	AFTRA Contractor $56.00	AFTRA Contractor $56.00	None Required or Negotiated
Studio Rental	Master Studio	Project/Mini Post-Production Studios	Project/Mini Post-Production Studios	Demo Studio	Demo/Garage Studio
	$150.00 (Per Hour)	$125.00 (Per Hour)	$125.00 (Per Hour)	$50.00 (Per Hour)	$50.00 (Per Hour)
	$350 (Per Session)	$300 (Per Session)	$300 (Per Session)	$125 Per Session	$125 Per Session
Per- Diem (Royalty Artist Only)	Per- Diem $250.00 (Per-Day)	Per- Diem $75.00 (Per-Day)	Per- Diem $50.00 (Per-Day)	Per- Diem $25.00 (Per-Day)	None

Figure 10.2: The master scale and expense budget sheet show the various amounts of money labels pay the members of the recording team based on the type of session, scales, and the length of the sessions.[239] & [240]

Notice that the producer is paid by the side or one song, the royalty (label artists) is paid triple scale, meaning the SAG-AFTRA per-song or hour rate (whichever is greatest), times a triple scale, times the three hours. The musicians (AF of M) have a leader who is paid double scale, and the background (SAG-AFTRA) singers have a contractor who is paid an extra $56.00 per-hour or song.

Recording Team	Union Other	Tracking 10am-1pm	Overdub 1 2pm-5pm	Overdub 2 6pm-9pm	Mix 10pm-1am
Producer	None				
Audio Engineer	None				
Studio Rental					
Other	Cartage				
	Per-Diem				
	Other				
Musicians	AF of M	Leader	Leader		
		1	1		
		2	2		
		3	3		
		4	4		
		5	5		
		6	6		
Royalty Artist	AF of M	1	1		
	AFTRA	1	1	1	
Back Up Singers	AFTRA			Contractor	
				1	
				2	
				3	
				4	

Figure 10.3: Once you've got the cost of one song, multiple it by ten to determine your budget for your ten song album.

[239] " Recording Scale Summary Sheet 7/03/2017." AF of M Recording Scale Summary Sheet 7/03/2017. July 3, 2017. Accessed July 15, 2017. http://www.nashvillemusicians.org/sites/default/files/Media%20Root/AFM%20RECORD-ING%20SCALE%20SUMMARY%20SHEET2018.pdf.
[240] "SAG-AFTRA Sound Recording Code." SAGAFTRA.org Sound Recording Code at a Glance. Accessed July 15, 2017. https://www.sagaftra.org/files/sound_recordings_code_at_a_glance_2017.pdf.

The Technical Legal Requirements

AF of M musicians are hired "by the session call" (3 hours, except for demo sessions). SAG-AFTRA vocalists are hired by "the hour or number of songs recorded per-hour" with a two-hour minimum session call. Producers are usually hired "by the side" (one song) and paid half up front (when they agree to do the project) and the other half when the label accepts the final master tape. Some receive "producer points" (often between 1% and 3%) out of the royalty artist's points. Studios may be rented and audio engineers may be hired by the hour, session, day, or project.

A traditional master recording session is a three-hour call with a maximum length of 15 minutes of actual saved recorded time, four sides (songs) and a limited number of overdubs for corrections and sweetening. However, there are also 3.5-hour scales, 4-hour scales, and overtime rates. The AF of M lead musician and the SAG-AFTRA contractor provide a "card" that is signed by the musicians and vocalist that is turned into the unions, who then bill the label for the musicians' and singers work.

Labels commonly pay their SAG-AFTRA royalty artists a maximum of triple scale. However, that's a label decision not an SAG-AFTRA requirement. The low budget rate requires a "side letter" from the label and producer stating the project is limited to a total of $99,000, which allows them to pay a reduced fee to the musicians. Union demos are not allowed to be pressed and sold, they are only for demonstration of a song or artists being pitched to a label or other entity.

The Recording Budget all-ins

The all-ins are the expenses the label pays for (on the front end), that are 100% recoupable out of the artist's royalties. In traditional deals, the money was taken out of artists' royalties for album sales. The deals were often structured to the advantage of the label, which is why many recording artists never received a dime while the labels would often profit in the millions. However, as discussed earlier, the act could walk if the deal didn't work out and owe the label zip. In addition, the acts usually used the promotion, publicity, and marketing, paid for by the label, to create their own artist's management team and business. They often made millions of dollars of which the label received zip. As you already know, the 360 deals the labels have developed have terminated that side of the business with the major labels, as it's the only way they can survive. Remember, the all-ins at 100% recoupable rates were usually,

- **The recording budget expenses**

- **The pressing of recordings and Mechanical Licenses**

- **The advance money paid to the act for signing the deal**

The rest of the label's expenses including promotion, publicity, and marketing were usually at a 50% recoupable rate. However, if the act was paid tour support and the marketing, promotion, and publicity were in support of the tour, then they also were at the 100% recoupable rate. What's the point of all of this? Remember, the labels used the all- in budget (usually the 100% recoupable rate of the recording budget, pressings, mechanicals and advances paid) to determine the promotion and publicity budgets.

PROMOTION AND PUBLICITY BUDGETS

The recording budget is used not only to predict the total cost of the recording but also to determine future label promotion and publicity for the act. Promotion budgets are often based within a range of 100-200% of the all-in budget (recordings mechanicals, advances, and recording production plus mechanical licensing) and publicity is usually in a range of 50-100% of the all-ins. Famous acts may or may not fit into these estimates depending on the marketing plan, as superstar acts receive much larger advances, and lower tour support because they are already well known to consumers and fans. New act's budgets are often limited to a figure just high enough to determine if the albums, concert tickets and merchandise and brands sell well enough to demonstrate that the act has the potential to become highly profitable.

SUMMARY

Most of the major labels have a clause in the 360 deal contracts which requires the act to complete and submit a recording budget on approval. The final amount spent on the recording will depend upon the three variables of (a) the types of session, (b) the cost of each stage of the session, and (c) the expense of hiring the recording team. This team, which is approved by the label, includes the producer, audio engineers, union musicians and singers, and the recording studio expenses. The recording budget, as well as the advance monies paid to the act for signing the deal, and the mechanicals are considered "all -ins". The total costs of the recording will be charged to the artist's account as 100% recoupable.

Recording artists should know the amount of money the label is investing into their careers. Just think about all the stuff we had to know to complete a simple professional album. The value of recordings has declined with the decrease in record sales, yet they are still needed to break, promote, and market recording artists. In the past, labels made their profits from album sales. Now, it's the use of the recordings as promotion to increase profits from the live ticket events, streaming, and branding. Artists are often required to submit a recording budget to the label for its approval before the recording process begins. In addition, the act hires the producer with the approval of the label, who then hires AF of M union musicians and SAG-AFTRA member singers to backup on the session. There are five types of sessions - (a) Master sessions, (b) Low Budget sessions, (c) Limited Pressings, (d) Demos, and (e) The right- to -work state indie sessions. In addition, recording sessions are usually completed in stages or steps, including per-production, basic tracks, overdubbing, mixdown, and mastering.

Hopefully, the recording team of the producer, audio engineer, musicians, singers, and the royalty artists signed to the label together create the type of recording that inspires listeners and profits both the act and label. The labels use the all-in expenses (advances, recording budget, and mechanical licenses) to determine the marketing plan budget for promotion (100%-200%) and publicity (50%-100%). Thus, the recording budget is used not only to predict the total cost of the recording but also to determine future label promotion and publicity activities for the act.

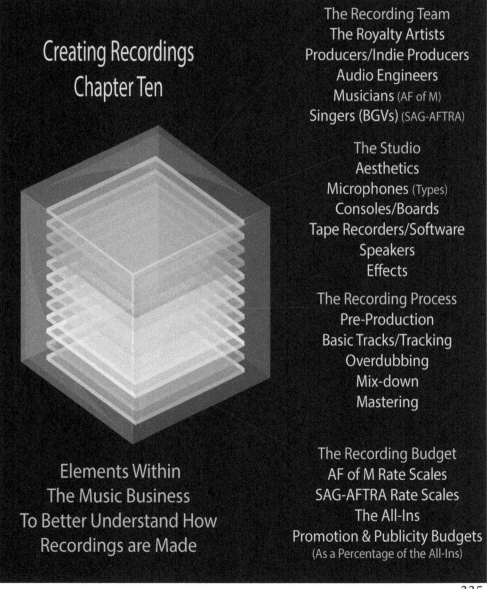

Creating Recordings
Chapter Ten

The Recording Team
The Royalty Artists
Producers/Indie Producers
Audio Engineers
Musicians (AF of M)
Singers (BGVs) (SAG-AFTRA)

The Studio
Aesthetics
Microphones (Types)
Consoles/Boards
Tape Recorders/Software
Speakers
Effects

The Recording Process
Pre-Production
Basic Tracks/Tracking
Overdubbing
Mix-down
Mastering

The Recording Budget
AF of M Rate Scales
SAG-AFTRA Rate Scales
The All-Ins
Promotion & Publicity Budgets
(As a Percentage of the All-Ins)

Elements Within
The Music Business
To Better Understand How
Recordings are Made

In order to motivate people, I must make sure that every time they try something different or try something special, whether its creative marketing or creative recordings, they should be aware they may be contributing to the culture of Nashville and to this nation.

What is exciting about the music business is that we can impact the culture for generations to come, particularly if we find the right artist and the right song.

When we create a record that people enjoy fifty years later, that is making an impact on culture.

It excites me when I hear many people taking credit for a hit because it takes lots of people to make a hit.

- Mike Curb[241]

---

[241] Mike Curb, with Don Cusic. Living the Business. Nashville, TN: Brackish Press, 2017: 301.

Chapter 11

Artist Representation

When artists have the support of a major label or a huge fan base they created themselves, then it's time to hire representation, better known as a personal manager and the management team. Once again, it's a situation where one depends on the success of the other, as the artist relies on the experience, supervision, and connections representation provides to them. The personal manager and the management team members, on the other hand, will only represent the types of acts who can pay their salaries, as they receive a percentage of the artist's gross revenues.

Figure 11.1: After the label has financed the act's career to the tune of $1-$2 million, then they turn over their "investment" to the Personal and other types of managers to help the act develop and control their artistic careers.

CHAIN OF EVENTS

One needs the others. Just as the songwriter needs the music publisher, the musicians and singers in the studio need the producer to create wow recordings. Now, the labels need the acts they sign to become iconic recording and performing artists idolized by consumers. The same is true for the other side of the coin. The music publisher is a non-entity without the songwriter's songs; the acts are extremely limited without the label's financial support, marketing and publicity, and the producer is dead in the water without the talents of the musicians and singers. Think back as all of these connections are driven by the label's financial investments in the artist's creativity, combined with the consumer's love of recordings and live music. In short, the success of one brings opportunities and success to the other individuals and businesses in the entertainment creative and business systems.

The second tier of events commence after the investment and development of the artist by the labels (image and brand) and the street date release (for the sale and promotion of the recording). *Promotion* of the act is linked to radio airplay and other forms of traditional media, with social media and commercial tie-ins giving additional exposure. The direct purpose of promotion efforts is to supply a "sample" of what the act's recordings (packaged as potential emotional stimulation for consumers)are which may help consumers "discover" the act. At the same time, *publicity* kicks in through interviews on TV talk shows, social media, and stories about the act's lifestyle (called a back-story), which supports the promotional campaign. It's the two to four weeks of exposure the act needs to be "discovered" and at the same time, the label will be watching to see if the act is catching on with the public.

"GETTING DISCOVERED" STARTS THE CHAIN

A number of business decisions have to be made when a new band launches their career with their first show or even with an established or super star acts out on a tour. The local act is on their own and will have to "wear" several different hats to set-up the show. In contrast, the established and superstar acts have their personal management teams do it all for them through a "power of attorney agreement" in the deal between the personal manager and the royalty artist.

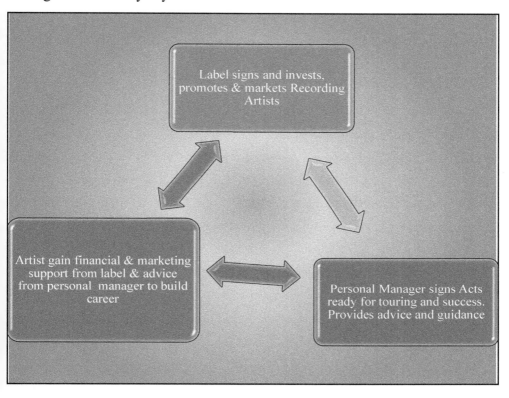

Figure 11.2: The label signs and markets the acts and then turns them over to the personal manager and the management team. The artist has received two vital industry-related supports most independent acts will never have. These are financial and marketing support from the labels; and, professional advice and guidance for building their career from a personal manager. In return, the artist usually owes 38%-47% of gross earnings to the label and management team.

The inexperienced local act's goal is *exposure* through live shows to start a buzz with the local fans tweeting and spreading their excitement through social media. If it works, because the fans enjoyed the band enough to tweet again and again, then label deals, record producers, studio musicians and world class audio engineers, plus marketing plans, promotion and publicity, and finally, representation may follow. Notice the chain of events again, as the process of "being discovered" starts in the local community with fans excited by a local band's performance, and then builds step-by-step to a label deal and professional representation. In other words, a local band's path to a label deal and professional artist management starts locally and depends on the band's ability to shake up the fans with their talent, songs, and shows.

The bottom line in financial. If things click, everyone becomes more successful. It's the domino effect that's found in almost every phase of the music industry, as the creative systems and the business systems meet to create opportunities for themselves through their corporate and entrepreneurial ventures. And, their success leads to other's financial success. For example, performance venues, restaurants, social media and mass media outlets who use the artists' images and their music in their work also profit. Take a look at what opportunities the labels have created for the management company, mass and social media, Internet streamers, and many other businesses. At the same time, consider how much money is then returned to the label, music publishers, songwriters, and recording artists.

THE LABEL/MANAGEMENT CONNECTION

As you already know, in 360 deals the artist's career goals are based on the commercialization or monetizing of their image and "brand" based on the consumer's emotional connections to the act's recordings and live shows. The Artist Manager's job is to exploit (a good thing in this business) the consumer's emotional connection to the act by providing point-of-purchase buying opportunities. These include tickets for live shows and branded merchandise. Of course, the personal manager is providing the advice and guidance to help the artist's build their successful career.

Why are they doing it? To be honest, it's to make money for the artists, themselves, and the label in 360 deal agreements. It's important that you understand the differences as in the traditional recoupment deal labels and management were separate business entities. They still are in 360 deals for legal reasons, but the labels now have an increased interest in the management company's success as they receive a percentage of the acts generated gross revenues. At the same time, the management company is using the label's financial investment in the development of the act, marketing, etc., to provide the type of artist they can advise who will generate profits for everyone.

The Strategic Management Plan

Personal managers provide representation, supervision, and administration to artist's business. They also advise and guide the emerging artist in the hopes of making the act into an iconic, long-term success. The personal manager, artists, and sometimes the labels develop a *strategic management plan* to determine the goals and strategies suitable for the act's success. Legally, labels are not allowed to manage their signed artists, but they can, at the request of the personal manager, consult with the act and personal manager, as all three collaborate to maximize everyone's profits. Once everyone is on the same page, the management team is established by hiring a booking agent, business manager, and a road manager for tours and shows. Usually an attorney (more as needed) is hired on an hourly basis to supervise and draw up contracts, and, provide general legal advice.

The Management Team

The artist management relationship is built on trust. The artist has to trust the manager to provide the right advice and to make the right decisions that will build the artist's career. The personal manager has to trust the artist to follow the advice given, stay healthy physically and mentally, work, work, work, and always exploit every opportunity to make use of shameless self-promotion.

It is the artist's responsibility to pick the right manager, someone who will make a great impression, be well respected by record label executives and talent agents, and well known by movers and shakers in the industry. Don't hire a friend or relative because their lack of experience and poor decisions will affect your career and income probably forever!

Personal Manager

Personal managers are hired by the act, and sometimes, the choice is made at the recommendation of the label. It is common for personal managers to have their own representation companies, and to manage several acts through their business. The artist is exclusively signed to one manager. Recording artist Mark Volman of the Turtles (2013) explains how the artist and personal manager relationship works,

> *A personal manager receives a percentage of what an artist earns. If the artist makes money, so does the manager. If the artist doesn't make money, the manager can still make money. What? You must understand that as an artist you sign an exclusive personal contract, which means the artist can work with NO other manager. On the other hand, a manager has NO exclusivity to the artist. He can manage as many acts as he can sign and that is why he can be making money while you might be waiting for your royalty check to get you out of trouble. Also, if one of his other acts is doing well, he might be, could be, probably is spending more time with the act doing well at the time. I have heard a great manager who handled many acts say that management is like spinning plates. You try to keep them all in the air so that none of the plates slow down so much that they stop spinning, fall, and break. You must keep them all spinning, albeit, some might be spinning faster than others and one might really come close to falling, you must keep them all spinning for everyone to survive.*[242]

---

[242] Wacholtz, Larry E., Mark Volman, and Jenifer Wilgus. Off the Record. 3rd ed. Vol. 1. Nashville, TN: Thumbs Up Publishing, 2013.

Representation	Industry	Job Description	Who They Represent	How They are Paid
Personal Manager	Music Industry; Tours, Image, Promotion, Publicity, Song Selection (Advice)	Advise Shows, tours, employees, performance, business opportunities, budgets, labels, branding	Major Recording Artist; Touring Musicians	Percentage 15-20% of Gross
Booking Agent AF of M	Music - for American Federation of Musicians	Tours, Musical Performances	Musicians for tours and performances	Percentage 10% of Gross
Business Manager	Music, Film, and Stage	Control money and financial investments, plus taxes	All	Hourly or 3-5% of Gross
Performance Union Agent SAG-AFTRA	Video - American Federation of Television Radio Artists;	Advice; Find employment	Film, Video, and Stage Actors	Percentage 10% of Gross
SAG-AFTRA	SAG for Actors in Film;			
Equity	Equity/Stage			
Attorney	Music, Film, and Stage	Negotiate, write Contracts, advise artist and managers.	All	Hourly, Salary or retainer
Talent Agent	Film & Visual Media; Tour Music industry	Advice; Connects musical acts to image and branding	Actors; Recording Artist Personalities; Writers; Film production	Percentage 10% of Gross

Figure 11.3: This table provides an example of the various types of representation found in the music industry. Personal managers head the management team for recording artists and may only provide advice, guidance, and counsel. The booking agent is often licensed by the AF of M; the union talent agents are sanctioned by SAG-AFTRA for singers, and Equity for stage performers. The other types of talent agents are those who represent film actors, and other types of personalities in mass and social media.

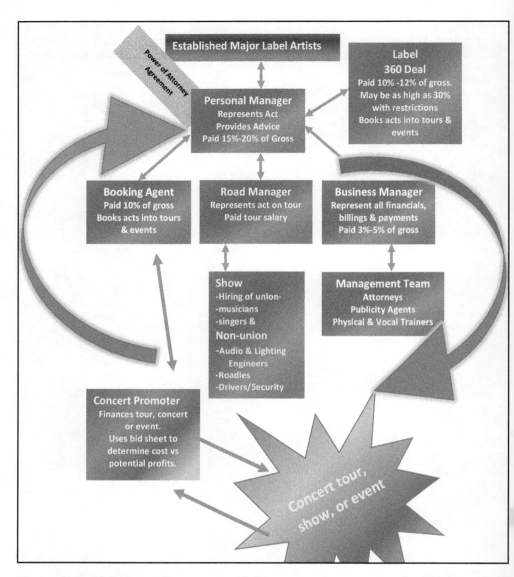

Figure 11.4: The personal manager and the management team work together to maximize an artist's potential income from the fame generated by the label's investments. This chain of events (all in red) is connected to selling the image and brand of the act to a promoter (green) who "buys" the show to perform at an event (concert) being established and funded by the promoter for the purpose of making a profit. The large red arrow indicates the money spend by the act (business manager) to fund the show's musicians and others. The large green arrow represents the money being paid by the promoter for the act to perform, which pay all of the acts bills and provides (hopefully) profits. Also notice the power of attorney agreement between the act and personal manager.

Personal Managers select the recording deals, concert appearances, and staff members who will best enhance the artist's long-term goals. Personal Managers supervise everything connected with the business of the act. They will make recommendations to the artist about whom to consider hiring as their booking agent, business manager, road manager, and sometimes even suggest the touring musicians. However, personal managers are restricted in most states, including California and New York, from actually securing jobs and gigs for the acts they represent. They are limited to only the advise and consent role.

THE ARTIST PERSONAL MANAGER CONTRACT

Nashville entertainment attorney Rush Hicks provided a sample contract between the artist and the personal manager. It will give you an idea of the language and the terms you can expect to read and commit to if you are the artist signing the agreement (2009):

> *WHEREAS, Artist wishes to obtain Manager's exclusive advice, guidance, counsel, and direction to promote and develop Artist's Career as defined herein; and*
>
> *WHEREAS, Manager wishes to provide such services on the terms and conditions set forth herein.*[243]

That expression establishes the purpose of the deal, which is in this case, is to state that the artist and personal manager mutually agree to form a business together. Key terms and corresponding responsibilities of the act and the personal manager are covered in the artist-personal manager agreement. Again, from attorney Rush Hicks (2009),[244]

- *Term-The initial term is usually for two (2) years commencing on the date first written above, and terminating as of the end of the last day of the second year thereafter. Artist hereby grants to manager*

---
[243] Rush Hicks, "The Personal Management Agreement," by (Rush Hicks Esq.: TN, Nashville, 2009).
[244] Rush Hicks, "The Personal Management Agreement," by (Rush Hicks Esq.: TN, Nashville, 2009).

three (3-5) additional one-year option periods (each year referred to as the "Option Period") automatically (approved) exercisable by manager unless manager on or before the end of the preceding Initial Term . . . notifies the artist in writing of its desire to terminate this Agreement.

Manager's Services-Throughout the Term of this Agreement, Manager agrees-

- *To advise, guide, direct and counsel Artist in any and all matters pertaining to employment, publicity, public relations, advertising, the selection of musical material, and all other matters pertaining to Artist's Career which are not specifically excepted herein.*

- *To advise, guide, direct and counsel Artist with relation to the adoption of the proper format for presentation of Artist's talents in the determination of proper style, mood, setting, and characterization in keeping with Artist's talent and best interest.*

- *To advise, guide, direct and counsel Artist in the selection of artistic talents to assist, accompany, or embellish Artist's artistic presentation.*

- *To advise, guide, direct and counsel Artist concerning compensation and privileges for his talent and similar artistic talent.*

- *To advise, guide, direct and counsel Artist concerning the selection of booking agencies, artists' agents, artists' managers, and persons, firms and corporations who will counsel, advise, seek, and procure employment and engagements for Artist.*

- *As pertinent to Artist's Career, to advise, guide, direct and counsel with regard to general practices in the entertainment, music and recording fields and with respect to compensation and terms of contracts related thereto.*

- *To advise, guide, direct and counsel Artist regarding hiring publicists, marketing consultants, advertising agencies, and similar consultants and service providers hired to further Artist's Career.*

- *To meet with Artist when reasonably requested by Artist.*

- *"Artist's Career"-shall mean and refer to Artist's career worldwide in the entertainment and related businesses, including without limitation, work done by Artist in the recording, acting, literary, theatrical, music publishing, music composing, personal appearance, advertising, entertainment, amusement, music, music performance, music video, television, radio, motion picture, motion picture sound track, commercials, endorsements, video, internet and merchandising fields and otherwise related to Artist's career in the entertainment field, as now known or hereinafter devised in which Artist's artistic talents and/or name, voice, likeness, and/or public image are developed and exploited.*

- *Non-Exclusivity-Manager's services under this Agreement are non-exclusive. Manager shall at all times have the right to render the same or similar services to others whose talents may be similar to or may be in competition with Artist, as well as engage in any and all other business activities, however, Manager agrees to be reasonably available to render the services to Artist hereunder.*

- *Territory-Artist's engagement of Manager under this Agreement is exclusive throughout the world.*

- *Agencies and Publicity-Artist may from time to time enter into agreements with talent agencies, theatrical agencies and employ-*

ment agencies whose function and obligation shall be to procure employment and engagements for Artist. Any compensation (which Artist may be required to pay to these agencies) shall be at the sole cost and expense of Artist. If requested by Artist, Manager agrees to supervise and screen the selection and activity of such agency. All expenses of persons of companies specifically retained by Artist to do publicity, public relations or other work on behalf of Artist shall be at the sole cost and expense of Artist.

- *Manager's Authority-Artist hereby grants to Manager the right to approve and permit any and all publicity and advertising and to approve and permit the use of Artist's*

- *Name, pre-approved photograph(s), pre-approved likeness(es), pre-approved voice, pre-approved sound effects, pre-approved caricature(s), and*

- *Pre-approved artistic and musical materials, for purposes of advertising and publicity in the promotion and advertising of Artist's products and services.*

- *Manager agrees to consult with Artist about tour plans and other activities on a regular basis.*

- *Manager shall reasonably attempt to obtain Artist's signature directly or via facsimile (considering Artist's actual availability and the turnaround time with respect to the particular matter concerned), or Manager shall attempt to obtain Artist's written approval . . .*

- *Receipt of Artist's Compensation-Artist shall engage at its expense a business manager to receive all Gross Income for Artist and shall account and remit to manager in each month when there is either*

> *Compensation or expenses due manager out of Gross Income including;*

- *Artist business manager-. . . shall keep accurate and complete books of account and records with respect to all amounts received by Artist and manager in connection with Artist's Career,*

- *Both Artist and Manager-may audit up to three years at a time but may audit any given year only once.*

- *Artist shall cause-to be delivered to manager a full statement of account showing the monthly Gross Income . . .*

- *Manager's Compensation-. . . a sum equal to fifteen percent (15%) of all Gross Income . . . directly or indirectly by Artist or by any other person or entity on Artist's behalf, . . .*

- *After the Term (end of the deal)-Manager shall be paid, in lieu of the Fee, a sum (the "Post-Term Commission") equal to fifteen (15%) percent of all Gross Income (except for items excluded under the paragraph 7 above) received or accrued by Artist for the first five (5) years after the Term has ended, which Post-Term Commission shall be reduced to ten (10%) percent for the five (5) years thereafter, and then further reduced to five (5%) percent for the next five years.*

Before you have the opportunity to sign a Personal Manager-Artist Agreement make sure you take a look and thoroughly understand all the terms and clauses you see in the contract samples above. It is to your advantage to have a clear understanding before you talk to an attorney of what each of these mean.

POWER OF ATTORNEY

Personal managers may legally represent artists through a *power-of-attorney agreement*. Usually, it's part of the artist-personal manager deal granting the personal manager legal authority to control the business and career of the artist. Booking agents, tour or road managers, business managers are then hired to support the personal manager's decisions, as approved by the artist. The *power of attorney* agreement should be limited only to the act's business, and not their financial or personal issues.

TYPES OF PERSONAL MANAGERS

There are several types of personal managers in the business, and their success is generally based on their ability to help artists become rich and famous. Timing is everything, as the act's position in their career (new, established, superstar, etc.) usually determines the types of managers they can employ. If you are a new artist without label or music company support, securing a major personal manager is unlikely. If you're an established artist with a career buzz and consumer fan club momentum, then an established management company may be interested. In the end, the artist and manager relationship is a partnership, sometimes similar to the emotional commitment of a marriage, based on trust, and for the purpose of achieving business goals (making money) that each could not have attained without the other.

COMMISSION BASE AND RATES

Personal managers are typically paid 15-20% of an artist's royalty base, which includes income from record deal sales but not advances or any money from the recording budget. They also receive a percentage of the concert tours, movie appearances, and corporate sponsorships, and in some cases, branding. The standard is 15% for single artist representation and 20% for groups or bands. However, the rates may be more or less depending on what is negotiated based on reputation, and potential success.

GROSS REVENUES

Management payment rates are based on the *gross income* of all or part of whatever the act earns. This too is negotiable, but the more powerful the managers, the less likely they are going to negotiate down the percentage of what they are paid or which types of incomes they are to be paid on which is called "a commission". In addition, most managers will not agree to work for net, which is the amount of money an act is paid after all expenses (touring, recording, agent fees, taxes, etc.) are deducted. Also, the personal manager's typical business expenses (in the name of the artist) are paid out of the artist's gross income, not by the personal manager. Business office expenses, travel, payments to business managers, road managers, and booking agents, who are recommended to be hired by the personal manager in the name of the artist (remember the power-of-attorney), are paid by the artist, not the manager.

BUSINESS MANAGERS

Business managers are the financial experts who provide the accounting, tax planning, and investment advice for the acts. In good management situations, all the money earned by the act goes first to the business manager who then pays everyone. Business managers should be paid a flat or hourly rate for the amount of work they accomplish and for the success of their financial investments. However, expert business managers working for major recording artists are paid a percentage of the gross income (3-5%), as they are more than worth it, considering the amount of paperwork required for the millions of dollars the acts are grossing. It is desirable for a business manager to have a degree in finance or accounting, plus a successful track record in investments and money market funds, and experience with industry professionals.

BOOKING AGENTS

Booking agents for the major label acts are licensed by the AF of M to represent the musicians employed as recording artists, session musicians, and concert performers. The singers, just as the situation was in the recording studio, are represented by SAG-AFTRA. If the recording artist ever wants to be in a theater stage play, then they will need the representation from an Equity licensed agents, who represent professional live theater. The unions, of course, bring the power of collective bargaining and legally supported contracts to encourage businesses to hire union musicians, vocalists, actors, and others, to fulfill their financial and contractual obligations to the artists they employed, as originally stated in the deal.

The licensed booking agent is allowed to employ sub-agents under the unions' agreements. They are paid between 25-50% of the 10% gross income the acts receive when "booked" and paid to perform. Basically, the booking agent's job in the music industry is to connect with Live Nation, AEG-Live, or the independent concert promoters to book the act for a tour or concert event being created by the promoters. The booking agents cannot approve the date, price, or the booking without the approval of the personal manager. If approved, 100% to 50% of the artist's payment is deposited into an interest-bearing account until the act arrives, stands on stage, and starts the performance. At that point, there is an electronic transfer of the funds from the first account into the artist's business manager's account.

Tour or Road Managers

Road managers are responsible for the daily business decisions dealing with concerts and personal appearances on the tour. As a result, road managers handle the local press as well as questions and concerns from promoters, local radio stations, and record retail promotions. They also have to be on top of branding, merchandise, and any issues with corporate endorsements, such as road banners and advertising connected to the tour. In addition, they may have to make hotel and restaurant reservations. They also may have to act as go-betweens and address problems or concerns that may arise among the recording artist(s), band members, roadies, and tour support. Many established artists outsource all hotel and dining reservations to an independent company who make the reservations instead of expecting the personal manager to do so.

ATTORNEYS

Attorney are hired at the recommendation of the personal manager to supervise all legal issues associated with the act's business, including their contracts. Attorneys are central to an act's success in the business. It is well worth the time and money on the front end of the deal to pay for expert legal advice as that may save millions of dollars later. Attorneys charge hourly rates of ($250-1,000 per-hour) or are placed on a retainer, which is a monthly minimum fee. Unless the attorney will be very busy with the client's work, by-pass the retainer and pay the hourly fee.

OUTSOURCING

Most of the management team members have their own businesses and are simply "hired" by the artists through the personal manager as a work-for-hire. In other words, the personal manager will "outsource" as many positions as possible in order to reduce the payroll when the act is not touring. As an example, the road manager, security, drivers, roadies, tour supervision (people who make the hotel reservations, etc.,) musicians, and backup singers are only used when they are needed. Remember, this industry is highly entrepreneurial, and thus, the musicians, drivers, road managers etc., have their own businesses and often work several different shows (acts) during the year.

TERMINATION OF THE DEAL

Sometimes the breakup of an artist and manager is similar to a divorce as lawsuits and counter lawsuits are not uncommon, with the manager claiming commissions on the artists' future royalties. Unless there has been some kind of criminal conduct by the manager, he or she usually wins, gaining partial royalty payment for a limited time. Also, at the end of some deals, the manager may continue to receive a part of their commissions based on the idea that the act's future success is based on decisions the management team made during their tenure.

THE LABEL CONNECTION

The purpose of representation is to monetize the artist's career created by the label's investments and then to manage every opportunity created for the maximum potential profits for the act. Remember, the labels operate by funding the development of the act, their recordings, and then by providing marketing, promotion, publicity, and tour support. What they've created for the personal manager and the management team is an opportunity to turn their investments in the artists into additional profits for everyone. And also remember the label is providing the seed money to fund the tour through tour support.

Labels, under 360 deals, are paid 10-15% of the artist's gross royalties derived from the act's activities, as managed by the personal manager. It's a win/win situation if the artist develops a significant fan base, willing to spend money for the live ticket, merchandise, and product brands. Additional money is often dropped by corporate endorsements, if the act connects to the types of fans (lifestyles) that fit into a company's target market.

PROMOTERS

Promoters are the next step in the equation as they provide the money, research, and personnel to stage concerts, events, and festivals. The artists started this journey by playing local clubs and shows to become as successful as possible in their local markets. If that works, they take a step up in the process and start touring the region or short-hop tours of clubs in visiting cities and states. At the same time, as we've already discussed, they should be attempting to build a fan base from Internet sites and social media. The promoter, in the beginning is really the night club owners and managers who "book" them for shows. The problem is trying to land a gig when you're unknown in your local city or state. The club owners are afraid that no one will show up and they'll lose money.

THE CATCH-22

The club managers, and even Live Nation and AEG-Live, are not going to sign unknown acts to play their clubs, bars, festivals or tours, as they know the unknown acts can't draw a crowd, which means no money! The catch -22 is: How can an unknown band become known, if they can't get the gig where they will be seen by potential fans?

It's expensive to create a show even in the small clubs, as the building, employees, booze, food, licensing, taxes, and other costs of doing business add up. Thus, the club manager wants the biggest, most famous acts they can pay the least amount of money to play, in order to bring in the largest possible crowd. The major independent promoters and national touring companies have the very same approach concerning artists and tours. They have a very hard time supporting unknown and unsigned acts to labels, as they know the infrastructure to establish a fan base is missing. What that means is that beginning acts need to create a win/win situation for the club owners and themselves by helping generate an attendance, and contributing to the promotion and social media outlets in a manner that will benefit both the club and band.

SUMMARY

The power has shifted in the industry from the traditional major label model to a cooperative team effort between record label executives and artist's representation to launch and support the iconic artists. Labels spend the usual $500,000 to $2,000,000 breaking the acts, and that was cool when they could sell enough albums to make a sizable profit. However, with album sales fading fast, both the labels and management team members had to change their thinking toward helping each other succeed. Without the

10-12% additional revenues from the artist's gross income, labels would probably not survive. And without the significant financial investment from the labels on the front end to launch the act's career, both would fail.

In the past, the artist's representation team, consisting of the personal manager, booking agent, and business manager fought for their artists with the label executives trying to secure more money, and promotional support from the labels. It's still somewhat the same under the 360 model, except now the labels are demanding more from the management team, as they've spent the money to launch the act and they expect the management team to understand that they are now part of their business (revenues).

At the same time, artist management has come to realize that without the label's financial investment in the artist's recordings, development, promotion, publicity, marketing distribution, and tour support, they would probably not have anyone to manage as nobody would have ever heard of the artists. It costs money, serious money, to launch an act's career; or, if you're an indie artist, then it's going to take lots of time, usually years. And in this industry, time is money! Thus, it's a new day as the label executives and the members of the artist's management team have readjusted their business models to include each other as team members, who serve as consultants by working together to increase the profitability of the act and their own business interests.

The personal manager's job is to advice and guide (meaning give advice) to the artists about how to build a successful career. The booking agent's job is to sell the live ticket show to promoters for as much money as possible. The personal manager usually receives 15% for a solo act and 20% for a band. However, Elvis's manager reportedly made 50% of everything, so anything is possible. The booking agent is often franchised by the AF of M as the labels are signatories to both SAG-AFTRA and the AF of M and the artists are union members. Booking agents receive 10% of the live ticket show's gross. The business managers for major artists also get a piece of the action which is about 3-5%. So, let's add it up, as the personal manager of a band receives 20%, the booking agent 10%, the record labels 10-12%, and the business manager 3-5%. By the way, the top industry labels and management team members are worth everything you have to pay them, as they have the resources, time, experience, knowledge, contacts, and abilities to take the artists from local success to world superstar.

Take a couple of minutes to review the "Block of Knowledge" layers and how they relate to each other before moving on to the next chapter.

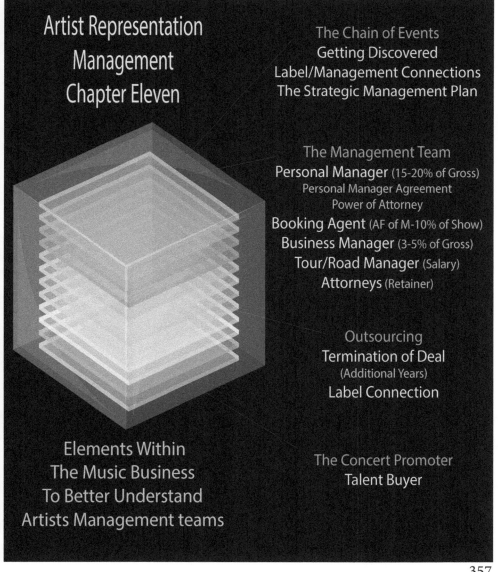

Artist Representation
Management
Chapter Eleven

The Chain of Events
Getting Discovered
Label/Management Connections
The Strategic Management Plan

The Management Team
Personal Manager (15-20% of Gross)
Personal Manager Agreement
Power of Attorney
Booking Agent (AF of M-10% of Show)
Business Manager (3-5% of Gross)
Tour/Road Manager (Salary)
Attorneys (Retainer)

Outsourcing
Termination of Deal
(Additional Years)
Label Connection

Elements Within
The Music Business
To Better Understand
Artists Management teams

The Concert Promoter
Talent Buyer

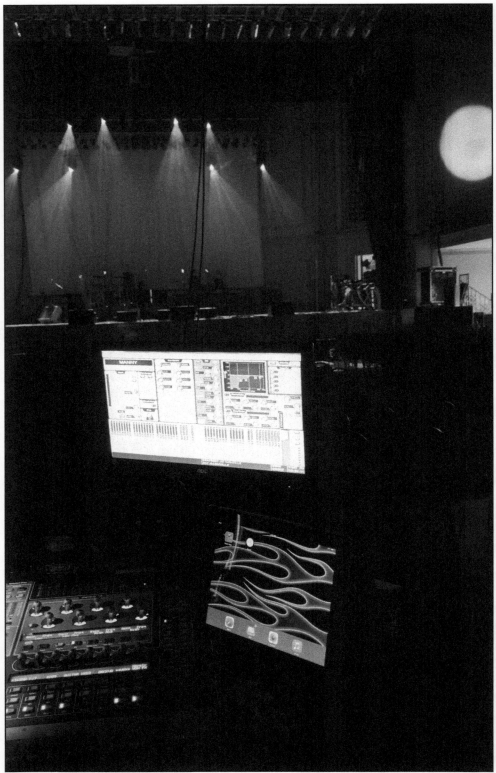

Chapter 12

Creating a Stage Show

Once the artist has the "machine" supporting them (label and representation), then it is time to build the live show with the booking agent's pitch to the promoters. The cost, size, type, etc., of the show depends on where the act is on the "entertainment business chain of events". If they are at the beginning, then the cost of the show is basic; if they are building a new fan base and have a label and management team in place, then they are somewhere in the middle; and, if they are superstars, then they are at the end; or, as we like to say in the business "at the top".

Beginning acts are seeking exposure and will probably break even or lose money on the shows and tours. Experienced and professional artists have learned the system, have the connections, and reputations to make a very good living preforming locally or on the road. Major label acts usually spend the first year, as you already know, preparing to launch their careers, but once on the road success builds to a point where the money is more than significant. Superstars have expensive tours, but end up making millions of dollars.

CREATING A SHOW

You'd think creating a show would be easy, but it's not. Beginning acts learn quickly that playing a gig in a local bar, nightclub, or small venue is much more than moving out of the garage onto a larger stage. A series of decisions and events have to happen first, as you read about in this chapter. Start by reviewing a business plan to quickly understand what steps you'll need to complete to launch your band as a business and to secure a venue for a performance.

The Band's Legal Business

You're a legal business as soon as you start receiving money from performances. The entertainment business description of legal business includes licensing, band agreements, employment contracts with club managers, etc., and, an agreement between the band members. It's important to decide who owns the band and the name of the band. Remember in Chapter 5, we covered the different types of legal businesses including Sole Proprietorships, Partnerships, Limited Liability Corporations, and, Corporations. If the members are all members of the band's business, then an LLC or a Corporation is best. A Partnership Agreement is fine except there are less legal protections provided against lawsuits. With LLCs and Corporations, you receive the legal protection, but you get taxed twice. If the members of the band do not own the band's business, then they are probably Sole Proprietorships working as independent contractors.

In addition, depending on the type of business selected you may need to file a DBA (doing business as) with the state and you may also need to file for a business license from the city where you reside. Don't forget to also clear the name of the band by searching and then trademarking the name of the band with the state and federal government.

The Band, Crew, & Equipment

Depending on your decisions about who owns the band and the band's name you may or may not want to hire additional musicians and singers for the show. The band members and additional musicians and singers will probably be independent contractors meaning you may provide whatever deal you want with them. In most cases, when performing in local venues few of you will be members of the AF of M or SAG-AFTRA. Musicians usually supply their own gear, but you'll still have to figure out who is going to pay for the audio equipment, lighting, and merchandise you'll want to sell at the events.

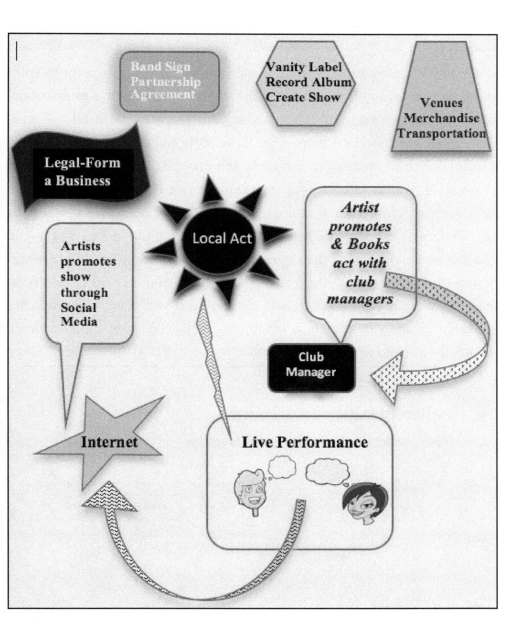

Figure 12.1: The local band has to follow a chain of events by forming a business; having the band members sign a partnership (or LLC) agreement; rehearsing the show; buying the needed audio and lighting gear. The band functions as its own manager, booking agent, and promoter to pitch the act to local venues. The purpose of live shows in local venues is to create an opportunity to build a fan base through word of mouth and social media.

The Live Ticket Show

When you're just getting started, in most cases, you've got a lot to learn about the business of putting on a show. You won't have a professional booking agent or personal manager, so you'll have to do it all yourself. Before you get frustrated, remember its actually fun and you'll be meeting a lot of new and interesting people in the process. Rehearse for the type of stage and venue in your local market that you'll be playing. Shows in large arenas before 10,000 fans are much different than the nightclub or bar. Rehearsal space can often be rented with sample stages and sound gear for you to determine the sequence of the songs and your stage presentation. Most importantly, think about who the customers will be and what they might want to hear. They will determine if you'll get a second shot at each club and venue by how much they enjoy the show and how much money they spend on booze and food.

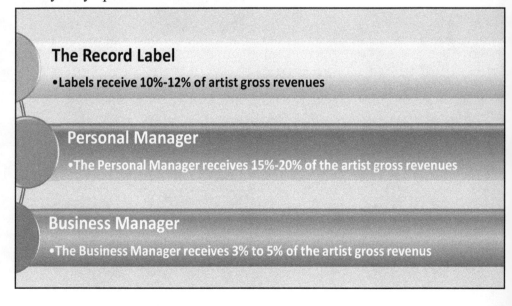

Figure 12.2: In 360 deals, the labels receive a percentage of the artist's gross revenues, as they have underwritten the marketing, promotion, publicity. The Personal Manager receives 15%-20% and the Business Manager 3%-5%. In total, that means that 38%-47% of whatever the act generates in revenues is already owed to the label and management.

TRANSPORTATION

Only major label recording artists can usually afford a bus and semi-truck for their shows and tours. Settle for a trailer or rent a van and just be glad you don't have to pay the gas or diesel bill while using a rented bus. If you keep notes of all the expenses in your business plan, you'll be able to write them off in your annual tax reports, and, that includes insurance and gas.

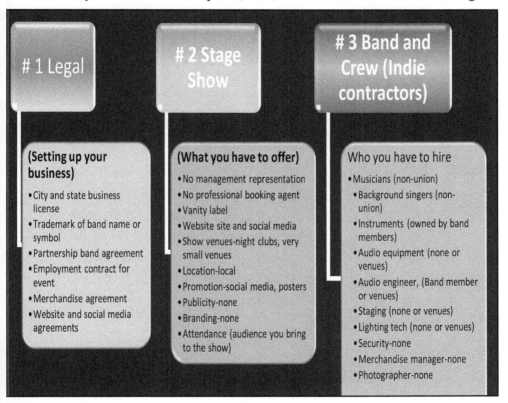

Figure 12.3: Breaking into the industry as a new band in a local community is a step- by -step process. Moving from the garage to a live stage takes preparing the show and making decisions that establish the band as a legal business.

HOTELS & FOOD

Sadly, many new acts lose money when starting out as a band performing live, so try to avoid the overnight hotel bills and expensive booze and food. When launching your act by performing, the purpose of the show is not to make money but to give the consumer a chance to discover you.

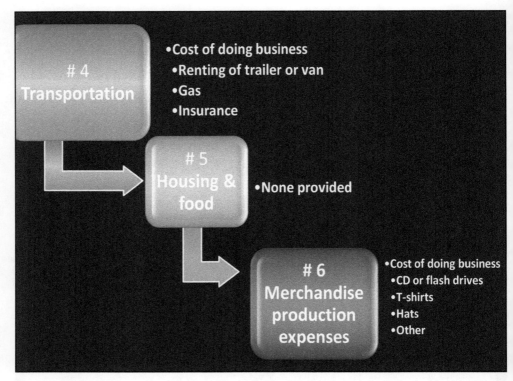

Figure 12.4: Planning to put on a show takes additional steps in the chain of events as the band now has to consider the economics of their show opportunities. When breaking into the business, exposure is the name of the game. The question is why would the manager or promoter hire this unknown band to perform in their establishment?

MERCHANDISE

Most new artists first record an album using ProTools or some other type of software and then upload it to the Internet, usually giving it away free. Two things to remember, if you give it away, it's hard to sell CDs at a club performance as merchandise, and the label won't be interested in signing you if the recordings don't score millions of sales or streams. However, you may create a vanity label as streaming companies pay labels for the streams (and you are the label). Then join SoundExchange, which will pay you as the label, artist (you again), and the musicians (you, one more time) digital royalties for satellite radio and streams. Also, remember to register your claim of copyrights for your songs and the claim of copyright for the recordings of the songs as you own both of them. If you're also the music publisher or songwriter join ASCAP, BMI, or SESAC. If you do not join all these organizations in the system, you will not be paid.

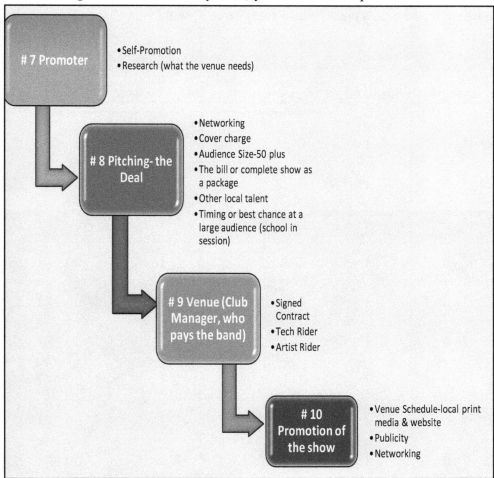

Figure 12.5: The last steps in the chain of events are really a checklist of things the band has to accomplish to book the gig. They have to act as self-promoters, researching the best venues for their target market of consumers. They have to pitch the deal to the bar or night club managers or event promoters; get a signed contract; and, provide the artist and tech riders.

Typical merchandise items sold by new artists are a few T-shirts, key chains, and hats. You'll have to pay for them on the front end and then crank up the price when selling them at shows. However, remember that a fan wearing your T-shirt or hat is also a traveling advertisement for the band. Make sure, as you become more successful, to have a link on your home page to a store website where viewers may purchase merchandise, and leave their emails so that you can send them discounts and notices when you'll be playing again in their area.

SELF-PROMOTING

Kicking off your band's career means that you'll be wearing several hats.

Process	Beginning of Career	Established Artists	Super Star
Legal	(Setting up your business) As a Sole Proprietor or LLC Band pays upfront expenses City and state business license Trademark of band name or symbol Partnership band agreement Employment contract for event Merchandise agreement Website and social media agreements	Attorney as a LLC or Corporation	Attorney as a Corporation
Business of the Stage Show	Band pays upfront expenses No management representation No professional booking agent Vanity label Website site and social media Show venues-nightclubs, very small venues Location-local Promotion-social media, posters Publicity-none Branding-none Attendance (audience you bring to the show)	Personal Manager & Management Team	Personal Manager & Management Team
Band and Crew	Work for free or percent of door Musicians (non-union) Background singers (non-union) Instruments (owned by band members) Audio equipment (none or venues) Audio engineer, (Band and member or venues) Staging (none or venues) Lighting tech (none or venues) Security-none Merchandise manager-none Photographer-none	Union Members of AF of M & SAG-AFTRA Staging covered in Tech & Artist Rider	Union Members of AF of M & SAG-AFTRA Staging covered in Tech & Artist Rider

You're a member of the band. You are acting as the booking agent and concert promoter. When they are getting their start, a lot of band's think the first chain in the business chain of events is to tie into the established infrastructure of the entertainment and music industry, unaware that booking agents and personal managers are paid on a percentage of what the band makes.

Process	Beginning of Career	Established Artists	Super Star
Transportation	Band Pays upfront expenses Renting of trailer or van Gas Insurance	Bus & Truck	Airplane & equipment & crew bus, truck
Housing & food	None	Per-diem	Per-diem
Merchandise production	Band pays upfront expenses CD or flash drives T-shirts Hats Other	Outsourced or label fulfillment	Outsourced or label fulfillment
Branding	None	Outsourced or label fulfillment	Outsourced or label fulfillment
Booking Agent	Self-booking	Union licensed (10% of gross)	Union licensed (10% of gross)
Promoter	Self-Promoter	No cost to band	No cost to band
Venues	Nightclubs Bars Small theaters Private parties	Small venues 1,000-5,000 seats plus	World venues 12,000-plus seats
The Deal	Non-union agreements Networking required by band Cover charge Audience Size-50 plus Bar bill Billing-local talent Timing (local events)	Personal Manager & Management Team (25-35% of gross revenues)	Personal Manager & Management Team (25-35% of gross revenues)
Show Promotion	Venue Schedule-local print media & website Publicity Networking	Label Management Team Promoter	Label Management Team Promoter

Figure 12.6 & 7: Next, consider the products your selling which are the stage show to the promoter and your merchandise to the fans.

Since the band can't make any money because no one knows who they are, it is a mistake to expect industry professionals to provide you with representation at this point in your career. However, a start-up band still needs a booking agent, manager, and a promoter to find the gigs to play. Guess who that is going to be? Do more research to determine the club's availability for shows, who are the main contacts, and the numbers of people who typically attend each night of the week. With that information, you'll be able to understand from the club manager's perspective what the best possible deal is for them.

Venues

People like different types of clubs and venues including bars, small theaters, private parties, festivals, and, don't forget, colleges. Bands need to play shows in locations where the target market is, not where the people in the audience will not be interested in that musical genre or type of show. Research and locate the venues that can help you the most by putting you in front of the types of consumers you want to become fans.

Pitching the Deal

To review, you're a member of the band, a business owner, a booking agent, promoter, and now you've got to become a sales person. What you're really becoming is an entrepreneur and that's a good thing. But now you've got to sell the band's live show to a nightclub, bar, and some other type of event planner. Try to create a win-win situation where you can expect to increase the club's attendance by about 50 people. To the manager that's music to their ears as the booze and food sales increase profits. Consider the ways you'll be paid such as a cover charge or a percent of the door. Don't ask for any money from food sales or booze as that is not possible. Also, consider the timing of the show, such as the day of the week, as you don't want to perform when most people are at another event or away for summer instead of attending classes.

Show Promotion

The new band is expected to deliver the extra customers to the club, which just adds the name of the band to their website schedule. It's up to the band to generate a local buzz about the show through the social media, posters, networking, contacts, and tweets to drive the fans to the performance. If enough fans show up, have a great time, spend money, and love the sound and show, the act will be invited back by the club manager. A couple more times if the crowds keep getting larger and then, at the next show, you can charge more money for each show. When that happens, you've created a solid fan base excited to see you and who will pay more.

Website & Press Kits

Press kits have become a thing of the past; yet, you'll still need some type of electronic press and promotion pack to send to potential clients. The purpose is to get them to your website where they can catch your recordings, news, and videos to see if you'd fit their establishment, venue, or program.

Creating the Tour

The steps our beginning band had to accomplish to generate a buzz are taken care of for the establish major label artists and superstar acts by their personal manager and the corresponding management team members. The labels provide the tour funds that get the band on the road. Setting up the business, show creation, transportation, hotels, concert deals, venues, and promoter's offers are evaluated with the final decision being made by the personal manager. Then, the management team completes the difficult work of rehearsals, contracts, staging the show, transportation, marketing, promotion, and publicity. If you've ever question what professional representation does for their 30-35% of the artist's gross revenues, now you know.

The Rehearsal

The personal manager and the management team will prepare the artist they represent for a show on tour. A road or tour manager, musicians, backup singers, audio, lighting, and road crew members will be hired and rehearsed. Union musicians and rehearsal staging personal must also be paid union scales (if they are members of the union) for each day of work, which will usually run for several days to two weeks depending on the complexity of the show. Rehearsals can be expensive for established and newly signed acts. The following is an example of the two-week rehearsal budget for a mid-level act with six musicians, taking four back-up singers, with additional lighting and audio out on the road.

Item	Union/ Minimum	Hours	Sub-Total	Days	Sub-Total	#	Total
Musicians	Side $40-per hour	8	$320	10	$3,200	5	$16,000
	Leader $80-per hour	8	$640	10	$6,400	1	$6,400
Cartage	$12-36.00 per day	1	$24 (Ave)	10	$240	6	$1,440
Royalty Artists as Musician	Triple scale leader $240-perhour	8	$1,920	10	$19,200	1	$19,200
Back-up Singers	$50 per hour	4	200	5	$1,000	4	$4,000
Royalty Artists as Singer	Triple scale $150-per hour	4	$600	5	$2,400	1	$2,400
Audio Engineer	$500 per day rate	8	$500	10	$5,000	1	$5,000
Lighting	$400 per day rate	8	$500	4	$2,000	1	$2,000
Rehearsal Hall/room	$400 per day rate	8	$400	10	$4,000	1	$4,000
Food Beverages	$25 per person	Breakfast & Lunch	$25	10	$250	15	$3,750
Total							About $65,000

Figure 12.8: Rehearsing for a road tour can be expensive. In the above example, we paid six AF of M musicians scale rehearsal rates for ten days and four back-up singers for four days. The musicians also received cartage for their instruments, the audio engineer and lighting were paid top scales, as they would be highly regarded and hired to match the extra staging required for an upscale show. We also had to pay for a rehearsal room with stage, audio, and lighting already provided. Union requirements provide for a light breakfast and lunch, so they are also budgeted.

AF OF M ROAD SHOW SCALES

The AF of M has minimum wage scales and pension requirements for touring musicians. Contracts include the L-1, LS-1, and AFM T-2, which are the three types of live performance scales and contracts for everything from concerts to parties and weddings. For tours, the AF of M recommends the AFM T-2 for live performances (on tour) in the United States and Canada. The requirements include a minimum wage of $200 per 50-minute show, plus a 10% payment to the pension or EP fund. In addition, a per-diem of $35.00 per-day and $70.00 per- non-performance days, plus travel expenses and hotel accommodations for each musician. The lead musician receives double scale just as in the recording studio sessions.[245] Obviously, for the show we are pricing the musicians will be paid a weekly salary or a per-show payment in excess of the union minimum requirements.

PRICING THE SHOW

The staging equipment and transportation trucks and buses must be rented and leased. Hotel rooms will be booked, and security hired if the act is at the status to need one or more. What's known as the "asking price for the show" is determined by pricing the seven parts of the "staging budget":

- Travel to the venue

- Transportation of performers, crew, and equipment

---

[245] "Nashville Musicians Association American Federation of musicians local 257 Nashville Road Scale." Nashvillemusicians.org. Accessed July 25, 2017. https://www.nashvillemusicians.org/sites/default/files/Road%20Scale.pdf.

- Equipment leases or rentals

- Union scale salaries for performers and weekly salaries for all others (road crews, drivers, security, etc.)

- Road or tour manager's salary

- Hotels

- Per-diem for all personnel associated with the show

The routing of the show is important, unless you're Lady Gaga, who performed almost every 2 to 3 days a week for months at a time. You'll want to get 3 to 4 shows in a week, at best. And out on the road means gone from home for an extended period of time until the tour is over. The exception is the main royalty artist, who may fly from show to show or fly home once in a while for a short stay between shows. In addition, some independent promoters may offer a "pickup" show which is usually staged in smaller markets between two larger cites. Those shows are last minute deals and often at a lower price, as the promoter offers a way for the act to collect extra money instead of just driving through the town. The following budget is an example of a "baseline tour budget" for an act on a 28 show, 40 day tour. Notice that we've included union musicians and singers, the cost of manufacturing the merchandise, and travel.

BASELINE BUDGET

Pricing a show is difficult. The acts want the most amount of money possible for their show and the promoter (who is hiring the act to perform) wants to pay as little as possible. It all comes down to the fame of the act and how many fans will want to buy tickets at various prices. And our baseline budget show us that it'll cost about $35,000 to put on the show paid for by the act's company out of his or her pocket or the acts financial backers. We are using the average expenses and weekly salaries for an established act presenting an upscale show with extra lighting and sound effects, for mid-size 5,000 to 15,000 seat arenas and venues over the 40-day tour.

Item	#	Cost				Shows	Debt	Revenue
Rehearsal	1	Total cost of rehearsal for show					$65,000	
Royalty Artist	1	$12,500 reserve for royalty artists				28	$350,000	
Musicians	6	$1,000 per-show				28	$168,500	
		$250 non-show days				11	$16,500	
Backup Singers	4	$700 per-show				28	$78,400	
		$150 non-show days				11	$6,600	
Road Manager	1	$200 per-show days				28	$5,600	
		$150 non-show day including rehearsals				26	$3,900	
Audio Tech	1	$500 per-show				28	$14,000	
		$100 non-show days				11	$1,100	
Lighting Tech	1	$500 per-show				28	$14,000	
		$100 non-show days				11	$1,000	
Merchandise Salesperson	1	$100 per-show day				28	$2,800	
		$25 non-show day				11	$275	
Merchandise For sale	5	Merc Item	Cost	Price	Sold		Total Expense	Profits
		T-shirt	$4.00 with logo	$12.00 profit of $8.00	125,000	350,000 Seats/Tickets	$500,000	$1,500,000 -$500,000 **$1,000,000**
		Sweat Shirt	$8.50 with logo	$35.00 profit of $26.50	35,000	350,000 Seats/Tickets	$297,500	$1,225,000 -$297,000 **$928,000**
		Hat	$6.00 with logo	$15.00 profit of $9.00	80,000	350,000 Seats/Tickets	$480,000	$1,200,000 -$480,000 **$720,000**
		Key Chain	60¢ with logo	$5.00 profit of $4.40	15,000	350,000 Seats/Tickets	$9,000	$75,000 -$9,000 **$64,000**
Taxes in local market	28 at 10%							Total $2,712,000 -$271,200 Total Merc **$2,440,800**

Item	#	Cost				Shows	Debt	Revenue
Air Travel Royalty Artist	1	Show #	Day	City	Ticket		Expense	
		Rehearsal	Thu	Gainesville, FL		1	$425	
		1	Fri	Atlanta		1	$399	
		2	Sat	Charlotte		1	$564	
		3	Sun	Travel		-------		
		4	Mon	Louisville, (pickup)		1	$769	
		5	Tue	Cincinnati (pickup)		1	$517	
		6	Wed	Travel		-------		
		7	Thu	Pittsburgh		1	$538	
		8	Fri	Buffalo		1	$995	
		9	Sat	Toronto, ONT		1	$191	
		10	Sun	Montreal, QUE	home	1	$621	
		11	Mon	Travel	home	-------	-------	
		12	Tue	Travel	return	1	$557	
		13	Wed	Boston		1	$287	
		14	Thu	New York		1	$389	
		15	Fri	Philadelphia		1	$607	
		16	Sat	Alexandria		1	$499	
		17	Sun	Newport News (pickup)	home	1	$733	
		18	Mon	Travel	home	-------	-------	
		19	Tue	Travel	home	-------	-------	
		20	Wed	Travel	return	1	$433	
		21	Thu	Minneapolis		1	$287	
		22	Fri	Chicago		1	$287	
		23	Sat	Indianapolis		1	$621	
		24	Sun	St. Louis		1	$508	
		25	Mon	Travel		-------	-------	
		26	Tue	Kansas City		1	$276	
		27	Wed	Travel		-------	------	
		28	Thu	Oklahoma City		1	$288	
		29	Fri	Dallas		1	$331	
		30	Sat	Austin		1	$794	
		1	Sun	San Antonio (pickup)		1	$523	
		2	Mon	Travel		-------	------	
		3	Tue	New Orleans		1	$570	
		4	Wed	Travel		-------	------	
		5	Thu	Memphis		1	$667	
		6	Fri	Jacksonville		1	$997	
		7	Sat	Tampa		1	$1,028	
		8	Sun	Fort Lauderdale		1	$619	
		9	Mon	Travel	home	1	-------	
Total for plane flights	31	-------	---	-------	---	-------	$16,320	
Limo	36	$100-per day	---	-------	---	36	$3,600	
Bus (Leased)	2	$1,000 per-day per bus. Musicians and singers will have hotel rooms as required by union agreements. Bus one will sleep 6 and bus two 5.				40	$40,000	
Driver- also provides security	2	$150 a day for driving				40	$12,000	
		$100 for security duties				28	$5,600	

Staging Equipment	1	One minor leased package of extra lighting, staging, effects and audio	40	$30,000
Road Crew	5	$200 load in and load out days	28	$28,000
		$50.00 travel days (sleeping)	11	$2,750
Per-diems show days	7	$35 Musicians (includes royalty artists)	28	$6,860
	4	$35 Singers	28	$3,920
	11	$25 All other personal	28	$7,700
Per-diems non-show days	7	$70 Musicians (includes royalty artists	11	$5,390
	4	$70 Singers	11	$3,080
	11	$50 All others	11	$6,050
Hotel room	1	$300 Royalty artists (flies home for 5 night during extended travel)	35	$10,500
Hotel rooms	10	$150 Musicians and singers	40	$60,000
Legal	1	One-time expense for legal supervision and approval of all contracts.	1	$2,500
Insurance	1 policy	$2,500 for only 60 days, plus a million-dollar bond for personal manger, artists, and management team	60	$2,500
Cost of Tour	1	Total cost of tour		$975,735
Average	28	The average cost of each show (includes rehearsal and travel days)	28	**$34,847**

Figure 12.9, a, b, & c: The show will cost about $975,000.00 to complete the 40-day tour and could gross a little more than $7,500,000, depending on the asking price and how much money the promoters pay. This is a situation of risk vs. an opportunity based on the assumptions of the value of the act to the fans and how much they are willing to spend on the live ticket event.

This baseline tour budget provides an estimate of what it will cost to put on a tour with 28 shows over 40 days. However, that does not cover the cost of representation which includes the personal manager, business manager, and the booking agent. This is where the budgeting process get tricky. On top of the baseline budget, which we determined is about $35,000 per show, we have to add money the band will owe to the management representation team (excluding the booking agent). Here is how that looks:

- Personal manager - 20%

- Business manager- 5%

The estimate for the show must include the personal manager's and business manager's percentages of the gross as a reserve, which means their payments are included in the asking price. Remember, they are paid off of the gross instead of the net. Thus, if the asking price for the show only covered the cost of the show, there'd be no money to pay the personal and business manager. Don't forget that the cost of your representation team is calculated in addition to the baseline budget of the show. In our example, that mistake would cost the artist $7,000 and $1,750 to pay the personal manager and the business manager per show. Therefore, we need to add $8,175.00 to the asking price.

We can't figure the booking agent's 10%, because we're still in the process of determining the asking price for the show. Remember, the booking agent receives 10% of the gross amount promoters pay for the show.

The Asking Price

The personal manager and booking agent are still trying to determine an "asking price" for each show. Promoters usually book an act by the asking price for a show unless it's Live Nation, AEG-Live or one of the other major promoter companies setting up a tour. As you've seen, the cost to the band or artists for putting on each show is $34,847, which we'll round up to $35,000. We also had to add the personal's and business mangers' percentage of gross payments of $8,175 on top of the per-show cost for a total of $43,715. We'll also round up that to $45,000.

The Value of the Act

You may have thought that figuring out the "asking price" the booking agent quotes to promoters for hiring the act or band to perform was simple. My guess is you are now starting to understanding that it's not as easy as you'd think. However, our journey to find our asking price is almost complete.

What's the value of the iconic act is the next issue. Are their recordings on the top charts on broadcast radio? Are they getting millions of hits on streaming sites? Is their fan base increasing quickly? The record labels executives know the answers to these important questions and they will share them with the personal manager. What is the psychographic lifestyle(s) of their fan base? How much money do they make, their age, preferences, and the other acts they enjoy most?

If the personal manager handles Taylor Swift, the asking price is in the neighborhood of a million dollars per show. If it's a new, just breaking major label act, the asking price is often around $50,000 or less. In this instance, we have an established act that is rising on the charts and building a very sold fan base. How much should the asking price be? Our basic rule is to triple the budget line plus the expenses of the representation team. So in our situation, we would think that the asking price is $45,000 times 3, or, $135,000. But we are not done yet!

If we get $45,000 plus another 10% for the booking agent, we have covered all of our expenses, everyone got paid, and we made money on selling the merchandise. Remember, we have to add 10% of the final price per-show to cover the booking agent's percentage for acquiring the gig. That means we are now at $45,000 plus $4,500, which we'll round up to $5,000, so our final base price is $50,000, meaning that $50, 000 will cover all the bills. Now, based on the value of the act, we can triple the $50,000 to $150,000 and we have our FINAL asking price of $150,000 per show.

The Price Range

The promoters, with the personal manager and the management team, work together, to varying degrees, on the band's tour schedule and venues, the housing and cartage arrangements, the characteristics of the show itself, and the merchandise and vending set-ups. The booking agent opens the negotiation with the promoter by announcing the asking price. Promoters rarely pay the asking price, unless you're a superstar, and, then they try to construct a deal in their favor. In this example, unless the act or band gets hot, hot, hot in the very near future, we may/ may not always get our asking price. If two or three promoters want the act or band for the same night, the price goes up. If only one is interested, then the booking agent and manager are more flexible on the price to accept.

In this band's situation, a price of $150,000 is in the middle of what similar bands are also getting. Therefore, we now have a range of our asking price of $150,000 which is fair and competitive with the other bands out touring. We now have the ability to play for a lower price and still make significant profits. Most of the shows will book at $145,000 to $130,000. The pickup shows, which are last minute on the tour route, will book for as low as $75,000 to $111,000. Now, it's up to the booking agent to get the shows booked and the final approval is up to the personal manager.

BOOKING AGENT'S FEE

In our situation, the personal manager can now predict a range of gross revenues generated from the tour. Let's take a look at an example, from the expense sheet provided earlier. Remember, our first show in Gainesville was used as the final rehearsal so we only grossed the $50,000.00.

OPPORTUNITY VS RISK

The 28 shows in our example grossed $3,510,000. The highest gross, if all shows had sold at the asking price, would have been a little over $4 million and the lowest gross, if sold at the bottom rate of $75,000, would have been a little over $2 million. From the gross, we have to deduct the booking agent's 10% or $351,000. The risk vs opportunity for the label is the total investment of $500,000-$2,000,000 vs the multiple rights royalties generated by branding, streaming, the live ticket, album and single sales and other revenue sources. For the artist, the cost (risk) of the label deal is zip, yet, the financial potential is huge (opportunity).

As we can see in our example, the risk vs opportunity is a $975,000,000 upfront cost vs a possible gross return of about $8,175,000. But with the cost of the musicians, singers, tech, roadies, staging, representation, the O/R is closer to a one ($975,000) to four ratio (possible gross of over $4,000,000) after paying management and before taxes. The promoter's level of opportunity vs risk is high, as the amount of money made or lost may be significant. The hired musicians, singers, techs, etc., have the least risk, as they often have union representation, and, are paid as independent contractors.

The label has the highest risk over a period of years, while the promoter has a short-term risk, which is the evening of the event. In the following *Figure 12.10 look at the Opportunity vs Risk* and *in Figure 12.11* observe the different amounts of money concert promoters paid for the shows.

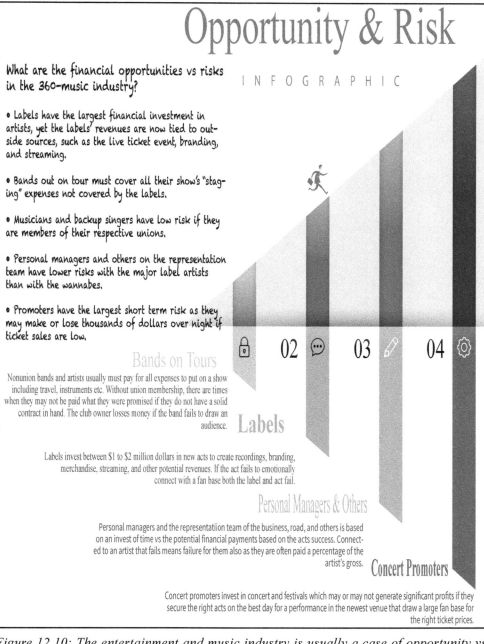

Opportunity & Risk

What are the financial opportunities vs risks in the 360-music industry?

INFOGRAPHIC

• Labels have the largest financial investment in artists, yet the labels' revenues are now tied to outside sources, such as the live ticket event, branding, and streaming.

• Bands out on tour must cover all their show's "staging" expenses not covered by the labels.

• Musicians and backup singers have low risk if they are members of their respective unions.

• Personal managers and others on the representation team have lower risks with the major label artists than with the wannabes.

• Promoters have the largest short term risk as they may make or lose thousands of dollars over night if ticket sales are low.

Bands on Tours
Nonunion bands and artists usually must pay for all expenses to put on a show including travel, instruments etc. Without union membership, there are times when they may not be paid what they were promised if they do not have a solid contract in hand. The club owner losses money if the band fails to draw an audience.

Labels
Labels invest between $1 to $2 million dollars in new acts to create recordings, branding, merchandise, streaming, and other potential revenues. If the act fails to emotionally connect with a fan base both the label and act fail.

Personal Managers & Others
Personal managers and the representatiion team of the business, road, and others is based on an invest of time vs the potential financial payments based on the acts success. Connected to an artist that fails means failure for them also as they are often paid a percentage of the artist's gross.

Concert Promoters
Concert promoters invest in concert and festivals which may or may not generate significant profits if they secure the right acts on the best day for a performance in the newest venue that draw a large fan base for the right ticket prices.

Figure 12.10: The entertainment and music industry is usually a case of opportunity vs risk for all involved. I once had an executive from United Records tell me that if I wanted a safe "risk" go to Las Vegas where the odds of winning are better. The music and entertainment industry is a business where we really need to understand how it works and we should always understand the financial and emotional risk if we want to achieve success.

Show #	Day	City	Ticket	Shows	Expense	Show Price
Rehearsal	Thu	Gainesville, FL		1	$425	$50,000
1	Fri	Atlanta		1	$399	$125,000
2	Sat	Charlotte, NC		1	$564	$150,000
3	Sun	Travel		-------		-------
4	Mon	Louisville, (pickup)		1	$769	$90,000
5	Tue	Cincinnati (pickup)		1	$517	$75,000
6	Wed	Travel		-------		-------
7	Thu	Pittsburgh		1	$538	$135,000
8	Fri	Buffalo		1	$995	$110,000
9	Sat	Toronto, ONT		1	$191	$145,000
10	Sun	Montreal, QUE	home	1	$621	$145,000
11	Mon	Travel	home	-------	-------	-------
12	Tue	Travel	return	1	$557	-------
13	Wed	Boston		1	$287	$135,000
14	Thu	New York		1	$389	$145,000
15	Fri	Philadelphia		1	$607	$150,000
16	Sat	Alexandria		1	$499	$150,000
17	Sun	Newport News (pickup)	home	1	$733	$110,000
18	Mon	Travel	home	-------	-------	-------
19	Tue	Travel	home	-------	-------	-------
20	Wed	Travel	return	1	$433	-------
21	Thu	Minneapolis		1	$287	$130,000
22	Fri	Chicago		1	$287	$140,000
23	Sat	Indianapolis		1	$621	$125,000
24	Sun	St. Louis		1	$508	$130,000
25	Mon	Travel		-------	-------	-------
26	Tue	Kansas City		1	$276	$125,000
27	Wed	Travel		-------	-------	-------
28	Thu	Oklahoma City		1	$288	$130,000
29	Fri	Dallas		1	$331	$145,000
30	Sat	Austin		1	$794	$140,000
1	Sun	San Antonio (pickup)		1	$523	$80,000
2	Mon	Travel		-------	-------	-------
3	Tue	New Orleans		1	$570	$120,000
4	Wed	Travel		-------	-------	-------
5	Thu	Memphis		1	$667	$125,000
6	Fri	Jacksonville		1	$997	$130,000
7	Sat	Tampa		1	$1,028	$140,000
8	Sun	Fort Lauderdale		1	$619	$135,000
9	Mon	Travel	home	1	-------	
-------	---	-------	---	-------	$16,320	
$100-per day	---	-------	---	36	$3,600	

Item	#	Cost	Shows	Debt	Revenue
Staging Equipment	1	One leased package of extra lighting, staging, effects and audio	40	$30,000	
Road Crew	5	$200 load in and load out days	28	$28,000	
		$50.00 travel days (sleeping)	11	$2,750	
Per-diems show days	7	$35 Musicians (includes royalty artists)	28	$6,860	
	4	$35 Singers	28	$3,920	
	11	$25 All other personnel	28	$7,700	
Per-diems non-show days	7	$70 Musicians (includes royalty artists)	11	$5,390	
	4	$70 Singers	11	$3,080	
	11	$50 All others	11	$6,050	
Hotel room	1	$300 Royalty artists (flies home for 5 nights during extended travel)	35	$10,500	
Hotel rooms	10	$150 Musicians and singers	40	$60,000	
Legal	1	One-time expense for legal supervision and approval of all contracts.	1	$2,500	
Insurance	1 policy	$2,500 for only 60 days, plus a million-dollar bond for personal manager, artists, and management team	60	$2,500	
Cost of Tour	1	Total cost of tour		$975,735	
Average	28	The average cost of each show (includes rehearsal and travel days)	28	$34,847	

Figure 12.11: This page and the previous one indicates that in our example, the tour grossed about $3.5 million dollars. The average gross per show totaled a little over $125,000 and the shows cost an average of about $34,000 to play. That leaves a profit of over $90,000 per show.

MERCHANDISE

It's not unusual to make as much money selling merchandise at the live ticket event as the band makes for each show.

Merchandise For sale	5	Merch Item	Cost	Price	Sold	Seats	Total Expense	Profits
		T-shirt	$4.00 with logo	$12.00 profit of $8.00	125,000	350,000 Seats/ Tickets	$500,000	$1,500,000 -$500,000 $1,000,000
		Sweat Shirt	$8.50 with logo	$35.00 profit of $26.50	35,000	350,000 Seats/ Tickets	$297,500	$1,225,000 -$297,500 $928,000
		Hat	$6.00 with logo	$15.00 profit of $9.00	80,000	350,000 Seats/ Tickets	$480,000	$1,200,000 -$480,000 $720,000
		Key Chain	60¢ with logo	$5.00 profit of $4.40	15,000	350,000 Seats/ Tickets	$9,000	$75,000 -$9,000 $64,000

Figure 12.12: Comparing the cost of the merchandise to the manufacture and sale price with 350,000 ticket holders as buyers indicates a potential gross of about $4 million. The profit to cost ratio is about 3 to 1. The merchandise sales often make as much money as the show performance. Notice the T-shirts net $1,000,000, the sweatshirts $928,000, the hats $750,000, and, the key chains $64,000.

TOUR FINANCIALS

Let's take a look at how much money the tour made by looking at the following figures. As you can see from the three figures, the total cost of the tour was $975,735.00 paid by the band or investors for the cost of putting the show on the road. The gross revenues from the show performances totaled $3,510,00.00. The average cost per show (paid by the act if self promoting or by investors) is $34,847.00 and the potential profit from each show (the amount paid by the promoters minus the cost of the show) averages $90,510.00.

- **$125,357.00 per show gross**

- **$34,847,00.00 minus the average cost of the show**

- $90,510,00.00 profit per show

TOUR GROSS

Booking agents do not often make any money from merchandise and other revenue streams associated with the tour. But others do, including the personal manager (20%), the business manager (5%), and the record label (10-15%).

Industry Role	Payment from Gross	Percentage	Remaining Amount
Personal Manager	$1,502,000	20%	$7,510,000 gross
			PM-$1,502,000
			$6,008,000
Record Label	$901,200	12%	$6,008,000
			Label-$901,200
			$5,106,800
Business Manager	$375,500	(5%)	$5,106,800
			BM-$375,500
			$4,731,300
Booking Agent	$351,000	10%	$4,731,300
			BA-$351,000
			$4,380,300
Royalty Artists	----------	53%	$4,380,000

Figure 12.13: This is a somewhat shocking table as the $7.5 million gross is quickly reduced to $4.3 million when the artist must pay the personal manager, record label, business manager and booking agent.

First, we need to find the tour gross, which includes all the revenues from the sale of the shows ($3,510,000), plus the merchandise (gross, not net), which is, about $4,000,000. Remember, it is not that unusual for the merchandise sales to total about the same or more than the gross of the sales price of the shows to the promoters. That's what we have in our example, the shows grossed $3.5 million and the merchandise $4 million.

Paying the Label, Personal & Business Managers

Thus, the gross of the tour is $3,510,000 paid by the promoters and $4,000,000 from the merchandise sales for a total of $7,510,000. The booking agent received 10% of the gross of the monies promoters paid for the shows, usually excluding merchandise and all the other generated revenues. The percentages paid to the representation team members and to the label are a portion of the gross revenues, including the monies paid by the promoters for the tour, plus revenues from merchandise and other sources. Let's finish this up with the personal manager receiving $1,502,000 (20%), the business manager $375,500 (5%), and the record label $901,200 (12%). If we include the 10% paid to the booking agent off of the gross from the shows only, that figure is decreased to 4% over all gross revenues generated. That reduces the amount of mail box money paid to the artist from 51% to 47% of the overall gross revenues generated.

Mail Box Money

How much did the royalty artist end up making? Any guesses? The total tour grossed $7,510,000, of which the personal manager was paid $1,502,000; the label (for the 360 deal) $901,200; the business manager $375,500; and the booking agent $351,000. That leaves the artists with $4,380,300. But we are not done yet! We can't forget the tax man and with a net income of $4,380,300, the federal tax rate is about 40%. If the act lives in a state where taxes are required on earned income, such as in California, then add another possible 13.3% for income and another 9.5% for sales taxes on parts of the merchandise.[246]

In general, the tax rate could be as high as 53%. However, more than likely, the act will have a business manager who understands the income may be deferred, tax exmpt, or may be subject to lower capital gains rates or

---

[246] "California Income Tax Calculator." SmartAsset. Accessed August 17, 2017. https://smartasset.com/taxes/california-tax-calculator.

not subject to FICA taxes. Thus, the act whose net from the tour could be as high as $4.3 million may actually only receive a little over $2 million dollars after taxes. Still not bad for a 40 day tour.

*****

The entertainment industry uses a variety of print and online services to help them keep track of touring artists are booked, which you can also use to discover where you would like to tour.

Artist Growth

Artist Growth is a venture capital subscription-based company that has created a unique niche for itself for beginning and traveling artists and bands. It uses a Cloud-based software to provide access to information about clubs, agents, and promoters. Acts or the agents can use the software for scheduling, developing merchandise and sales reports, and accounting. The software tracks the band's expenses and revenues, creates and manages budgets, schedules and contacts.[247]

Celebrity Access

Celebrity Access is a subscription service that provides (just as its name implies) access to celebrities. Touring acts are posted on Celebrity Access with a brief bio and contact information including the artist's agent's name and email, the act's availabilities (for promoters who are seeking talent), contact information for the personal managers and booking agents, tour dates, tour promoters, and venues. It also provides contact information for other types of celebrities, labels, and many other industry links. It runs the *Box Office Scores,* a listing of all touring acts' gross revenues, tickets sold, and ticketing information. It allows booking agents to post dates of acts planning tours. Lastly, talent buyers and promoters may also post for the types of acts they are seeking.[248]

---
[247] "The Platform." Artist Growth. Accessed July 27, 2017. https://artistgrowth.com/site/the-platform/#manage-pricing.
[248] "CelebrityAccess." CelebrityAccess. Accessed July 27, 2017. http://www.celebrityaccess.com/.

Talent Agencies

Creative Artists Agency (CAA), International Creative Management (ICM), United Talent Agency (UTA), and William Morris Endeavor Entertainment (WME^2) are the major talent agencies who manage many of the most famous acts, recording artists, authors, and other public personalities. Talent agents are in a different aspect of the industry from personal managers and the music business management teams. They usually represent film, movie, TV, and sports personalities. The talent agencies focus is often "booking" talent on other types of media and branding. Pan and King (2016) claim talent agents,

> ... put... together content and talent in new ways to make new entertainment properties. In that sense, agencies serve as a "broker for information and opportunities".[249]

Talent agents also work with labels, personal managers of other acts and their management teams to support marketing plans, promotion, publicity, that may, in turn, contribute to their own iconic artists in various types of entertainment products such as live shows, events, movies and film.

Some of the major talent agencies have become event producers themselves, as they now set up the tours and fulfill all the roles of the typical concert producers. Some also act as booking agents for music talent on gigs and tours if the act is well enough known to also appear (be seen as a valuable assess to the agent) in other types of media. Another advantage is that they have offices in many capitals around the world.

Creative Artists Agency (CAA)

CAA was formed in 1975 and has a powerful list of actors and entertainment personalities, including famous directors, sports, business, and celebrity motivational speakers.[250] According to Answers.com & Hoover's

---
[249] Jonathan Pan, John King, "Are Esports Stars Born or Made? – The Nexus." The Nexus. September 11, 2015. Accessed July 21, 2017. https://nexus.vert.gg/esports-stars-born-or-made-4d771b1fe17f.
[250] Creative Artist Agency (CAA), "Creative Artist Agency LLC." Hoover's Company Profiles, http://www.answers.

Company Profile (2010), CAA is

> *Arguably the most powerful talent agency in the business. ...Represents clients working in film, music, television, theater, sports, and literature. The firm's client list reads like a who's who of A-list stars, including such luminaries as Steven Spielberg, Tom Cruise, Brad Pitt, George Clooney, LeBron James, Simon Cowell, David Beckham, Will Ferrell, and Sandra Bullock. It has also works with commercial clients such as Coca-Cola and toymaker Mattel. Supplemental services include strategic counsel, financing, and consulting. Its Intelligence Group/Youth Intelligence unit tracks and conducts behavior research for consumers from ages 8 to 39.*[251]

International Creative Management (ICM)

ICM was formed in 1975 by the merger of Creative Management Associates and The International Famous Agency.[252] Hoovers (2010) describes them as follows,

> *...The agency represents film and television actors and directors, as well as artists in theater, music, publishing, and new media. A major "ten percent" (along with CAA and William Morris Endeavor), ICM represents such A-list clients as Halle Berry, Rosario Dawson, Robert Duvall, Beyonce Knowles, and Chris Rock, as well as emerging performers. It has offices in Los Angeles, New York, and London.*[253]

United Talent Agency (UTA)

UTA represents major stars and the behind-the-scenes creative artists in the entertainment industry who make the entertainment products we love to watch.[254] According to Hoovers (2010),

---

com/topic/creative-artists-agency, (accessed August 24, 2010).
251 Creative Artist Agency (CAA), "Creative Artist Agency LLC." Hoover's Company Profiles, http://www.answers.com/topic/creative-artists-agency, (accessed August 24, 2010).
252 International Creative Management Agency, (ICM) Answers.com, http://www.answers.com/topic/international-creative-management-inc, (accessed March 29, 2011).
253 International Creative Management Agency, (ICM) "International Creative Agency," Hoovers Company
254 United Talent Agency, (UTA), "Production Department," http://www.utaproduction.com/, (accessed August 24, 2010).

Started in 1991 and different in Hollywood as some of its best agents own part of the company, clients include Harrison Ford, Miley Cyrus, Rachel McAdams, and Johnny Depp, as well as a client list of directors, producers, and screenwriters... Beyond the celluloid, the company represents literary authors, journalists, musicians, and creators of mobile, online, and gaming content. It also provides branding, licensing, and marketing services.[255]

UTA also represents many of the behind-the-scenes workers in the film and production business. UTA productions.com (2004) says they

...Represent famous producers, directors of photography, production designers, costume designers, film editors, first and second directors, stunt coordinators, visual effects supervisors, production service providers, (including animatronics) and the Mediapro Studios in Romania which includes 19 fully equipped film and TV stages (four of which have water tanks, various workshops, approximately 100 acres of property on the shore of a lake, a park, and satellite uplink equipment).[256]

WILLIAM MORRIS ENDEAVOR ENTERTAINMENT (WME²)

WME2 takes a different niche, as it represents talent, public personalities (speakers), and authors. It was formed in 1898 to represent vaudeville acts and currently has offices in New York, Beverly Hills, Nashville, London, Miami Beach, and Shanghai.[257] Bloombergbusinessweek.com (2010) explains,

...It provides commercials and endorsements in the areas of print, on-camera, voiceovers, animation, video games, licensing and merchandising, infomercials, PR campaigns and satellite media tours, and non-performing personal appearances; and offers lecturers in the fields of national and global affairs, media, business and economics, health and science, humor, and sport and motivation. The company represents

---

[255] United Talent Agency, (UTA), "United Talent Agency," Hoover's Company Profiles, http://www.hoovers.com/company/United_Talent_Agency_Inc/hytrxi-1.html, (accessed August 24, 2010).

[256] United Talent Agency, "Mediaprostudio," United Talent Agency, http://www.mediaprostudios.com/, (accessed March 29, 2011).

[257] Willaim Morris Endeavor Agency "Locations," http://www.wmeentertainment.com/, (accessed August 24, 2010).

clients for music and personal appearances in various musical genres, including rock, pop, urban contemporary, country, comedy, Latin, Christian/gospel, and adult contemporary; and secures endorsement, sponsorship, commercial, marketing, licensing, motion picture, television, digital, publishing, and broadcasting opportunities. It provides screenwriters, producers, directors, and actors for motion pictures; represents reporters and anchors on network and cable outlets, covering news, sports, weather, and entertainment, as well as television and talk show hosts, and producers in the news arena; provides writers, composers, lyricists, directors, choreographers, actors, and producers for theaters.[258]

TALENT AGENTS

Talent agents may own their own agencies, as they provide some career advice and guidance, just as personal managers in the music business. Their main job is to seek and acquire employment for their acts. A good example would be local talent agents who represent models. However, in today's music industry, the talent agent's job description is blending with some of the personal manager's traditional roles.

IEBA

If you're a new act, with a buzz, momentum, and a possible label deal, how can you get discovered by promoters? Remember, promoters and promotion companies, such as Live Nation and AEG Live, are the key to concerts, festivals, and tours. Promoters use The International Entertainment Buyers Association (IEBA) and The National Association of Campus Activities (NACA) and other showcase opportunities to discover, arrange, and set up concert tours with new and established acts. Basically, the organizations hold annual events that bring the buyers of talent (promoters) and the managers and acts together. The International Entertainment Buyers Association (IEBA) is the top nonprofit organization in the nation that annually sponsors a conference for buyers to view acts and buy tours.

---

258 William Morris Endeavor Agency "William Morris Agency, Inc," Bloomberg Businessweek, http://investing.businessweek.com/research/stocks/private/snapshot.asp?privcapId=872395, (accessed August 24, 2010).

NACA

The National Association of Campus Activities (NACA) is a nonprofit organization that sponsors national and regional conferences for college representatives to view and book entertainment tours on college campuses. Both IEBA and NACA are great organizations who offer newer bands and acts an opportunity to be discovered by industry professionals.

Real Name	Stage Name	Real Name	Stage Name
Stefani Joanne Angelina Germanotta	Lady Gaga	Born Steveland Hardaway Judkins; later renamed Steveland Hardaway Morris	Stevie Wonder
Ray Charles Robinson	Ray Charles	Anthony Dominick Benedetto	Tony Bennett
Tracy Morrow	Ice-T	Katheryn Elizabeth Hudson	Katy Perry
Cordazer Calvin Broadus Jr.	Snoop Dogg	Beyonce Giselle Knowles	Beyonce
Selena Quintanilla-Perez	Selena	Shawn Carter	Jay Z
Marshal Bruce Mathers III	Eminem	Madonna Louise Veronica Ciccone	Madonna
Chubby Checker	Ernest Evans	Richard Starkey	Ringo Starr
Eleanora Fagan Gough	Billie Holliday	Lester Polfus	Les Paul
Cameron Jibril Thomaz	Wiz Khalifa	Wladziu Lee Valentino	Liberace
John Francis Bongiovi Jr.	Jon Bon Jovi	Carlos Ray	Chuck Norris
Alecia Moore	Pink	Frank Castelluccio	Frankie Valli
John Anthony Gillis	Jack White (White Stripes)	Farrokh Bulsara	Freddie Mercury
Reginald Kenneth Dwight	Elton John	Steven Victor Tallarico	Steven Tyler
Gordon Matthew Thomas Sumner	Sting	Alicia Augello Cook	Alicia Keys
Victoria Caroline Adams [Beckham]	Posh Spice (Spice Girls)	Marvin Lee Aday	Meat Loaf

Figure 12.14: Many acts wisely use a stage name for publicity and try to live a normal life with their birth names.[259]

---

[259] Thompson, Eliza. "48 Musicians Who've Been Lying About Their Names This Whole Time." Cosmopolitan. July 14, 2017. Accessed July 22, 2017. http://www.cosmopolitan.com/entertainment/celebs/a41076/musicians-real-names/.

Summary

Once an artist has the potential to "blow up" into the next big thing, they will need a personal manager and the corresponding management team. Unknown acts are simply not ready for major artist representation, as the personal manager and team members are usually paid a percentage of the artist's gross revenues. Obviously, if the act is making zip, so would the management team. Therefore, timing is important, as once the act has hundreds of thousands of fans, a potential major label deal, then it is time to seek representation.

Personal managers usually work for themselves, signing acts into their own companies, though the act is only hiring one manager. The contract between the artist and the personal manager has a power of attorney clause, which gives the personal manager and the management team the legal right to conduct the artist's business. Booking agents are hired to pitch the act to promoters who create concert events and tours. Business managers control the revenues and take care of the accounting, payroll, taxes, and investments. Road or tour managers hire security, roadies, and others to control all aspects of the tour. Attorneys are hired for legal opinions and representation concerning legal issues. Publicists and marketing experts may be added to create artist interviews for promotional purposes for the mass and social media.

Launching a career as a new act or band in your local area is very difficult. It starts with forming a legal business and acquiring the required business licenses. In addition, the band members should sign a partnership agreement stating who owns the band's business and name. After rehearsing for a show, the band has to sell themselves to potential clubs, bars, and other types of establishments, through the venue's manager in order to land a gig. The band will need to have their website up and running and have recorded music and video available for the prospective club promoters and managers to determine if they want to pursue a deal.

Personal managers provide advice to the act about the business decisions that need to be made. In the next chapter, we'll learn how promoters hire talent through booking agents or talent agencies, rent venues for concerts, and, then, promote and advertise the event.

Generating the Stage Show
Chapter Twelve

Elements Within
The Music Business
To Better Understand How To
Create a Live Ticket Show

The Recording Team
The Band's Legal Business

The Live Ticket Show-Costs
Transportation
Hotel & Food
Merchandise
Self Promotion
Venues

Infrastructure
Pitching the Show
Show Production
Website/Press Kit/Social Media

Creating the Tour-Business
The Rehearsal
(AF of M/SAG-AFTRA Scales)
Pricing the Show
Baseline Budget
The Asking Price
Booking Agent's Fee
Financials
Gross-vs-Net
Mail Box Money

System
Celebrity Access
Talent Agencies
I.E.B.A & N.A.C.A

Chapter 13

The Live Ticket

Time to cash in! We started our long journey with an understanding of the value of the song. Then, we matched that song to the perfect act to establish their image and brand in the studio. The label, which signed the act with its own significant fan base, funded the recordings, marketing, promotion, and publicity. The launch included the uses of mass and social media through the traditional methods of distribution, and, also on the Internet. A personal manager was hired with the corresponding management team members. These are the booking agent, business manager, and a road manager. The live show was developed and rehearsed to pitch to promoters. Time to roll the dice.

Concert promoters use a bid sheet to estimate, then project, the cost of putting on the event. The bid sheet is divided into four sections- (a) Pre-Show Expenses, (b) Show Expenses (for live show), (c) Production Expenses, and (d) Post -Show Expenses. It's important for the promoter to make realistic estimates in each of the four areas. Needless to say, mistakes are literally costly. Price the event wrong, and you could lose a considerable amount of money, and earn a bad reputation in the process, thus, jeopardizing your ability to continue to work in the industry.

THE TWO-WEEK NOTICE

If the artist's recordings connect with consumers psychologically and emotionally, as we discussed earlier in the book, then the act has an opportunity to have a lasting, profitable, performing career as a public personality. And it's at the end of this journey when we'll discover if the artist is going make it or not. It takes years for artists to fine tune their talents and build a fan base. It takes about another year after being signed by a label to develop the act, record the album, to work up and implement a marketing plan. Then, the recordings are unveiled to the public through the media and the Internet and the act is revealed as on opening act for the live ticket.

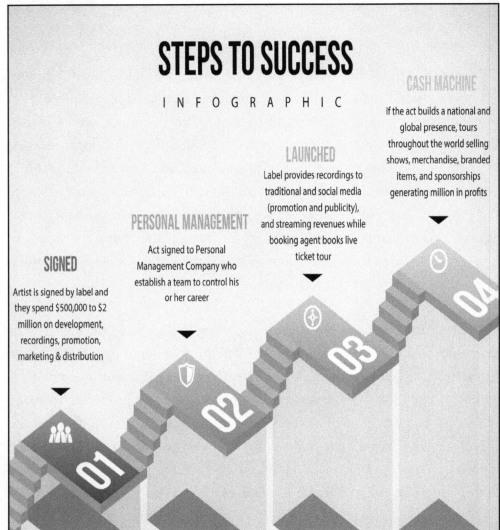

Figure 13.1: After a year of a step-by-step process and spending $500,000-$2 million, labels hand over the career of the artist to a personal manager and the corresponding representation team. Before 360 deals, labels made their profits on the sale of albums and singles, but now that is disappearing. As a result, the management team has become even more vital to the success of the act and the label, as they receive a percentage of the artist's gross revenues.

CREATING DEMAND

Labels and the personal manager initiate the marketing plan for a two to four-week period of time with supporting promotion. Typical outlets for promotion are radio airtime, videos, and advertisements through the electronic, print, and social media. When we add publicity, such as interviews on media and social media, and tweets, emails and other forms of publicity distribution, we provide a range of opportunities for the target market audience to "discover" the artist and their recordings.

Remember, on a million dollar deal the labels often budget 40-60% or more on promotion and publicity to unveil the new act and recordings in an attempt to give the public a chance to emotionally "buy into" the act's persona, image, and brand. And, it will only take about two weeks before the label executives know if the act is going to make it or not. They've been through this before, and they know what the data should tell them. They look at all the numbers, the analytics, and the trend lines on sales and streams to determine which direction the profit or loss arrows are pointing. Should nothing move, meaning few sales of albums, zero or few streams, poor audience responses to the acts live ticket shows, and poor merchandise sales, then these are indications of failure.

CONNECTING THE DOTS

However, such catastrophes rarely happen, as the label's executives know what they are doing. They have worked hard to find the best material possible (songs), hired the top producers, musicians, and singers to record the album, and paid for the promotion, marketing, and publicity needed to give the artist a triumphant launch. The only question they generally have at the two to four-week mark is determining how large the act's potential success is and what can they do to make it better. Capturing a larger part of the market share usually means spending more money on the front end to increase the fan base and profits on the back end.

Once the act and the recordings have been successfully launched, the strategic management process is turned over to the personal manager and the management team. The personal manager and label usually work together to sync executive decisions in an attempt to positively exploit the artist's success, image, and brand to the highest level with the established fan base, as they turn additional consumers into passionate fans.

In the previous chapters, we observed how the personal manager and the management team provide representation for label's acts. We also reviewed how the acts, through their personal manager, hire musicians and backup singers, plus a road manager to go on tour. The booking agent's job is to sell the act's show to the independent promoters or promotion companies. Without the promoter, there's no show. Thus, just as the label's investment in the artist supports the artist's career for recordings and the live ticket performance, it's the promoter or the promotion company's investment in a show or event that provides the opportunity for the act, management team, and label to receive profits from the artist's performance.

REVENUE STREAMS

The live ticket and streaming, as we've already learned, are the future of the music business revenues. Let's be honest, vinyl sales are not going to save the quickly decreasing popularity of owning CDs. Smart people always follow the money, and in this case, it's the use of the 360 deal to launch the act, their recordings, live ticket and streaming that will hopefully generate the funds required to pay all the bills and provide a hefty profit.

We've already explored the streaming aspect in the record label chapter, now let's take a look at the live ticket market and process. The important concept to understand is how much money and work have been put into the act on the front end before the artist is ready to become a part the popular culture mindset where they can become profitable.

The Live Ticket

Each concert or "event" is organized, funded, and promoted by the promoters, who invest their own capital to monetize consumers' emotional connection to the artist's personae. Once again, remember, that the music business is really the emotion business and as such, the concert business is really a created "event" in a special "place in time and location" for the sole purpose of generating money based on the ticket buyer's emotional connection to the acts performing. According to *Pollstar* (2017), the leading trade magazine for the concert business,

> *The best metric for determining an artist's true popularity is their ability to sell tickets for a live performance. There was a time when radio airplay and recorded music sales were the best measure of who is hot, but today's world of fragmented music consumption also includes on-demand audio or video streams, commercials, video games, and fashion shows. Artists ability to pay their mortgages now relies predominately on touring revenues generated from ticket and merchandise sales. While recorded music revenues have been in steady decline, live music dollars continue to grow despite sharp increases in ticket prices.*[260]

Just as the record label funded the recording artist's career, now we have the promoters who fund the live ticket events, which offer the artist, representation, and the label profits. Without the promoters, there's no show! And at this point, we'd have far fewer acts, labels, and personal managers if the promoters failed to fund the events as the existence of the labels, representation, and the acts themselves are now tied very closely to the live ticket business, as everyone shares in the profits.

*****

---

260 Pollstar. "2016 Year End Special Features." Pollstar.com. January 06, 2017. Accessed July 24, 2017. https://www.pollstar.com/article/2016-year-end-special-features-130308.

Music itself is going to become like running water or electricity. So it's like, just take advantage of these last few years because none of this is ever going to happen again. You'd better be prepared for doing a lot of touring because that's really the only unique situation that's going to be left.

-David Bowie[261]

*****

The Concert Business

The live ticket industry is usually understood as concerts, festivals, and tours. However, in today's music business, "live events" may include professional sports, politics, and other types of staged events that may attract consumers. Concert sales (excluding sports and other events) in 2016 (as reported in *Pollstar.com* in January 2017) set an all-time record. Here is their data:

- $9 billion in detailed 2016 concert grosses.
- The Top 100 Worldwide Tours generated $4.88 billion in sales
- The Top 100 Tours of North America grossed a record $3.34 billion which was up 7% over last year's $3.12 billion.
- The Top 100 acts sold a record 43.63 million tickets. That is over 1.5 million
- More tickets or 4% higher than the previous year.
- The average ticket price also hit record levels at $76.55, which is up 3% or $2.30 over 2015.[262]

The Staging Process-Recap

[261] "David Bowie Quotes." BrainyQuote. Accessed August 20, 2017. https://www.brainyquote.com/quotes/quotes/d/davidbowie451750.html.
[262] Pollstar. "2016 Year End Special Features." Pollstar.com. January 06, 2017. Accessed July 24, 2017. https://www.pollstar.com/article/2016-year-end-special-features-130308.

In the previous chapter, we analyzed how the personal manager and the management team prepare the artists they represent for shows to be sold to promoters, whether as single shows or as a tour. In our example, a road or tour manager, musicians, backup singers, audio, lighting, and road crew members were hired and rehearsed. Union musicians and rehearsal staging personal were paid union scales (if they are members of the union) for each day of work which ran for two weeks. We also set up the 40-day tour and then went through several steps to determine an asking price of $150,000 for the show. The acceptable price range was from $75,000 for small pick-up shows to the $150,000 asking price.

The Label's Buy In

The label is in the touring or live ticket derby as they provided the front money for the tour. Remember that it takes about a year to accomplish the long list of items for the act to learn, adhere to, and cause things to happen. It's in the act's best interest to aggressively take advantage of all of the career opportunities made available through the major label and the advice of the personal manager. Besides, label executives and personal managers will expect the artists to toe-the-line and understand how important the steps are to both the act's success and the label and representation company's profits. To put it bluntly, if the act is blowing them off, they will not waste their time helping the act in the future.

Selling the Show-Recap

Booking agents list the act and all of the contact information on Celebrity Access and an outsourced publicity company is hired to provide the "tour news" to the traditional and social media and other sources. Record labels support the act's tour by providing the start-up tour support money and also additional promotion and publicity. In the previous chapter, we observed how the personal manager and the management team provide representation for label's acts. We also reviewed how the act hires and signs musicians and backup singers, plus roadies and a road manager to go on tour. Now, look at the other side of the deal to determine what a promoter has to accomplish before buying the show.

Promoters first research the market to determine which acts will "sell well" in their local markets. They use bid sheets to determine their break-even points and projected expenses on the concert. They use *Billboard Magazine's* research and charts, information from *Pollstar Magazine's* concert reports and news, plus sales and streaming figures, and analytics from Nielsen and other firms to determine which acts may be profitable. However, an act that is successful in one market may not be in another, so the promoter has to understand the types of consumers (lifestyles), who live in the projected concert area.

BID SHEET

Promoters use a bid sheet to determine a fair price for the show. The bid sheet helps the promoter determine a reasonable bid price for the show in their local market before talking to the booking agent. Remember, the game we're playing is the promoter wants to pay as little as possible for the show and the booking agent wants the highest price possible, as they receive 10% of whatever the final price. The Creative Artist Agency (2011)[263] recommends a bid sheet be submitted online when requesting purchase of any of their signed talent.

SIGNATORY

The signatory is the individual at the promotion company who is the authorized person to issue the money and sign the deals. If it's an independent promoter or a new promoter to the industry, then the booking agent and personal manager may run a full background investigation to determine the financial solvency, history, key people with whom the promoter claims to have worked, and also gather general information about promoter before they consider an offer.

---

263 Creative Artists Agency (CAA), "Touring", CAA.com, CAA%20Creative%20Artists%20Agency.webarchive, (accessed April 7, 2011).

Venue

The location for the show in a local market must be up to certain standards for the artist, the crew members, and most importantly, the fans. The larger venues are usually IATSE houses, which means the stagehands' union must be used for the load in (of the band equipment, staging, audio and lighting). They are also responsible for the load out, which is the breaking down of the equipment and staging and loading it back into the vans or semi-trucks. Booking agents know that if the venue is an IATSE house, this show including the road manager, major royalty artist, musicians, singers, and roadies will be well treated and respected. The audio and lighting members of the show crew will be allowed to operate the venue's equipment and union members may assist. If the tour doesn't have audio and lighting techs (rare), the IATSE crew members provide engineers for both the sound and lighting.

Promoter's Projected Expenses

After the information section of the bid sheet is completed, the promoter must determine the actual cost of putting on the show. There are obvious and less obvious costs that cover renting or buying the talent, renting the venue, advertisement, insurance, bonding, fees for the IATSE crew, and rider expenses. This part of the bid sheet is divided into predicting (a) Pre-Show Expenses, (b) Show Expenses (for the live show), (c) Production Expenses, and (d) Post-Show Expenses.

It's imperative for the promoter to make realistic estimates in each of the four areas or they may lose a ton of money from their mistakes when selling tickets at the wrong price. Everything is negotiable. However, smart booking agents and promoters will attempt to establish long-term relationships that will provide future profitable events and opportunities for both.

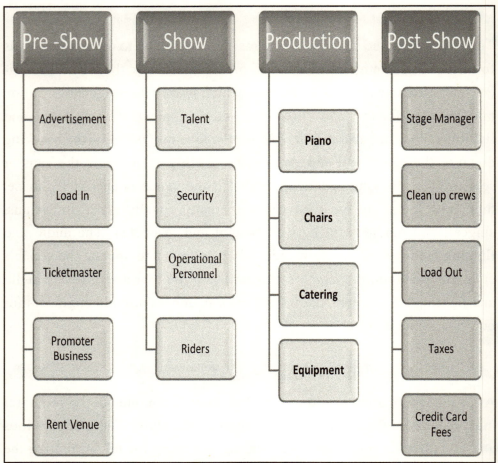

Figure 13.2: What does it really cost to stage the concert? The bid sheet divides the cost into (a) Pre-Show Expenses, (b) Show Expenses (for live show), (c) Production Expenses, and (d) Post- Show Expenses.

PRE-SHOW

Labels want their artist out touring to promote their latest recordings, streams, merchandise, and brands, as the money they bring in helps with advertising expenses. However, as we already know, the costs are usually charged to the recoupment fund in the artist's name at the label. Pre-show expenses include alerting the public through advertising and selecting a sponsoring radio station.

Sponsoring Radio Station

Promoters and labels often work together to select a local radio station to sponsor the concert. The promoter receives a break on advertisements and the station is allowed to claim it's co-sponsoring the concert with the promoter's company. The station often receives comp tickets to the concert and the promoter gets the event or concert that is being set up advertised on the station.

Social Media

The best way to connect directly to the fans is through social media. Promoters now use fan club lists and social media platforms to connect with the fans to notify them of the upcoming tickets for the concert. Credit card companies and other branding sources also connect with the social media sites to increase the fans' interest in the act, concert, and their products.

I.A.T.S.E. Crew

As stated earlier, the International Alliance of Theatrical and Stage Employees (I.A.T.S.E.), represents audio engineers, lighting technicians, set designers, and stagehands for live shows and events.[264] A union house is the venue, studio, etc., that has signed an agreement with unions (SAG-AFTRA, AF of M, Equity, and I.A.T.S.E.) to use only union members for various entertainment productions. Most Broadway venues, sports complexes, and movies made in Hollywood are considered union jobs made or performed in union houses. Exceptions include the production facilities in right-to-work states that often allow for nonunion productions.[265] However, in this situation, if the promoter is using a union house, then the cost of the stagehands' union must be estimated on the promoter's bid sheet.

Ticketmaster

---

264 International Alliance of Theatrical Stage Employees, Moving Picture Technicians, Artists and Allied Crafts of the United States, Its Territories and Canada, (IATSE), "Welcome to IATSE", "http://www.iatse-intl.org/about/welcome.html, (accessed April 7, 2011).

265 International Alliance of Theatrical Stage Employees, Moving Picture Technicians, Artists and Allied Crafts of the United States, Its Territories and Canada, (IATSE), "Welcome to IATSE", "http://www.iatse-intl.org/about/welcome.html, (accessed April 7, 2011).

Ticketmaster was started in 1976 by Albert Leffler and Peter Gadwa (two college staffers) and Phoenix executive Gordon Gunn.[266] Today, the company controls almost all tickets sold at over 3,000 U.S. venues, including those of more than 50 professional sports teams.[267] It grew its business by offering many of the venues front money (in some cases millions of dollars) for the exclusive right to sell tickets to all the events scheduled at the venues. In 2010, the company merged with Live Nation and according to their website (2011),

> ...Ticketmaster is the global event ticketing leader and one of the world's top five eCommerce sites, with over 26 million monthly unique visitors. Live Nation Concerts produces over 20,000 shows annually for more than 2,000 artists globally. Front Line is the world's top artist management company, representing over 250 artists. These businesses power Live Nation Network, the leading provider of entertainment marketing solutions, enabling over 800 advertisers to tap into the 200 million consumers Live Nation delivers annually through its live event and digital platforms.[268]

Ticketmaster, in the past, has bought out most of its competitors through mergers and buyouts. In addition, Ticketmaster is currently offering services over the web and through many other ticketing venues.

The Promoter's LEGAL Business

Some of the bid sheets decisions are related to the promoter's own business including legal, insurance, and bonding fees. The promotion company must figure the cost of creating the show or event into the bid sheet, as it will affect the company's money flow from the legal expenses as contracts need to be reviewed and approved. Usually, a damage deposit is also required by the venue and an insurance policy and a personal bond for the promoter is may also be purchased. The insurance policy is in case of

---

266 HEIDI EVANS | Times Staff Writer. "Rival to Ticketron: Ticketmaster Emerging as Force in L.A." Los Angeles Times. January 31, 1985. Accessed July 29, 2017. http://articles.latimes.com/1985-01-31/business/fi-5143_1_ticketmaster.
267 Our History::Ticketmaster. Accessed July 29, 2017. http://www.ticketmaster.com/about/our-history.html.
268 Ticketmaster, "Our History" ticketmaster.com, http://www.ticketmaster.com/history/index.html?tm_link=abouttm_history, (accessed April 7, 2011).

personnel problems caused by the event and the bond is for legal expenses if sued. A personal bond for a two to three- day event is often only a few hundred dollars.

PROMOTER'S SHOW EXPENSES

The actual show expenses are defined as the cost of hiring the artists, musicians, security, operation personnel, and the fulfilling of the tech and artist's riders request. The promoter is buying a "package" or total show from start to finish for a specific price. A "rider" is an additional set of instructions for the promoter regarding the specific artist and staging requirements for the setting up and show operation.

TALENT

The biggest expense for concerts and events is the talent. Therefore, the promoter has to negotiate the best deal possible for the top billing artist and opening act. What's really difficult is to determine the value of the talent and show (the promoter is buying) to the ticket price consumers may be willing to pay. This time the game is for the promoter to get the highest ticket prices for the show that will also generate a sold-out crowd. The key is to match the best show available to the highest ticket prices fan and consumers are willing to pay in the local market. A ticket priced too high and the show will fail, too low and the promoter will not make as much money as they could have. In the last chapter, the band in our example, would cost this promoter between $75,000 to $150,000 to perform depending on the market size and if the show is scheduled or a pickup.

SECURITY

Most promoters hire three types of security for their events and concerts. A uniform police presence is usually required by the governing city. It's usually one uniform police officer for every certain number of fans. T-shirt security are the big football types of men who are there as "bouncers" to keep the fans in order. Last, and at every concert or event, is the undercover security. Undercover security is not present to break up fans having a good time. They are there to catch the drug pushers and violent types who want to cause problems. If something happens that results in lawsuits, the promoter can point to the three types of security that were present, and that on the back of the ticket "enter at your own risk" type of legal verbiage.

OPERATION PERSONNEL

Ticket takers, ushers, and box office personal provide services to the fans and consumers by helping them find their seats, answer any questions, and providing additional suggestions and advice. Just some more money the promoter has to budget.

ARTIST RIDERS

A rider is an additional set of instructions for the promoter regarding specific artist's requirements. Riders usually include the staging, lighting, security, and food, drinks, or other necessities for the artist including phone, security sweeps, and the color of the walls (rare, but it does happen). Even the type of and color of the furniture in their dressing room may be described in the rider. The costs of the rented furniture, food, booze, and if the walls need to be painted a different color, are paid for by the promoter. By the way, the walls will have to be painted back to the original color after the show and the promoter will pay for that also.

PRODUCTION/TECH RIDER

The production rider provides instructions for the I.A.T.S.E. crew on specific technological processes and steps required for staging and putting on the show. I.A.T.S.E. crews use the tech riders for setting up the stage, lighting, sound, and other show processes including stunts (for an example, a motor bike the act rides over the crowd). Items include the size and height of the stage, cues for audio effects, where to place instruments, the number of super troopers (spot lights) and lighting cues during the show.

MEDICAL STANDBY

In the riders, the artist often has a long list of high carb foods, booze, and other items to boost their energy for the show. Some acts have a medical doctor give them a vitamin shot before the show. In addition, if not required by local laws or the operating terms of the venue, promoters, and some acts, like to have an ambulance at the show, just in case there is a medical emergency, which has happened in the past and lives were saved.

Fireman (as required by codes)

Most cities will require a fireman to inspect the venue before the show for any situations that may cause a fire and to also check every exit to make sure they have not been blocked.

I.A.T.S.E. Crew (Show)

The I.A.T.S.E. stagehand crew unloaded the equipment before the show; set up the staging for the show; and, run most of the audio and lighting equipment during the show. If the act has its own audio and lighting people, which is a smart thing to do, as they know all the cues and songs, then the union crew assist when needed. Both are paid for being there, and, if the union stagehand is not required for the audio or lighting, they are still paid by the promoter.

Piano Rental

Many of the venues do not have an acoustic grand piano available for the musicians, so if the rider calls for one, we know who's going to rent one and that's the promoter. In addition, the piano is tuned before rehearsal and then also before the show. Heat, cold, humidity, and moving the piano a few feet on the stage can mess up the tuning. Acoustic grand pianos are less frequently required as electronic keyboards often sound fine; however, if it's in the rider, then it must be provided. In some venues, a tuner is expected to remain during the show to handle any sound issues with the instrument, which is an additional expense for the promoter to add into the costs of the show.

Chairs

What is the basic price for renting a venue for one evening? The quick answer is about $1.00 a seat. Of course, the price will vary from venue to venue, but one dollar a seat is a great place to start the negotiation. Also, if the promoter has to rent chairs, the price is the same, about one dollar a chair.

Catering

The riders provide a list of foods and drinks required for both the act and the rest of the show's crew, including the road manager, audio and lighting engineers, roadies, and in most cases, the union crew members. Remember, when we were constructing the asking price of the show in the last chapter, the union requirement for per-diem for the AF of M musicians was raised from $35 per-day to $70 per-day on non-show days. The reason is the promoter has food and drinks catered for the show, but on non-show days the members have to buy their own food out of the per-diems.

Equipment & Extra Professionals

The promoter also funds the additional expense of renting cement barricades if required; a forklift for the load in and out; and of course, the licensed forklift driver. Professional riggers, or the stage crew, who attach the over-head lighting for the stage show, are expensive. Last is the professional electrician, as the amount of electricity for the show is intense. The last thing a promoter needs is a fire caused by an electrical component getting too hot or circuit breakers popping, killing the show in the middle of a song.

Post-Show Expenses

Promoters also have to budget for the post-show cleanup crews. The house stage manager is paid, and depending on the rider, the promoter may have to pay for the transportation, and hotel of the act (which you should not do).

The I.A.T.S.E. crew will need to complete the load out of all the equipment and staging. Then we have to pay taxes to the city, and often, to the state. If consumers used credit cards for their merchandise purchases (and most do), the promoter will have to pay part of the credit card kickback fees, if they received any of the money from sales. In addition, the credit card companies are paid their 3-5% on ticket sales kickback when consumers used the cards for the tickets, usually through Ticketmaster.

PROJECTED EVENT EXPENSES

Using the following Projected Bid Sheet Expense Sheet, the promoter can now estimate the total cost of putting on the show. As long as the expenses are not hyped and close to correct, the promoter will know the cost of the show. Now it's time to figure out how much to charge for the tickets, and to estimate the potential profits or losses at 50%, 80%, 90% and 100% of the tickets sold. Deciding what to charge per-seat is called scaling the house.

Figure 13.3 on the following page provides an example of a bid sheet that allows the promoter to determine the projected expenses for the concert or event being creating. It's the first step required before deciding the ticket prices and scaling the house.

Bid Sheet Projected Expenses

Pre-Show Expenses	Show Expenses	Production Expenses	Post-Show Expenses
Advertising & Sponsoring Station (Ads & Comp Tickets) $_____	Major Artist $_____	Piano Rental $_____	Stage Manager $_____
Social Media Promotion $_____	Opening Act $_____	Piano Tuner $_____	Rider $_____
I.A.T.S.E. Crew load In $_____	Security- [] Police [] T-shirt [] Private $_____	Catering $_____	I.A.T.S.E. Crew Load Out $_____
Ticketmaster $_____	Ticket Takers (show) $_____	Chair Rental $_____	Clean-Up $_____
Promoter Business Legal: Administration: $_____	Ushers (show) $_____	Electrician & Power Fireman (As required by Codes) $_____	Credit Card Fees $_____
Venue/Damage Deposit $_____	Box Office $_____	Riggers $_____	Housing (Acts) $_____
Insurance Bond $_____	Artist Rider Production/Tech Rider $_____	Forklift Operator $_____	Limo: Other: $_____
Licenses & Permits ASCAP/BMI &SESAC: $_____	Medical (on Standby) $_____	Equipment Rental Super Troopers & Lighting $_____	Transportation $_____
City & State forms/Taxes $_____	I.A.T.S.E. Crew Operation of Super Troopers & Audio $_____	Barricade Rental $_____	Taxes: Federal: State: Local: $_____
Total	Total	Total	Total

TICKET SALES PROJECTED REVENUES

Once the promoter knows the cost of putting on the show, it's time to figure out how much money can be generated. Time to cash in, as stated at the top of this chapter! Again, pricing the tickets and "scaling the house" are the responsibility of the promoter. The promoter reviews the basic research again, looking at comparing ticket prices for the band (show) to hire at other locations, to determine if they were sell outs and the various ticket prices. The goal is to charge the maximum price for the seats and then "scale the house" (ticket prices for various sections of venue seating), based on the fans perceptions and emotional connection to the act.

Scaling the House-Bid Sheet Projected Ticket Prices

Type of Ticket # 1	Type of Ticket # 2	Type of Ticket # 3	Type of Ticket # 4
% Of Venue ____	% Of Venue ____	% Of Venue ____	% Of Venue ____
[] Premium [] Average [] Discount [] Comp (Free) [] Other Number of Seats ____	[] Premium [] Average [] Discount [] Comp (Free) [] Other Number of Seats ____	[] Premium [] Average [] Discount [] Comp (Free) [] Other Number of Seats ____	[] Premium [] Average [] Discount [] Comp (Free) [] Other Number of Seats ____
Ticket Price $ _____ 100% gross $ ____	Ticket Price $ _____ 100% gross $ ____	Ticket Price $ _____ 100% gross $ ____	Ticket Price $ _____ 100% gross $ ____
90% gross $ ____	90% gross $ ____	90% gross $ ____	90% gross $ ____
80% gross $ ____	80% gross $ ____	80% gross $ ____	80% gross $ ____
50% gross $ ____	50% gross $ ____	50% gross $ ____	50% gross $ ____
		50% gross $ ____	

Figure 13.4: The Scaling the House-Bid Sheet Projected Ticket Price form allows the promoter to analyze the various options for ticket prices at 100%, 90%, 80, and 50% of the tickets sold.

The trick is to determine ticket prices that will allow the promoter to financially break-even (recoup the invested money) at different opportunities including the 50%, 80% and 90% of tickets sold. The promoter needs this information to set the ticket prices and to negotiate the cost of the show with the booking agent. We know in our example from the previous chapter the band's asking price is between $75,000 to $150,000. However, the promoter doesn't know that, as all he or she knows is what's found on Celebrity Access. Remember, on that site, the asking price is $150,000. The promoter may also check other resources to compared how many tickets were sold and at what price range for the act's show at previous concerts. Of course, none of that matters until he finds out what he can pay for the show based on the bid sheet's expenses and the projected revenues from ticket sales.

Scaling the House/Ticket Prices

Scaling the house, as we've already noted, is the process of determining the ticket prices for various seats (in a variety of locations) in the arena or venue. Festivals often bypass the process by simply charging one ticket price for the entire festival, which often includes many acts over a period of days or weeks. At concerts, fans pay more money for the seat tickets closer to the stage. Once the promoter has estimated the total projected cost of "putting on the show" by using the bid sheet, then they have to determine "how much money" they can make by estimating ticket prices. The "hotter" the act, the higher the ticket prices!

The Scaling Formula

A simple formula is to divide the total cost of the show by 50% of the seats. The idea is that by selling half of the venue seating, the promoter should financially break-even. Those ticket prices become the "average" ticket price for seats in the middle of the venue. Then, the promoter will determine the price of the back of the house seats (in either one or two levels) of "cheaper tickets" depending on the size of the venue and the total number of seats available.

As an example, the promoter may reduce seat ticket prices behind the middle of the "average" seats by 25%, and, then reduce the really distant or "bad" seats 35-50% off the average ticket price. To determine the "best seat" ticket prices, promoters simply add the average, poor, and bad ticket prices together to determine a premium ticket price. Sometimes super premium ticket prices are offered on first and second row seats or standing room areas next to the stage. Of course, this is a simple method, and what the promoter wants to do is charge whatever the customers will pay.

Now, let's say the total cost of the show from the bid sheet is $200,000 and the venue has 5,000 seats. The 2,500 seats (50% of the house) will be at the average ticket price. Another 1,500 are at the discounted (cheap seats) price, and 1,000 at the premium ticket price. How much will the tickets to the show cost? In this case, we'll divide the $200,000 by 2,500 seats to get a price of $80.00 for the average ticket, reduce the discount tickets to $60.00, and price the premium tickets at $140.00. How much money would the show produce at 50%, 80% and 90% of ticket sold?

Determine a sold out gross first by just doing the math. The average priced tickets will bring in $200,000 ($80 x 2,500 seats). The discounted tickets will bring in $90,000 ($60 x 1,500 seats), and the premium tickets yield $140,000 ($140 x 1,000 seats). That's a total gross of $430,000.00. Now, look at the percentages. At 50% sold, the tickets would generate only $215,000 with the show costing at least $200,000. That could be a serious problem as a few tickets less and the promoter is losing money. At 80%, the gross is $344,000 and at 90%, $387,000.

The question is a simple one, will the fans pay that much money for the tickets, yes or no? The promoter now has the information required to call the booking agent and make his best deal.

Projected Revenue from Ticket Sales			
Revenue Tickets @ 100% Sold	Revenue Tickets 90% Sold	Revenue Tickets 80% Sold	Revenue Tickets 50% Sold
Ticket # 1 $____	Ticket # 1 $____	Ticket # 1 $____	Ticket # 1 $____
Ticket # 2 $____	Ticket # 2 $____	Ticket # 2 $____	Ticket # 2 $____
Ticket # 3 $____	Ticket # 3 $____	Ticket # 3 $____	Ticket # 3 $____
Ticket # 4 $____	Ticket # 4 $____	Ticket # 4 $____	Ticket # 4 $____
Projected Gross from Ticket Sales @ 100% Sold	Total Gross (100%) $		
Projected Gross from Ticket Sales @ 90% Sold	Total Gross (90%) $		
Projected Gross from Ticket Sales @ 80% Sold	Total Gross (60%) $		
Projected Gross from Ticket Sales @ 50% Sold	Total Gross (50%) $		

Figure 13.5: Scaling the House with the projected ticket prices provides the concert promoter with an estimation of the total gross of the concert if it sells out. From there, they can determine lower break even points and make their final decisions about the show's financials.

THE TYPES OF DEALS

Concert promotion is a very risky business, so there are many types of deals that can be often structured. However, according to Mark Volman of the supergroup The Turtles (2008), there are four types of deals- *the straight guarantee, guarantee plus a percentage of the gate, guarantee plus a percentage of the net, and, guarantee plus a bonus.*[269]

STRAIGHT GUARANTEE

With the *straight guarantee* deal, the act receives a guaranteed amount of money regardless of the success or failure of the promoter to generate an audience. This type of deal leaves the promoter with an opportunity to lock in the act at a fixed cost, reducing the risk increasing his or her potential profit based on the success of the event. A straight guarantee can also be negotiated for a percentage of the house revenues, which superstar acts often require as in 90% of the profits after all concert cost are paid. However, that is a risky move for unknown or beginning acts, as the percentage of zero is zero, meaning if the promoter loses money or just breaks-even the band is paid zip.

GUARANTEE PLUS A PERCENTAGE OF THE NET (GATE)

The act receives the *guarantee plus* a certain percentage of the net after the break even point (all expenses have been paid). The percentage of the net becomes a negotiation point for the band to receive additional income on a very successful event and increases the negotiated leverage for the promoter to land or sign a more successful act for the event.

GUARANTEE VERSUS A PERCENTAGE OF THE NET

The act receives either the fixed guarantee or a *percentage of the net*, whichever is the greater. This type of deal is a mixture of the straight guarantee deal and the guarantee plus a percentage of the net deal. It creates a little more financial security to the act. If the event is poorly attended or a loss of money for the promoter, the act is still paid the guarantee. If the event is very successful, then the act is paid an amount of the guarantee plus a little extra.

---

269 Mark Volman, "Types of Concert Tour Deals," Survey of Music Business Course Pace, (Belmont University, Nashville, TN, 2008).

Guarantee Plus a Bonus

With the *guarantee plus a bonus*, the act receives the guarantee plus a negotiated bonus payment based on the number of tickets sold. The bonus is a variable amount that increases as the number of seats sold hit various levels. This type of deal provides more security to the promoter.

Concert Promotion Process

Once the promoter determines which acts or packaged shows to book (employ), then the process becomes a little crazier as several more things have to fall into place. Will the venue have an open date on the same day the act is available to perform? Will the act be on tour near the promoter's location when the available venue dates are open? It cost too much money to travel across the country for one show. Are there any other events happening in the local area that might decrease the potential ticket sales?

Bad weather, an artist's poor health, or some other uncontrollable situation can negatively determine the final concert attendance also. Hopefully you're now starting to understand what promoters experience each time they produce a show. But let's not forget, a successful concert can make hundreds of thousands of dollars in one evening. It's easy to see why the concert promotion business is considered a high profile, somewhat risky, yet very profitable business. . . if you know what you're doing!

Profit Margins

Promoters subtract their total projected expenses from their projected gross ticket sales revenues to determine their break-even points and profit margins. Knowing their profit margins helps the promoter make the decision to go for it or pass. Profit margins are based on how many seats must be sold to break even or make a profit. Many concerts require 50-80% of all tickets to be sold to break even financially. Promoters hope the profits will be much greater than the 20% depending on the acts booked, promotion, and publicity. However, other types of margins are common depending on what is negotiated on the front end, and, of course, the type of deal and the number of tickets sold.

MERCHANDISING

With the advent of 360 deals, much of the merchandise sold at concerts is provided as a fulfillment item by the major label. The artist and the personal manager determine the types and quality of items to be sold and then the label outsources the work to private companies. The label pays for the items and adds the bill to the act's recoupable account at the label. When items are sold, the label takes their cost of manufacturing, plus their share of the profits and sends a check to the artist's business manager for the remaining amount. The advantage in this type of deal is that the artist does not have to pay for the manufacturing of the merchandise out of their own pockets.

Companies such as EMI, Brockum, FMI, Nice Man, Winterland, and Missing Link provide and sell merchandise for artist(s) who do not have the label fulfillment deal.[270] The artists receive between 15-35% of the gross income from merchandise, while the providing company pays for all the merchandise, shipment, sales personnel, booths, tables, and advertisements. Artists approve the design of the merchandise and receive quarterly checks for their percentage of each item sold.

Sometimes, the concert venue may receive part of the total merchandise profits for providing space, tables, and advertisement opportunities to the merchandising company. Soft drinks, food, and candy are considered concessions that are sold by the venue with all profits remaining with the venue.

*****

---

270 Missing Link, "Who We Are," Missinglink.com, http://www.missingink.com/who_we_are, (accessed April 7, 2011).

Serious Music Market

While much of what we have studied here has to do with popular music and commercial music acts, symphony orchestras, opera companies, dance troupes, and Broadway shows also go on tours both nationally and abroad. They follow the same processes regarding promotion and development of bid sheets, as do the bands we have used in our examples. Known as the serious music market, symphony orchestras, opera, Broadway and dance companies contribute billions annually to the United States economy. Many opportunities are available for classically trained, consummate musicians and vocalists. Private and public organizations, churches, universities, public and private grants, donations, businesses, and local volunteer organizations often finance orchestras and various types of choral groups. Many serious music organizations are dependent on these political, social, and music-supporting groups to provide financial support for local musicians.

Concert Industry Trade Magazines

Billboard Magazine is the most powerful weekly publication covering all aspects of the music industry. *Pollstar Magazine* covers the concert business. Promoters use the agency rosters to select and locate the artists they want to book. Venues use the trades to publicize their auditoriums for acts, managers and promoters. Domestic and international news stories detail the artists' lifestyles and their successful businesses.

Live Nation

Live Nation Entertainment is ranked at #330 in the Fortune 500 business charts (2017). Its top competitors are Entertainment on Stage and SMG Holdings, Inc. According to Hoovers (2017),

> Live Nation Entertainment holds center stage as the world's largest ticket seller and promoter of live entertainment. The company significantly expanded its ticketing services with the purchase of Ticketmaster Entertainment. The 2010 deal, worth some $889 million, created a

powerful live-music conglomerate. The firm owns or operates about 165 venues in North America and Europe. Annually, about 530 million people attend some 250,000 Live Nation events. Live Nation also owns House of Blues venues through HOB Entertainment and dozens of prestigious concert halls. In addition, Live Nation owns a stake in about 350 artists› music, including albums, tours, and merchandise . . . and about 8,300 employees.[271]

AEG LIVE

AEG Live is really a bunch of individual companies flying the same flag. As an example, AEG Present is London based, AEG Presents is in New York, AEG Live Productions is based in St. Louis, AEG Live/The Messina Group is out of Nashville, Chuck Morris Enterprises is in Denver, and the list goes on. AEG-Live, in London, has partnerships with Concerts West, the Bowery Presents, Marshall Arts, Madison House, and the Messina Touring Group in the United States. They own over twenty venues in the U.S. in major cities, as the company is a soft LLC working as a partnership with the top touring and promoters in the United States and global markets.[272]

ON STAGE ENTERTAINMENT

On Stage Entertainment likes to focus its live presentations on iconic superstars, some of whom have already passed on (as examples, Elvis Presley, and Marilyn Monroe). However, their profit margins are competitive with Live Nation in some cases. Again, according to Hoovers (2017),

> *Elvis hasn't left the building; he's waiting on stage. On Stage Entertainment produces and markets live theatrical entertainment, including its flagship Legends in Concert tribute shows, which feature impersonators who pay tribute to celebrities of the past and present like Elvis Presley, Cher, Marilyn Monroe, and many others. The show has toured in 15 countries and plays nightly in Las Vegas; Atlantic City, New Jersey;*

---

[271] "!company_name! | Company Profile Report." Sales leads, Company Profiles, Business Database & Sales Acceleration Solutions - D&B Hoovers. Accessed July 29, 2017. http://www.hoovers.com/company-information/cs/company-report.live_nation_entertainment_inc.f0b688de4dc5a036.html.
[272] "AEG Presents." AEG Presents. Accessed July 29, 2017. https://www.aegpresents.com/.

Branson, Missouri; and Myrtle Beach, South Carolina. The company also performs Legends at casinos, state fairs, and amusement parks, as well as traveling productions, cruise ship shows, and corporate entertainment events. On Stage Entertainment was founded in 1983.[273]

FELD ENTERTAINMENT

Feld Entertainment's niche is based on the old circus business and the owner of the private company was a father who started the company after being a clown with Ringling Bros. and Barnum and Bailey Circus. D&B Hoovers claims (2017),

> *A lot of clowning around has helped Feld Entertainment become one of the largest live entertainment producers in the world. The company entertains people through its centerpiece, Ringling Bros. and Barnum & Bailey Circus, which visits about 120 cities in North America each year. Through a partnership with Walt Disney, Feld also produces touring Disney On Ice shows, such as Treasure Trove. In addition, its Disney Live! produces live Disney-themed touring stage productions. Chairman and CEO Kenneth Feld, whose father, Irvin, began managing the circus in 1956, owns the company and personally oversees most of its productions. Ringling Bros. and Barnum & Bailey Circus made its first performance in 1871.*[274]

CIRQUE DU SOLEIL

Cirque du Soleil is the modern version of Feld Entertainment's Ringling Bros. and Barnum & Bailey Circus. Again, Cirque de Soleil is a private company owned by a fire eating former circus performer, who has reinvented the circus business by merging acrobatics and the traditional circus shows into a very profitable business. Hoovers say (2017),

> *Cirque du Soleil ("Circus of the Sun") is probably the only organization where you can get away with calling the founder a clown. The group has turned the circus on its ear, blending street entertainment, eccentric*

---

273 "!company_name! | Company Profile from Hoover's." Entertainment On Stage Inc | Company Profile from Hoover's - D&B Hoovers. Accessed July 29, 2017. http://www.hoovers.com/company-information/cs/company-profile.entertainment_on_stage_inc.d9d3ab34ccc20fe2.html.

274 "!company_name! | Company Profile from Hoover's." FELD ENTERTAINMENT, INC. | Company Profile from Hoover's - D&B Hoovers. Accessed July 29, 2017. http://www.hoovers.com/company-information/cs/company-profile.feld_entertainment_inc.6b8499d51b8d95cf.html.

costumes, and cabaret. Its shows have been seen by more than 100 million spectators in nearly 300 cities on five continents. Among its 20 productions are "O" (an aquatic show at MGM Resorts' Bellagio); LOVE, a Las Vegas show featuring Beatles music (with support from Sir. Paul McCartney and Ringo Starr, and from the widows of George Harrison and John Lennon); and touring shows Quidam and Alegría. Accordionist, stiltwalker, and fire-eater Guy Laliberté owns Cirque du Soleil, which he co-founded in 1984.[275]

VIRTUAL CORPORATIONS

Virtual Corporations are sole-purpose companies set up to run the tour, ticketing, and merchandising. Promoters run the businesses out of their hotel rooms using multiple phone lines, cell phones, social media connections, fax machines and email. These corporations often gross millions of dollars during the tour, and when the tour is finished, the companies are closed and "out-of-business".

*****

AWARDS SHOWS

Winning a Grammy, Oscar, Tony, Emmy, ACM, Country Music, Golden Globe, or any other type of award means MONEY! Winning the top award in your industry is instant prestige, and, it also increases profits from streaming, CD sales, tour tickets, merchandise, and branding. Voting for some of the awards is limited to members only. Some others are by consumers who phone, email or use social media to vote for their favorite recording artist.

THE GRAMMYS

The Grammys are presented by the National Academy of Record Arts and Sciences (NARAS). The founding nonprofit organization (NARAS) is located in Los Angeles with chapter offices in Atlanta, Chicago, Florida

---

[275] "Cirque du Soleil Inc Company Information." B&D Hoovers. Accessed July 28, 2017. http://www.hoovers.com/company-information/cs/company-profile.cirque_du_soleil_inc.b6db0f5285d5f6c2.html.

(Miami Beach-area office), L.A., Memphis, Nashville, New York, the Pacific Northwest (Seattle-area office), Philadelphia, San Francisco, Texas (Austin-area office) and Washington D.C. Voting members include singers, musicians, producers, songwriters, engineers, managers, and business professionals who work at the highest level in the industry.[276] According to Grammy 365 (2011),

> ...The GRAMMYs are the only peer-presented award to honor artistic achievement, technical proficiency and overall excellence in the recording industry, without regard to album sales or chart position. ...Over the last decade particularly, The Academy has expanded its goals from the important work of recognizing the best in music through the GRAMMY Awards to establishing itself as the preeminent arts advocacy and outreach organization in the country. The Academy's mission statement is simple, but represents the heart and soul of the organization's efforts: to positively impact the lives of musicians, industry members and our society at large.[277]

The Emmys

Both the Emmys and the Oscars have awards for songs and music in their entertainment productions. The Emmys are the ultimate award in the television industry presented by the National Academy of Television Arts and Sciences (NATAS), and its sister organization the Academy of Television Arts & Sciences (ATAS). Emmys and Global Media Awards are presented for excellence in news, documentary, sports, daytime programming, creative and digital entertainment, public and community service, technology, engineering, business, and primetime programs.[278]

The Oscars

The Oscars also have their music connection, as many hit songs got their shot in a film or movie. As examples, "Silver Bells" was first in the Bob

---
276 Grammy Awards, (National Academy of Recording Arts and Sciences), "About Us," NARAS, http://www.grammy365.com/about, (accessed April 19, 2011).
277 Grammy 365, "About Us," NARAS, http://www.grammy365.com/about, (accessed April 19, 2011).
278 The Emmy Awards, (National Academy of Television Arts and Sciences), "History," NATAS, http://www.emmyonline.org/academy.html, (accessed April 19, 2011).

Hope movie, *The Lemon Drop Kid*, and the rock group Paramore had their song "Decode" in the movie *Twilight*. The Oscars are presented by the Academy of Motion Pictures Arts and Sciences. They're the top award for filmmakers, producers, actors, scriptwriters, editors, songwriters, musicians, technical operators of cameras, lights, audio, effects, and of course, the directors.[279]

SUMMARY

Labels provide the initial funding to get the act's show ready for the tour with the act's personal manager and representation team members guiding the act as they rehearse. They also prepare and sell (known as the pitch) the show to the promoters. Live Nation, AEG Live, and many independent concert promoters fund most of the concerts, shows, and festivals in the United States, and in many other locations in the world. Booking agents who represent the artist, pitch the act to promoters who act as talent buyers. The act is then (once the deal is maded), required to show up and perform (for a negotiated amount of money) at the place and time, as required by the promoter in the contact between the act's representation company and the promoter.

The most important question for the promoter to answer is *what is an acceptable price for the show?* To determine their bid for the artist's services, promoters use a bid sheet to estimate the cost of putting on the concert. Hiring the act is usually the largest expense. Once the promoter knows the cost of putting on the show, the next step is to price the tickets and "scale the house" to determine the possible profits and try to protect against losses. Promoters use basic research from *Billboard*, and *Pollstar Magazines* and additional information from Nielsen Research and others before considering the amount of money to pay the artist. They also look at comparative ticket prices for the band or show from their previous performances at other locations.

---

[279] Oscar Awards, (Academy of Motion Picture Arts and Sciences), "History and Organization," AMPAS, http://www.oscars.org/awards/governors/index.html, (accessed April 19, 2011).

Once the promoter has a better understanding about the financial situation from the bid sheet, the next step is to negotiate the deal with the booking agent. Everything is negotiable. But, there are four types of "typical" deals usually discussed. A straight guarantee locks in an amount of money the band will earn for performing at the event. A guarantee plus a percentage of the net or gate means that the band will receive the guarantee amount of money, plus additional money from the door or other business. The guarantee versus a percentage of the house is an either-or situation. Here, the act receives whichever figure is the larger of the two. The guarantee plus a bonus is the last deal. This time, the band receives the guarantee and a bonus based on the success of the event. If you apply the block below to *Figure 13.6* on the next page, you will grasp the thinking that goes into how the money is spent to make the 360 deal in the music industry.

Entity or Business	Product Created	Service Provided	Revenue Streams
Songwriters	Wow songs	Networking	Royalties (From sales and licensing of songs)
Music Publishers	New Songs (Staff writers)	Agent to songwriters	Royalties (From sales and licensing of songs)
		Distribution of wow songs to industry	Ownership of Copyrights (Catalogs)
Labels	Iconic recording artists	**Funding of artist career**	N/A-usually an investment in artist of between $500,000-$2 million
		Artist development	
		Image development	
		Branding	
	Recordings	**Funding of master recordings**	**Royalties & Licensing Fees** (From sales and licensing of songs) including retail-with points to act **Streaming-with no payment to acts/maybe in the future**
		Approval of recording team & master recordings	
	Website	**Marketing plan** Promotion Publicity Distribution of recordings & Advertisements	**360 Deal Revenues** 10-12% of gross revenues generated by recording artist, plus: (depending on deal) 10%-20% of Merchandise fulfillment 10%-40% of Branding depending on deal 10%-20% of Corporate Sponsorship
	Music videos		
	Branding products & endorsement opportunities		
	Live ticket events	**Tour support funding**	**360 Deal Revenues** 10-12% of gross revenues generated by recording artist
	Merchandise fulfillment		
Recording Artists	Recordings Videos Live Performances Brandings Charities Endorsements	Shameless self-promotion	360 Deal Revenues Recording & streaming royalties (if any)
			The remaining generated revenue after all payments to label, management, supportive musicians, etc., and taxes
Production team of recordings & live ticket events	Recordings	**Live ticket performances and show production**	Wages (From independent contractors, scale wages from unions, rental or lease fees for equipment and studio rentals)
	Staging of Productions Live ticket events		
Performance Agencies (Managers)	Live stage shows	**Representation of act** Personal management Booking agent Business manager	**Commissions paid by act** (Percentage of artist's income such as 15-20% for personal management, 10% for booking agent & 3-5% for business agent)
	Employment for artists and supporting musicians, singers, & supporting employees		
Promoters	Concert events for consumers	Create marketplace for live shows and sale opportunities of merchandise and brands	Profits (Depending on the type of deal and breakeven points after all expenses are paid)
	Markets for Acts & performers (Musicians/singers)		
	Markets for IATSE crews & others		

Chapter 14

Careers

Now you know where the industry is headed- at least for today! When you figure out where your passions are your job is to build the music business and entertainment industry of the future. What a great opportunity and blessing to you for going for it! The world is waiting! So, where do you fit in and how many different types of careers are available? And, how can you use the information you gained in this book to build your own career?

HOW WE GOT HERE

There are many ways to analyze the music industry. My suggestion, as you've discovered, is to use the empty cube or block to visualize how to think about what the industry, its products, people, business models, and careers look like from an abstract perspective.

Of course, a clear cube is too simple and doesn't really say anything about anything. So, at the end of each chapter you found another cube with layers representing important items or "layers of knowledge" to help you understand *what you need to know* to become valuable in the music industry.

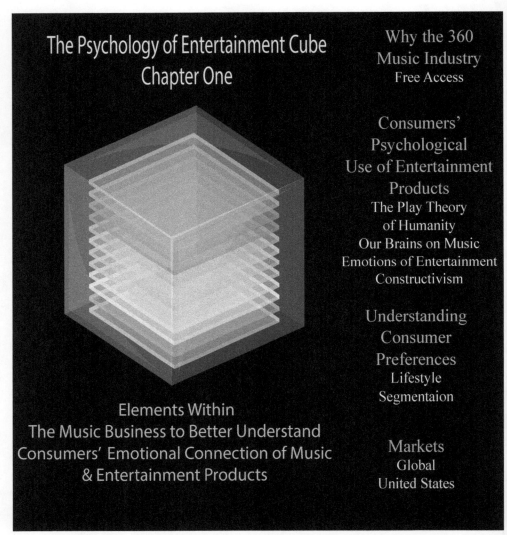

In Chapter One, the empty cube is filled with the layers of (a) why we now have the 360 music industry; (b) theories on understanding how consumers use music and entertainment products; (c) how consumers have different preferences for different formats of music and other related entertainment products; (d) how labels and research firms divide consumers into different lifestyle typologies for marketing, promotion, publicity, and sales; and, (e) trends in the industry sales totals in the global markets. Reading each cube this way let's you see the key ideas' applications.

Consider which chapters clicked with your passions and desires to be in the business. Then, blend all of the information with the various career opportunities shown in the image below to see where you might fit and find a rewarding career. Remember, music helps us enjoy our life and daily events. So, be a part of this great industry that provides music for the world to enjoy.

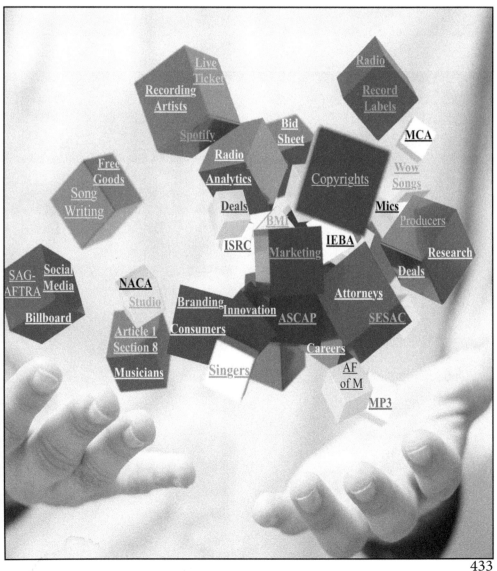

The following information from the United States government provides an example of the types of jobs, the number of employees, businesses, and average salaries. The latest information for the United States (2012) illustrates many of the different types of careers available in this industry. Notice the NAICS code and the related information including the number of people currently employed in the industry in specific careers, the number of businesses, and the average salaries. The second chart provides more specific information on careers in the creative system.

THE NORTH AMERICAN INDUSTRY CLASSIFICATION SYSTEM (NAICS)

NAICS Code	Types of Industry or NAICS Sub Code	Sub Industry	Annual Number of Business	Annual Average Employed	Total Annual Wages	Annual Wages per Employee
10	Total, all industries		9075876	115557595	$5,927,513,234,040	$51,295
	1026	Leisure and hospitality	793468	14625406	$307,030,768,985	$20,993
334	NAICS 334 Computer and electronic product Manufactory		18992	1047250	$110,975,227,966	$105,968

434

NAICS Code	Types of Industry or NAICS Sub Code	Sub Industry	Annual Number of Business	Annual Average Employed	Total Annual Wages	Annual Wages per Employee
	3343	Video equipment	691	19764	$1,777,226,456	$89,923
443	Electronic and appliance stores	Retail	48854	488418	$21,883,743,168	$44,805
451	Sporting goods, hobby, book and music stores	Retail	53041	614563	$12,038,486,442	$19,589
	45114	Musical instrument and supplies stores	3858	31408	$870,021,275	$27,701
	4512	Book, periodical, and music stores	8285	89050	$1,753,846,505	$19,695
	451211	Book stores	7229	81601	$1,547,692,857	$18,967
	45122	Recorded tape, CD, and record stores	No Data	No Data	No Data Available	No Data Available
	45392	Art dealers	5228	17104	$863,487,829	$50,483
511	Publishing industries,		37116	721441	$70,516,770,871	$97,744
	51113	Book publishers	3790	64228	$5,046,029,724	$78,564
	5112	Software publishers	14931	310895	$44,004,443,247	$141,541
512	Motion picture and sound recording industries		29164	384839	$25,732,739,262	$66,866

NAICS Code	Types of Industry or NAICS Sub Code	Sub Industry	Annual Number of Business	Annual Average Employed	Total Annual Wages	Annual Wages per Employee
	5121	Motion picture and video industries	25553	368763	$24,512,755,283	$66,473
	51211	Motion picture and video production	17916	214321	$20,351,259,680	$94,957
	51212	Motion picture and video distribution	535	7398	$961,729,997	$130,000
	512131	Motion picture theaters,	4289	127489	$1,678,289,191	$13,164
	512132	Drive-in theaters	230	1950	$21,065,077	$10,801
	51219	Post production and other related industries	2583	17605	$1,500,411,338	$85,225
515	Broadcasting, except Internet		9744	282264	$23,094,579,171	$81,819
	5151	Radio and television stations	8334	219765	$16,685,933,164	$75,926
	51511	Radio stations	5616	90136	$4,935,153,650	$54,752
	5152	Cable and other subscription programs	1410	62500	$6,408,646,007	$102,539
516	Internet publishing and broadcasting		No Data	No Data	No Data	No Data

436

NAICS Code	Types of Industry or NAICS Sub Code	Sub Industry	Annual Number of Business	Annual Average Employed	Total Annual Wages	Annual Wages per Employee
517	Telecom		39772	850936	$68,613,325,877	$80,633
	5172	Wireless carriers	8630	155470	$11,588,339,241	$74,537
	5174	Satellite	777	9077	$917,657,647	$101,092
518	Data processing, hosting and related services		16418	276773	$25,591,467,578	$92,464
	54181	Advertising agencies	19057	189809	$17,844,822,786	$94,015
	54192	Photo services	13780	56767	$1,615,495,060	$28,458
	61161	Fine arts schools	12094	83313	$1,557,985,472	$18,700
71	Entertainment recreation		132631	2094689	$73,013,251,195	$34,856
	711	Performing arts and spectator sports	51724	444794	$36,387,475,968	$81,808
	7112	Spectator sports	6309	135853	$17,558,490,642	$129,247
	7111	Performing arts companies	9844	114631	$5,171,624,756	$45,115
	71111	Theater companies and dinner theaters	3332	62607	$2,128,557,135	$33,999
	71112	Dance companies	898	10933	$414,846,261	$37,945
	71113	Musical groups and artists	4961	34208	$2,316,709,316	$67,725
	7113	Promoters of performing arts and sports	7174	120052	$4,461,483,891	$37,163

437

NAICS Code	Types of Industry or NAICS Sub Code	Sub Industry	Annual Number of Business	Annual Average Employed	Total Annual Wages	Annual Wages per Employee
	713	Amusements, gambling, and recreation	74734	1503654	$31,884,622,282	$21,205
	7114	Agents and managers for public figures	4548	22139	$2,509,519,307	$113,353
	7115	Indie artists, writers, and performers	23849	52119	$6,686,357,372	$128,290

Figure 14.1: The North American Industry Classification System (NAICS) is the latest federal government statistical data on the number of jobs in the entertainment and related industries. Jobs have a unique number and sub-codes related to similar career jobs. You'll find the number of businesses, the average number of employees, the total annual wages, and the annual wages per employee.

The occupations list, based on the latest figures available (2012-2014), shows the number of small entrepreneurs, work-for-hire, and independent contractors such as producers, musicians, camera operators, etc., and the average wages. The news for creative, innovative, skilled, bright, educated artists, technician assistants and bookkeepers is a shockingly high 12.5%. If you're part of the creative systems, you'll probably be hired as a "work-for-hire," so you'll need to focus on entrepreneurship and how to run your own business. As you'll see, there are lots of opportunities for creative individuals; however, you also need to understand how the business operates and who will hire you and how that process works. Remember to check the legal forms of business and the licensing requirements in your state before venturing out of your own.

NAICS Jobs for Creative Artists, & Technicians

Occupation Title	Code	2012 Employment (in thousands)	2012 Percent of Industry	Projected 2022 Employment (in thousands)	Projected 2022 Percent of Industry	Employment change 2012-2022 Number (In thousands)	Employment Percent of change 2012-2022
Total, all occupations	00-0000	46.6	100.0	52.4	100.0	5.8	12.5
Fine artists, including painters, sculptors, and illustrators	27-1013	3.9	8.3	4.3	8.3	0.5	12.5
Actors	27-2011	3.9	8.4	4.4	8.4	0.5	12.5
Producers and directors	27-2012	3.0	6.4	3.3	6.4	0.4	12.5
Writers and authors	27-3043	2.9	6.2	3.3	6.2	0.4	12.5
Secretaries and administrative assistants, except legal, medical, and executive	43-6014	2.1	4.5	2.5	4.7	0.4	18.3
Audio and video equipment technicians	27-4011	2.0	4.3	2.4	4.5	0.4	18.1
Public address system and other announcers	27-3012	1.9	4.0	2.1	4.0	0.2	12.5
Craft artists	27-1012	1.8	3.9	2.1	3.9	0.2	12.5
Office clerks, general	43-9061	1.8	3.9	1.9	3.7	0.1	6.9

Occupation Title	Code	2012 Employment (in thousands)	2012 Percent of Industry	Projected 2022 Employment (in thousands)	Projected 2022 Percent of Industry	Employment change 2012-2022 Number (In thousands)	Employment Percent of change 2012-2022
Musicians and singers	27-2042	1.7	3.7	1.9	3.7	0.2	12.5
General and operations managers	11-1021	1.1	2.3	1.2	2.3	0.1	12.5
Laborers and freight, stock, and material movers, hand	53-7062	1.1	2.4	1.3	2.4	0.1	12.5
Executive secretaries and executive administrative assistants	43-6011	1.0	2.1	1.0	1.9	0.0	0.3
Multimedia artists and animators	27-1014	0.9	2.0	1.1	2.0	0.1	12.5
Agents and business managers of artists, performers, and athletes	13-1011	0.8	1.8	0.9	1.8	0.1	12.5
Entertainers and performers, sports and related workers, all other	27-2099	0.8	1.7	0.9	1.7	0.1	12.5
Bookkeeping, accounting, and auditing clerks	43-3031	0.8	1.7	0.9	1.7	0.1	12.5
Business operations specialists, all other	13-1199	0.7	1.4	0.7	1.4	0.1	12.5

Occupation Title	Code	2012 Employment (in thousands)	2012 Percent of Industry	Projected 2022 Employment (in thousands)	Projected 2022 Percent of Industry	Employment change 2012-2022 Number (In thousands)	Employment Percent of change 2012-2022
Photographers	27-4021	0.7	1.5	0.8	1.5	0.1	12.5
Self-enrichment education teachers	25-3021	0.5	1.1	0.6	1.1	0.1	12.5
Public relations specialists	27-3031	0.5	1.0	0.5	1.0	0.1	12.5
Technical writers	27-3042	0.5	1.1	0.6	1.1	0.1	12.5
Film and video editors	27-4032	0.5	1.0	0.5	1.0	0.1	12.5
Sales representatives, services, all other	41-3099	0.5	1.2	0.6	1.2	0.1	12.5
Accountants and auditors	13-2011	0.4	0.8	0.4	0.8	0.0	12.5
Graphic designers	27-1024	0.4	0.8	0.4	0.8	0.0	12.5
Set and exhibit designers	27-1027	0.4	0.8	0.4	0.8	0.0	12.5
Sound engineering technicians	27-4014	0.4	0.9	0.5	0.9	0.1	12.5
Security guards	33-9032	0.4	0.8	0.4	0.8	0.0	12.5
Museum technicians and conservators	25-4013	0.3	0.6	0.3	0.6	0.0	12.5
Dancers	27-2031	0.3	0.7	0.3	0.7	0.0	12.5
Music directors and composers	27-2041	0.3	0.7	0.3	0.7	0.0	12.5

Figure 14.2: NAICS jobs for creative artist, technician involved in production is important as they are the professionals who make the recordings, movies, books, computer games that brings enjoyment to consumers and profits to the industry.

THE FUTURE

My hope is that by now you're starting to understand how much of the traditional business in entertainment has shifted towards the 360 music industry and why that is the case. We all know the only thing in life that is certain is CHANGE. Keep an open mind and consider *all* of the amazing opportunities the new 360 music industry brings to you. Reflect on what author Paul Wissmann, national sector leader of KPMG media and telecommunication practices, says is the challenge that lies ahead (2017),

> *In a world where we can look up anything we want, and find it through a search bar or an algorithm that tells us-based on our likes or past viewing habits-what's out there, traditional entertainment providers are losing market prominence and need to reinvent themselves to be relevant in the emerging ecosystem.*[280]

*****

---

[280] Leonard Brody, " Coming Soon To A Device Near You," *Forbes* September 5 2017: 64-65.

EPILOGUE

As the editor of this book, having read through it, I thought it might be helpful to give Larry a sample of an Epilogue he could use to close the book. I wrote this late one night, read it to Larry, and he said, "It is better than I could have done. It is a very positive review of what you remembered and what you learned from editing the book. I could only hope that everybody who reads it has gained the same insights. Thanks for doing it, Beverly, and stick in the back as the Epilogue".

By now, you should recognize the entertainment and music industry is complex. Since you started reading this book, the *Billboard* charts have changed, the *New York Times* bestseller list is published with new authors added weekly, the TV lineups have changed, and at least six new movies have premiered. In addition, artists have retired, new acts have been signed, and money has been made and lost- sometimes in the blink of an eye. As was said earlier, there is a lot of Vegas in this business! You need only think about what entrepreneur Leonard Brody writes in *Forbes* to remind yourself how rapidly things are changing in entertainment, "The media landscape is undergoing a massive rewrite on every level, from the formats that content is taking to how it is distributed and consumed".[281]

What are your takeaways now that you have studied this book? You should have your own lists of more to learn, ideas to pursue, and gaps to fill in, but let me offer, in closing, a few thoughts.

- *First, be a career entrepreneur.* Keep in mind your goal as a member of the music business is to contribute to its artistic and/or its business structures. What this is means is learn how to become a good researcher, promoter, publicist, and business manager yourself. Read the trade magazines, use the entertainment websites, and the government websites to stay up to date on changes in the law, in finance, and in consumer taste. Gain suf-

---
281 Leonard Brody, " Coming Soon To A Device Near You," *Forbes* September 5 2017: 64-65.

ficient statistical knowledge to understand data analytics, and how to use corporate reports, consumer research data, and marketing trends analysis to suggest directions for your business and how much money you will need to profit on your creativity.

- *Second, talent is a gift for you to develop and apply.* If you want to make it in the industry as an artist, you have to be practical. Know who runs the labels, how to get noticed by having a product you can draw fans into wanting, and understand how lifestyles, education, and money influence consumer choices.

- *Third, don't let others determine what you want to do in the business and how you are going to do it.* Know the differences between the types of deals and music licenses, the copyright laws, and your rights as a content creator. Demonstrate you know your value with the confidence that comes from broad learning and multiple types of experience. Practice creating your own budgets and develop your people skills. You will need to be a good spokesperson for yourself, and you will need to communicate to others in the business. Also, because you will be either directly hiring people (or consulting with your label and personal manager as people are hired), know what the jobs are in the industry and what you should expect from your representation team. It's unnecessary for you to be a part of everything that goes on in the business, but you do want to know that your business is ethically and legally managed.

- *Lastly, approach your career in the industry with an open mind and an open heart.* Listen to what others have to offer, make your own choices and decisions, and remain flexible, as you will have to change if your career has any length to it. In fact, the innovations and changes in the music industry can be seen as a mirror and a measure of how well your products are being received by your fans. Expect to take risks, and you can adapt more quickly to both failures and successes as you try to capture that lightning in a bottle. Good Luck!

Index

360 3, 4, 15, 16, 21, 27, 28, 37, 57, 72, 83, 86, 96, 99, 100, 138, 141, 160, 191, 200, 201, 208, 211, 214, 218, 226, 227, 228, 236, 237, 241, 242, 243, 251, 252, 253, 258, 259, 262, 266, 269, 271, 272, 275, 277, 278, 295, 300, 301, 335, 336, 342, 343, 356, 358, 364, 388, 396, 400, 402, 423

360 Deals, 83, 226, 252, 253, 258, 262, 295, 356, 400, 423

A

ABC 67

Acts 20, 22, 111, 209, 246, 389

Administration deal 155

AEG Live 425, 429

AF of M 26, 28, 248, 306, 322, 323, 324, 325, 327, 328, 330, 333, 334, 336, 345, 353, 358, 362, 373, 409, 414

AF of M Road Show Scales 28, 373

AF of M Sound Recording Labor Agreement 26, 325

Agents 27, 28, 353, 393

All-ins 252, 334, 335

Alpert, Herb 66

AM 69, 253, 254

A&M Records 66, 67

Apple 63, 133, 222, 226, 229, 320

A&R 22, 38, 146, 150, 209, 216, 231, 232, 233, 242, 243, 244, 248, 249, 250, 251, 271, 272, 282, 284, 305, 309

Article 1, Section 8 109, 111, 116

Artist Growth 28, 389

Artist Personal Manager Contract 26, 347

Artist Representation 26, 339

ASCAP 19, 70, 147, 166, 173, 178, 179, 180, 181, 182, 183, 184, 185, 191, 253, 367

Asking Price 28, 379

Attorneys 27, 355, 395

Audio Home Recording Act 73

Authorship 119, 122, 126

Azoff, Irving 269

B

Basic Tracks 25, 319

Bell, Alexander Graham 60, 68, 73

Berliner, Emile 65

Bertelsmann 63

Bezos, Jeff 275

Bid Sheet 29, 406, 415, 417

Billboard 5, 24, 145, 170, 225, 227, 251, 258, 264, 271, 293, 294, 295, 296, 301, 316, 317, 318, 406, 424, 429, 445

Blanket License 184

BMI 19, 70, 147, 166, 173, 178, 179, 181, 182, 183, 184, 185, 191, 253, 367

Booking Agents 27, 353

Bowen, Jimmy 250, 251, 300, 301, 315, 316, 317, 318

Bowie, David 65, 404

Brandenburg, Karlheinz 76

Branding 23, 252, 271, 280

Branson, Richard 85, 426

Brody, Leonard 442, 443

Bronfman, Edgar 66

Brooks ,Garth 84, 85

Brown, L, Russell 143, 145

Budgets 26, 214, 250, 252, 330, 334, 335, 336

Business Managers 27, 28, 353, 388

Business Models 41, 64, 67, 73, 83, 96, 134, 135, 138, 220, 228, 263, 271, 358

Business Plan 20, 200

Business System 16

C

Capitol Records 65, 84

Career Launch 214

Career Timeline 197

CBS 63, 67

CDs 34, 36, 40, 171, 219, 231, 248, 262, 263, 322, 327, 366, 402

Celebrity Access 28, 389, 405, 418

Certificate of Recordation 18, 126

Certificate of Registration 17, 125, 126

Charisma Records 84

Cirque du Soleil 31, 426, 427

Citibank 85

Clapton. Eric 52

Claritas 45, 46

Columbia Records 62

CON 123

Consent Decree 19, 184

Controlled Composition Clause 19, 173, 174, 226

Co-publishing deal 155, 163

Copyright Acts Chart 111

Copyright Law 3, 105, 109, 126, 175

Copyright Registration 17, 120, 123

Copyright Royalty Board 170

Corporate sponsorship 100

Corporation 65, 66, 84, 206, 362

Cover Songs 19, 175

Creating a show 361

Creating the Tour 28

Creative Artists Agency (CAA) 28, 390, 406

Creative Destruction (Joseph Schumpeter) 86

Creative System 16, 91, 94

Creative Work 95, 121, 122, 123, 126, 127, 131, 149, 171, 312

Crewe, Bob 145

Curb, Mike 14, 88, 194, 274, 338

D

DBA -Doing Business As 362

Deal Points 22, 246

Deals 37, 66, 83, 85, 90, 96, 99, 101, 130, 131, 135, 143, 154, 155, 156, 158, 159, 160, 161, 162, 163, 164, 167, 168, 182, 190, 191, 196, 214, 218, 226, 227, 237, 240, 243, 246, 248, 250, 251, 252, 253, 258, 262, 263, 269, 271, 272, 278, 295, 300, 301, 328, 334, 335, 341, 342, 343, 347, 355, 356, 364, 371, 374, 400, 406, 420, 423, 430, 446

Demo 35, 143, 147, 302, 305, 308, 309, 318, 319, 334

Deposit Copies 18, 127

DeSylva, Buddy 65

Dickson, William 61

Digital Downloads 21, 23, 219

Digital Millennium Copyright Act 115

Disney, Walt 47, 168, 426

Distribution 35, 38, 49, 57, 74, 90, 106, 107, 110, 119, 134, 162, 173, 183, 197, 208, 210, 219, 220, 222, 230, 251, 259, 262, 264, 281, 299, 326, 358, 399, 401

Domingo, Placido 7

E

eCo (Electronic Copyright Filing) 17, 123, 124, 127

Economies of Scale 21, 96, 214

Edison, Thomas Alva 60, 61, 62, 63, 67

Effects 25, 313

EMI 65, 84, 85, 86, 307, 423

EMI Group 84, 85, 86

Emotions 15, 18, 43, 142

Entrepreneur 63, 200, 204, 208, 370, 445

Entrepreneurship 53, 200, 201, 210, 220

Exclusive Recording Agreements 247

Exclusive Rights 3, 59, 117, 123, 129, 132, 173

Exploit 91, 163, 342, 343, 402

F

Fanning, Shawn 74

Faxon, Roger 85

Federal Communication Commission (FCC) 253

Feld Entertainment 31, 426

Festivals 418

Fifty/fifty 154

Film 63, 67, 71, 72, 81, 84, 91, 95, 110, 127, 129, 131, 143, 147, 154, 158, 161, 167, 180, 185, 186, 191, 220, 233, 235, 294, 324, 345, 390, 391, 392, 428

Financial support 231, 340, 424

FM 69, 70, 253, 254

Folio Licenses 19, 167, 186

Formula 77, 108, 142, 184, 240, 242, 248, 418

Free Goods 23, 263

Freemium 21, 220

G

General Electric Corp (GE) 63

Global 35, 36, 49, 115, 168, 181, 207, 231, 232, 233, 234, 235, 236, 249, 251, 293, 294, 392, 410, 425

Gordy, Berry, Jr. 65

Gullah Language 83

Gutenberg, Johannes 58, 106

H

Hadden, Briton 58

Harry Fox Agency 166, 169, 171, 173, 175, 183, 191

Hicks, Rush 347

HMV 62, 65

Honeyman, Thomas 34

Huizinga, Johan 41, 42

I

I.A.T.S.E. 29, 409, 412, 413, 414

IEBA 28, 29, 393, 394, 395

I.F.P.I 37

Innovation 15, 57

International Creative Management (ICM) 28, 390, 391

Internet users 38

ISRC Codes 264

J

Jobs, Steve 63

Johnson, Eldridge 65

Jones, Quincy 205, 206, 300

Jukebox 83

K

Kawakami 48

Kelly, George 44, 46, 58

L

Labels 7, 34, 37, 38, 40, 48, 49, 62, 64, 66, 67, 70, 71, 73, 75, 78, 81, 82, 83, 84, 86, 90, 91, 92, 95, 99, 100, 101, 102, 109, 119, 120, 121, 122, 127, 128, 129, 131, 132, 134, 135, 143, 146, 148, 149, 150, 154, 158, 161, 169, 170, 171, 173, 174, 177, 190, 191, 195, 196, 197, 200, 203, 207, 208, 209, 213, 214, 215, 216, 218, 219, 220, 221, 222, 224, 226, 227, 228, 229, 230, 231, 232, 233, 237, 239, 240, 241, 242, 243, 244, 247, 248, 249, 252, 253, 254, 258, 259, 260, 261, 262, 263, 264, 265, 266, 267, 268, 269, 271, 272, 277, 278, 282, 284, 292, 293, 294, 295, 300, 301, 302, 305, 308, 321, 323, 325, 326, 327, 328, 332, 334, 335, 336, 337, 340, 341, 342, 343, 346, 356, 357, 358, 359, 364, 366, 371, 380, 389, 390, 400, 401, 403, 405, 409, 446

Langer, Susanne K. 43, 46, 142

Levitin, Daniel 43, 142

Lifestyles 45, 46, 252, 267, 356, 406, 424, 446

Limited Pressings 330, 336

Live Nation 354, 357, 379, 393, 410, 424, 425, 429

Live Ticket 29, 34, 37, 135, 146, 195, 197, 200, 201, 233, 237, 240, 241, 262, 271, 275, 277, 278, 282, 284, 299, 300, 301, 306, 336, 356, 358, 364, 378, 382, 400, 401, 402, 403, 404, 405

LLC 89, 206, 362, 363, 390, 391, 425

Low Budget 330, 336

Luce, Henry 58

M

Mail Box Money 28, 388

Marconi, Guglielmo 62, 68

Marketing 23, 24, 35, 38, 216, 231, 242, 251, 258, 259, 262, 272, 281

Mastering 25, 322

Master License 19, 167, 186, 295

Master Session 330

Matsushita Electrical Industrial 66

MCA 5, 66

Mechanical Licenses 166

Media Base 181

Media Monitors 181

Merchandise 27, 34, 40, 50, 83, 90, 96, 98, 100, 135, 201, 210, 214, 219, 220, 236, 240, 246, 247, 248, 249, 252, 262, 263, 267, 271, 278, 281, 284, 295, 336, 342, 354, 356, 362, 366, 367, 368, 374, 380, 381, 386, 387, 388, 389, 401, 403, 408, 414, 423, 425, 427

Merchandising 30, 423

Microphone 60, 310, 311, 312

Miendlarzewska 48

Mixdown 25, 321

Monetizing 145, 342

Morse, Samuel 68

Moss, Jerry 66, 67

Motown 65

Multiple Rights 21, 213, 218, 220, 269, 272

Music Business 5, 37, 38, 39, 40, 49, 52, 57, 63, 68, 72, 74, 84, 86, 106, 127, 143, 147, 195, 197, 200, 204, 207, 208, 209, 231, 266, 275, 302, 304, 306, 325, 390, 393, 402, 403, 404, 445

N

NACA 28, 393, 394

Napster 74, 75, 89, 119

NARAS 5, 300, 427, 428

NBC 67

Netflix 34, 81

Networks 35, 67, 69, 72, 74, 179, 184, 254, 255, 258, 280, 281

News Corp 71

Nielsen 24, 201, 256, 259, 293, 294, 295, 406, 429

NMPA 19, 167, 168, 188

North 48

Notice of Intent 175

NSAI 20, 188

O

On Stage Entertainment 425, 426

Overdubbing 25, 320

Ownership 3, 67, 85, 105, 106, 107, 108, 109, 110, 111, 115, 119, 120, 122, 123, 126, 132, 152, 153, 156, 158, 160, 161, 162, 163, 167, 187, 190, 230

P

PA 123

Partnership 206, 362

Patents 17, 120

Personal Manager 26, 344, 347, 364

Philips, Sam 66, 67

Phonograph 60, 62, 325, 326, 327

Player Piano 170, 171

Point of Purchase 237, 281

Pollstar 403, 404, 406, 424, 429

Pollstar Magazine 406, 424

PolyGram 66, 67

Power of Attorney 26, 352

R

Radio 34, 35, 36, 57, 60, 62, 66, 67, 68, 69, 70, 71, 75, 77, 78, 79, 81, 83, 121, 122, 148, 153, 154, 156, 166, 167, 179, 180, 181, 182, 183, 184, 191, 230, 233, 235, 236, 252, 253, 254, 255, 256, 257, 258, 262, 275, 280, 281, 282, 294, 323, 324, 349, 354, 366, 380, 401, 403, 408, 409

RCA Records 65

Recording Artists 20, 197

Recording Budget 26, 216, 249

Recording Rate Scales 26, 332

Recording Studio 35, 82, 83, 141, 200, 296, 300, 304, 308, 309, 314, 322, 336, 354, 373

Recording Team 25, 304

Record Labels 35, 38, 170, 196, 222, 271, 405

Record Physical Sales 219

Recoupment 90, 96, 101, 210, 214, 218, 236, 252, 301, 314, 343, 408

Rehearsal 28, 364, 372

Retail 21, 23, 219, 263, 275

Revenue Streams 29, 402

R.I.A.A. 37, 219, 293

Richardson, Eileen 75

Riders 30, 412

Roster Artist 241

Royalties 168, 182, 248

Royalty Artist(s) 25, 174, 248, 249, 268, 308, 309, 327, 329, 330, 334, 341, 374, 388, 407

S

Safe Harbor 35, 132

SAG-AFTRA 26, 248, 322, 323, 325, 327, 328, 329, 330, 333, 334, 336, 345, 354, 358, 362, 409

SAG-AFTRA National Code of Fair Practice for Sound Recordings 327

Sampling 19, 177

Scaling the House 30, 417, 418

Schumpeter, Joseph 86

SE 123

Serious Music Market 424

SESAC 19, 70, 147, 166, 169, 170, 173, 178, 179, 182, 183, 184, 191, 253, 367

SGA 188

Shakespeare, Wiliam 52

Shark Deal 155

Signatory 29, 406

SOCAN 178

Social Media 29, 78, 256, 409

Sole Proprietorship 205

Sole Proprietorships 362

Song Formulas 18, 142

Sony Music 85, 213, 227, 229, 237, 244, 272

SoundExchange 269, 285, 286, 366

Sound Recording Trust Agreement 26, 325, 326, 327

Special Payments Fund 26, 325, 326

Spotify 23, 34, 37, 51, 81, 133, 134, 208, 222, 225, 226, 229, 247, 256, 267, 268

SR 123

Staff publishing deal 155

Stage Names 29, 393

Stages of a Recording Session 25, 318

Statute of Anne 17, 107, 108, 109

Statutory Rate 19, 171, 174

Streaming 21, 23, 35, 133, 134, 201, 209, 220, 221, 222, 224, 225, 226, 227, 266, 267

Stream rates 224

Streams 35, 37, 83, 98, 135, 163, 208, 209, 222, 227, 236, 241, 246, 261, 264, 268, 278, 284, 293, 294, 295, 296, 366, 387, 401, 403, 408

Studio(s) 23, 24, 25, 279, 300, 302, 303, 305, 306, 308, 315, 334. 392

Swift, Taylor 380

Synchronization Licenses 19, 167, 185, 187

T

Talent Agencies 28, 390

Technology 34, 38, 39, 49, 52, 57, 62, 67, 68, 74, 77, 82, 83, 86, 92, 96, 100, 118, 132, 134, 138, 146, 182, 183, 186, 230, 236, 428

Termination of the Deal 27, 355

Terra Firma 85

Terrestrial 69, 70, 166

Tesla, Nikola 60, 68

The AF of M Sound Recording Labor Agreement 325

The Avalon Project of the Yale Law School 107

The Beatles 65, 84, 307

The Filtering System 18, 145

The Four Seasons 145

The Future 228, 230, 444

The Grammys 31, 427

The Management Team 26, 343

The National Music Publishers Association of America 19, 168

Theory of Personality (George Kelly) 44

The Oscars 31, 428, 429

The Production Matrix 18, 146

The SAG-AFTRA National Code of Fair Practice for Sound Recordings 26, 327

The Scaling Formula 30, 418

The Sound Recording Trust Agreement 26, 327

The Sparrow Corporation, 84

The Statutory Rate 19, 171

The Types of Concert Promotion Deals 30

Ticketmaster 409, 410, 415, 424

Time Warner 58, 100

Tour Expenses 214

Tour Financials 28

Tour Gross 28, 387

Tour or Road Managers 27, 354

Tours 254, 404

Trademarks 3, 17, 119, 120

Trost 48

Turing, Alan 72

TX 123

Types of Businesses 20, 205

Types of Personal Managers 352

Types of sessions 325, 330, 336

U

UHF 69, 70, 253

UMG 85, 213

United Artists Records 84
United States Constitution 17, 109
United Talent Agency (UTA) 28, 390, 391
Universal Music Group 85, 227, 229, 240, 272
UPC Codes 264

V

VA 123
Variety 24, 294, 295
Vega, Suzanne 76
Velvet Tone 62
Venues 27, 181, 370, 424
VHF 69, 70
Vinyl 63, 82, 214, 222, 248, 262, 263, 293, 327, 402
Virgin Music Group 85
Vivendi 66
Volman, Mark 142, 344, 420, 421

W

Walichs, Glenn 65
Warner Bros. Records 65
Warner Music 58, 59, 219, 220, 225, 227, 237, 240, 272
Warner Music Group (WMG) 58, 59, 213, 219, 220, 225, 227, 237, 272
Website & Press Kits 28, 371
William Morris Endeavor Entertainment (WME2) 28, 390, 392
Wissmann, Paul 442
Witt, Steven 89
WMG 213
Work-for-hire 155, 157, 160, 200, 249, 308, 355
Wow Songs 18, 149

Y

YouTube 36, 57, 106, 119, 132, 133, 134, 167, 183, 185, 191, 198, 200, 201, 222, 224, 225, 226, 229, 269

Z

Ziv 48

CPSIA information can be obtained
at www.ICGtesting.com
Printed in the USA
LVHW09s0440220918
590842LV00007B/8/P